THE BATTLE FOR PUBLIC OPINION

THE BATTLE FOR PUBLIC OPINION

The President, the Press, and the Polls During Watergate

GLADYS ENGEL LANG
and KURT LANG

COLUMBIA UNIVERSITY PRESS
NEW YORK   1983

This publication was prepared under a grant from the Woodrow Wilson International Center for Scholars, Washington, D.C. The statements and views expressed herein are those of the authors and are not necessarily those of the Wilson Center.

Library of Congress Cataloging in Publication Data

Lang, Gladys Engel.
  The battle for public opinion.

  Includes bibliographical references and index.
    1. Watergate Affairs, 1972–   —Public opinion.   2. Public opinion—United States.
3. Press and politics—United States.
I. Lang, Kurt, 1924–   . II. Title.
E860.L36   1983   973.924   82-12791
ISBN 0-231-05548-X
ISBN 0-231-05549-8 (pbk.)

Columbia University Press
New York   Guildford, Surrey

Clothbound editions of Columbia University Press books are Smyth-sewn and printed on permanent and durable acid-free paper.

Book design: Ken Venezio

In Memory Of
E. Matthew Engel 1893–1968
Jean Gratz Engel 1900–1976
Ernst Lang 1891–1976
Ilse Kass Lang 1895–1979

Contents

PREFACE

End (handwritten)

Hardly anyone is likely to forget Watergate. Like others, we were fascinated, often puzzled, and perturbed by what we watched on the TV screen, heard on radio, and read in the press. Unlike most others, we had a professional interest in following the story as it unfolded. Watergate was to us a dramatic demonstration of how the news media might intrude into a political controversy and expand it into a crisis of confidence.

What was the effect of the media on the creation, the course, and the resolution of Watergate? The answer is not as obvious as it may appear. Despite the heroic efforts of some journalists, Watergate had no visible effect on the 1972 Presidential election. Yet six months later, even before the televised Senate Watergate hearings, the nation's attention had become riveted on the issue, and for more than a year thereafter, until Richard Nixon's dramatic exit, Watergate dominated the headlines and the network news. Then followed a succession of televised political events, enacted with "the whole world watching," that students of mass communication and public opinion could hardly resist. By studying what happened, how it was reported, what audiences perceived, and how they reacted, they could infer effects. They could also conduct mental experiments to tell them what the outcome might have been if the event had not been televised or had been reported some other way.

We began studying media effects in 1951, when General Douglas MacArthur, recalled from his Korean War command by Harry Truman after years spent in the Philippines, Japan, and Korea, was welcomed home to America with parades and ceremonies. Our study of MacArthur Day in Chicago is usually cited as demonstrating how the "reality" experienced through television differs from the "reality" of being there. The study did stress this difference, but explanation pointed beyond the unique characteristics of television that structured the event to the *political* context that shaped the expectations of both journalists and their audience. In some ways the political climate surrounding MacArthur Day resembled that during the

Watergate era. Truman, after his surprise victory in 1948, had become a beleaguered President, plagued by scandals in his official family, charged with indifference to communist infiltration into high places and responsibility for the fall of the nationalist government in China. The Republican opposition depicted MacArthur's dismissal as an act of sabotage bound to have adverse effects on the American effort in Korea. By their focus on crowded parade sites, by their selection of interviewees, by the way they dramatized the occasion, telecasters conveyed and thus confirmed this impression of popular sentiment overwhelmingly against Truman and in favor of MacArthur. In this atmosphere, created by what we then called a "landslide effect," politicians supporting Truman's action felt a need to proceed cautiously. Some were intimidated from speaking out, and for a time the 71-year-old General became a serious contender for the Republican nomination. Nothing comparable would happen during Watergate, where the depiction of where the public stood was much more ambiguous.

The following year we studied the televising of the 1952 conventions, the first shown to a national audience. We were able to document more specifically how the presence of television entered political strategy and how different styles of coverage made a difference in what viewers perceived. We also explored the meaning of participation in the conventions via television and its implications for citizens' involvement in politics. These and other studies of media events—including presidential debates and election night—can be found in two books, *Television and Politics* and *Voting and Nonvoting,* and in journal articles.

With our predilection for using critical political events to study media effects, it is easy to see why we should have gone on to study Watergate. An invitation from the *Columbia Journalism Review,* soon after the end of the Senate hearings, to contribute to a special Watergate issue was a further impetus. The editor wanted to know what social scientists had to say about the impact of 37 days of televised testimony and interrogation. We were surprised to find that numerous studies of the hearings had been conducted, many without any funding. This was a high point, never again to be equaled during the rest of Watergate. It was not that the research effort ceased. Individuals here and there generated data on how the media covered and how people responded to Watergate. Their work, much of it never published, has also been of great help to us.

Despite the reams of literature on Watergate, mostly written by media and political insiders, the connection between public opinion and media coverage during Watergate years has never been definitively charted. Nor has there been a comprehensive study from a social science point of view of how public opinion affected the development and resolution of this controversy. This book is an attempt to fill that gap by weaving together the evidence from a broad range of sources: from empirical studies, some of them our own, some by other communication researchers; from data routinely collected in polls on a month-to-month basis and used to track shifts in attitudes; from published recollections; and from newspaper and television content analyses. We have also interviewed members of government, public opinion analysts, and journalists, all of whom followed the movement of public opinion during Watergate from their special vantage points.

The analysis of this material presented fewer problems than how to present what we found. While—like almost everyone—we continue to speak of "Watergate" as if it were one event, the term subsumes a series of events, few of them fully predictable. The immediate response of the public or of political actors to any one of these events can be understood only in the context of prior events, to which it was a delayed response. We therefore felt we might be compelled to choose between two alternative modes of presentation: to write a history of Watergate, tracing chronologically the major events, the way the media reported them, the public response to the events known through the media, the political moves and reactions provoked by these events, and the movement of public opinion; or to organize the material conceptually, without regard for time sequencing, into chapters, each of which would examine and illuminate one or more aspects of the effect of mass communication on public opinion. Our decision to combine the two modes of presentation may have resulted in two books within a single binding. On one level, the Watergate story is told chronologically, with some media events described in considerable detail. We think this necessary since for a large and continuously increasing part of the population, Watergate is an unknown. We have found college students truly entranced by accounts of what is history for them. Many who were young teenagers when Nixon resigned are familiar with only the general outline of the story and with such stock phrases as "expletive deleted." And even the rest of us can use a refresher on the "battle for public opinion" in which, as our title implies, the media provided the arena on which the controversy was fought out.

On a less concrete and more theoretical level, however, the book is about public opinion and the democratic process. Each chapter uses a major event (or events) in Watergate to shed light on some basic issue, such as: what are the limits to the power of the media to determine the public agenda? has the role of public opinion changed with the coming of quickly disseminated continuous polling? what kind of a say does the public have in the decision-making of political elites? what is a pseudo-event, and what does it mean to say the media are biased?

The news media were not an outside or extraneous force whose influence on the course of Watergate can be isolated from other influences. To be sure, one can show how the early media reports first brought to light the hidden dimensions of the break-in at the Watergate headquarters of the Democratic National Committee. The media were the first to signal that this was only the tip of an iceberg, but their effect on the subsequent course of the Watergate controversy is more complicated and can be understood only by looking at the whole political process. Some readers may hope that we shall conclude with a rebuke to the news media, finding that Nixon was hounded from office by a hostile press; others may want us to celebrate the democratic process by confirming that, in resigning, Nixon bowed to the will of the people. We have consciously resisted the temptation to be sensationally assertive. Research seldom supplies the simple answers that make for simple headlines. The media were there and the people approved; had the media not opened privileged political negotiations to public scrutiny or had the polls failed to record public opinion as supportive, Congress might never have moved against Nixon. Yet the media did not impeach Nixon, nor did the people, although both had a part in the extended maneuvering at the end of which an American President left office "voluntarily."

No book ever takes shape in the mind of a single individual as if by immaculate conception. This one is not only jointly authored but involved collaboration far more extensive than any title page can possibly indicate. Our first acknowledgment rightfully goes to our students who, at various points during Watergate, helped us monitor television newscasts, recorded some of the live coverage, distributed questionnaires, participated in the tabulation of media content, and performed one or more of those routine tasks indispensable to the success of any research project. We should like here, in particular, to acknowledge the assistance of Janice Engsberg, Larry Levine, Susan Levine, and Norman Prusslin (now station manager of WUSB, Stony Brook). In addition, Glenna Engel Lang and Alexander von Hoffman spent part of one summer replaying and analyzing some of the videotapes from the impeachment debate.

Another debt of gratitude is owed to academic colleagues on whose studies we were able to draw. Citations throughout the text are testimony to our dependence on their work. But special thanks are due to Lawrence Lichty, University of Maryland, for sharing with us his log of network news during Watergate, an invaluable resource; to Jack Orwant, American University, for the use of his file of polls and constituent letters sent out by congressmen in 1973/1974; and to Josephine R. Holz for sharing with us the worksheets used in her thesis on the *New York Times* Watergate coverage. Polls by commercial poll-takers were another rich source of data. Although most of this information is in the public domain, we are grateful for additional help, information, and/or copies of original press releases provided by Irving Crespi, formerly of The Gallup Organization; to Mervin Field of the Field Research Organization, which conducts the California Poll; to Burns W. Roper of The Roper Organization; to the staff of Louis Harris Associates; to Stephen Cole of Social Data Analysis, which conducts the *Newsday* poll, and last but not least to Harry W. O'Neill of Opinion Research Corporation, who let us have the tabulations from previously unpublished polls that firm conducted for the Republican National Committee and the White House. Albert E. Gollin, Newspaper Advertising Bureau, also helped with some poll data from a study he had conducted in Washington.

We benefited immeasurably from our stay at the Woodrow Wilson International Center for Scholars. In addition to the Fellowship, which relieved us from teaching for an academic year, the Center provided a congenial atmosphere, conducive to discussion with those who shared our good fortune. Especially rewarding were the many incisive observations generously offered by scholars from neighboring disciplines. We gained many an insight from Michael Les Benedict, Ohio State University; Jeff Fischel, American University; Alan Henricksen, Fletcher School of Diplomacy at Tufts University; Rei Shiratori, a visiting scholar from Japan; Peter Braestrup, editor of the *Wilson Quarterly*; and we received invaluable assistance from both Zdenek David, the Center librarian, and Stephen H. Haber, a volunteer researcher at the Center. Also not to be dismissed lightly is the easy access our Washington location gave us to some of the actors in the televised Watergate drama and to members of the Washington press corps. No one we approached denied us an interview.

Drafts of chapters were read and critiqued by Albert E. Gollin, Alexander von Hoffman, Glenna Lang, and Kevin Engel Lang, and the whole manuscript by some anonymous reviewers. Their comments and those of Barry

Sussman and Lawrence Lichty, who served as discussants for the first formal presentation of our study at the Center, were most helpful. There should, however, be no doubt in readers' minds on whose shoulders to lay the blame for sins of omission as well as commission.

Our survey after the Nixon resignation could not have been undertaken without CBS support dispensed through Professor Sidney Kraus, chairman of the Department of Communication at Cleveland State. We are equally grateful to him for his unrelenting enthusiasm about "critical event" research at a time when others refused to recognize its soundness as an approach to the study of media effects. Other financial aid came in the form of a small grant from the John and Mary R. Markle Foundation. This, together with a grant-in-aid from the Research Foundation of the State University of New York, enabled us to move ahead with the statistical analysis of previously collected data.

Finally, we are indebted to Charles P. Webel, assistant executive editor at Columbia University Press, for his confidence in the manuscript and to Leslie Bialler whose meticulous copy editing detected needless errors. Glenna Lang donated the graphics and jacket design.

Gladys Engel Lang
Kurt Lang
June 17, 1982

CHAPTER 1

OVERTURNING A LANDSLIDE
From Reelection to Resignation

On the evening of November 7, 1972, Richard M. Nixon was reelected President by a landslide, losing only Massachusetts and the District of Columbia. The vote was a clear reflection of public opinion, yet when Nixon quit the Presidency less than two years later, most Americans approved. According to every poll estimate, no more than two of every ten Americans, and possibly as few as one in ten, were unhappy with the outcome, and even this minority, while somewhat disillusioned, accepted the resignation as inevitable and necessary. Few were bitter or vengeful. Indeed, seldom except for national emergencies has there been a greater display of national unity than when Nixon took the unprecedented step of resigning the Presidency of the United States.

This almost universal approval of such an extraordinary turn of events is itself extraordinary. The legitimacy of the Presidential changeover could have been open to serious challenge. After all, his successor was Gerald Ford, picked by Nixon himself to succeed Spiro Agnew, who had been forced to resign in disgrace from the office of Vice President. Ford had been one of Nixon's staunchest defenders almost to the very end. Nor were people as enthusiastic or unanimous in their support for Ford as media reporting implied. His approval rating just after he took office was 71 percent according to Gallup—a percentage below that of Lyndon Johnson (79) and Harry Truman (87) after their sudden elevations from the Vice Presidency under equally extraordinary circumstances.[1]

Throughout the long months of controversy over Watergate, there was constant talk in and by the press of a "nation torn apart." Both Richard Nixon in resigning and Gerald Ford on taking office had stressed the need to "heal the wounds" of a nation divided by a shattering political scandal. Yet, contrary to some dire predictions, the unprecedented succession did not provoke the constitutional crisis some had feared. There was continuity. Foreign relations remained unimpaired. Even more noteworthy was the strangely muted public response. Some fifteen months of apparent polarization suddenly ended without any serious political clashes or much visible dissent, without joyful demonstrations or dancing in the streets. If there were wounds to heal, they were only surface scratches.

A BATTLE FOR PUBLIC OPINION?

Of one thing we can be certain: the transition would not have taken place so quietly—indeed, it might not have taken place at all—had it not been preceded by a dramatic reversal of public opinion. Who, at the beginning of the second Nixon administration in January 1973, would have dared suggest that a President reelected with a lopsided majority and at the peak of his popularity could be forced out of office eighteen months hence? Or that the most sacred secular office in the world would be turned over, with the nation's blessing, to a man with as little national recognition as Ford?

Richard Nixon himself believed that public opinion was the critical factor in what he called the "overriding of my landslide mandate." For him, the struggle to stay in office, especially after the firing of Special Watergate Prosecutor Archibald Cox, when impeachment first became a real possibility, was a "race for public support." He called it his "last campaign," only this time it was not for political office but for his political life.[2]

As the President saw it, the main danger of being impeached resided in the public's becoming conditioned to the idea that he was going to be impeached. This was a good enough reason for Nixon's strategists to keep a close watch on all indicators of public sentiment—letters, telegrams, telephone calls, editorials, television commentaries, press reports, and, especially, what the polls showed. At the same time, the President developed a media strategy specifically and directly aimed at winning the battle of the polls. The media were the principal battlefields on which the major confrontations took place. Television, because of how it was used by all sides, played a most active role in the conflict.

Many observers of Watergate agree that it was Nixon's defeat in the battle for public opinion that forced him to retreat at crucial points when he failed to rally support for his stand to limit the scope of any probe into the Watergate break-in. Ultimately, it left him no alternative but to bow out. In this view, the way public opinion made itself felt exemplified "democracy at work," a favorite cliché of the news media. Ford lent it official sanction in his inaugural address when he told the nation, "Here the people rule." The view in the Nixon camp was less benign. Public opinion was seen as an ever-present danger. Stirred up by the media, deliberately manipulated by his enemies, and tracked by pollsters, public opinion was to become the hostile force that ultimately *drove* Nixon from office.

Not everyone believing that public opinion influenced the resolution of Watergate agrees that it hastened the end. In fact, an argument can be made that public opinion had exactly the opposite effect, that it slowed the process and prolonged the crisis. Some members of Congress, reluctant to move against the President unless assured that they had a majority solidly behind them, felt restrained by public opinion. Polls that continued to show most people opposed to Nixon's removal from office failed to provide this reassurance, though these same polls also showed large majorities believing that the President was somehow involved in a "serious" scandal and not just caught up in the usual politics. Critics of opinion research have gone so far as to argue, some most vociferously, that during most of Watergate the major polls, whether by inadvertence or design, exaggerated the extent of opposition to impeachment. Consequently, the media were slow to register the groundswell for impeachment.

A third group of political analysts regards this emphasis on public opinion as totally misplaced and the Nixon strategy as misdirected. To them the battle for public opinion was only a sideshow. The media, in treating the issue as a political struggle for public support, diverted attention from the one crucial element in the downfall of Richard Nixon: the accumulation of incriminating evidence. If Watergate was a political contest, as it obviously was, the stakes consisted of information. Those pressing the case on legal grounds had to be mindful of public reaction but only insofar as people had to have confidence in the fairness and objectivity of the process by which the President was being judged.

Clearly the nation had experienced a dramatic shift in public opinion during the more than two years of controversy, which began with a break-in and ended with Nixon's resignation. What could account for such a reversal? The first place to look for an explanation is in the behavior of the media. TV, radio, and print are essential to the formation of public opinion in the modern nation in two ways. They disseminate information that allows members of the public to form opinions and, just as important, they convey to politicians and to others an image of what public opinion is, thus giving it a force it would not otherwise have.

Our primary purpose is to observe public opinion in action—to see how it is formed and how it changes and what impact it has on national political life. Because of their importance in shaping and reporting public opinion, the media become a central focus in our inquiry. We shall be considering in relation to Watergate such recent developments as expanded television coverage and the increased emphasis on opinion polls as news. Expanded television coverage speeds up and dramatizes the day-to-day flow of events to which the public bears witness, so that occasionally the citizenry learns about important political developments and negotiations at the same time as closely involved public officials. Rapidly collected and analyzed opinion polls have replaced newspaper editorials as the "voice of public opinion" and gained a prominent place in news reporting. In what has been designated as "precision journalism," polls themselves become news events, so that it sometimes becomes difficult to separate the impact of the issues on which people have been polled from the impact of the published responses.

WATERGATE AS A CASE STUDY

Watergate was one of those rare occasions when the public is sufficiently agitated to directly influence political decisions. It therefore offered an excellent opportunity for tracing how public opinion is aroused and how it exerts its influence. While the process could be described and analyzed as it operated within a unique historical event, it could also be related to general theories of how public opinion operates. There were, however, few models from which to borrow since, surprisingly, few scholarly case studies have dealt with the mass media as they relate to the development and outcome of political controversies—other than during electoral campaigns. There are exceptions, such as the imaginative case study by W. Phillips Davison of the Berlin blockade and airlift of 1948–49.[3] In that study, Davison was able to document how the West Berliners, surrounded in their enclave by Soviet troops who threatened to cut off the vital arteries by which they received food and other supplies, were made conscious by the media that the eyes of the world were upon them, viewing their struggle as a valiant effort to hold this outpost of the "free world" against the Soviet effort to expand its hegemony. Others are by Bernard C. Cohen, who dealt with the drafting and adoption of the American-Japanese peace treaty that officially terminated World War II, by Leon Sigal of the controversy over the Skybolt ground-to-air missile, and by Todd Gitlin, who (in a somewhat different vein) dealt with the effect of media coverage on the development of the New

Left movement in the 1960s and 1970s.[4] None of these episodes were anything like Watergate.

The need to examine public opinion in relation to events during Watergate was underscored by controversies over the role of the news media at every stage of the crisis. Some have claimed that the media's inattention during the 1972 election prevented a majority of the public from taking the Watergate break-in seriously. Others have charged that Watergate was nothing but a media-created issue, at least one that would never have emerged without Woodward and Bernstein and company. Disagreement arises over whether such media events as the coverage of the Senate Watergate hearings in the summer of 1973 created public concern or whether they did little more than play on partisan dispositions and thus polarize the nation along usual political lines. Equally problematic are the reasons for the failure of Nixon's media strategy of stonewalling and political counterattack. The President had only recently proven himself a master political strategist who knew how to manipulate the media. During Watergate did the media become too formidable an "enemy" or did Nixon misread the public mood? The television coverage on resignation night is still another subject in dispute. The networks are said to have abandoned their critical reporting role in covering the events that functioned as ceremonies of transition. In this book we attempt to shed some light on these and other matters as well as inquire about the long-term effects of Watergate. Is it likely to affect future political attitudes? or lead to institutional reform? or change the political climate?

MEDIA EFFECTS

We have also used the Watergate controversy to consider some theoretical issues about the influence of the mass media on public opinion. Specifically, we deal with four perspectives from which the nature of media effects has been viewed. These can be summarized as the minimal effects theorem, agenda-setting effects, the refraction principle, and the study of critical events.

The minimal effects theorem is based largely on evidence derived from the observation of individual responses, focusing on differences in the responses of those exposed and those not exposed to certain media content. It holds that changes due to exposure tend to be incremental and mostly to strengthen existing dispositions by making people more convinced of views they already hold. With regard to public opinion, this means that substantial attitudinal change in response to persuasive messages is the exception or, as Joseph T. Klapper has put it,[5] communications more often reinforce than convert.

Much of the evidence in support of the minimal effects theorem in politics comes from studies of electoral campaigns, a time when mass media influence is reduced by the conventional nature of the campaign debate. People are apt to be more persuasible during primaries, when they are first learning about candidates and their choices have not yet crystallized, as well as during periods of political upheaval, when the things people take for granted are called into question by events. However, the erosion of party loyalties during the 1960s and 70s caused electoral preferences to become more volatile than they were years ago, when the by now classic campaign studies on mass communications were conducted.[6] The role of the media in the public opinion process needs studying in situations where the potential for opinion change is greatest, and Watergate certainly meets this criterion. Americans were confronted with a situation that was unfamiliar and with facts that strained their credulity. Yet, most Watergate studies have failed to establish a direct link between a pattern of media use and opinion about Watergate. They seem only to confirm the theorem of minimal effects by demonstrating that most changes were predictable from and consistent with long-standing political convictions reinforced by media exposure. Responses to Watergate coverage were thus seen as determined by the individual's party affiliation and whether he or she had voted for Nixon in 1972. But we also note that most of these studies were undertaken more than a year before the resignation, at the time of the televised hearings of the Senate Watergate Committee. They could take no account of the gradual but massive shifts of opinion over the entire two-year period, as a retrospective study like ours can.

Some researchers have emphasized the active role of the audience as a counterweight to the power of the media. Effects, as Elihu Katz put it, depend not on what the mass media do to people but on what people do with the mass media.[7] What use do they make of the content or medium? What gratifications do they seek? The effect depends on what is sought. Where a need is not met by the content, when it fails to divert or to inform, the message is likely to be ignored or its import discounted. But it seems to us that the media content can also create a need or signal a problem of which users had not previously been aware. Some gratifications sought through media use are themselves media-generated. Thus it was that the important, often puzzling, and sometimes exciting events during Watergate aroused new needs for information among persons not ordinarily active followers of political news. Moreover, when the Watergate fare was the only offering on the major networks, as when all three were covering the Senate hearings, some "captive" members of the audience found themselves following developments as they would a televised soap opera.

The agenda-setting hypothesis derives from the observation that the mass media, while perhaps not very effective in persuading people *what* to think, do seem to tell people what to think *about*. Research has looked for correspondences between the amount of attention an event or issue receives in the media and the importance members of the audience assign to it. Content is usually measured by the emphasis (amount of time and space) on some issue or issues in the news; response by the perceived importance of the issue among the public. A high correlation between the two suggests that the media, collectively, steer attention to certain issues, events, and personalities. Or, as McCombs and Shaw describe the agenda-setting function, people learn from the mass media what the important issues are.[8]

Studies of agenda setting have had a special attraction for students of mass communication discouraged at the failure of audience research to demonstrate "scientifically" the media influence their common sense tells them is there to be found. The Watergate case seems to illustrate just such a correspondence between the prominence of Watergate-related news and the amount of public concern expressed in response to poll questions. Watergate's failure to become a serious issue during the 1972 election campaign has been blamed on the failure of most newspapers to follow the *Washington Post*'s lead in publicizing the scandal. Later, once it became a "big story," it was the zeal with which the press pursued Watergate that was widely considered the major factor in making it into a massive scandal. Upon closer examination, the media were themselves responding to events and not acting as prime movers. By examining how Watergate did become an issue and how that issue underwent redefinition, we try to illuminate the role of the media in what we refer to as the agenda-building process.

The refraction principle points to the creation of a symbolic environment by the organized news media. One cannot understand the formation of political opinion without taking this into account, for all of us live in a world of meanings, some of which are *mediated*, which is to say that the objects, events, and personalities these meanings refer to are outside the range of direct experience and known only insofar as knowledge about them is communicated. Most of what most people know about politics and much of what they react to refers to distant events known only through the mass media. But news organizations are more than transmitters of messages about "reality." Their role as producers, even creators, of news is of equal importance.[9] They are geared and functionally specialized to monitor the increasingly complex world from many different vantage points, but they must single out some observations and reports from a much larger number. Inevitably, any focusing involves blowing up some aspects of the "reality" while others are unreported. Too close a focus will put some out of range altogether. What the organized news system yields can best be described as a refracted image; at its worst it results in reports deliberately slanted to fit some self-serving interest or what official spokesmen believe the public needs to know. But whether intentionally distorted or not, the image of the world is always depicted from some perspective, brought into focus through some lens, including the various lenses of the television camera. Hence, we prefer the more neutral term "refraction" to that of "bias" to designate the influence of the communication system on the content disseminated.[10]

In crises like Watergate the news media provide the common point of reference. Anyone seeking information and trying to understand what is going on depends upon what is fit to print or to transmit electronically. Besides the way the news media report events and what they include, there is the language through which they describe them, of the metaphors employed to refer to the subject at issue at various points in time. We note the potential power of such labels as the "Watergate caper," "the Saturday night massacre," "the smoking gun," and so forth to condense under a simple epithet matters that are highly problematical. As the meaning of Watergate changed over time, the language of the public opinion polls—both the wording of questions and the words used to sum and convey their findings to media audiences—also came to reflect these changing metaphors. The public, politicians, and even journalists themselves responded to the symbolic world created by the media. The sociologist Fred Davis has suggested that the depiction of the most extraordinary events through the everyday routines and practices of news coverage familiar to audiences everywhere helped make the extraordinary ordinary, thus contributing to the tranquil, unemotional response to the end of Watergate.[11]

This is not to say that the political environment to which the public responds is an invention of the media. The media are neither all-powerful nor beyond any control other than that of their managers. The limits become evident when a one-sided attempt to define "reality" is contested. The ability of the President to co-opt the airwaves on command and to dominate the news is at least somewhat balanced, as it was during Watergate, by reportage not under White House control. Through its investigative reporting, through "instant analysis" of Presidential speeches, through its coverage of Presidential initiatives as well as events to which he can only react, television gives prominence to political forces that act as a counterweight to Presidential power.

Through the intensive examination of such critical events—of what happened, how this was reported, and of the public response—one can illustrate refraction and analyze its consequences. These events are larger than the political actors and activities under scrutiny. Also involved are the many anonymous people who make up the audience. Watching, listening, or reading about political activity is also a form of political activity. What meaning does this activity have for the individual? Does viewing a political blockbuster—like the Senate hearings or the House Judiciary Committee debates—give the viewer a sense of having participated in the affairs of the country? Do members of the audience see themselves primarily as spectators or as part of the process? The significance an event has for people is affected by their realization that the same event is also being watched by millions of others at the same time.

Our analysis traces the changing public definitions of Watergate ("crime"), Nixon's involvement ("guilt"), and impeachment ("punishment") and the determinants of these changes. Following an overview of public opinion and the media in chapter 2, each chapter from 3 through 9 takes up, in chronological order, events that appear to have been critical in the movement of opinion. Each is used as a testing ground for some aspect of theory about communication and public opinion. Chapter 10 considers the question of long-range effects of Watergate while chapter 11, using historical comparison, asks whether there was anything unique about the role of the media and of public opinion in the creation and resolution of the crisis.

CHAPTER 2

THE PUBLIC AS BYSTANDER

Political leaders, advocates of reform proposals, persons speaking for special constituencies, and even the "man (or woman) in the street" continually invoke public opinion to legitimate positions they themselves favor. The press nowadays gives big play to opinion trends. Governments track these carefully and commission polls tailored to their needs. What the public thinks is judged important, since responsiveness to the popular will remains, after all, the cornerstone on which the edifice of popular government rests.

Just what is "public opinion" and how does it influence the decisions of government? Was it more than rhetoric when Gerald Ford, on assuming the office of President of the United States, declared that "here the people rule"? Traditional doctrines of popular government start from the single premise, stated in one form or another, that sovereign authority resides with the people, that their will is supreme. Yet, if sovereignty is vested in so vague a collectivity as an entire "people," the concept of public opinion loses much of its utility as a diagnostic tool.[1] If the will of the people is only what everyone agrees to, such unanimity is rare, and the supposed mandate that the people hand their government amounts to nothing more than a willingness to be ruled in accordance with custom and law. Even at that, people often disagree on which customary or legal practices they believe to be workable and of some benefit to everyone. Also, if public opinion as the will of the people stands for nothing more than an underlying consensus, this hardly helps explain how it influences the passage of particular laws, the choice among alternative policy decisions, or political decision-making in general.

Evading this conceptual problem, some political theorists specifically identify public opinion with the decisions of representative bodies functioning as agents of the people. This leads them only to the unpalatable conclusion that ultimately all government, however despotic, is legitimated by popular consent, a position brilliantly argued by David Hume some two centuries ago, long before the advent of modern totalitarianism made a mockery of it.[2] Consent, in this formulation, can be assumed as long as the governing bodies in which power is vested act in accordance with persistent attitudes that go deeper than opinions of the moment.

If public opinion is a force that counts for anything, one should be able to distinguish between despotic rule based on coercion and the kind of management of consent characteristic of popular government. The problem of consent is apparent whenever a government in making a decision cannot count on universal approval but actually expects opposition, either because the decision accedes to the demands of a special interest group or because, though deemed to be "in the public interest," it may be not be popular. The force that inheres in public opinion can then assert itself in one of two ways: by a reluctant willingness to go along with the decision or by a refusal to follow the lead of the legislative body or other authority. It is in the latter case, when it causes problems and raises the prospect of protest, that the role of public opinion as a source of legitimate authority becomes most clear.

FORMS OF SOCIAL CONTROL

Public opinion, custom, and law, are the three basic forms of social control. In social science, the term "social control" has nothing to do with compliance imposed from without; it stands for the very opposite, for the means through which any society regulates itself and coordinates the behavior of its members.[3] The authority inherent in each form of social control has a different basis. That of custom resides in habits acquired over time. Hence, the older the practice, the more hallowed it is likely to be. As a rule, customs change slowly, sometimes so slowly that people are not even aware that they are changing. A customary practice may simply fall into disuse as the circumstances that gave rise to it disappear, without provoking the discussion and debate that are the hallmark of public opinion.

Law consists of a body of more or less codified rules usually with specific sanctions for violation. Sanctions imply coercion but this, too, is subject to strict rules. Moreover, in law, the rule itself is not subject to argument; it is only the facts, and which rule they come under, that are at issue. Differences on these points are normally resolved through the courts, whose rulings and decisions must be insulated from the pressure of public opinion if they are to retain their "objective" character. That, in any event, is the rationale for the opposition to recent changes in regulations that in some jurisdictions allow live television coverage of trials and thereby enlarge the audience for them. That public pressure can overcome objections is evidenced by the vote of the full House, just before Nixon resigned, to permit live broadcast coverage of its upcoming impeachment debate. The Senate, too, was ready to permit the public at large to witness its trial, had one occurred.[4]

Public opinion comes into play in problematic situations where none of the rules of law apply or where there is a dispute about their suitability. Legal and political arguments are frequently in contention, as they were during several phases of the Watergate controversy. It is then, when consensus can no longer be taken for granted but must be actively sought, that opinion takes over as the dominant form of social control. Even impeachment, despite its imposing legal façade, is essentially a political process. Richard Ben-Veniste and George Frampton Jr., two members of the Special Watergate Prosecution Force, have concluded that the total course of the investigation by the House Judiciary Committee, though fair and judicious, only exposed the "extreme political nature of impeachment" revealing the "unwillingness of many in Congress to recognize objectively the stark facts of criminal wrongdoing that were put in front of them."[5]

Law and politics, nevertheless, each employ a characteristic language of discourse. Legal language, in its appeal to fixed rule, in its emphasis on precedent, in its endeavor to appear precise and dispassionately objective, emphasizes logical necessity. Political language is more rhetorical, with sentences framed to appeal to sentiment, to lofty motives, or even to crass self-interest as long as it simultaneously persuades the opposition to settle for what it can get rather than to stand on some alternative principle.[6] Acquiescence in a political decision, in contrast to a legal one, can never be taken for granted. It is through bargaining that one discovers where the points of possible agreement lie.

The difference between public opinion and these other forms of social control should be clear. Public opinion, insofar as it is opinion and not custom or law, tends to be unstable and in flux. It also tends to be less than unanimous. Not only does public opinion incorporate divergent viewpoints but, because opinions diverge, what is at issue at one time or in one place may not be at another. A belief is relevant to public opinion only if there are acceptable grounds for holding a contrary one, where disagreement cannot be considered sheer folly or unacceptable heresy, like the notion that witches inhabit the night. As deviant beliefs acquire acceptability, their merits may become a matter for wider discussion. If people take sides, the belief enters the realm of public opinion.

For opinions to be relevant, they must also concern public rather than private matters, a distinction that is far from absolute and can change both with time and circumstance.[7] Marriage, for instance, seems an eminently private affair between two individuals and, possibly, their families; but when King Edward VIII wished to marry a twice-divorced commoner whose husbands were still alive, the mere intent was enough to provoke a public reaction. The King, after all, was a symbol of national sovereignty and of the unity of the British Empire. The first concern of some key political leaders was that the monarchy continue to enjoy the highest respect among the masses and thus ensure social peace in a period of economic crisis, while others (among them Winston Churchill) rallied to the King's side. A public formed quickly, almost spontaneously, composed of all those interested in and taking sides on the question. The boundaries of any public may shift as more people are aroused or become weary and lose interest. But insofar as the attention of many people is focused on the debate about any issue, these constitute a collectivity—a single public—despite the division of opinion that separates the two sides.[8]

During a crisis public opinion is apt to shift, especially as leaders compete for approval and support. What at one point seems to be the popular mandate may later turn out to have dwindled into a minority point of view. This is well illustrated by the precipitous decline in Richard Nixon's ratings in the opinion polls just months after winning reelection. By summer 1973 it was becoming doubtful that Nixon would even have won the election had it been held then.[9]

DETERMINING THE PUBLIC WILL

The elusive nature of public opinion has created a problem for the "devotee of democracy [who finds himself] in much the same position as the Greeks with their oracles. All agreed that the voice of the oracle was the voice of God, but everybody allowed that when he spoke he was not as intelligible as might be desired."[10] Even when an election results in an unambiguous majority, it is not always clear on what grounds the voters have arrived at their judgment or what mandate they mean to hand their chosen representatives. The nature of the mandate becomes more dubious with the passage of time.

How can leaders determine the public will to which they should be responsive? Two divergent solutions have been suggested. One derives from a view that is essentially elitist. It stresses the inevitable limitations on mass intervention in political decision-making which reside in the general public's lack of expertise, ability, or a strong desire to follow closely and continuously the matters under discussion. The second stems from populist tradition and calls for direct and frequent consultation on policies with the largest possible number of citizens, whatever their level of information or degree of concern. Folk wisdom rooted in practical experience is considered an essential counterweight to the esoteric considerations and vested interests that lead to the betrayal of the common interest.

A highly sophisticated version of the elitist position was set forth by Walter Lippmann, first in his *Public Opinion* (1922) and, most forcefully, in *The Phantom Public* (1925). His critics have emphasized what he said public opinion could not and should not do. For Lippmann, the idea that the public could deal with the substance of public policy and of law was simply wrong. When the public attempted to do so, he argued, it merely became the "dupe or unconscious ally of special interest." The theory of popular government that expected "insiders" (those with the information necessary to formulate a complex policy) to allow "outsiders" (ordinary citizens without such knowledge) to help direct public affairs was a "false ideal." One could hardly expect the average member of a mass public to grasp the details of the problems of the day; he had neither time, interest, nor knowledge. The notion of the public as a mass of citizens directing the course of events was, for Lippmann, a "mere phantom." However, he paid attention not only to what the public was not but also to what it was, not only to what public opinion could not do but also to what it could do. The public, for him, consisted of only those individuals interested in the matter at hand. That kind of public did indeed have a role to play: it could provide guidance to its representatives in identifying problems and areas in need of remedial action of some sort, whatever this might be. Further, it could and should decide which party, institution, or agency was to be entrusted with working out policy solutions. The public was, in his view, little more than a "reserve force" that could be mobilized on behalf of the method and spirit of "law and morale." [11] Over and above the conflicting interests found within the polity, there was one, but only one, interest common to all and that was "that all special interests shall act according to settled rule." [12] In this sense, the public could act, not to assure that their own viewpoint prevailed but to protect their common stake in democratic rule from assault by special interests and determined extremists.

The populist approach takes the opinions of the mass public more seriously. In equating the "public" with the "populace," it embraces the plebiscitarian principle of seeking direct guidance from the people on the details of policy; for example, asking the public to authorize or disallow expenditures for some particular purpose, such as the building of roads, or to empower specific legislation, such as prohibiting the sale of alcoholic beverages or allowing legalized gambling. Inasmuch as a voter referendum is cumbersome, slow, costly, and participation often too low to justify the expense, this device is employed less often than those enthusiastic about this form of popular rule might wish. Also, it has become clear that the outcomes of such plebiscites are frequently less than an accurate expression of the "public will." Not only is the result often foreordained by the wording of the proposition put to the electorate but the collective decision is open to undue influence by a determined minority with a special stake in winning.

Both modern-day "elitists"—a designation not used in the pejorative sense—and modern-day "populists" agree on the need to get an accurate reading of the public will. What they disagree on are the resources and energy to be devoted to such readings, the authority with which they are to be endowed, and the use to be made of them. Those who push for maximum input into governmental decision-making look to the continuous monitoring of public opinion through scientific polling, which they see as a faster, and thus more timely, and possibly more accurate, though less binding, method of soliciting opinion than the referendum. Their stress is on the improvement of polling techniques, on compressing the time gap between the solicitation of responses and the determination of results, and on more refined analysis of the findings.

Others—not all of them "elitists"—concede that polling can be scientific but are concerned that, like other scientific instruments, polls can be misused. The rapid ascertainment of public reactions to political developments, made possible by improvements in communication technology, can subject policy-makers to pressure from a public that is uninformed or even misinformed. The distribution of opinions in a poll can also be misleading if some alternatives are left unexplored or if one aspect of the findings is overly emphasized at the expense of others. Some worry even more that policy-makers themselves will misuse the polls to document support for their own policy positions.[13]

The limitation of the political poll as a measure of public opinion is not only a matter of its use or potential misuse; it is also implicit in its procedural logic. Polls are designed to elicit from a sample representative of some population an accurate and complete expression of the views they hold. Although there is nothing capricious either about taking a poll or about the way people generally answer poll questions, this activity is not free from certain pitfalls. Survey researchers take care that those they interview are representative of the population about which they want to generalize; they are careful about how they construct their questionnaires, about how to obtain a response that is not biased by the interviewer, and about how best to analyze these responses. Yet different polls sometimes yield different results, and the assessment of the opinion climate can depend on which poll is being read or cited. Researchers know all too well that such things as wording questions—the ambiguities, the alternative answers from which the respondent must choose, the context in which a question is presented—and the date of the interview can make a difference in the image of the public mood drawn from seemingly "hard" poll figures.[14]

How the context in which a question is asked affects the picture of public opinion is well illustrated by measures of support for continued American intervention in Vietnam. Asked in 1971 whether they favored or opposed the withdrawal of all American troops from Vietnam by the end of the year, two of every three Americans said they favored such a course. Yet when those in favor were then asked whether all troops should be brought home *regardless* of what happened in Vietnam, a sizable number changed their minds. The overwhelmingly favorable 66–26 percentage split in support of the troops' return was reduced to a mere 44–41 percent plurality.[15] The policy-maker in search of guidance must rely, as did his Greek predecessor, on his own interpretation of what the oracle meant: What was the *real* division of opinion? Were 22 percent (the difference between 66 and 44 percent) ready to be done with the war, regardless of consequences, but not yet prepared to admit it? Or, taking the results most literally, had their initial expression of support for troop withdrawal been an off-the-cuff response, which was readily reversed when reminded of possible consequences? Alternatively, were those who changed their minds still quite confident that South Vietnam would not fall and only responding to a purely hypothetical situation?

One cannot interpret such results unless one can distinguish between responses that express firmly held convictions and those that are highly volatile gut-level reactions to topical issues. While everyone seems to know this and to admit as much, any summary statistic of current opinion tends to assume an authority all its own. The press seeks unambiguous, straightforward news to report, while politicians and interest groups look to these figures for self-justification or to plot strategy. A case in point was the announcement, in 1980, by the League of Women Voters that its decision to invite Representative John Anderson, who had entered the Presidential campaign as an independent, to participate in the televised debates would be contingent on his achieving a 15 percent standing in at least two national preference polls. That "objective" criterion was to legitimate the decision to exclude or include Anderson in the debate by making it appear to be not an arbitrary judgment by one citizens' group but one made by the public at large.

DOMINANT VS. MAJORITY OPINION

For a political leader to adopt a position or to pursue a policy simply because the polls show it to have majority support would be sheerest folly. At best, responses to poll questions provide a guide to what various segments of the population will tolerate or support under certain conditions. The sheer weight of numbers does not guarantee that, put to test, the majority will prevail. As much, and perhaps more, depends on the intensity with which people on either side hold their beliefs, on how willing they are to assert them and thereby create a climate of opinion. A determined minority prepared to press its opinions against all opposition may well prevail over a majority whose members are largely indifferent.[16]

If not all opinions carry the same weight, then public opinion as a form of social control is not the same as the numerical aggregate of individual opinions that polls present. Public opinion is a collective representation, a shared image of the likely response that elite actors see themselves forced to take into account. It is, in essence, the dominant opinion. Quite often this is indeed the opinion of the majority, but it can be less if the minority view has sufficient logic, prestige, resources, or commitment to carry the day. Opinions held without real conviction have less significance, whereas those based on legal, scientific, or other expertise are assumed to carry more than their numerical weight. Yet popular clamor can at times override expert authority based on status or specialized knowledge if, and perhaps only if, the mass public is sufficiently aroused and mobilized by those with some axe to grind.

Recently, Elisabeth Noelle-Neumann has shown that persons who believe their own views to be in the majority more readily engage in conversations with strangers who disagree and press their views on them.[17] This is so, no doubt, in many instances and under specifiable circumstances. Therefore, if a determined and vocal minority can make its view *appear* to be that of a majority, those without a strong conviction one way or the other may concede. Minority opinion then becomes dominant without commanding an actual majority. If majority and dominant opinion are often confused and perceived as one and the same thing, it is in part because in most elections that have been studied the opinion split has been quite close and the major parties have had near-equal legitimacy in the eyes of the public. The party that draws a majority vote also becomes the dominant party.

The vote is, indisputably, the single most important and most visible way for the mass public to influence decisions. Yet the way public opinion operates during an election campaign may be quite different from the way it operates most of the time. For one thing, during elections, campaigners are most open in their efforts at persuasion and the public somewhat suspicious, and even cynical, about being wooed. For another, what counts in the election campaign is who gets the most votes; the numerically preponderant and dominant opinion are one and the same. But this is not necessarily what determines the outcome of a political controversy.

These caveats notwithstanding, more effort has gone into the study of election campaigns than into studies designed to show how public opinion influences the outcomes of other political contests, in which public support is not quite so openly courted, even though there may be as much or even more at stake for the country. To be sure, those in office inevitably keep an eye on the electorate they will face at the end of their terms. And many seek the sort of acclaim for their actions and decisions that will assure their place in history. Even nonelected officials generally avoid, if they can, stirring up an adverse public reaction that can reduce their influence as power-wielders. It may even cause enough embarrassment to force such officials out of office. The point is that the pressure of public opinion exists as a potential force even when no election is imminent. To understand the role of public opinion in the political process, we have to look beyond its impact on voting decisions and electoral outcomes.

PUBLICITY AND OPINION

To have influence, opinion has to be visible. It has somehow to gain the attention of those responsible for shaping and making policy. Visibility can be achieved through other than plebiscitarian instruments—by demonstrations, boycotts, campaigns of civil disobedience, special petitions, and the like. The mere articulation of opposition to present or pending policy, even by only a few people, can be a portent of things to come. The opposition must somehow be discredited, isolated, or made less vociferous. Neither must it be allowed to feed on concessions. The way office holders deal with private representations by special interests is, in principle, no different from their response to opposition that enjoys sufficient publicity to be a threat. Yet the public often regards the two differently. Concessions, in the one case, will be viewed as favoritism or selling-out; those made to calm the highly publicized opposition are more likely to be perceived as a legitimate response to a grievance. The essential difference is between what Schattschneider calls the "pressure system" and the system of electoral politics.[18]

While specific opinions may have no impact without publicity, the power of the mass public always exists as a latent force, even when its opinions are not well articulated. It is always there and capable of being mobilized to confront political leaders when there is a policy failure or when the public trust has been breached. Yet how much public opinion can be said to lead those delegated to lead and how much it is led, if not manipulated by them, is an open question. Except on those relatively rare occasions when people take to the streets to protest, deluge their representatives with mail and telephone calls, or withhold the cooperation necessary for a policy to work, public opinion remains quiescent, working its influence subtly and indirectly, usually by little more than expressions of praise or blame.

There are, of course, limits to this influence. These depend not only on the means available for the expression of opinion, but also on the distance that separates the political centers from the rest of the world.

Outside these centers where decisions are actually made and a wide array of expertise is available, people live and work with limited access to necessary information and little awareness of all the complex considerations that go into the formulations that constitute a policy. Contemporary society differs greatly from the face-to-face community that is still taken by many as the guiding model for democratic decision-making. In that largely self-sufficient community, specialization was limited and the salient facts needed to arrive at decisions were equally available to all. Opinions would normally be formed and sharpened in discussion with neighbors, with everyone able to intervene in a dispute.

It is not that talk about politics and public issues has necessarily diminished with the destruction of that sense of community fostered when work and residence are joined in the same locality. Politics as a topic of conversation has certainly not been banned. But there is a difference in the manner of political discussion, and it reflects a division of labor within the political world as great as that in industry.[19] When people talk about politics today, they usually have in mind a remote government, with which they have little direct contact. Difficulties arise because government decisions are perceived by people as affecting their well-being, indeed the very quality of their lives, yet very few have either the time or the access to information needed to familiarize themselves with the concrete merits of the alternatives among which their leaders constantly decide.

None of this need inhibit anyone from taking a stand on a public issue. On most issues opinions tend to develop along predictable lines defined by perceived group interests and expressive of ideological dispositions rather than dispassionate inquiry.[20] Thus, the initial alignment of opinion over Watergate was more or less coincident with support for Nixon or McGovern in 1972, between traditional civil libertarians and the "law and order" advocates, between opponents of the Vietnam war who approved the purloining of the Pentagon papers and others who believed Nixon's actions, however questionable, were motivated by his overriding concern for national security, between participants in the counterculture and "Middle America," and so forth.

That public debate during such controversies as Watergate can be far removed from the real political bargaining through which elite decisions evolve is not in and of itself anything new. Popular government on the national level, even in earlier times, has always been remote and impenetrable. The mass of the people never had much chance of affecting the course of events. What is "new" is the increased number of layers that intervene between the interested citizen and the discussion within government, making the seat of government appear remote and even "foreign." For many Americans, the nation is made up of "Washington" and "the rest of the country." As government has grown, the networks within which the discussion of policy takes place have become ever more specialized. Although some nongovernment experts, especially those hooked into "issue networks," participate in policy formulation and are called on for advice from time to time, the mass public takes no part in these negotiations.[21]

This widening gap between actors and bystanders has seemingly been bridged by the new media of mass communication. Some facets of the political process have unquestionably become more visible to more people than ever before. Who would ever have dreamed, at the turn of the twentieth century, that an American President would hold press conferences in plain view of millions of people, answering questions on all sorts of political and personal matters? Or that, as part of the normal news delivery system, millions would watch Congressional committees conduct hearings? Both the executive and the legislative establishments find publicity a powerful weapon for political defense or political attack, depending on circumstances. The emergence of television as the dominant news medium forces us to examine the effect of making political negotiations so visible.

VISIBILITY AND THE BYSTANDER PUBLIC

The mere fact that activities formerly not seen by the public have become so widely visible changes some things but not others. The type of "contact" made possible by television does not actually reduce the distance between the esoteric elite level and the exoteric mass level at which matters up for political decision are discussed. Now a witness to events once remote and inaccessible, the mass public is still condemned to a bystander role. Living in their own world, the members of that public are privy to, but not part of, the give-and-take through which parties with conflicting interests hammer out an acceptable policy, though not always a workable one, by balancing the weight of evidence against political considerations. As bystanders, members of the public make judgments on the basis of what information they have, judgments they are inclined to identify with the public interest. These preferences are then communicated to poll-takers (or to the press) and through them to the relevant politicians.

The preferences of the mass public do not, however, translate directly into executive decisions.[22] The bystander public is in no position to make policy, to draft a law, or even to commit a public body to follow through on a decision. To be sure, there are binding plebiscites, through which the mass public can obstruct or approve but not directly implement. The "decision" they make when they vote is nothing beyond the expression of a judgment, a judgment on what others have done or are proposing to do. If a large majority concurs, political leaders accept this as a mandate to continue; at least the prospect of massive defections is temporarily assuaged.

This ever-present possibility that the reactions of the public, as bystanders to negotiations, will affect bargaining positions gives it a "third party" function. Its role in a political dispute is hardly that of a neutral arbiter but of a potential ally or enemy; it can shift the balance of power by the way it throws its weight around.[23] Political posturing for the media can mobilize a public as an ally when other political resources to make one's viewpoint prevail do not suffice. It can also be used by a dominant coalition to contain any possible challenge.

To speak of two, and only two, sides in the formation of policy is, of course, to oversimplify. Most political problems are too complex to be presented as clearcut two-sided alternatives to be voted on by legislators or by an eligible electorate. The number of viewpoints has first to be reduced and the diverse interests, always present in a pluralistic society, amalgamated. This "interest aggregation," as Almond has called it,[24] is normally a function performed by political parties, which are themselves coalitions of constituencies and factions that have compromised differences to maximize their power. Such coalition-building is as indispensable to the conduct of politics on the elite level as it is to the mounting of an electoral campaign. There is no other way to govern when no party holds an absolute legislative majority or when party loyalty alone cannot assure the passage of legislation. As for the mass public, when aroused, it can intervene in this process; and it occasionally does, but only to the extent that it has been mobilized under some banner or behind some cause. Both the lines along which political coalitions then form and which coalition emerges as the dominant one will depend on the perception of where the public stands—whether it is perceived to have clearly rallied to one side, whether its position appears frivolous and likely to be ephemeral, or whether it seems to be based on convictions serious enough for people to act on. The image that emerges from these assessments is that accepted as the "popular will."

THE MEDIA AND PUBLIC OPINION: A WORKING MODEL

The political effects of the mass media have to be considered within the context of the bargaining through which political coalitions are built and held together. Yet this elementary point has all too often been neglected.

Research, mainly preoccupied with the number of voters swayed by political communications during campaigns, has adapted a persuasion model in which an electoral decision is treated much like any other market decision. This overlooks the reality: election outcomes are in a very practical sense collective decisions. The difference between a market decision and a collective decision is absolutely fundamental. Political action of any sort must take account of opposing viewpoints in ways that implementing a market decision need not. If elections have failed, as they have over the past three decades, to produce workable majorities, one explanation lies in the targeting of campaigns at voters as individuals rather than the forging of durable coalitions. Falling electoral participation and the erosion of party loyalties are symptomatic of the limits as well as the social cost of this strategy. To repeat, the direct effect of mass communications on the electoral decisions of individual voters is only one element in a far more intricate set of relationships through which the media influence public opinion and political outcomes.

Let us therefore outline, as a working model, the ways—other than by direct persuasion—in which mass communication affects how political coalitions are built and how public opinion functions as a form of social control:

1. The news media give greater visibility to certain political activity and political actors and thereby immeasurably enlarge their potential forum.
2. Any publicity creates an audience of bystanders whose actual size varies but who, regardless of size, intrude insofar as those involved in political bargaining are aware of them.
3. Most of the time, these bystanders do little more than observe. They may or may not form opinions, but unlike those who make political decisions and formulate policies, whatever opinions they form cannot be directly implemented. Even when they write letters to representatives, sign petitions, join a demonstration, or participate in an organized campaign, they are only asking others to heed their advice. Their opinions, basically, are expressions of praise or censure of others, indicating how they should act or whether they have acted correctly.
4. The distinction between actors or agents and bystanders, between those who act and others who merely react, between insiders who participate in the give-and-take and outsiders who do nothing beyond giving or withholding approval, is fundamental to the conception of public opinion as a form of social control. To be sure, participants can change roles and the lines between actors and reactors can become so thin

that they can hardly be discerned, but the difference in roles remains and points to the limits of public opinion as a political force.

5. Bystanders play an important third-party role in any political transaction, even when they hardly appear to be "present" and are unable to make themselves heard. But should they later take sides and mobilize, they can change the power relationship. And even when they refrain from any overt demonstration, their acquiescence may be essential for the success of a policy.

6. The media of mass communication present political actors with a "looking-glass image" of how they appear to onlookers.[25] They know that the published reaction does not always accurately express public reaction, but this does not reduce their intense concern with media reports as the first clue to the responses of the public and a factor in that response. Favorable media recognition becomes an important resource in political bargaining. The converse is also true. Some bargains can never be struck unless they can be kept private.

7. With or without publicity, the bystander public functions as a significant reference group for political actors who seek consent or at least acquiescence. They therefore invest much effort in their media appearances, always hoping to align themselves with the largest possible constituency and to avoid stirring up opposition. Many activities are deliberately framed with an eye to how these may be reported. As politicians have generally become more sensitive to their image, especially as projected on television, the influence of the media on the actions and reactions of those whom they publicize—the so-called newsmakers—becomes crucial for the course of a political controversy.

8. Finally, media publicity is a resource not only for those who decide and make policies but also for any person or group seeking to pressure the decision-makers. One way a view gains attention is through the press.

This outline indicates a direction in which research must move and is in fact moving. The news should be treated as if it were a map of the political landscape. Such a map is, to be sure, a moving map with contours of political figures, policies, failures, impending problems, and threats. But like all maps, it cannot reproduce the political world in all its richness and variety. Inevitably it depicts the world from a particular perspective that determines what is selected and highlighted. The labels it gives to events locate otherwise unknown territory and make the world appear more familiar. Herein lies one of the costs of this enlargement of consciousness beyond one's immediate world—the dependence on maps provided by the mapmakers.

These media maps have to be a focus of investigation. They make up the symbolic environment that orients not only the mass public but also the circle of "insiders," who also depend on the media in charting their political course. Although the image has become more vivid and more personalized, there still is "refraction." Some elements are blown up; others appear distorted or are diminished in size by their proximity to the vanishing point. The same applies to the image of public opinion. The indicators of public opinion have changed over the years and the image of the public depicted through the media has become a most important reference group not only for political actors but also for the public itself and even for the media.

It is this model that guides our analysis of public opinion in the Watergate controversy.

CHAPTER 3

1972: THE WATERGATE "CAPER"

Political attitudes, beliefs, and behavior do not easily change in response to the mass media, and even when they do the link is difficult to demonstrate. Yet the conviction survives that mass communications are a powerful political force. Since the early 1970s this conviction has gained new strength, in part from studies that document a correspondence between the amount of media attention a problem receives and the amount of public concern about the problem. Noting this connection between press concern and public concern, social scientists have arrived at a reformulation that holds that "people learn from the media what the important issues are." [1] Or, as Bernard Cohen in his study of the press and American foreign policy put it two decades ago, "the press may not be successful much of the time in telling people *what to think*, but it is stunningly successful in telling its readers *what to think about*." [2] Applied to the media as a whole, this process has been called agenda setting.

Watergate provides a prima facie case through which to illuminate the role of the mass media in setting the public agenda. If Watergate was not a significant factor in the outcome of the 1972 Presidential campaign—and it was not—was this because the media gave it too little coverage? When it did erupt into a major focus of controversy just five months later, was this simply a matter of stepped-up press attention?

In the case of Watergate, folk wisdom supports the agenda-setting hypothesis. On the one hand, the press (or most of it) has been critized for having buried the issue during the campaign, or at least for providing insufficient coverage; on the other, the news media have been lavishly praised for their key role in mobilizing the public. Without the dogged pursuit of the facts by enterprising newsmen, it is widely believed, the scandal would have expired and the Nixon administration would not have been held accountable. Neither evaluation of the media role quite accords with the evidence.

We start from the assumption that the agenda-setting hypothesis—that bland and unqualified statement that the mass media set the agenda during election campaigns—attributes to the media at one and the same time too much and too little influence: "Too much" because it ignores the contextual and political factors that limit the power of the media to set the public agenda; "too little" because it sheds little light on the process through which public agendas are built or through which a problem, having caught public attention by being big news, gives rise to a political issue.

PRESS COVERAGE: 1972

James Perry, who covered the 1972 campaign for the *National Observer*, thought "Watergate should have been an issue in the election and it really wasn't. If we had worked harder and dug deeper, could we have made Watergate the issue it should have been?"[3] In saying this, Perry implied a direct causal relationship between press inattention and the lack of public concern.

It is true that most of the press failed to follow the *Washington Post* in its effort to get at the full facts behind the break-in at the Democratic National Headquarters. But it is also true that much of the basic Watergate story was in the public domain by the time the 1972 campaign reached its climax. That story included not only the details of the bungled break-in on June 17, 1972 to the headquarters of the Democratic National Committee but also such related matters as the deliberate circumvention of campaign finance laws, "dirty tricks" perpetrated by persons in the employ of the Committee to Reelect the President (CRP), and the illegal use of Federal agencies by the White House against its political "enemies." To be sure, during the campaign, some of these stories surfaced only as unverified press exposés or as allegations by persons with axes to grind. But they had been publicized before election day.

If coverage of Watergate during the campaign was far from negligible, it was also highly uneven. The regional and local newspapers gave it much less space than such "cosmopolitan" papers as the *New York Times* and the *Los Angeles Times*, which have their own bureaus in Washington. In this initial phase of Watergate reporting, the *Washington Post*, as everyone seems to know, led all other papers in its investigative reporting of various aspects of the story. Following the break-in on June 17, the *Post* was:

the first to make a connection between the burglary and the White House; the first to show that Nixon campaign funds were involved; the first to describe the "laundering" of campaign money in Mexico; the first to involve former Attorney General John Mitchell; the first to involve former presidential appointments secretary Dwight

Chapin; the first to explain that political espionage and sabotage were an intrinsic part of the Nixon campaign; the first to trace the Watergate affair to the very doors of the President's Oval Office—to his White House chief of staff, H. R. Haldeman.[4]

These initial efforts to "get the story" and to "get it out" have been celebrated in print and on film. Both the editors of the *Post* and their energetic reporters, Carl Bernstein and Bob Woodward, won Pulitzer Prizes for their performance. The whole world, it sometimes seems, knows how a routine police story, apparently of only local interest, became the big story of the decade.

With a few notable exceptions, the rest of the press did not join the *Post* in its dogged pursuit of the Watergate story. During the campaign fewer than 15 of the 433 reporters assigned by 16 leading news bureaus to the Washington area devoted their full time to Watergate developments.[5] Of the three networks, only NBC, with 25 Washington reporters, assigned one person full time to Watergate, and it did this only after the Republican convention in August.

The political character of a newspaper affects its coverage. Unlike the electronic media, newspapers are unregulated, under no legal obligation to serve the public interest, and often subject to strong pressure from local interests, advertisers, and their publishers. In 1972, about seven of every ten newspapers (71.4%) had endorsed Nixon, while the others remained neutral (23.3%) or backed McGovern (5.3%).[6] While Doris Graber, in her study of campaign reporting, did not find that political endorsements affected the total *amount of space* a newspaper devoted to various issues,[7] Ben Bagdikian, in a more detailed and intensive analysis, showed that newspapers endorsing Nixon more often downplayed stories reflecting adversely on the President than did papers that had remained neutral. Thirty papers that he examined had, together, 90 opportunities to print news items about three crucial Watergate stories—an exclusive tape-recorded interview with Alfred Baldwin, a lookout-man for the Watergate burglars; an investigative report on the scope and technique of political sabotage; and a story linking Haldeman with the sabotage project. Of these opportunities, 31 were missed, mainly by the pro-Nixon press. The failure rate was 52 percent for the papers endorsing Nixon compared to 23 percent for the "neutrals." And those pro-Nixon papers that did carry any one of these stories were less likely to make them front page news.[8]

This pattern of downplaying Watergate could produce some striking differences in coverage. Between June 17 and November 6 the *Los Angeles*

Times, which had no special local interest in the Watergate affair and endorsed neither candidate, gave the story front page treatment, according to our own count, four times as often as the *New Orleans Times-Picayune* and more than twice as often as the *Chicago Tribune,* both of which had come out for Nixon. It was not until August 27, a full twelve weeks after the break-in, that the *Tribune* put a Watergate-related story on the front page.

Still, if the treatment of Watergate news was downplayed by some newspapers, it was not buried. Between August 27 and the end of the campaign, the story was to appear on the first page of the *Tribune* another twelve times. And the coverage in some influential papers might, at the time, have been considered "overkill." Watergate made the front page of the *Washington Post* almost one day out of every two—79 days altogether; it made the front page of the *New York Times* about one day of every three—33 times.[9]

In contrast to most of the print media, network television joined the *Post* in giving the Watergate break-in big play from the start. The *NBC Nightly News* Saturday June 17 reported that the burglars "apparently were unarmed and nobody knows why they were there." The next night, it ended its report with these prophetic words: "I don't think that's the last we're going to hear of this story."[10] *CBS Sunday News* carried an essentially similar report and by Monday, June 19, all three networks had broadcast filmed reports. Next day, after the *Post* had named an employee of CRP as a link between the "bugging" and the White House, and Lawrence O'Brien, the Democratic National Chairman, had filed a million dollar damage suit against CRP, the burglars, and other as yet unnamed defendants, ABC and CBS made this their lead story, and NBC included it as a news item.[11]

Thereafter, the amount of television news time devoted to the Watergate affair was substantial. When we combined results from three separate analyses of television news coverage during the 1972 election,[12] it turned out that Watergate, compared to other political news, fared quite well, considering that it was competing not only against election stories designed by campaign headquarters to command television attention but also against the air war in Vietnam and news about the peace talks being conducted by Henry Kissinger. On the average evening, more than one network was likely to carry such an item and overall Watergate received far more publicity than most political developments. The time devoted to Watergate, during the 11 weeks monitored by Lawrence Lichty, was almost identical to that given Vietnam and, according to a Patterson-McClure count over a shorter seven-week period, Watergate was second only to the Paris talks in the number of stories "clearly relevant to the campaign though not about the campaign itself." No other story—measured by number of items—came close; over 11 weeks, 17 percent of all political items carried by ABC evening news were about Watergate, 19 percent of those on CBS, and 20 percent on NBC. (Appendix, table 1)

Statistics of this sort are hardly infallible. Results can be influenced by the choice of news categories, by the time period covered, and by the definition of what constitutes an item. We are, nevertheless, reassured by the consistency in the conclusions of three independently conducted analyses, the third being that supervised by Edwin Diamond. The picture painted is buoyant enough to exonerate the networks from charges that they deliberately downplayed the story throughout the campaign. Yet we also note that the average time devoted to Watergate was about 75 seconds per television news program—surely a paltry amount and hardly one that permits penetrating analysis. But that is the nature of news treatment on regularly scheduled broadcasts. Indeed, there was sufficient similarity in the amount and content of Watergate coverage among the three network programs to infer some kind of "structural bias" stemming from the unique character of the medium, with its time constraints and insistence on visual components to any story.[13]

Still, despite this broad uniformity, the networks differed both in the style and in the tone of their coverage: in the length of items; in the political context within which events were reported; and in the language of presentation, for instance, the use of such buzzwords as "caper" and "bugging incident." On all counts CBS surpassed its commercial competitors in the depth of its coverage while the large number of items on NBC is deceptive; more than half, according to Diamond,[14] lasted less than a minute. The network differences in these and other more subtle elements of style should not be minimized. They can, as past studies show, introduce a considerable amount of refraction into the image of reality to which people react, resulting in different meanings being conveyed by "identical" content.[15]

Whatever the deficiencies of television news, the networks put more emphasis on Watergate during the campaign than did newspapers. That was the conclusion Graber drew from a systematic content analysis comparing "campaign stories" on the three networks with those in 20 newspapers chosen so as to be representative of the American press.[16] Her mildly startling result: Watergate accounted for 8 percent of all "issues" alluded to in some

5000 campaign stories in newspapers during the last 30 days before election; on television the proportion was about three times as large—about 23 percent.[17] Moreover, while the newspapers emphasized Vietnam, television emphasized Watergate. Though the total informational yield was probably higher in newspapers, the dominant treatment given Watergate by television gave the story attention value.[18]

Differences in network treatment of the Watergate story were less striking than differences between newspapers and could not be traced to a consistent pattern of downplaying or overplaying Watergate news likely to hurt Nixon's chances for reelection. While CBS gave more time per newscast and more total time to Watergate-related news, this is largely accounted for, according to both Diamond and Lichty, by two long special reports that CBS *Evening News* broadcast on October 27 and October 31. Later in this chapter we consider how their airing became a subject of controversy both within and outside CBS, revealing the vulnerability of the broadcast media to charges of biased reporting.

By putting more emphasis on Watergate news than did the press, especially the regional press, the networks also helped the newspapers, which carried the burden of investigatory reporting, to go "national" with their stories. If, during the campaign, there was sufficient media coverage of Watergate to have brought it to most people's attention, this must be attributed not mainly to either television or newspaper coverage but to the symbiotic process whereby they are linked. Network news editors often take their cues about what stories to pursue from the journalists and the newspapers they esteem. And, in recognizing their stories, network news adds to the visibility given stories first appearing in print. If major stories in the *Washington Post* were not picked up by the more local and regional press or if they were reported only within the context of White House denials, the networks, by picking these stories up, turned them into national news. Thus, after CBS aired its two-part special in October, based mainly on Watergate stories worked up by the *Post*, Katherine Graham, its publisher, is said to have remarked to CBS news head, Richard Salant, "You turned our local story into a national story."[19] Others at the *Post* called the CBS stories a "lifesaver"; they believed that it was harder after that for the rest of the press to dismiss the attention to Watergate as a vagary of one Washington newspaper.[20] Still, one must not exaggerate the ability of television to force press attention. The CBS presentations were no doubt a real boost to a much harassed *Post* staff, but we could find no evidence that there was any significant change in the amount of play papers across the nation gave Watergate following the CBS specials.[21]

PUBLIC AWARENESS: 1972

There is no reason to conclude that the media during the campaign draped a curtain of silence over Watergate. Certainly the coverage was sufficient to have made clear majorities of the public aware of it by late summer, when the matter had caused enough of a stir for polling organizations, which look to the news for cues, to start asking questions about it.

When Gallup asked in September 1972, "Have you read or heard about Watergate?" 52 percent of a national sample said they had. While this level of awareness may not stagger the imagination, it is not unimpressive when put into context. It accords roughly with the proportion of Americans who, in 1970, could correctly name their Congressman or who, in 1971, had "read or heard about the articles first published in the *New York Times* about how we got involved in the Vietnam War" (that is, the Pentagon Papers). On the other hand, by this same measure, the public at this time, three months after the break-in, was less aware of Watergate than it had been of Nixon's new welfare proposals in 1969 and his new economic program to fight inflation in 1971, both of which achieved awareness scores in the 70 percentile range a week after their unveiling on television.[22]

This Gallup reading, taken in mid-September, may actually underestimate the extent of awareness, inasmuch as "Watergate," as a code name for the break-in and its ramifications, may not yet have caught on among many people aware of the incident. For instance, when a Harris poll, conducted at about the same time, asked more specifically, "Have you heard, or not, about the men who were caught trying to install wire-taps in the Democratic National Headquarters in Washington?" 76 percent indicated their awareness.[23] And by October, 87 percent of the voters in Summit County, Ohio, said they were aware of the "Watergate break-in."[24]

Awareness is only a precondition for taking a stand in a controversy. Polls taken during the campaign provide no evidence that, for the most part, citizens were outraged and prepared to charge the Nixon administration the political price for its various trespasses. Rather, most people regarded this kind of wiretapping, which most believed to be an invasion of individual rights, as a commonplace occurrence, the usual kind of skullduggery to be expected, especially during a campaign.[25] Moreover, the various Watergate stories led very few voters to link the break-in to the White House. In late August, when the Opinion Research Corporation (ORC) asked a series of questions about the incident, very few (17%) thought that the Republicans or CRP had put the men up to the break-in and even fewer—a mere one percent, mainly Democrats—suspected Nixon. Most people were content to reserve judgment about who was to blame for the incident.[26]

None of this means that nearly everybody accepted Republican disclaimers. A study in Ohio found four of every ten voters, as election day drew near, at least willing to entertain the possibility of White House involvement: only 12 percent were free of all doubt.[27] Yet there is no evidence that the Watergate revelations had caused many people to question the honesty of the Nixon White House. In late September when the Gallup Poll asked about the "most important problem facing the country today," corruption in government was far down the list. And when the Democratic candidate, George McGovern, late in the campaign called Nixon's administration "one of the most corrupt in history," his argument did not have much impact.[28] Surveys do show that as a "man of high integrity," Nixon lost some ground between September and October, but his performance ratings remained just about where they had been—with about three-fifths of the public approving the way he was handling his job.[29]

Nor did Watergate play any perceptible role in the outcome of the election. When the University of Michigan Center for Political Studies asked a nationwide sample of eligible voters what they liked or disliked about the Presidential candidates, fewer than one percent volunteered anything about Watergate.[30] Equally revealing of the general attitude is the response to a question by ORC in its October 13–15 survey: "If it were proven that the charges against the President's re-election committee are true, will this [make you] less likely to vote for President Nixon, or wouldn't it have any effect on your vote?" Only 21 percent said it would affect their decision while 68 percent said it would make no difference. Throughout the campaign Watergate remained, first and foremost, an argument for confirmed Democrats. Though potentially explosive, it caused very few Republican defections, and very few voters found the Watergate break-in "personally important" in making up their minds how to vote.[31]

Clear majorities were therefore aware of Watergate developments during the campaign. The national media had given Watergate sufficient attention for it to have become a matter of some considerable public concern. Yet the majority of the eligible electorate considered what they read and heard about the break-in "just more politics." Only a minority were personally concerned about its implications for civil liberties or saw in what they had learned evidence of corruption in the administration. While there were doubts about the Republican version of the break-in, hardly anyone connected the incident with Nixon. Though the basic facts that later became such a familiar part of the Watergate saga had been publicized and were in the public domain, media attention had failed to put Watergate on the public agenda. It had neither tarnished Nixon's Presidential image nor played any perceptible role in the outcome of the election. Most people did not find the Watergate affair important in making up their minds about how to vote. Why didn't they?

WHY WATERGATE DID NOT BECOME AN ISSUE

Obviously, the amount of coverage given a matter of political relevance does have some bearing on public reaction, but to posit a simple correspondence between amount of news coverage and amount of public concern is to ignore two other conditions that affect the power of the media to set the public agenda: (1) Some issues in some situations for some people require more coverage than others to cross the threshold of inattention and to displace other concerns, and (2) the context in which the news is presented determines to a large extent whether a problem comes to be perceived as important and politically relevant.

Issue Thresholds

What is an issue? Issues have been variously conceptualized: as *concerns*, the things about which people are personally worried; as *perceptions of key problems facing the country* and about which the government should do something; as the existence of *policy alternatives*, such as SALT II or an anti-abortion amendment, which people may choose to support or oppose and which may influence how they vote in an election; as *public controversies*, such as that over Watergate; and as the *underlying causes or determinants of political cleavage*, as when one talks of a "race issue" or a "law and order issue," even when these symbols do not openly enter the debate.

In the last analysis, an issue is whatever is in contention among a relevant public. The objects of potential controversy are diverse. A policy, a party and its platform or past performance, a political personality, a particular act, or even a theory about such matters as the state of the economy or the causes of a disease can stir public debate. Yet many controversies, even political ones, remain invisible to the general public. Discussion remains confined to the political bodies legally charged with decision-making responsibility although they may seek expert advice or be responsive to special interests. This kind of esoteric debate is largely ignored by those involved in isolating the agenda-setting effects of the mass media. They are concerned primarily with the public agenda, which is to be distinguished from the various institutional agendas. It consists of only those issues on which "the people" form opinions and are inclined to take sides.[32] This degree of participation can hardly develop except through some medium of communication that links the polity and the public at large.

In assessing the role of the media, we have to note the considerable differences in the amount and kinds of attention required to convert personal concerns, social problems, policy decisions, intragovernmental controversy, or fundamental cleavages among the population into public issues.

Some issues arise out of conditions that *directly affect nearly everybody* in the same way—such as inflation, high taxes, gasoline shortages, and so forth—and therefore exhibit a strong propensity to show up as personal concerns. A different type of issue is related to a situation whose effects are *selectively experienced*, such as urban congestion or draft calls. Last, there are conditions and developments whose effects are *generally remote from just about everyone*, such as the plight of refugees from Vietnam or wrongdoing high up in the government. The three categories have vastly different thresholds of sensitivity,[33] and the nature of the influence exerted by the media varies accordingly.

Problems that affect nearly everyone tend to have low thresholds. Thus, unfavorable economic conditions, such as inflation, would be of general concern even without attention from the news media. However, concern is apt to be boosted in two ways: through media recognition that puts the problem into the public domain and through statements by political figures trying to mobilize certain constituencies with promises, by fixing blame, or courting support for some kind of political action. The economic issue moves onto the political agenda quite naturally. As it does, the political relevance of the voter's own economic position compared with that of the previous year recedes while the relevance of the voter's perception of the state of economic affairs increases.[34] These perceptions are basically media generated, though as the number of individuals feeling personally worse off continues to increase, it becomes more difficult for anyone to believe prosperity is just around the corner, however optimistic media reports may be.

On matters that are more selectively experienced, like urban crime, the problem itself is made more visible and concern increased by media recognition. Reports of a crime wave can make even those not personally victimized cautious about walking the streets, even when the individual's chances for being attacked remain slim. Sensational media coverage can exaggerate the dimensions of a problem; it can also create a problem where none exists. For instance, speculations about an impending oil shortage can precipitate a run on existing supplies that leads to a real shortage.[35] While continuing attention by the media helps keep a problem alive, lagging media recognition can slow the rise of concern, particularly when those most directly affected are few and/or powerless. The majority either remains unaware of the problem or downgrades its importance, as in the case of ghetto conditions that suddenly erupt into riots.[36]

The potential influence of the media is greatest when the public has no direct contact or no first-hand experience with the matter in contention. Most of the perceptions people have of the larger universe, of the things they cannot see for themselves, are rarely the result of direct observation and experience but are known only second-hand, derived mostly from mass media reports. This includes most of the perceptions people have of the political environment. Important as other organized and interpersonal channels of communication may be in the political realm, they play only a supplementary role, operating within the larger symbolic context provided by media messages. Whether or not a major event, like the launching of the first Soviet sputnik or an American moon landing, gives rise to a political issue depends on whether it is reported in a context of crisis and partisanship or as a unifying achievement. The style of coverage reflects, in turn, the existing political situation and the ability of political figures to seize on the event as an issue. (In chapter 7, where we consider the impact of the televised impeachment debate, we shall have more to say about the rhetorical context of public affairs coverage.)

Also, problems compete for attention.[37] Therefore, the salience an issue has for elites or for the mass public is to some extent a relative matter. A potentially explosive issue surfacing at the "wrong" time, when other controversies are dominating the polity and the news media, is apt to be ignored until the time is ripe. Here, too, thresholds are relevant. High-threshold issues encounter greater difficulty in gaining the attention of the news media, and even when they do, as through some sensational exposé or foreign policy crisis, much depends on the ability of an administration, party, or candidate to identify with the cause or to steer clear of its negative implications. The controversy may affect political support without entering the list of most important problems. By contrast, low-threshold issues, because of their link to personal concerns, almost compel the attention of political elites and of the news media. This increases the likelihood that they will either displace or become assimilated into issues already on the public agenda.

Watergate as a High-Threshold Issue

Watergate was one of those issues requiring more than the ordinary amount of news recognition to break through the threshold of inattention. The problem it signified was outside the range of and remote from most people's immediate concerns. The details of the break-in at the Watergate complex seemed outlandish and their import difficult to fathom. Surfacing during a campaign, the whole story could even more readily be dismissed, since denunciations of the opposition for unfair electioneering methods and low-level campaign tactics are endemic to American politics. Still, it is not unheard of for such charges as those leveled by McGovern to stick and for "corruption" and "dirty politics" to provoke controversy and even become major public concerns in the heat of a campaign. This eventuality, in the case of a problem that does not directly impinge on almost everyone, requires more than routine recognition by the media. It requires a build-up, which is a function of more than the amount of space or time that the news media devote to the story. The facts have somehow to be translated into terms that make their implications personally meaningful and closer to the citizen's own concerns.

To understand why Watergate failed to become a major issue despite the considerable news coverage, we have to consider the context in which it surfaced: during an electoral contest and in competition with other political controversies for public attention.

The Media Situation. To belittle the significance of Watergate was an obvious and essential part of the Nixon strategy. The media, however unintentionally, played into his hands. Both the terminology adopted in the Watergate coverage and the way editors seemed to lean over backward to be fair and balance every story by presenting "two sides," even when there may have been only one, made it easier for the public to dismiss the incident and the charges growing out of it as just the usual campaign politics.

For one thing, the press gave big play to language that made the break-in seem frivolous, even foolish. Thus, Ron Ziegler, the White House press secretary, made headlines a few days after the burglary. When parrying with reporters, he dismissed the affair as a "third-rate burglary attempt," a phrase destined to haunt him. The President later referred to it as "this very bizarre incident." Before that, on June 22, he had told reporters at an impromptu press conference that such a raid "had no place in our electoral process or in our governmental process." A week after the break-in, June 24, the New York Times reported that the break-in was being popularly referred to in the nation's capital as the "Watergate caper." "Caper" was not, however, so far as we have been able to trace its origins, a Republican put-down. It first appeared (June 19) in the headline of a story by Ronald Kessler in the Washington Post. Since the phrase did not appear in the text, we assume it was the invention of a headline writer. Thereafter the label stuck. On June 21, a Post editorial took for its title a paraphrase of a then-popular CBS series, Mission Impossible. Under the headline Mission Incredible, the newspaper called the incident "an example of life imitating art right down to the taped locks, the rubber gloves, the tear gas pens, the array of electronic equipment, and the crisp new hundred dollar bills in the hands of the five men who stole into Democratic Party headquarters the other night under cover of darkness and something less than impenetrable aliases."

The term "caper" quickly gained currency among the attentive public. Eric Sevareid, in his commentary (CBS, September 7) noted the wide use of the term and NBC's venerable anchorman, David Brinkley, discussed the "caper," remarking that it had fallen flat as an issue, had influenced few votes, and was having no effect on the important issues of the election campaign (September 13). Indeed, it was to discredit this epithet that Walter Cronkite opened his extended discussion of Watergate, as part of the October 27 CBS Evening News, with the words: "At first it was called the Watergate caper. . . ." The rest of this 16-minute "news enterpriser" and its briefer sequel four days later, which alarmed the White House, pulled together bits and pieces of information to demonstrate that there was more to the break-in than just a bungled effort to bug a telephone. But, by that date, the campaign was virtually over except for the voting.

Few can doubt that by attacking the press, the White House dampened its enthusiasm for carrying exposés that could not be incontrovertibly documented. The response of many papers, during the 1972 campaign, was to retreat to some kind of mathematical balance, whereby stories favorable to the Republicans and stories favorable to the Democrats were given equal play and space each day. This "twinning," as Bagdikian calls it, was a popular practice.[38] Mainly this meant holding back a Watergate story damaging to the President until it could be coupled with a denial that generally neutralized its impact; where denials were not forthcoming, reporters often sought them out.

Bagdikian has supplied some examples, both from newspaper and television coverage. One example concerns the handling of a *Washington Post* story about a $25,000 campaign contribution that was "laundered" and wound up in the bank account of a Watergate burglar. ABC held back on the story for a day until it could be coupled with news that Nixon had given instructions for a Government Accounting Office probe into the matter. Using this same "twinning technique," the *Chicago Tribune* report on August 2 was captioned "GAO To Audit Finances of Nixon's Campaign Committee." Another of Bagdikian's illustrations: when the *Washington Post* on October 25 disclosed that White House aide H. R. Haldeman had been among those authorized to make payments from the Republican secret campaign fund to finance political sabotage, the story was immediately denied both by the CRP chairman and Nixon's press secretary. Next day the *Chicago Tribune* headlined the story: "Ziegler Denounces Post Spy Stories, Denies Link." Two of the story's 18 inches concerned the accusation, the rest the denial. The *Minneapolis Tribune* did not print the Haldeman story but put the denials on its front page.[39]

This balancing of publicity fitted the Republican strategy in yet another way. Throughout the campaign, Nixon had tried to make news only in his capacity as President, keeping as much distance as possible between himself and reporters, thus forcing them to settle for surrogates in reporting the Republican side. Charles Guggenheim, McGovern's media advisor, urged Democratic National Chairman O'Brien to write the networks and say the Democrats would not accept responses to McGovern from surrogates as constituting equal time, since this practice put them at a disadvantage.[40] Being matched against the President's men, rather than the President himself, could only make their candidate seem less Presidential. The media, for their own part, made little effort to expose this strategy by making an issue of the President's nonappearances. Their responsibility as journalists, as they saw it, was to reflect the "reality" of the campaign.[41] Paradoxically, that "reality," as later became clear, was greatly influenced by a media strategy which was an integral part both of Watergate and its coverup.

It is well documented that the networks were a special target of the Nixon administration. Just how much the administration tried to intervene directly in the networks' coverage of Watergate during the campaign has been the subject of some debate, the most rancorous involving the two-part CBS news enterpriser in late October. Suspicions were aroused when the second part was delayed for a day and then, when broadcast, cut by about half. Rumor had it that this was a response to White House pressure, beginning with a call from Charles Colson, known as a troubleshooter and key political advisor to the President. Both William S. Paley, Chairman of CBS, and Richard Salant, then President of CBS News,[42] have acknowledged Colson's complaint that CBS was discriminating against the administration in favor of McGovern, but they have also insisted that the decision to cut the second report was based on sound news judgment and was not in response to White House threats. Daniel Schorr, then a CBS correspondent, maintains, however, that Colson at a cocktail party told him: "Well, Mr. Schorr, we didn't stop your goddam Watergate spectacular, but we sure cut you down a bit, didn't we?"[43] The White House made other less clumsy attempts to manage the news through such tactics as feeding questions to journalists for use in questioning Democrats on television public affairs programs such as *Issues and Answers* and *Face the Nation.*[44]

White House intimidation of the press paid dividends, but their efforts at deceiving both press and public investigators and heading off investigations that could have made headlines, especially that of the House Banking and Currency Committee, paid larger dividends. For, in preventing damaging news from developing, CRP avoided publicity that could have increased the salience of Watergate and thereby affected the electoral preferences of some voters. Whether this media strategy, which was an integral part of the coverup, would have succeeded to the extent it did had the news media given it more attention remains moot.

The Political Situation. In explaining why Watergate did not make the public agenda in 1972, we must also consider the concrete circumstances under which Watergate was injected into the electoral campaign. Much of Richard Nixon's first term had been dominated by controversy over Vietnam, a problem that continued to be perceived as important and politically relevant by a large number of people. It remained prominent in the news throughout the summer and autumn. Yet, even had more of the press acted so as to make Watergate the big issue that it ought to have been, it is unlikely that it would have become decisive for the outcome. For, the overriding issue of the 1972 campaign, the perception most salient for voters' choices, was the relative credibility of the two candidates: which of the two could be counted on to achieve peace in Vietnam? to cope with worsening economic conditions? to deal effectively with the crime and drug problems that were uppermost in the minds of most people? In 1972, most voters, no matter what their major concerns might be, were prepared to vote for the man or for the party they believed had their own best interest at heart or simply for the one they believed would do the better job.[45] To become a major factor in the election Watergate would somehow have had to be perceived as relevant to Nixon's credibility. Yet it was not so identified and, again, the question is "why not?"

The answer lies, first, in the loss of credibility suffered by McGovern in the course of his fight to win the nomination and during the campaign, which made his charges against the Nixon administration appear as a desperate attempt to divert attention from problems plaguing his own candidacy. The campaign had begun with McGovern the clear underdog. Every poll showed Nixon with a big lead. Still, Nixon's lead was no greater than it had been at the same point four years earlier in an election that he eventually won by the smallest conceivable margin over Hubert Humphrey. McGovern, however, was unable to devise a strategy to close the gap.

If Watergate did not become an issue in the campaign, it was not for want of McGovern's trying. Speaking to a United Automobile Workers local August 15, he labelled the break-in "the kind of thing you expect under a person like Hitler," a charge readily dismissed by the Republicans as "character assassination" and political hyperbole. He raised the issue again, in mid-September, after having been encouraged by party leaders frustrated by their unsuccessful attempts to use the courts and government investigations to expose the break-in as something more than the usual politics. By mid-October a new stridency marked the McGovern campaign rhetoric. Not only did his speeches place more emphasis on corruption and honesty in government but Watergate was featured in a new series of spot commercials. One referred to the ten million dollars received in secret campaign contributions from men whose names and interests the Republicans refused to reveal. "Who," the viewer was asked, "are these men and what do they want?" With the campaign effectively over, McGovern in a major speech, spotlighted Watergate as the main issue before the public: voters, in voting for Nixon, he said, would be voting for Watergate corruption.

But nothing McGovern had to say about Watergate alarmed the public.

Earlier mistakes had cost the Democratic nominee dearly in credibility and damaged his reputation for decisiveness. In the end, many people even lost confidence that McGovern, who had gained his prominence as a peace candidate, could do a better job than Nixon, always considered a "hawk," in ending the war in Vietnam.[46] Especially, McGovern had been irretrievably hurt by his handling of the Eagleton affair less than two weeks after his nomination. When the press revealed that Senator Thomas Eagleton of Missouri, McGovern's Vice-Presidential running mate, had previously been hospitalized for psychiatric treatment, McGovern's inept handling of the problem (he first said he was 1000 percent behind Eagleton but asked the Missourian to take himself off the ticket a few days later) did not exactly improve his image. Most people, including many Democrats, reacted negatively.[47] The issue dominated the news for some days, into early August, and Republicans had little to do but exploit it for all it was worth. In his July 27 press conference, Nixon was asked four questions about the Eagleton affair but none about the investigation of Watergate.

But if one reason why Watergate did not "take off" as a campaign issue was McGovern's lack of credibility, we have also to explain why Watergate did not "rub off" and tarnish Nixon's image. First, we have noted the success of the strategy whereby Nixon sequestered himself in the White House, venturing out only to address audiences guaranteed to give him an enthusiastic reception that could be recorded by the television cameras and the press corps. By distancing himself from the press, he managed to escape the close scrutiny given McGovern's every move and statement. This also enabled him to stonewall on Watergate. By letting his Vice President, Spiro Agnew, and leaders of CRP carry the burden of responding to McGovern's charges of "whitewash" and corruption, he managed not only to stave off suspicions concerning his personal involvement but also to stay Presidential and personally above the whole affair.

There is a second more basic explanation for the reluctance of the public to point a finger at the President. This is found in the phenomenon of incredulity.[48] There is no greater fallacy than the belief that facts speak for themselves. The charge that a President could have involved his own staff in a "third-rate burglary" or in the "laundering of campaign funds" or could have promised the people the "most thorough investigation ever" that would later prove pure fiction seemed outlandish to most people. This skepticism alone gave a certain weight to the official denials of White House complicity. In 1972 the American people may have been ready to believe that a mayor or a governor might so sully the office he held but not a President who had taken a sacred oath of office at the beginning of his term.

This awe of the office of President, which rubs off on the incumbent, was shared by a large part of the press corps and inhibited them from pursuing the case as hard as they might have. The same was, of course, true of most politicians. The McGovern camp long remained hesitant about exploiting Watergate as an issue, afraid that a frontal attack on corruption and abuse of power in the administration might misfire.[49] A national poll by ORC in early October confirmed their forebodings: 51 percent of those questioned agreed that McGovern's attack was "simply a political charge by a desperate politician who is behind"; only 29 percent thought that Nixon needed to "answer and explain these charges" while the remaining 20 percent had no opinion on the matter. When the question was repeated three weeks later, after news stories had linked Haldeman to the break-in, the gain scored by McGovern was but a slight one.

News coverage, then, had created awareness of Watergate, but this did not translate directly into a politically relevant response. With the evaluation of the candidates' suitability for office clearly the decisive factor for voters, Watergate never became linked in most people's minds with Nixon's fitness to be President. It did not appear to intrude directly into people's lives. While few would consider illegal electronic eavesdropping and political sabotage to be acceptable campaign practices, the crime was perceived as that of politicians against other politicians and thereby too remote from everyday concerns to agitate the ordinary voter.

CHAPTER 4

HOW WATERGATE MADE THE PUBLIC AGENDA

A half year after Richard Nixon's landslide victory, Watergate had become the center of a full-blown political controversy. Nearly everybody was aware of it, and many more people were now taking to considering it an "important problem."

Public awareness of "Watergate" had risen from 52 percent in late September 1972 to 83 percent by early April 1973. This near-saturation level of awareness, which Gallup found when it resumed polling on Watergate five months after the election, may actually have been reached as early as mid-February.[1] At any rate, by the middle of April, the awareness figure stood at 91 percent and climbed to 96 percent by mid-May, just before the Senate Watergate Committee was about to begin its public hearings (May 17).

Along with growing awareness had come growing concern. Even before these hearings, Watergate had made its way, for the first time, onto the Gallup list of "most important problems facing the country today." Though clearly still lagging behind such low-threshold issues as "the high cost of living," mentioned as a concern by 62 percent of adult Americans, "Watergate and/or corruption in government," named by 16 percent, was in close competition with "crime and lawlessness" (17%) and on a par with "drugs" (also 16%), two matters apt to impinge more directly on the day-to-day lives of citizens.[2]

As late as March 25 a *New York Times* editorial had despaired of what it called the "monumental apathy" of Americans in the face of this serious trend in corruption. Yet, the number of people willing to play ostrich and simply write the whole matter off as "just more politics," though still a plurality, had been steadily dwindling, and the number for whom the "bugging attempt" was "really something serious" had been going up correspondingly. Two national polls came up with similar findings in April: only about half the nation still believed Watergate to be "just politics," the kind of thing both parties engage in.[3] And, apparently, even many of those not yet ready to say they were seriously concerned were somewhat uneasy for, by April, a new element had entered the controversy. There was a rather pervasive feeling that the President was being less than candid with the public. At issue now was how to proceed so that the full truth could be flushed out. Nearly two-thirds (63%) of the citizenry believed Nixon had "withheld important information" about Watergate and only 9 percent thought he had been "frank and honest" about it.[4]

The suspicion that the President might have been actively involved was gradually growing. As late as February, few people—just 3 percent, according to a private poll for the Republicans—believed Nixon himself had ordered the break-in and another 11 percent, most of them Democrats, though doubting the President's direct involvement, held him responsible for the atmosphere that had made it possible.[5] Yet by early April all this had changed; far more people now suspected a tie-in between the once "bizarre incident" and the White House; more than four of every ten persons interviewed in a nationwide survey now believed that Nixon knew about "the Watergate situation in advance."[6] Given these nagging doubts and increasing suspicions, it is not surprising that Nixon was also receiving a strongly negative rating on his "handling of the Watergate case."[7]

Was Watergate leading people to lose confidence in the Nixon administration? Here answers are hard to come by. Few pollsters or survey researchers had been asking questions about Watergate between October 1972 and April 1973. Only the month-by-month ratings of the Presidential performance—measured by responses to questions such as "Do you approve or disapprove of the way Nixon is handling his job as President?"—provide some clues.

These ratings, routinely tracked by polling organizations, suggest that Watergate did not rub off on Nixon until early in April. In that month, there was an abrupt drop in the proportion approving the job he was doing and an abrupt rise in the proportion clearly disapproving. Thereafter, Watergate continued to take its toll. Two surveys, taken just a week apart, the first ending April 2 and the other on April 9, indicate a nine-point decline during that short period in Nixon's *net* approval rating. Although the press usually headlines the rise and fall in the approval rate when tracking Presidential popularity, the net approval rating—the percent approving minus the percent disapproving—provides a more sensitive barometer of public sentiment. By this measure, ten more points were lost in the three-week period ending April 30. By the end of the first week in May net approval, according to Gallup, had fallen from +27 to +3—all within about one month. The same decline is evident in responses to Harris questions. By Spring 1973, net approval ratings were well below those Nixon had been receiving throughout the year beginning June 1972.

Such trend data have, however, to be read with caution. In February 1973 Nixon was enjoying peak ratings. It was the beginning of his second term and just after the peace agreement was signed with North Vietnam on January 25, resulting in the return of the American prisoners of war after years in North Vietnam. He was bound to slip from this pinnacle of popularity, even without the albatross of Watergate around his neck.

Nor should the strength of public disapproval be overestimated. It is true that Nixon on his relatively rare public appearances was now apt to be confronted with placards protesting Watergate. Yet as a much-favored Presidential front-runner, he had seen other placards deploring his role in Vietnam. At neither time was there a public clamor for his head. Reporters visiting college campuses in the spring found national issues, including Watergate, being all but ignored by students.[8] Congressmen were not subjected to the spontaneous outpouring of letters, phone calls, and telegrams that was to be their lot when the controversy heated up, though many found their constituents, when asked about their opinions on Watergate, wondering just where it would all end.[9] Most people still regarded the President as "a man of high integrity" whom they held in high repute. Not only did he rate high on this measure to begin with, but the decline was not nearly so drastic as it was in such categories as on inspiring confidence personally or handling corruption.[10]

This conservative assessment of public indignation over the Watergate disclosures was apparently shared by the President himself. In a telephone conversation with H. R. Haldeman on April 25, he told his White House Chief of Staff that "despite all the polls . . . I think there's still a hell of a lot of people out there, and from what I've seen . . . they want to believe. That's the point, isn't it?"[11] It was indeed. Some five months after the Presidential election fewer people than before thought Watergate was nothing but another routine political squabble. There had been some erosion of Presidential credibility. But the majority of the public, unable to understand what was going on, still wanted to believe in Mr. Nixon. It was getting at the truth about Watergate that was becoming an issue. How had the media contributed to this growing concern?

EVENTS AND SATURATION COVERAGE

The Watergate story appeared to have been all but buried in the immediate post-election period. Was it the renewed attention the news media gave it the next spring that accounted for its emergence as an issue? First, Watergate as a news story, even immediately after the election, never altogether disappeared from sight. Things kept happening. In December 1972, when Dorothy Hunt, the wife of Watergate defendant H. L. Hunt, died in an airline crash in Chicago, her purse was discovered to contain a large sum of money, all in hundred-dollar bills. This brought Watergate briefly back into the headlines. Other Watergate news centered around Judge Sirica, whose court had jurisdiction over the trial of the defendants in the Watergate burglary case. In December, Sirica became involved in a dispute with the *Los Angeles Times* over its publication of an interview with a former FBI agent, Alfred Baldwin, who had been a member of the unit responsible for the Watergate break-in and a key witness in the upcoming trial. Then, through most of January, it was the trial itself that drew attention. When the defendants, over the objections of their own counsel, decided to change their plea to guilty on all counts, Sirica openly questioned their motives, noting that this would remove the accused permanently from all questioning in open court. A spate of stories in the press alleged that Hunt was behind the change, that the men were being paid for keeping silent by persons unnamed. These stories originated mainly in the *New York Times*, the *Washington Post*, *Time*, and in the syndicated columns of Jack Anderson. Judge Sirica, aware of these allegations, sharply questioned the defendants but could not shake them. All denied that they were being coerced in any shape, manner, or form, insisting that they were not being paid by anybody for anything. Sirica made it clear that he did not believe them, and at the end of the trial, on January 30, declared that the full facts behind the break-in had yet to be unearthed.[12]

By the big play it gave Sirica's suspicions and through editorial comment, an important part of the press was beginning to convert the story of Watergate from a "bungled burglary" into a "coverup" and a quest for the truth. For example, a January 13 editorial in the *New York Times* said the question in need of an answer was who had hired the defendants. It called for the appointment of a special and independent prosecutor. At issue, as the editorial put it, was the "integrity and credibility" of an administration that, for the next four years, had to be "accountable to the American people."

Soon, the Senate's first steps toward an investigation of its own also made news. In early January, its Democratic caucus voted to ask Senator Sam Ervin, a North Carolina Democrat, to head a probe of the Watergate affair, a move Sirica supported by publicly hoping, on February 2, that the Senate committee would be granted sufficient power "to get to the bottom of what happened in this case."[13] On February 7, the Senate, miffed at Nixon's failure to deliver his State of the Union message in person, unanimously adopted a resolution to establish a seven-man select committee to probe all aspects of the bugging case and other reported instances of attempted political espionage against the Democrats during the 1972 election campaign.

In January and February, these and other Watergate items often made newspaper headlines as well as the network news on television. Yet they were to be overshadowed by dramatic events that underlined Nixon's role as President and world leader. On January 20 he was inaugurated for his second term. The ceremonies, estimated to cost more than four million dollars, were more expensive than any previous American inaugural. "We stand," the President told the nation in his televised address, "on the threshold of a new era of peace in the world." Three days later, in a nationwide television report, the President announced that Henry Kissinger and the chief North Vietnamese negotiator, Le Duc Tho, had initialed an agreement "to end the war and bring peace with honor in Vietnam and Southeast Asia."

The release of Americans held prisoner in Vietnam began on February 12. With the arrival of the first group of men at Clark Air Force base in the Phillipines, it became a national television production. The first man out of the plane paid homage to home and country and, also, to Richard Nixon. "We are," said Navy Captain Jeremiah P. Denton, "profoundly grateful to our Commander-in-Chief." Air Force Colonel James Kasler was even more explicit, sounding a theme that Nixon would make very much his own. "President Nixon," he said, "has brought us home with honor."

During February and most of March Watergate developments also competed with other big stories. In February there was the devaluation of the dollar by 10 percent, then a continuing dollar crisis, which worsened in March and temporarily closed foreign exchange markets in Europe and Japan. Of less personal concern to most of the public but more sensational and good news copy was a 37-day confrontation between militant Indian leaders and federal troops around the Oglala Sioux hamlet of Wounded Knee, South Dakota. When the last POWs did come home late in March, the President again went on the air to announce that "for the first time in twelve years no American military forces are in Vietnam" but, by that time, developments in the Watergate story were dominating the news.

If Watergate never completely disappeared from view after the election, it was only in March that levels of coverage once again reached those of the previous fall and soon surpassed them. After late March time and space devoted to Watergate rose rapidly. By May the *New York Times* was carrying an average of 14 items a day, nearly eight times the average of the previous October and coverage in other major newspapers rose correspondingly.[14] The increase in television coverage was even more dramatic, considering the time strictures of the network newscast. In the two weeks before the televised Senate hearings began, between 20 and 25 percent of the roughly 20 minutes available for hard news on the typical program was devoted to Watergate items.[15]

This expanded coverage was not simply an increase in amount, but a change in kind. It marked the onset of the sort of *saturation* coverage that had been devoted to Watergate for only brief intervals in 1972. Saturation is the combined effect of *prominence* with *continuity*: Prominence, as operationalized here, means placement on the front page of a newspaper or devoting at least 60 seconds to an item on television; continuity requires such prominence on at least four out of five successive weekday telecasts or, in the case of newspapers (where one must make allowance for Sunday and Monday doldrums in the news) on four successive days, or five out of seven, or six out of nine.[16] In no case can there be a break in front-page placement for longer than three days.

Prominence gives a news item the visibility that facilitates one's attention. Continuity allows for the kind of reiteration and development of news angles that help to fix the basic elements of a story in one's mind. Both are conducive to the emergence of an issue. Both are necessary before a high threshold event like Watergate can break through the barrier of public inattention to become a dominant concern. How much prominence and continuity are necessary to move an issue onto the public agenda depends on the political context.

We have charted, in Figure 1, the periods from June 1972 through May 1973 when Watergate was given saturation coverage. There is a marked difference in pattern between the earlier and later months. In the campaign phase, periods of saturation coverage hardly overlap; beginning in the early

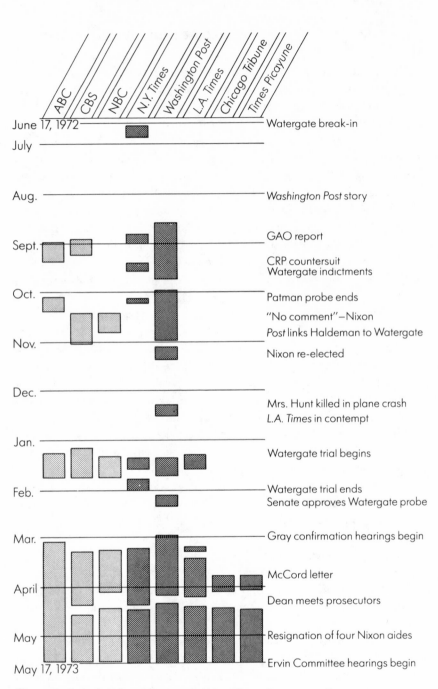

Figure 1. Periods When Watergate Was Given Saturation Coverage (June 1972–May 1973)

months of 1973, they more nearly coincide and from early April on every one of the networks and papers examined was indeed "saturated" with Watergate. This continued with little interruption until Nixon resigned.

Through most of the 1972 campaign, whenever a network or a newspaper gave prominent and continuous coverage to Watergate, as several did from time to time, it tended to be alone in this. Most of the big Watergate stories in this period were developed by investigative reporters flushing out information the Nixon camp had been eager to hide. Competing newspapers and management were not always eager to feature what they themselves had not developed, and many of the exposés derived their news value from being tied to a specific deadline. This helps explain why even in October 1972, when all three networks gave saturation treatment to essentially the same events, the items were broadcast on different days. CBS was "Watergate-saturated" from October 13 through November 1, ABC from October 3 through 12, and NBC from October 13 through 25. The only Watergate-related development to receive saturation coverage simultaneously from at least two networks and the *New York Times* was the controversy in late August over the release of a report by the GAO on illegal campaign contributions.

In 1973 the pattern changed. The media ceased in any sense to act as prime movers on Watergate. Breaking stories not initiated by the press mandated timely coverage so that periods of saturation coverage began to more nearly overlap. What first breathed new life into the story was the start of the trial of the Watergate defendants, held in Washington with its unique concentration of news staffs. For much of January it provided a continuous flow of news. Other developments were the confirmation hearings of Patrick Gray as FBI director and the civil suits by attorneys of Nixon's reelection committee against 14 members of the press. But the real breakthrough did not come until March 23, the day before the Watergate defendants were to be sentenced. A letter by James McCord, one of the seven defendants, was read by Judge Sirica in open court. A bombshell, it spoke of "political pressure" on all the defendants to remain silent, of perjury during the trial, of higher-ups—not named—who were implicated in the Watergate operation. From this point on, the disclosures began to fit together. They had too much plausibility to be dismissed and calls for a detailed explanation from the Administration came from both politicians and journalists. The possibility that a major scandal was brewing could no longer be ignored, even by the regional press, many of whose editors and publishers had been and remained strong believers in the President.

The number of Watergate headlines briefly declined in early April. But after this hiatus, every one of five major newspapers we examined gave prominent coverage to every development for the entire month before the Senate hearings began. From mid-April through mid-May, 56 percent of the evening newscasts (on 23 weekdays) led off with a Watergate story. With Watergate generating so many damaging stories, the White House could no longer afford to appear unresponsive to demands that the President do something to clear up suspicions, especially since these demands also came from Republicans concerned about their political futures. Events were moving so fast that the White House, previously reluctant to comment on the subject, itself became an important generator of Watergate news.

One by one persons close to the Oval Office began to be implicated. As news of McCord's testimony before the Watergate grand jury leaked out, the earlier Nixon strategy of diverting attention to other national issues no longer sufficed. The President finally (April 17) went on the offensive with two dramatic announcements of his own: first, he had initiated a "new inquiry" into the Watergate case leading to "major developments . . . concerning which it would be improper to be more specific"; second, in a partial retreat from a prior stand, he would permit testimony by White House aides before the Senate select committee under certain conditions. In adding that none of those who testified should expect immunity from prosecution, Nixon was talking as much to John Dean as to his own critics. He meant to cast Dean, whose lawyers were seeking such immunity in exchange for his testimony, in an unfavorable light as someone trying to shield himself from the consequences of past wrongdoing.

This effort failed to divert the media from pursuing the Watergate story. If anything it stirred interest in the newly developing controversy between the President and the Senate committee about the extent of its investigatory authority. Senator Sam Ervin, its chairman, made the front page when he insisted his Committee alone would be the final judge on whether White House aides could or could not refuse to answer questions. Ronald Ziegler, Nixon's press secretary, made equally big news when (April 17), after relaying Nixon's statement about "major new developments," he referred to all past statements about White House noninvolvement as "inoperative." Incidentally, this phrase, which quickly became part of the expanding Watergate vocabulary, was not altogether Ziegler's invention but practically put into his mouth by reporters who had been badgering him to tell why the President was backtracking on his old insistence that no one in the White House had been implicated.[17] Ziegler repeatedly avoided an answer by assuring them that "the president's statement today" is the "operative" statement. Finally, someone asked whether he was then saying that "the other statement . . . is *inoperative*" "Yes," Ziegler replied, making Watergate history.[18]

The rash of resignations by persons high up in the Nixon administration, all duly reported by the press, told its own story. Then, on April 30, the White House announced the resignations of Nixon's two closest aides, John Erhlichman and H. R. Haldeman, along with those of Attorney General Richard Kleindienst and White House counsel John Dean. That evening, in a televised address, Nixon accepted responsibility for "those whose zeal exceeded their judgment" while denying any complicity either in the break-in or any attempt to cover up. He now conceded, that "there had been an effort to conceal the facts." In pointing out that in 1972 he had not, for the first time in his long political career, run his own political campaign, he suggested not only that he had been unaware of what CRP had been up to, but also that his own investigators had lied to him. From here on, he would leave Watergate to his new Attorney General, Elliott Richardson. Then, in a somewhat emotional appeal, he expressed his desire to be free of Watergate so he could spend his remaining 1361 days in office dealing with grave foreign and domestic matters.

Again, despite the President's attempt to put Watergate behind him, sometimes dramatic developments compelled more news coverage. One bombshell was the dismissal on May 11 of government charges of espionage, theft, and conspiracy against Daniel Ellsberg and Anthony J. Russo Jr., defendants in the Pentagon Papers trial, which ended abruptly because of an "unprecedented series of actions" by a special unit established in the White House. The reference was to a surreptitious entry into the office of Ellsberg's psychiatrist in search of confidential medical records to be used, as it later turned out, to discredit his patient politically. The opening of the televised Watergate hearings, on May 17, and the appointment, on May 18, of Archibald Cox as Special Watergate Prosecutor, placed the Watergate scandal and many things related to it on the agenda of several public bodies. Watergate would have to be dealt with. What still remained unsettled was how the issue would eventually be resolved.

THE MEDIA CONTEXT

Does saturation coverage in response to the march of events suffice to explain changes in the perceptions of Watergate and the increase in public concern? The concomitant increase in coverage lends credence to the hypothesis that the media force attention to certain issues. But the mere discovery that there is a parallel between the attention given an "issue" and its salience for the mass public tells us little about the process by which this occurs. It is our contention that more than direct learning is involved.

We know of only two empirical studies that directly address the influence of the mass media on attitudes toward Watergate during this period. One is by Weaver, McCombs, and Spellman. In May 1973 they recontacted people in a North Carolina community whom they had first interviewed in an election survey the previous October.[19] Comparing respondents' perceptions of Watergate during the campaign with their perceptions at this time, the researchers found that those most exposed to political news during the campaign were least likely to have changed their minds about the importance of Watergate, and that the amount of change was negatively correlated to the frequency with which people had discussed politics.

Both correlations are weak but worth noting, because they contradict the basic assumption underlying the agenda-setting hypothesis: exposure to and interest in media coverage should strengthen its effect. Neither did these researchers find any evidence that the amount of media use or political discussion in the more recent period was in any way related to the amount of change. In plainer language, those who had followed the campaign most avidly in 1972 were least apt to have changed their minds about the importance of Watergate during the half year since the election, and those who had changed their minds were not now following Watergate developments either more closely or less closely than those who had not.

What is one to make of these findings? Other evidence from the study suggests that, among those who had followed the campaign most closely, openness to change was limited by a *ceiling effect*, which is to say that some people, having already been influenced, no longer were open to influence. Watergate had already broken through the threshold of their inattention during the electoral campaign, and once they had identified it as a serious problem, further exposure to Watergate news could produce little more change. It was those who had not been paying attention earlier whose perceptions were more likely to be affected by the spate of Watergate stories in the spring. The saturation coverage compelled their attention, forcing them to recognize that there was a problem and that the problem was serious.

Also, campaign communications, which are designed to persuade, can put people on their guard if they are aware of this intent. So long as the election was being contested, Nixon supporters had every motive to accept the White House belittling of Watergate. Once it was over, however, the issue resurfaced in a different, less patently political, context. With the McCord letter, the Watergate issue was becoming more bipartisan, with prominent Republicans joining in the demand that Nixon clear up the matter. Senator Barry Goldwater, leader of the conservative wing of the party, had likened Watergate to the Teapot Dome corruption scandal when Warren Harding was the White House occupant. Senator Charles Mathias of Maryland, a liberal Republican, said Watergate posed a moral question; it threatened public confidence in government. Senator John Tower, a conservative Texas Republican, said it was "in the best interests of the White House that the whole thing be bared."[20] Calls for investigations from Senators once solidly in the Nixon camp could no longer be dismissed as mere campaign rhetoric.

Still another factor is the nature of the information that people were being asked to accept. Where the situation that gives rise to an issue can be known only through the media—where the news is about events that are totally outside the range of most people's direct experience—the believability of the events being reported or, as in this case, of charges being leveled is an important determinant of what people will believe. The distinction between credibility, which is an attribute of the source of information, and credulity, the individual tendency to believe or disbelieve, helps make understandable the process through which Watergate made the public agenda.

Edelstein and Tefft, who have made this distinction, found that the break-in and related events seemed at first to have no relation to the lives of people they had been interviewing during May and June 1973 in Longview, Washington.[21] There was something about the things that were supposed to have happened or to be happening that many people found hard to believe. Any tendency toward disbelief was reinforced by skepticism about the sources from which the information came. Many of the charges were emanating from politicians whose credibility could be discounted and from journalists suspected of bias against Nixon. They also noted that people's disbelief, in first reading or hearing about Watergate, centered more on the facts of the case—that is, on the events and actions described as having taken place within the President's own circle—than on the credibility or trustworthiness of the media or of any specific medium from which the information came. Least believable was the idea that this was all part of a high-level political espionage effort and that the government would go out of its way to protect those responsible. Only somewhat more believable was the suggestion that "political parties" or "other officials" could have been involved in breaking and entering. There were so many things people found hard to believe that, even before they could ponder the importance of the Watergate issue, they first had to be convinced that a number of facts were indeed believable or, at least, beyond disbelief.

The level of credulity had gradually changed. By late March and April many more people had come to accept that some of the things they were reading or hearing about could have happened or, at least, were ready to grant them enough credence to want them clarified. This suspension of disbelief did not necessarily mean that they were ready to accept as fact either that the White House was involved or that Nixon was untruthful. What they had come to believe was that the President was not revealing all he knew. To many, this meant that he was shielding those who had served him.

That "getting the facts out" had become both a concern and an issue is also apparent from responses to Nixon's April 30 speech. While most political leaders, speaking for public consumption, expressed relief that the President had broken his long silence on Watergate, spokesmen for both parties continued to press for the appointment of a special prosecutor. On the other hand, when Representative John Moss, a California Democrat, called for a formal inquiry into possible impeachment, the House Democratic floor leader Thomas P. O'Neill Jr. of Massachusetts dubbed this a "bit premature."

As for the public, response to the speech was not only split but also ambivalent. Those who had watched or listened divided four to three against Nixon's having "told the whole truth" (Gallup, May 2). A Harris telephone poll, spanning three days (May 1–3), found just about half agreeing that Nixon's speaking out had gone a long way toward restoring public confidence in the integrity of the White House. Most of the rest disagreed, and some 12 percent withheld judgment. This response makes it appear that most Americans wanted to believe Nixon's story, even though parts of it strained their credulity. What the public found hardest to believe was that it had taken the President a full nine months to find out about White House involvement in the cover-up.[22] The issue had changed from whether there should be an investigation to what kind of an investigation there should be. On this matter there was a striking consensus: 78 percent of those telephoned agreed that "there are still so many unanswered questions left about Watergate that only a completely independent investigation of the affair by people not controlled by the President will get at the truth."

THE AGENDA-BUILDING PROCESS

By Spring 1973 Watergate was on the *political* agenda. Congress had launched an investigation into illegal campaign practices. A newly appointed Special Prosecutor was given full authority to investigate and prosecute offenses arising out of the break-in to the Democratic National Headquarters and just about any other offenses relating to the election. By this time also, Watergate was on the *public* agenda. A significant segment of the citizenry was seriously concerned about the disclosures and wanted the government to do something, while opinion about the nature of the problem and what needed to be done was divided.

As yet, not many people saw in Watergate, as they would later, a personal threat to their own well-being, closely touching their lives. Public opinion four months into Nixon's second term could hardly be called "outraged," but neither could it be depicted any longer as "apathetic," as it had been as late as March. Gradually this public was making its presence felt. Politicians were becoming aware that as more and more people came to take Watergate seriously, most would react negatively to the appearance that anything was being covered up. Those in Congress pressing for a full investigation were able to ride the crest of this feeling. Public reaction to Nixon's April 30 speech supplied the ammunition they needed to outmaneuver those opposed to, or at least not enthusiastic about, a formal inquiry.

Watergate had broken into public consciousness only after the coverage had created a sense of crisis. This is not to say that the Watergate issue was something that the electronic and print media had created out of whole cloth. The coverage, which had stirred interest in Watergate, was dictated by events but the media themselves had become part of the field of action. Political figures with a stake in the outcome were using whatever publicity they could attract to advance their own goals and interests, thereby providing grist for the media and adding to the number of Watergate-relevant events there to be covered. As a result, the coverage reached saturation levels with

Watergate on the front page and on the evening news day after day after day as well as on early morning, late evening, and Sunday public affairs programs. But the headlines alone would not have sufficed to make a serious issue out of a problem so removed from most people's daily concerns. Continuity was necessary to rivet attention to new facts as they emerged. The process is circular. Media exposure and public attention generate responses at the elite level that produce still more news in a cycle of mutual reinforcement that continues until politicians and public tire of an issue or another issue moves into the center of the political stage.

Once again we revert to the distinction between low-threshold and high-threshold issues. On matters of concern to people, because they fall within their direct experience, as is the case with various bread-and-butter, sickness-and-health, life-and-death issues, the media clearly lack power to suppress concern. But they can do more than stimulate interest. By directing attention to these concerns, they provide a context that influences *how* people will think about these matters—where they believe the fault lies and whether anything (and what) should be done. Publicity given to essentially private concerns transforms them into public concerns. Whether or not it increases the problem for those affected, it does increase morale and legitimates the will to protest.

With regard to high-threshold issues like Watergate, the media play an even more essential role. Had it not been for the news reports about Watergate, hardly anyone would have known about campaign finance violations, "dirty tricks," illegal surveillance by persons connected with the White House, and the lot. Media attention was necessary before Watergate could be considered a problem. Yet, in publicizing a high-threshold issue like Watergate, the media do more than direct attention to a problem; they influence how people will think about it. They supply the context that, by making the problem politically relevant, gives people reasons for taking sides and converts the problem into a serious political issue. In this sense the public agenda is not so much set by the media as built up through a cycle of media activity that transforms an elite issue into a public controversy.

None of this should be read to mean that the media, all on their own, dictate the public agenda. They cannot "teach" the public what the issues are. They certainly do not operate in total autonomy from the political system. The gradual saturation of news content with Watergate depended on political developments in which the press itself was only one of several movers. Agenda building—a more apt term than agenda setting—is a collective

process in which media, government, and the citizenry reciprocally influence one another in at least some respects.

Let us, in conclusion, sketch out how the news media affect this agenda-
building process.

First, they highlight some events or activities. They make them stand out
from among the myriads of other contemporaneous events and activities that
could equally have been selected out for publicity. Making something the
center of interest affects how much people will think and talk about it. This
much is only common sense.

But, second, being in the news is not enough to guarantee attention to
an issue. The amount and kind of coverage required varies from issue to
issue. Different kinds of issues require different amounts and kinds of coverage to gain attention. Where news focuses on a familiar concern likely to
affect almost everyone, this almost guarantees instant attention. In the case
of a high-threshold issue like Watergate, which also surfaced at the wrong
time, it takes saturation coverage to achieve this result. Specifically, recognition by the "cosmopolitan" media was not enough. Only after the more
locally oriented press had become saturated with news of Watergate developments did it emerge as an issue that would remain on the political and
public agenda for nearly 16 months.

Third, the events and activities in the focus of attention still have to be
framed, to be given a field of meanings within which they can be understood. They must come to stand for something, identify some problem, link
up with some concern. The first exposé of the political fund used to finance
the unit responsible for the break-in was publicized during a Presidential
campaign. It was reported and interpreted within the context of that continuing contest. The Democrats' effort to change this context by interpreting
Watergate as a symptom of widespread political corruption within the Administration was not very successful. Watergate remained, at least for a while,
a partisan issue. The context had first to be changed.

Fourth, the language the media use to track events also affects the meaning imputed to them. Metaphors such as "Watergate caper" and "bugging
incident," which belittled the issue, disappeared that spring under an avalanche of signs of a high-level political scandal. The press, along with politicians, adopted less deprecatory codewords. "Watergate" or "Watergate
scandal" came to denote the various questionable activities now being disclosed. The words stood for nothing specific, yet for anything that could
possibly happen.

Fifth, the media link the activities or events that have become the focus of attention to secondary symbols whose location on the political landscape is easily recognized. They also weave discrete events into a continuing political story, so that the lines of division on the issue as it develops tend to coincide with the cleavage between the organized political parties or between other sharply defined groups. The public is informed about what is the "Republican" or the "Democratic" position, or the position of any other group—for instance, producers vs. consumers, have vs. have-nots—so that potential partisans can align themselves. Often the lines of division around an issue about to surface are unclear. And they are likely to be fluid. When Watergate first surfaced during the 1972 campaign, it was defined primarily as a partisan clash between Democrats and Republicans. By Spring 1973 opinion still divided along political lines, but a realignment was under way as the issue changed and sides began to shape up around the "need to get the facts out," over the public "right to know" vs. "executive privilege," and on the question of confidence in the integrity of the government.

Finally, there are the prestige and standing of the spokesmen who articulate these concerns and demands. Their effectiveness stems in good part from their ability to command media attention. Democratic politicians like Larry O'Brien and George McGovern had been lonely voices in the wilderness when, during the campaign, they pressed for a full investigation. Their demands, though publicized, were neither much heard nor much heeded. They were known as people with an axe to grind. But as the controversy escalated, the publicity given Judge Sirica's admonishment that the full truth had not been told led prestigious Republicans to call for explanations, and their various attempts to get at the facts put pressure on the White House. The bystander public was being wooed.

The process of agenda-building, as we conceive of it, goes on continuously and involves several feedback loops. The most important of these are (1) the images through which political figures see themselves and their own activities mirrored in the media, (2) the pooling of information within the press corps that fosters similarities in the imagery disseminated, and (3) the various indicators of the public response, especially opinion polling, towards which press and polity alike are oriented. As the controversy over Watergate continued, the nature of the issue continued to change, just as it had changed in the five months that followed the election.

As for the agenda-setting hypothesis: the media do play a vital role in calling attention to a problem, but neither public awareness nor public concern suffices to convert a problem into a public issue. It becomes a public issue only when the public can locate it on the political landscape and see reasons for taking sides. The news media help build these issues by establishing the necessary linkages between the polity and the public that facilitate the emergence of a problem as an issue. Once such linkages exist, even a high-threshold issue such as Watergate can retain its place on the public agenda against strong competition.

CHAPTER 5

THE ERVIN COMMITTEE HEARINGS

On May 17, 1973, eleven months after the five burglars were apprehended at Watergate, the electronic media took over what before then had been mainly a print story. Beginning that day the hearings of the Senate Select Committee on Presidential Campaign Activities, known as the Ervin Committee, were televised gavel-to-gavel. There would be 37 days of hearings, not ending until August 7 after 237 hours of coverage.

Remarkable about the proceedings were not only the revelations and the high standing of the persons implicated in Watergate but also the opportunity afforded the public to see for themselves as much they cared to see. The cross-examination took place before the cameras, where the exchanges between the seven-man committee and the 33 witnesses, mainly former members of the White House staff or employees of the Nixon reelection committee, could be watched close up by an audience whose size and sustained interest exceeded all expectations. In every major city, one station broadcast the hearings by day. Then, at night, some 150 to 160 public television stations carried a full replay of the day's hearings. Whatever transpired during the day inevitably made the evening news and the next morning's headlines to enter everyday conversation. Those unable to watch could listen to radio or catch the highlights on news specials and newscasts. Few people, however uninterested or bent on avoiding the hearings, could extricate themselves entirely from their pervasive influence.

Compared to most public affairs broadcasts, these hearings achieved extraordinarily high ratings. The best estimate of total exposure, based on Nielsen statistics, was some 30 hours per television home. By the second week of hearings, almost three out of four had tuned in to some part of the coverage and by early August, according to a national Gallup survey, nearly 90 percent of all Americans had watched some part of the hearings. Moreover, the *total* daytime TV audience had remained practically the same when all three networks carried the hearings, though viewing usually tends to fall off whenever popular entertainment is displaced by public affairs specials. When the networks subsequently began to rotate coverage, the total daytime audience actually picked up, an indication that the hearings had been attracting viewers not ordinarily reached by daytime TV.[1] Meanwhile, the hearings were outdrawing the regular entertainment fare; the average rating was 8.2 for the Watergate coverage and 7.4 for entertainment in the same time slot.

Nor, contrary to expectations, did the popularity of the hearings fall off as they continued on into July and August. There is of course a normal reduction in televiewing during the summer months, but the average *share* of audience for the first twelve of the 24 days when just one commercial network carried the Watergate broadcast was practically the same as that on the second twelve days—surely a sign of lively interest. So intently were so many people following the Committee's activities that jokes began to circulate about "addiction" and enthusiasts referred to themselves as Watergate "junkies." That a certain proportion of the audience watched only for lack of an alternative and that others simply stopped watching because they were no longer interested cannot be denied. The continued coverage did draw some viewer protest, the significance of which should not, however, be exaggerated. Such objections inevitably occur when a popular entertainment program is preempted—whether for a nominating convention or a Presidential press conference or even for Americans held hostage returning home. According to network reports, the mail and telephone response was, on balance, favorable. A CBS analysis of more than 1000 letters received showed 60 percent of the writers approving the coverage.[2] Those watching the rebroadcasts on public television were even more accepting. Of the more than 70,000 letters received by NPACT (its political service) only 573 were negative![3] And on-the-air solicitations of funds by WNET, the New York public television station, were so successful that they more than paid for the $5000 that these daily rebroadcasts were costing.[4]

Many members of the press, as well as senators on the Watergate Committee and their staffs, speculated at the time that this television spectacular was somehow shaking people up and would lead to massive shifts in opinions. Some, like Sam Dash, chief counsel for the Committee, believed that this opportunity to watch "live" testimony was making people less lethargic about Watergate.[5] They were having to think about and even rethink some of their taken-for-granted assumptions about the political process and restraints on the Presidency. Hearing about massive sums of money paid for political espionage and, later, for "hush money" was leading them to ponder the process by which a President is nominated and elected and to wonder what kind of personal loyalty or political commitment to any one man's election could lead to breaking and entering, to bugging, and to dirty tricks. Some observers even thought, or hoped, that as the hearings progressed, the public might develop a deeper concern about the infringements of civil liberties being revealed in the testimony. And, when they did end, the televised hearings were widely heralded as having provided a "unique civic lesson in American democracy."

The press was certain of one television effect: faith in the President had been shaken. Summing up the public's verdict after what the press called a "trial by electronic jury," a Newsday headline read: GUILTY, WITH THREE YEARS PROBATION.[6] The people, this implied, were afraid Nixon might not be telling the truth, but were not yet prepared to revoke the mandate he had been given. His rating in the Harris poll had fallen from 57 percent positive before the hearings to a mere 32 afterward.[7] The decline recorded in the Gallup ratings was less precipitous but yet considerable—from a prior 44 percent approving his performance to just 31 percent.[8] "Replays" of the 1972 election in which voters were asked how they would now cast their ballots, suggested that Nixon might not have won had the full story been out at the time of the election the previous fall. A national poll by Oliver Quayle, released in August 1973, showed McGovern with 51 percent of the vote against 49 percent for Nixon.[9] And a Harris poll similarly found Nixon trailing McGovern by 38 to 36 percent in a September replay.[10] Still, only a small minority of the public, asked about resignation or impeachment after the hearings ended, accepted the idea of so drastic a punishment.

THE INFLUENCE OF TELEVISION

If many participants, viewers, and reporters assumed a direct connection between changing opinions and the televised hearings, those involved in communication research tended to be more skeptical. Their skepticism derived both from an examination of patterns of Presidential popularity and from past experience in trying to pin down the direct effects of comparable television events on political attitudes.

For one thing, Presidential popularity as a measure of response to events has proved less than satisfactory. A somewhat volatile indicator, it tends to fluctuate in response to many influences, one being the general tone of the news. "Good news"—of new achievements, of progress in solving longstanding problems, of peace offensives—usually benefits the President, even when nothing he has done can account for its occurrence; "bad news"—of loss of life, economic recession, seemingly irresolvable problems, and even drought, or crop damage, which the President cannot prevent—may have adverse effects on his standing in the polls. There is a notable exception to the "bad news" syndrome: adverse tidings that are, or can be made to appear as, an attack on the nation can help the Presidential reputation as the nation rallies in defense of the flag and of the incumbent leader. Thus, the attack on Pearl Harbor sent Franklin Roosevelt's political stock soaring while the invasion of South Korea similarly improved Harry Truman's.[11] Likewise, Gerald Ford's performance rating went up after the *Mayaguez* incident, in which an American ship was seized by the Cambodians, as did Jimmy Carter's in the early days of the hostage crisis in Iran.

In the summer of 1973 there was no international crisis to shore up Nixon's standing in the polls. To be sure, in June, the hearings were discontinued for a week as the President met with Soviet leader Brezhnev for talks in Washington. And, again, in July the state visit of the Shah of Iran and his wife drew media attention to the symbolic importance of the Presidency, with Nixon playing the kind of ceremonial role that unifies and can give a boost to national pride while, incidentally, improving his performance ratings. On other occasions, Nixon directly invoked the need for national unity as he tried to contain the effects of the ever more divisive scandal. Yet even in the absence of a great deal of "good news," the "bad news" coming out of the Watergate hearings could hardly have accounted for all the slippage in his popularity. While on his "handling of the Watergate case" the President had received mainly "fair" or "poor" marks from the public from April on, when this question first made its way into the Harris poll, his ratings on handling of the economy were equally low, dropping to 15 percent positive in August. His ability to keep down the cost of living was judged even more negatively, with only 7 percent approving compared to 17 percent who approved his handling of Watergate.[12] An ORC poll (August 18–20) also suggests that not all of Nixon's loss of reputation can be laid to the televised hearings: 42 percent of those questioned believed that inflation and the cost of living were the "most important problems facing the country today"; just 20 percent mentioned Watergate, lack of confidence in government, or problems of Nixon and his administration.

Studies of the response to earlier televised political events had failed to reveal a pattern of dramatic changes in beliefs and behavior as a *simple* and *direct* response to what had been witnessed. Every audience, even a mass audience, is to a degree self-selected, which means that most viewers are watching because the content interests them and is congenial to their point of view. When people are exposed to contrary or unfamiliar points of view, these messages often fall on deaf ears and what they cannot avoid hearing can still be rationalized away or reinterpreted to fit what they already believe or want to believe. Individual reactions to the televising of such major public proceedings as political conventions and televised Presidential debates had generally fitted this pattern.

To say, however, that researchers had turned up little solid evidence of massive opinion change directly traceable to television exposure is not to say they had found the televising of political spectaculars to be absolutely without effect. For instance, our study of the nominating conventions in 1952 indicated that many viewers defined General Eisenhower as having won the nomination "in spite of the Republican machine" while Adlai Stevenson, Governor of Illinois, was looked on as the "hand-picked candidate" of outgoing President Truman, that is, chosen by the "political bosses." While neither definition accords substantially with the facts, the presentation of certain complicated events during the conventions led some viewers to such inferences. Then, during the election campaign, the image of Eisenhower battling the bosses at the Chicago convention reinforced the image of Eisenhower, the World War II hero, as a strong leader while Stevenson appeared "weak" because he had seemingly bowed to Truman's nod, having remained steadfast throughout the convention in his refusal to lift a hand in support of a grass-roots draft. Candidate images nurtured by what was witnessed on television affected voter responses to campaign rhetoric and ultimately how they cast their ballots.[13]

Research on viewer response to the precedent-setting Kennedy–Nixon debates in 1960 detected similarly subtle, indirect, and incremental changes through which media events affect political behavior. Thus, exposure to the first debate changed few preferences but helped Kennedy prove himself. His ability to "outscore" Nixon, known as a skilled debater, led many Democrats, hitherto reluctant to accept their party's choice, to believe Kennedy was Presidential timber. He acted like a President, which made him into a viable candidate. In this way, the first debate had cumulative effects. Kennedy's performance sparked the organization of viewing groups, generated enthusiasm, and led to greater campaign efforts, all of which together may have influenced the final vote as much as the debates.[14]

Before the Senate Watergate hearings, the televising of other Congressional probes had also had some unexpected consequences. In 1950, when television was still a novelty, a Senate subcommittee, under Estes Kefauver, Democrat of Tennessee, held an investigation into organized crime. Witness after witness from gangland was paraded before the TV cameras and questioned by the Senator and his chief counsel, Rudolph Halley. A pioneer study by G. D. Wiebe of the public response to the hearings indicated a high degree of emotional arousal and indignation, but when it came to doing something to remedy the situation, the study indicated, only a small minority of persons were sufficiently motivated to take even so modest a political action as writing to their Congressman.[15] Yet crime and corruption became one of the major issues in the 1952 elections and Kefauver, thanks to this television exposure, won many primaries to emerge as a leading contender for the Democratic nomination that year. In 1956, he became his party's Vice-Presidential candidate. Halley was elected President of the New York City Council, winning against the Democratic machine.

In 1954, the televising of the Army–McCarthy hearings appeared to be the Senator's undoing. These hearings, in which the Wisconsin Republican attempted to bulldoze with reckless charges several members of the establishment, certainly coincided with the turn in the controversial Senator's political fortunes, and their televising has often been cited as a major cause of his downfall and eventual censure by the Senate. In front of the pitiless TV cameras, it was alleged, Joseph McCarthy revealed himself to the public not as a patriot but as the demagogue he actually was.[16] We know of no study that substantiates any massive shift in attitudes in response to the Senator's antics. One empirical study, based on small samples in two cities, also by Wiebe, found that very few people had changed their minds about McCarthy because of what they had witnessed.[17] But the hearings did make an impression on his fellow legislators; they learned that McCarthy could be challenged. When, after the hearings, powerful political forces on Capitol Hill were finally stirred to action, McCarthy's public performance was among the evidence used to discredit him. Moreover, film clips from the televised hearings have been used ever since to educate new generations in what McCarthyism was all about. "McCarthyism" was even a disparaging term some Nixon supporters were later to apply to the impeachment hearings.

In assessing the impact of the Watergate hearings on the movement of public opinion, we then have to differentiate between their immediate impact and the delayed and more subtle shifts traceable to the televising. Assessing the immediate impact is facilitated by the abundance of data. No other development during the Watergate saga so galvanized communication researchers into action as did the summer hearings. But before reviewing the evidence—both as to immediate and more delayed effects—let us take a detailed look first at the controversy surrounding the televising of the hearings and then at the political reality portrayed during the two and one-half months of televised testimony. Both the context in which they took place and the content to which viewers were exposed are important in understanding their impact.

SHOULD THE HEARINGS BE TELEVISED?

Media coverage itself became an issue as the controversy over Watergate developed. The televising of the hearings had been hotly contested before they began and continuation of their full coverage soon came under attack. Prior to the hearings, the main opposition to live coverage was based on legal and political grounds, while the networks, anticipating losses among their daytime audiences, were hardly eager to participate. Some members of the Senate Committee and their staff were strong supporters of live television coverage. It was a central element in the strategy of both Senator Ervin and his chief counsel Sam Dash, though most Republican members were less enthusiastic. The public had also exhibited interest in the chance to witness the testimony. Later, as the summer wore on, the opposition to continued coverage came largely from Nixon supporters and the White House itself.

That the hearings would be telecast live and in their entirety was never a foregone conclusion. In questioning the legitimacy of parading witnesses continuously before TV cameras and radio microphones, the White House was only carrying one step farther a strategy conceived to counter the work of the Ervin Committee. Thus, John Dean, as he was later to testify, had hatched schemes, together with Haldeman and Ehrlichman, to derail the investigation. A briefing paper he had prepared included the following instruction: "Seek to get hearings over as quickly as possible because they really are a potential witch hunt. The President can note that hearings of this type damage all government officials and the institutions of the government. The public wants to believe the worst about all politicians and hearings of this type are going to damage all elected officials."[18]

In dealing with the hearings, the President's moves were guided by the principle that, if their televising could not be avoided, they could at least be made less than good box office. His strategy was directed at the media, as when he told Dean on March 15 that he was sure that committee Democrats, spurred by the media, would seek to "increase the drama" by drawing in as many higher-ups as possible. He intended—and on this both Dean and Nixon are in agreement—to take the steam out of the investigation with a comprehensive "Dean report" that, when made public, would serve a double purpose: first, it would be part of a strategy to define the degree of involvement of individuals in such a way as to delimit the number of witnesses subpoenaed; second, it could steal some of Ervin's thunder by setting out some of the "new facts" about Watergate so that they would have become "old facts" before the hearings began. If the White House could not kill the hearings, it could make them boring.[19] Years later Nixon claimed to believe, as he believed at the time, that most Senators on the committee, especially its chairman, were "publicity-mad" and expert in getting a favorable press. In his *Memoirs* he recalls that when Ervin was selected for the task in February 1973 some of his advisors thought this a lucky choice. The media, they argued, would be hard pressed to make much of a hero out of Ervin since his voting record was so downright segregationist but Nixon himself "knew better."[20]

A more formidable threat to live coverage came in the form of a legal challenge. Special Prosecutor Archibald Cox, in one of his first moves after confirmation by the Senate on May 23, argued in a letter to Senator Ervin that the continuation of hearings at this time would "create great danger that the full facts about the Watergate case and related matters will never come to light and that many of those who are guilty of serious wrongdoing will never be brought to justice." He suggested, among other things, that witnesses might be less likely to make full disclosures before television cameras than privately to prosecutors, that immediate hearings would impede the investigation and "make it impossible to get at the truth from bottom to top."[21] The Committee disagreed, holding with Woodrow Wilson that in the case of corruption in the executive branch the public-informing function of Congress was more important than its legislative function.[22] Thus rebuffed, Cox tried again to suspend the hearings by petitioning the U. S. District Court to require that testimony of two key witnesses—Jeb Stuart Magruder and Dean—be taken in closed session or, at least, without TV coverage. His attempt actually backfired. Senator Herman Talmadge, a Georgia Democrat, who until this time had been ambivalent about permitting live coverage, saw Cox's legal move as an assault on the prerogatives of the Senate, as trying "to get the judicial branch of the government to enjoin the legislative from functioning," which in his opinion was "without precedent in the history of the republic" (June 7). From here on, Talmadge stopped urging publicly that the hearings be brought to the quickest possible end.

The unusual amount of public interest in the testimony of former White House officials surely helped persuade network management to take on the gigantic task involved in continuous coverage. Yet even after the decision to go "live," they kept their options open. During the recess that followed the first five days of coverage, there were reports that full live coverage might not resume. What the networks did instead was to enter into an unprecedented agreement to rotate the coverage, with each network free to come in for testimony of unusual interest, as they did when John Dean was the witness.

Once the decision to broadcast the hearings had been made, news personnel had a stake in assuring their success. Thus, Sam Dash was the recipient of suggestions from television reporters on the order in which to schedule witnesses. To enliven the hearings, he was advised, the Committee should start off with a bang by leading with the "big guns." This conflicted with the Committee's own view that the hearings had to be more than a show. Since the prime goal was to educate the public, they opted for a "building block strategy" that would start with little-known witnesses who could provide the background necessary for understanding the testimony of the "big guns" when they did appear.[23] But there were those within the Committee who also worried that the public might tire of too much testimony and wanted the hearings kept as short as possible.

Still, if the continued coverage continued to be controversial and subject to debate in the press, this was partly because the White House had not abandoned its strategy for countering the influence of the hearings. Nixon was, of course, no longer in a position to fabricate a "Dean Report to Nixon" but had instead to contend with a "Dean Report to the Nation," witnessed by millions of Americans for five days, as the former White House counsel became the chief witness against the President. To minimize the influence of that report, a strategy of advance leaks was implemented. By one route or another, often from the Committee or members of its staff, nearly everything to which Dean and other witnesses were to testify found its way into the press the evening or the morning before their public appearance. Another Nixon strategy was the immediate denial of every charge, coupled, wherever possible, with an attack on the motives of the witness. Attacks were also directed at the media, especially for the "unfairness" of their Watergate coverage, partly to force an early end to the hearings but also to ensure that White House responses to unfavorable testimony were given at least equal publicity.

Perhaps the strongest attack on the fairness of televising the hearings came, as they neared their end, from Patrick Buchanan, a White House speech writer known for his earlier scathing assaults on the news media. Apparently provoked by the sharpness with which committee members cross-examined John Ehrlichman, the most combative witness so far, Buchanan, raised a question in a guest column of the Op-Ed page of the *New York Times* (August 2): Had not the media warned against the inevitability of injury to rights and reputations inherent in Congressional investigating ever since the days when the Senator from Wisconsin was at his worst? Yet, Buchanan pointed out, when the quarry was not domestic subversives but Nixon, the media forgot the old caveats. That so many people now believed that the President had prior knowledge of Watergate was a tribute to the power of the press.

While Nixon himself was dissuaded by his advisors from exposing the "illegalities" of previous Democratic administrations, on the grounds that it would look as if he were "trying to divert attention . . . by smearing others," [24] this did not preclude direct attacks by surrogates. For instance, on *Face the Nation* (June 10), a CBS public affairs program, Secretary of Interior Rogers Morton opposed further hearings since they tended "to try people in a forum which is not designed for that." On June 11 Spiro Agnew, still Vice President, in characteristic oratorical style, joined the campaign by using the media for an attack on the media. It was a deliberate part of the White House strategy to have these attacks and denials emanate from Nixon loyalists rather than from Nixon himself. In this way the President hoped to project an image of being above it all. Not only would he not comment until the hearings had ended but the word went out that he was not watching but attending to important matters of state.

On the Committee, it was Senator Edward Gurney, a Republican from Florida, who, as Nixon's most steadfast defender, carried the attack on the fairness of media publicity right into the hearing room. When Chairman Ervin evidenced outrage at the claim of Maurice Stans, the chief fund-raiser for the Nixon reelection campaign, that the destruction of certain financial records just after the break-in was "pure and innocent coincidence," Gurney seized the opportunity to provoke the first openly partisan clash of the hearings. "I, for one," he declared (June 13), in an obvious appeal to the television audience, "have not appreciated the harassment of witnesses by the chairman. . . ." The audience in the room, heedless of prior warnings, burst into applause as Ervin, the Senate's leading constitutional scholar, describing himself in his folksiest manner as "just an old country lawyer," responded, "I don't know of the finer ways to do it. I just have to do it my way."

Finally, Nixon could draw on one resource not available to the Committee: the media attention that a President normally enjoys simply by virtue of his office, the ability to make news that will compete with and draw attention away from "bad news." Some events—like the Brezhnev visit—could force postponements and drag the proceedings out interminably, until, it was hoped, the public finally lost interest. One news development, not of the President's own choosing, was his hospitalization for viral pneumonia in July.

MEDIA CREDIBILITY

Though the media themselves became part of the Watergate controversy, neither the televising of the Ervin Committee hearings nor press reporting of Watergate during this period seems to have diminished confidence in their integrity. In its annual summer poll of public confidence in major institutions, the Harris poll found the sharpest one-year rise ever in the rating of the press.[25] On the other hand, the reiterated White House charge that the media were giving Watergate "more attention than it deserved" did pay off: in June, Harris found 40 percent in agreement and by August, 50 percent. But very few people at either time accepted the more extreme notion that the "press is just out to get President Nixon on Watergate." Actually, during this three-month period, again according to Harris, there was an increase in the number who felt "if it had not been for the press exposé, the whole Watergate mess would never have been found out"—the proportion so congratulating the press had gone up from 56 to 66 percent.[26]

The public was, however, rather evenly split over whether the televising of the hearings should be continued when they resumed in September. A Gallup poll (August 3–6) found 58 percent supporting the idea while an ORC survey two weeks later (August 18–20) showed people by 44 to 50 percent against further full coverage. This opposition does not appear to signify an adverse judgment either on the job television had been doing or on the conduct of the hearings. In June the Committee had earned "excellent" or "pretty good" ratings on how it conducted its business from 61 percent of the public, with individual members all rated on the positive side, several winning accolades from over 80 percent. By the time the hearings ended, there was not so much a drop off in public approval as a firming up of negative opinion. The proportion rating the Committee's performance "only fair" or "poor" had increased from one out of five to one out of three.[27]

Opposition to further television coverage was mainly a political opposition to further hearings. Approval of the hearings had, from their beginning, run along partisan lines and, by the time they ended, Democrats and Republicans had become more polarized over their conduct and utility. Yet even if Republicans were much more likely to have reservations, few went so far as to call the *televising* itself "unfair." Asked by Gallup some two weeks after the summer hearings ended (and after Nixon had appealed to the public in a television speech) whether the hearings had been a "good thing" or "bad thing" for the country, the public—by 52 to 41 percent—judged them a "good thing." As to what was "good" about them, the main point was that "they kept the public informed." On the "bad" side they were most often judged a "waste of time" or "bad for morale." Eight percent justified their negative view with the argument, echoing one advanced by the White House, that the hearings had given the country a bad image abroad.[28] This contention was not supported by the facts. Although West Germany's conservative *Die Welt* openly doubted the sincerity and motives of the Watergate Committee—dubbing the hearings a "show trial" for the benefit of the television audience, a farce, and a mockery of the democratic process, and even, possibly, should Nixon be forced out, the first step toward a mild form of American fascism—the reaction of the rest of the world was generally positive. Japan's *Asahi Shimbun* and France's *Le Monde* were highly favorable. The *Times* of London, however, withheld judgment.[29]

TELEVISED TESTIMONY: TURNING POINTS

The televised hearings followed the planned "building block" plan for telling the story in sequence. In the first, "scene-setting," phase, witnesses testified that, contrary to the impression deliberately disseminated during the electoral campaign, the White House had retained overall direction over the Nixon reelection effort. The circumstances of the break-in to the Watergate headquarters of the Democratic National Committee and the apprehension of the burglars were also detailed. James McCord, the first witness with at least some "box office appeal," testified on the second day of the hearings, Friday May 18, relating how he had been offered executive clemency, financial aid, and eventually a job in return for his silence about what he knew of the break-in. The offer, he claimed, came from a former White House official, who said he was acting with President Nixon's knowledge. John Caulfield, the go-between, immediately denied this. Both McCord's accusation and Caulfield's response were big news. And Senator Ervin himself avowed on ABC's *Issues and Answers* that weekend that thus far "no competent evidence" had connected Nixon to the case. Not until Maurice Stans, the former Commerce Secretary and chief fund-raiser for the Nixon–Agnew campaign, took his seat before the committee was a real "star witness" paraded before the camera.

What was to be the "accusatory phase" began with the appearance of Jeb Magruder, deputy director of CRP, who followed Stans. Publicly contrite, Magruder admitted having perjured himself before the Watergate grand jury. Recalling how he and others had plotted the bugging and then tried to cover it up, Magruder not only confessed his own guilt but also implicated former Attorney General John Mitchell, H. R. Haldeman (the President's closest aide), and John Dean. Yet he also said that he personally still believed that Nixon had had no knowledge of the spying operation.

The stage was now set for John Dean's much-anticipated testimony, delayed for a week because of the Brezhnev visit. The appearance of Dean as Nixon's principal accuser was the next carefully planned building block. It was one of two events in the hearings that can be considered turning points in the history of Watergate as an issue.

Before Dean's appearance, the issue turned on his credibility. How substantial was his charge of Nixon's complicity? How well would it hold up under intensive scrutiny and cross-examination? For Dean and his counsel, this concern translated into whether he could project an aura of "credibility" for he was, to put it bluntly, pitting himself against the most powerful person in the United States. None of his testimony, his lawyers advised him, no matter how truthful, would be worth anything unless it could be made to appear credible. Or, as Dean later recalled it, "The White House . . . was betting that millions of people did not wish to believe a man who called the President a liar. It played upon emotions: no one likes a squealer, a Judas, an informant, a tattletale, especially one who is also guilty. Every base motivation was attributed to me: I had turned on the President for money, for publicity, for spite, because I was a perverted character. More commonly, it was stated that I was lying about the President to save my own skin."[30] Columnist Joseph Alsop, in a much-quoted phrase, called Dean a "bottom dwelling slug."[31]

That the public should question Dean's credibility is more than under-standable. To many he appeared trapped and ready to lie to save his own skin. From his point of view, there were only two choices, neither of them guaranteed to save him from a prison term. He could plea bargain with the Special Prosecutor, exchanging the promise of a light sentence for testimony sought by the grand jury, or he could testify under the most limited use immunity before the Ervin Committee—that is, with the guarantee that specific admissions could not later be used as evidence against him in the court room. Dean chose the public forum. The four reasons for his decision listed in his published account all relate to the need and opportunity to establish his credibility.

First, so he tells us, he was confident that he could give a credible per-formance. The setting was familiar; he had been employed on the staff of the House Judiciary Committee and knew how such hearings worked. Sec-ond, he counted on the format of the hearings to give him the chance to lay out his whole testimony—at his own pace and in his own words—with-out being bound to courtroom practice. Third, this allowed him to adopt a piece of President Nixon's own favored strategy, that of going over the heads of the hundreds of mostly unsympathetic print journalists to address directly millions of viewers, who would hang on his words yet not be prepared to scrutinize his testimony as critically as a trained lawyer. Finally, his accep-tance of limited use immunity was to help mute the squealer image, as he might still have to face prosecution for his role in the coverup. If people knew that he wasn't getting a free ride, he reasoned, that should make him more credible.

To assure that nothing in his TV performance would detract from his credibility as a witness, Dean watched a tape of his interview with Walter Cronkite, part of a special produced by CBS to mark the first anniversary of the break-in. He reviewed his mannerisms, jotted down criticisms, and made a studied effort not to appear "too cocky, too nervous, too mousy, too young." Heeding further advice from Sam Dash, he put his contact lenses aside in favor of an old pair of horn-rimmed spectacles that made him appear more studious and distinguished. He also mentioned that he trimmed his hair, because he had looked as if he needed a haircut when he talked to Cronkite.

Thus Dean made a studied appearance in the old Senate Caucus Room, site of the Kefauver and Army–McCarthy hearings. Once he had taken his seat at the witness table, the hearing took on the look of a courtroom for viewers familiar with TV dramas. The spotlight was on Dean. Where those preceding him had delivered their testimony flanked by lawyers who could whisper advice, he chose to sit alone, in order to dramatize the fact that, as he put it, "I was comfortable with my own words."[32] His lawyers sat some distance behind him, as did his photogenic wife, who thus appeared—as she was meant to—as backing her husband all the way.

Just about all of his first day in the witness chair was taken up by his reading from a 234-page typescript, the gist of which was that Nixon had actively participated in the effort to thwart the investigation of the Watergate break-in. Despite Dean's warning, in September 1973, that the Watergate case was a "cancer growing on the Presidency," Nixon had failed to appreciate the full implication of his involvement. Dean stuck steadfastly to his version of events through four consecutive days of questioning, some of it clearly hostile, that followed the reading of his statement. Challenges about certain details, about his overall veracity, and about his character hardly rattled him, not even when for a few brief moments he seemed to have been caught in an inaccuracy that could discredit his entire testimony. This concerned an alleged meeting at the Mayflower Hotel in Washington, where the payment of hush money to Watergate defendants was said to have been discussed. Senator Gurney, having coaxed the witness into reiterating that he was absolutely certain about his recollections as to time, date, and place of the meeting, triumphantly produced subpoenaed records that indicated the meeting had taken place at the Statler Hilton, not the Mayflower.

Gurney taunted Dean, who had flaunted his excellent memory during the long cross-examination: how much trust could one place in Dean's recollections of all those conversations with the President if, as he had just admitted, he couldn't even remember the name of a hotel in a city where he had lived for ten years? Dean, obviously flustered, was nevertheless able to turn this near disaster into a minor triumph. After the next break, he asked the Committee's permission to go back over one point; he explained that the coffee shop at the Statler Hilton, the site of the meeting, was called the Mayflower Room. The audience applauded—this was the kind of mistake anyone might make. Publicly, Dean thanked his lawyer for the information. Only later was it revealed that this tip had come from Daniel Schorr, a CBS reporter on Nixon's "enemies list," who was in the room covering the hearings.[33]

A more direct challenge came from Senator Talmadge. "What makes you think," he asked, "that your credibility is greater than that of the President, who denies what you have said?" Here is Dean's reaction, as he has recalled it, to a question so succinctly summing the central issue before the public:

I floundered, "Well, Senator, I have been asked to come up here and tell the truth. . . ." I hesitated and sighed. I was winging it. "You are asking me a public-relations question, really, in a sense. Why should I have greater credibility than the President of the United States?" I repeated his question. I couldn't say what I was thinking: Nixon is a goddamn liar, and if you put us both on the box [for a lie detector test] you'd find out who's lying. All I could add was "I'm telling what I know. I'm telling you just as I know it."[34]

Clearly, the time had not yet arrived when Dean, without tangible proof, could afford to make a direct charge against the President, the more so since he himself was so vulnerable to attack, having been fired from a Washington law firm for "violations of the canons of ethics" and having borrowed money from a White House safe to pay some of his honeymoon expenses. These blemishes on his character surfaced during the questioning and, though dismissed by Dean as simply bad judgment and not criminal intent, they were obvious ammunition for anyone sympathetic to the President.

Nevertheless, Dean seems to have emerged from his ordeal with his credibility less impaired than Nixon's other ex-aides. Gallup and Harris polls taken after all four had testified showed Dean being rated more favorably than Haldeman, Ehrlichman, and Mitchell and less likely than they to be thought "hardly truthful." Only a minority of the public accepted at face value a blanket denial of Dean's charges issued by the White House (June 25) or Charles Colson's allegation, meant to impugn Dean's motives in testifying, that it was Dean himself who had been at the center of a conspiracy to keep vital information from the White House.

Harris was the only national polling organization to ask the public to pit Dean's word against that of the President. "If it came down to it, and President Nixon denied John Dean's charges," a July question read, "who do you think has been more truthful about the Watergate cover-up—President Nixon or John Dean?" The number—38 percent—ready to believe Dean, even in the face of a Presidential denial, and the number—25 percent—not sure about whom to believe would be worrisome to any head of state. It seems even more significant that the question should even have been posed; Nixon was, after all, the President and the Presidency, though a secular institution, has its sacred components. Initially the issue of "credibility" had focused on Nixon's aides: who among them was telling the truth? Dean— or Haldeman, Ehrlichman, and Mitchell? With Dean's appearance, it became a question of accepting the sworn testimony of a former Presidential aide against the word of the President. More directly, was Nixon lying about his role in Watergate? This shift away from the credibility of the President's men to the credibility of the President himself was paradoxically hastened by the line of questioning pursued by Senator Howard Baker, the ranking Republican on the Committee and a strong supporter of the President. He prefaced his interrogation of Dean with a phrase that was to be endlessly echoed by the press and in recounts of the hearings:

The net sum of your testimony is fairly mind boggling. . . . . It occurs to me that at this point, the central question, and in no way in derogation of the importance of the great volume of material and the implications that flow from it, but the central question is simply put: *What did the President know and when did he know it?* [35]

To have asked in more straightforward fashion whether the President, and not Dean, might have been lying was unthinkable. Senators no less than most Americans regard that office with almost sacred awe. Yet from here on, the veracity of the President, who had gone to great lengths to remain aloof from the controversy by deflecting any blame from himself to subordinates, was ever more deeply an issue. The shift had begun ever so subtly, but after the testimony of John Dean there was no turning back. The shift was soon to gain momentum from the surprise testimony of Alexander P. Butterfield.

Both Republicans and Democrats on the Committee now agreed that it was within the President's power to achieve a quick resolution to Watergate. He alone could supply the evidence that could answer the burning question of what the President knew and when he knew it. It was only logical that the Committee, after Dean's testimony, should press for a meeting with Nixon. Yet the President had refused to meet with the Committee, or even the grand jury, on the constitutional grounds of executive privilege and the separation of powers. Meanwhile, Nixon's defenders kept playing politics with a dual message delivered to whatever audience they were able to reach: the press was "obsessed" with Watergate and the President, when he responded after the hearings ended, would be found uninvolved in Watergate. [36]

As pressure on Nixon to appear before the Committee mounted, the *New York Times* was able to report on July 12 that Nixon had consented to meet personally with Ervin to discuss his refusal to make documents available. The agreement followed a phone call Ervin had made to the President, during which, according to Ervin, Nixon was "emotionally distraught," claiming that the Committee was out to get him." "Mr. President," Ervin had responded, "we are not out to get anything except the truth." The President then told the chairman that he was about to enter Bethesda Naval Hospital with viral pneumonia but would meet with Ervin after his release.[37] As it turned out, the meeting never came about, for the issue about "how to get at the truth" took a new turn while Nixon was still recovering in the hospital.

This second turning point came on July 16 with the revelation by Alexander Butterfield of a secret recording system in the Oval Office of the White House. So unanticipated was his testimony that the session during which he appeared, unlike those where Dean starred, was covered only by a single network. And yet it was Butterfield who provided the key to "getting at the truth." A concealed device under the President's desk was automatically activated by voice to record on tape all of Nixon's conversations. This revelation was nothing short of sensational. It meant that the evidence existed, in the form of these tapes, with which to corroborate or refute the still undocumented charges by Dean. Now the credibility issue was linked not just to the quest for Nixon's personal testimony or the production of specified documents that might help get at the truth but to the release of the "truth" itself.

The reformulation of the issue was reflected in the news media. The *Washington Post* headlined its story next day: NIXON TAPE RECORDINGS SEEN AS ULTIMATE WATERGATE WITNESS (July 17). A week later (July 24), Howard K. Smith (ABC) commented that the Watergate hearings had been simplified: now the Dean, Mitchell, and Ehrlichman versions of the truth could be unraveled. Senator Baker and Fred Thompson, the minority counsel, shared these sentiments and expected the President would share them: would Nixon have taped these conversations if they contained incriminating statements? The more he thought about it, Thompson recalled, the more he came to believe that the President was "orchestrating the whole affair," that— clever politician that he was—he had intended the tapes to be discovered, and that at the appropriate moment he "would produce the tapes, or perhaps play them publicly; there would be nothing incriminating, and John Dean's testimony would be utterly discredited."[38]

Ervin (July 21) renewed his call to Nixon to make the evidence available to the Committee. With a wink at the television audience, he told the Committee that "those seeking the truth will draw the inference—and a justified inference—that the reason for not producing the tapes is because the evidence would be adverse to the President." Even Gurney, still loyal to Nixon, told UPI (and indirectly the President) that it would hurt politically should Nixon refuse all access to the tapes.

Heedless of this advice, the President headed for a confrontation in the courts. While still in the hospital, he issued an order to the Secret Service to withhold all information about the tapes. He rejected a formal Committee request on the legally highly questionable ground that the tapes "would not finally settle the central issues before your Committee," that he had "personally listened to a number of these" before their existence became known and had found them "entirely consistent with what [he knew] to be the truth." Others "with different perspectives and motivativons would inevitably interpret [them]," his July 23 letter went on, "in different ways." Faced with a subpoena from the Committee, he responded on July 26, through his deputy press secretary, that he would abide by a "definitive" Supreme Court decision but, so this implied, by nothing short of that.

Butterfield's revelation of the tapes had moved the issue of "getting at the truth" to "what the truth was." Thereafter, while the hearings ground to their end, the testimony of the "big guns" (Haldeman and Ehrlichman) had to compete with the struggle over the tapes for headlines. Of twelve *New York Times* front-page stories on Watergate during the period beginning July 17, the day after Butterfield's disclosure, and ending July 28, ten dealt with events related to this controversy.[39] On all three network evening news programs the tapes remained the lead item for four of the next five evenings following revelation of their existence. The following week, Ehrlichman's appearance gave the tapes story strong competition; yet nothing he said on July 26 could overshadow news of the President's formal refusal to heed the subpoenas for the tapes. Controversy over that refusal was to continue long after Phase I of the hearings ended on August 8.

Testimony of the key witnesses had refocused attention from a scandal for which Richard Nixon might have to shoulder some responsibility to the matter of the President's possible personal involvement in a conspiracy to obstruct justice. The testimony, especially the disclosure of the taped conversations, had put Nixon on the spot. With the hearings ended, a clearer answer and a fuller explanation than he had hitherto been willing to give were expected. While 33 witnesses had been heard from, both "Washington" and the members of the large television audience wondered what the one witness who had not testified might have to say. Would he be forthright? Would he relinquish the evidence needed to resolve the contradictions and tie up the loose ends in the 181 hours of testimony?

Nixon scheduled his "testimony" for August 15, in the form of a nationally televised speech. "Now that most of the major witnesses have been heard," he began, "it is time to speak out about the charges made and to provide a perspective on the issue." He refused to "deal with the various charges in detail," being even less specific than he had been in the statement issued May 22, in which, while denying personal complicity, he had admitted for the first time that some persons in the White House had attempted to cover up the Watergate scandal. He did list in detail all the things he had done to get at the truth, including his concurrence on May 18 in the appointment of a Special Prosecutor to handle the matter. The case, so far as he was concerned, was now before a grand jury.

Turning to the tapes, he said that "many have urged that in order to help prove the truth of what I have said, I should turn over to the Special Prosecutor and the Senate Committee recordings of conversations that I have had in my office or on my telephone." This, he insisted, he would not do because of a more important principle involved: "If I were to make public these tapes, containing blunt and candid remarks on many different subjects, the confidentiality of the Office of the President would always be suspect. It would make no difference whether it was to serve the interests of a court, or a Senate Committee or the President himself—the same damage would be done to the principle, and it would be irreparable. Persons talking with a President would never again be sure that recordings or notes of what they said would not subsequently be made public. No one would want to advance tentative ideas that might later seem unsound. . . ."

The message was clear: the tapes would not be released. Then, in the style for which Richard Nixon had been known ever since his "Checkers speech," when he appealed for public support over the heads of those who wanted him off the Republican ticket in 1952, he carried the attack to the enemy camp by blaming Watergate on the attitude that "became fashionable in the 1960s, as individuals and groups increasingly asserted the right to take the law in their own hands, insisting that their purpose represented a higher morality. Then," he went on, aiming a dart at the media, "their attitude was praised in the press and even from some of the pulpits as evidence of a new idealism. . . . The notion that the end justifies the means proved contagious. Thus, it is not surprising, even though it is deplorable that some persons in 1972 adopted the morality that they themselves had rightly condemned and committed acts that have no place in our national system." In other words, the responsibility for campaign espionage, the deliberate violation of campaign finance regulations, and the whole bag of dirty tricks and illegal retributions against political "enemies" unearthed during the Watergate investigation lay, in the last analysis, with those who had been its principal victims.

The Ervin Committee, the press, radio, and television, which had constantly been digging into the Watergate affair, he charged, were less interested in getting the facts than getting the President, so that now "after twelve weeks and two million words of televised testimony, we have reached a point at which a continued, backward-looking obsession with Watergate is causing the nation to neglect matters of far greater importance to all of the American people." He accepted the mandate the people had given him the past November, in the clearest possible choice of this century, to complete the initiative begun in his first term and to fulfill his promises for the second. He ended with the plea that "we cannot let an obsession with the past destroy our hopes for the future."

Response to the speech from key Republicans was not exactly reassuring. Senator Barry Goldwater said that the "President did not add anything to his other speeches that would tend to divert suspicion from him." Senator Edward Brooke of Massachusetts, a liberal Republican, used even harsher language: "The people want the facts. The President gave us rhetoric."[40] However, the large number of telegrams and telephone calls to the White House—described by Nixon as "the biggest outpouring since the days of his Vietnam speeches"—indicated that his plea had struck a "responsive chord."[41]

National polls indicate otherwise. While an unusually high proportion of adult Americans (77%) had viewed the speech, just somewhat over a fourth of these found his words "quite or somewhat convincing," according to a Gallup special telephone poll immediately afterward. A much larger number (44%) had found the President "*not at all* convincing."[42] A report based on an August 18–20 survey by the Opinion Research Corporation (ORC), a firm taking private polls for the White House, painted much the same picture: among those who had watched, heard, or read about the speech, unfavorable reactions outnumbered those favorable by 56 to 39 percent— the balance being toward the *very* unfavorable side. Only the results of a

Sindlinger poll released to the press told a different story: reactions were said to be 39 percent positive to 32 percent negative. That the exact wording of the question was not included in the release makes this appear an effort at manipulation rather than description, by a polling firm with close ties to the Nixon White House. This suspicion is supported by another Sindlinger release a few days earlier of responses to a national poll on the question, "Which action do you yourself feel is the more morally reprehensible— which is worse—the drowning of Mary Jo Kopechne at Chappaquiddick or the bugging of the Democratic National Committee?" Is it surprising that, in this forced comparison, Senator Ted Kennedy's role in the auto death of a young woman should have been found, by a 44 to 34 percent margin, more blameworthy than burglarizing the Watergate complex? [43]

None of this indicates that the speech was without effect. The speech did manage to halt, and even slightly reverse at least temporarily, Nixon's declining approval rating, as gauged by the national polls. Moreover, some of Nixon's arguments seem to have had a great deal of resonance among the public. The same ORC poll that had found general dissatisfaction with the Nixon speech also reported a high level of agreement with some of its main themes. A large majority (65–29%) agreed it was time to turn Watergate over to the courts. By 54 to 29 percent they agreed that the Senate hearings had hurt, rather than helped, the country. Almost half (49%) thought that the confidentiality of a President's conversations with his aides was similar to that between lawyers and clients, priests and penitents, or husbands and wives, while only 33 percent did not think so. A majority was also persuaded (46–39%) that forcing the release of the tapes might damage the office of the President and the country.

Louis Harris Associates in two post-hearing surveys—one right after the speech (August 18–19) and one a month later—documented a similarly schizophrenic pattern of opinion. The public, by a decisive 62 to 32 percent, endorsed Nixon's recommendation that "Watergate be turned over to the courts and allow the President to concentrate on more important things." Yet on every specific question that concerned Nixon's insistence on withholding the evidence, the public thought him more wrong than right, often by lopsided majorities. They especially disapproved his refusal to turn over White House files dealing with the bugging and coverup to the Ervin Committee while allowing H. R. Haldeman to take tapes of the White House conversations home where he could listen to them—an arrangement that Haldeman had testified to during his televised appearance.

If there was so much agreement with what Nixon had had to say, especially on depoliticizing the issue by turning it over to the courts, then why was the overall reaction to the speech so negative? Mainly, we believe, because he had failed to persuade the public on what really mattered to them. As throughout the summer, a large majority refused to believe that Nixon was not in some way involved in Watergate, that he had not planned or known about the bugging attempt or tried to cover it up. They remained unsatisfied with an undocumented explanation devoid of details. While they might agree that Presidential conversations should be confidential or that release of the tapes might damage the Presidency, the desire for information overrode these considerations. It was precisely because Nixon was still suspect that they approved turning the matter over to the courts. Some partisans on both sides of the issue hoped that subpoenas of the tapes by the Committee and by the Special Prosecutor would clear things up to their satisfaction.

The previously cited ORC mid-August survey also reveals that persons aware of the speech were no more likely to accept or reject the themes advanced by Nixon in his speech than those unaware of it. The best predictor of response was not party identification or self-definition along a conservative-liberal continuum but approval or disapproval of Nixon's performance in office. Over half of those who approved of Nixon's handling of his job as President declared themselves satisfied with the explanation he gave and only 18 percent of those approving wanted the tapes handed over to the Committee. (Appendix, table 2) Most of those who approved Nixon's Presidential performance yet were dissatisfied with his explanation, when asked what further explanation they wanted, mentioned the need for the tapes or a better explanation for not releasing them; at least, Nixon could give more facts about his involvement or mistakes. This general desire to find out "what the truth was" explains why there should have been so much agreement with Nixon's plea that the matter be turned over to the courts and yet so much dissatisfaction with the content of his speech.

Nixon's speech was followed seven days later by a televised press conference (August 22), his first in five months. Of 20 questions, 15 dealt directly with Watergate; of the remaining five, two concerned the scandal then brewing around Vice President Agnew which shortly thereafter led to his resignation; two asked about his recent accusation against the Kennedy administration for its alleged wiretapping—was this meant to justify such practices within his own administration? The remaining question—the last asked—was whether Nixon felt he owed an apology to the American people for having lied about the bombing of Cambodia. No one asked Nixon whether he had thought the hearings fair or about his thoughts on how the media had reported them. This did not, however, prevent Nixon from seizing the opportunity to counterattack. He expressed indignation at the "constant barrage—12 to 15 minutes a night on each of three networks for four months." The question on Agnew was used to illustrate the media practice of "convicting an individual—not only trying but convicting him—in the headlines and on television . . . completely contrary to the American tradition." The possibility that Nixon might resign, raised in another question, was rejected most emphatically and out of hand. Yet the very fact that such questions were being raised reveals the extent to which the atmosphere had changed since mid-May. When the Harris poll repeated in September the battery of questions about Watergate first asked in August, there had, if anything, been a slight deterioration in Nixon's standing with the public.[44]

IMPACT

Communication researchers, using "traditional" social science approaches, mostly surveys and experiments, do not expect individuals to change dramatically directly in response to media content. Opinions change, but seldom that quickly or profoundly. Television is powerful, but coverage of any one event rarely produces sweeping transformations. Most responses are in accord with dispositions, habits, norms, and interests already present in individuals or at least not in total contradiction. But research has also shown that pressure toward change builds up during severe crises when the whole world as one knows it seems to be crumbling, when individuals are pulled in opposite directions by conflicting allegiances, when they harbor within themselves several contradictory dispositions, or more generally when their commitment to a view is weak. The summer of 1973 should thus have been one of these periods in which the potential of television to change opinions was, if not great, then at least greater than usual.

Direct Effects

Opinions did change during the course of the hearings. But was it exposure to the televised hearings that accounted for a large part of that change? Did the opinions of those who followed the hearings on television change more than those of the others? If so, did some characteristics of viewers make them more susceptible to influence? One difficulty is how to distinguish between those exposed to the televised hearings and those not exposed. Anybody near a radio or with access to a newspaper had a hard time not knowing the hearings were being televised. And anybody with a television set would have found it difficult not to have been exposed to some part of the hearings as excerpts were a regular part of morning and evening news shows. For purposes of assessing the *direct* impact of the televised hearings, we choose to regard as *viewers* only those who more or less regularly followed the telecasts. All others we consider to be *nonviewers*, even though many, probably most, were subject to some spillover effect.

To some extent, whether one was a viewer or nonviewer depended on accessibility. The daytime Watergate audience, like the typical daytime television audience, included a disproportionate number of women, many of them a "captive audience" whose favorite programs had been preempted. Becoming fascinated, some "captives" soon became a willing audience. An undetermined amount of nonviewing was also for want of choice. Among those who might have watched but could not were some with daytime jobs living in areas where the nightly videotaped hearings were unavailable. (Of the nation's 220 public television stations, nearly a third, including those in such major metropolitan centers as St. Louis, Houston, and Minneapolis, did not carry the program distributed by PBS.)

Regular viewers of the proceedings were, on the average, better educated and of higher socioeconomic status than nonviewers. This would be as expected, given the usual composition of public affairs audiences, but there was a considerable overlap of these characteristics between viewers and nonviewers. What most differentiated viewers from nonviewers was their politics. Republicans and anyone who voted for Nixon in 1972 were more likely to be nonviewers, whereas the best predictor of viewing was having voted for McGovern.[45] The two groups also diverged markedly in their attitudes about a citizen's relationship to government. Nonviewers were also more likely to believe that there had been too much coverage of Watergate and that the hearings "weren't good for the country."

Nonviewing, however, did not necessarily reflect an exoneration of the President, a belief that he was innocent of any involvement in Watergate. For example, a study in Florida showed that nonviewers, though more likely to have voted for Nixon, were almost as likely as viewers to believe Nixon had prior knowledge of both the break-in and the subsequent coverup.[46] Still, if Nixon was guilty of something or other, they apparently did not want to hear about it. A nonviewer from Long Island, retired and with time to follow the hearings, recalled in an interview after the resignation—to which he remained unreconciled—that, during the hearings, he had watched only the evening news. The committee, for him, "was just going through the motions" and he kept hoping "it would all blow over. . . . there might be some fire to put out but it didn't amount to anything."

Paradoxically, nonviewers were more prone than viewers to say that the media coverage of the hearings was biased. This is because nonviewing, in many cases, reflected a deep-rooted distrust of politics and politicians. Such an attitude of generalized distrust, endemic in American life, helped many, during these long weeks of hearings to avoid ambiguities they might have found discomforting to face. Social scientists have long sought evidence of such chronic distrust or alienation, as some refer to it, by asking projective questions (for instance, about whether "People like me have no say about what goes on in government"). But these attitudes also find expression in spontaneous comments that "all politicians are corrupt" or, more specific to Watergate, "the only crime the Republicans committed was getting caught." Those revealing such attitudes were more likely than others to be nonviewers; our own study of response to the hearings showed distrust, as revealed by such comments, to have been especially typical of nonviewers who identified with no political party but had voted for Nixon in 1972.

Then, nonviewers were either those without access, for whatever reason, to the telecasts or those more likely than others to have closed off their minds to any potential influence. Given this tendency toward selective exposure and toward interpreting information received to fit one's own political frame of reference, was there much change in individual opinion as a direct response to viewing the hearings?

Despite the many studies at the time, information bearing on this question is limited. Like other researchers, McLeod and his colleagues, studying voters in Madison, Wisconsin, found the relationship between amount of exposure to the hearings and opinion change to be limited and elusive. Neither the level of exposure or the medium (radio or TV) most relied on appeared to have had any discernible effect on beliefs about Nixon's complicity in the break-in or accepting it as "typical of the things people do in campaigns." However, high exposure to the hearings, whether through radio or television, seems to have caused some voters to reevaluate the importance that "honesty in government" had had, or should have had, in the 1972 election.[47]

O'Keefe and Mendelsohn did identify one especially vulnerable group of viewers: those who had voted for Nixon in 1972 and were paying "a great deal of attention" to the hearings. They were somewhat less likely to find Nixon "truthful" than other Nixon voters paying less attention.[48] Our own Long Island study corroborates their finding: such voters, feeling let down by their candidate, were among those least inhibited in their expressions of shock and outrage at the whole affair. In Cleveland, Holm et al. also found the direct effect of the televised hearings to have been concentrated among a relatively small group of persons—those who began with a high degree of trust in government and viewed more than two hours of TV during the Dean testimony. Face to face with the murky reality of Watergate as portrayed by these televised proceedings, they came to acknowledge that Nixon's credibility and his ability to govern had been dealt a serious blow. Here, too, how people responded to the televised revelations was found to have been strongly influenced by how they were initially oriented toward them.[49]

Assessing Effects

To say that prior attitudes played a major role in shaping individual responses to the gavel-to-gavel coverage of the Watergate hearings is not the same as saying that no change resulted from it. A glance at polls from May through August does show movement in relevant opinions. Nixon's approval ratings, as noted earlier, dropped precipitously. There were also increases in the proportion of the public believing that Nixon was somehow involved in Watergate and that Watergate, whatever it stood for, was somehow a serious matter. It seems a reasonable assumption that these shifts were somehow connected with the testimony seen or heard by millions every day, then reported in newspapers and magazines, and mulled over in private conversations all over the land.

Still, one has to conclude that the immediate impact of the hearings was mainly to further, perhaps hasten, shifts in the public mood already under way before the hearings began. For the televised hearings had not begun in an opinion vacuum. Long before they started, the public had been forming judgments about the break-in. And events that occurred before the hearings went public—like the McCord letter sent to Judge Sirica, the firing of John Dean, and the resignations of H. R. Haldeman and John Ehrlichman—had set the stage by creating an interested audience already familiar with the names of witnesses who might testify about events they knew had taken place. By the time the hearings were to begin, awareness was nearly universal. Michael Robinson, a political scientist, whose interviewers called a sample of Oregonians on May 17, the evening of the first day of hearings, said many people just laughed when asked if they had heard about the "Watergate incident."[50] A Gallup poll taken just before the hearings went on the air showed that 96 percent had "read or heard about Watergate, one of the all-time high awareness scores recorded for a major news development."[51]

Not only did almost everyone know about Watergate but a large part of the people were already taking it "quite seriously." The Gallup Poll indicated that this proportion, 31 percent by early April, rose by some 16 percentage points even before the testimony of John Dean in late June, then rose by just another six points before the hearings adjourned in early August. Though using a somewhat different question, the Harris poll corroborated this trend. (Appendix, table 3) Both polls indicated that those who had initially withheld judgment—that is, the people who in April had "no opinion" about the seriousness of Watergate—had come to take it seriously. Their findings, together with those of the California Poll, confirm that the greatest impact of the hearings came during the early weeks of testimony, that those disinclined to take the matter seriously by early June were not likely to start taking it seriously later during the hearings. Something of a "ceiling" had already been reached.

None of these measures of "seriousness," however, tells us what it was about Watergate that people were beginning to take seriously. Where polls tried to solicit such perceptions, they generally asked whether or not people viewed Watergate as "corruption in the Nixon administration" or "dishonesty in the White House"—terms that cover a broad range of wrongdoing. Mervin Field's California Poll was an exception, spelling things out in an unusually lengthy and detailed question:[52]

Some people feel the alleged campaign law violations (failing to report large sums of money, using misleading ads, and paying people to infiltrate the opposing campaign) are *no worse than things that typically happen* in Presidential campaigns, while other people feel they are *a lot more serious than that*. In your opinion, do you feel the alleged campaign violations of the Committee are *worse than usual, about the same*, or *not as bad* as the usual campaign violations that occur in a Presidential campaign?

When the question was asked this way, the proportion judging such acts worse than usual increased from 40 percent the week before the hearings began to 50 percent during the last week of the hearings, while the proportion judging them about the same fell from 52 to 29 percent. Shifts in perceptions thus appear greater than those revealed by responses to the less specific questions used in the national polls. The conviction that Watergate stood for something beyond the ordinary was gaining ground during the hearings. It was not just that more people were taking the matter seriously but, among those taking it seriously, its meaning was being revised.

This new interpretation was difficult to pin down as it was occurring, though it did seem plain to researchers at the time that a significant change was taking place. "Shock" and "amazement" were terms often used by those asked about their reactions to the revelations. Many were "shocked" by evidence of how far the Nixon administration had been prepared to move against individuals to pursue its ends, by the testimony that tax audits were being used as a weapon against those considered "enemies of the White House," by plans to entice, compromise, and politically blackmail rival politicians, by White House–initiated wiretaps of unfriendly journalists' phones. Such allegations brought Watergate closer to home. No wonder that some 77 percent of those questioned (not all of them viewers) by the Yankelovich organization near the end of the hearings agreed that "Watergate shows how even the privacy of ordinary citizens is being threatened these days."[53]

Where, at the beginning of the hearings, Watergate had only stood for the bungled burglary and the attempted "bugging" at Democratic Party headquarters, by the time they ended, it had come to stand for a variety of acts, such as the burglary to obtain the psychiatric records of Daniel Ellsberg in order to discredit him for the unauthorized release of the Pentagon papers, for White House discussions of "hush money" to be paid to convicted burglars, for the White House secret taping of privileged conversations, to mention but a few of the revelations that had held so many enthralled during the summer. As the hearings continued, Watergate, which had begun as an impersonal wrong—with the break-in at the anonymous headquarters of a remote political party—became more personally threatening. Inasmuch as the basis for moral judgments of any "public wrongdoing" resides less in the social or public consequences it may have than in the personal harm that people can clearly visualize as being inflicted on themselves or others like themselves,[54] Watergate, for many, became not just a political but a moral issue.

Political wrongdoing also becomes more meaningful as responsibility for its occurrence is seen as residing less in some amorphous and impersonal "system" than in the specific acts of individuals. If perceptions of what was involved in Watergate and what it all meant changed during the hearings, so did the public understanding of who might be to blame. Even if "the hearings did not exactly bathe Nixon in guilt," as Michael Robinson found,[55] there was a 20 percent increase during the summer in the number of people believing the President was in some way involved. In May, the first time the question was asked by Gallup, it was simply put: do you believe that Nixon had prior knowledge of or participated in the coverup, or not? The next time around respondents were asked to choose among four statements about Nixon's involvement or noninvolvement the one that came closest to what they believed. By early August three-fourths of those questioned believed Nixon either had planned the break-in, knew about it in advance, or helped in its coverup. All others thought he had nothing to do with it or didn't know. (Appendix, table 4).

These national trends indicate that belief in Nixon's involvement was already widespread before the hearings, then gained currency in the beginning weeks of testimony, but thereafter increased only incrementally. Other data suggest differences in the patterns of response across the country. John Robinson, surveying two Michigan cities, found some increase between early May and late June in the proportion believing Nixon had advance knowledge of the wiretap attempt but a considerable decrease following Nixon's rebuttal in August.[56] The California Poll, comparing responses in May and August, noted that "the public does not appear to have materially changed its view of President Nixon from that which it held before the hearings started."[57]

"Presidential involvement" also took on a new meaning as the meaning of Watergate changed. To suspect Presidential involvement while considering Watergate the "usual politics" is different from suspecting such involvement in a serious wrongdoing. Yet a mere suspicion is a long step from convicting the President. By the end of the hearings, support for resignation or impeachment had increased, but the overwhelming majority of Americans still opposed Nixon's removal from office (Appendix, table 5). In early August only a quarter said they thought Nixon should "be impeached and compelled to leave the Presidency," and fewer than half thought he should resign even "if it were *proven* that he knew about the bugging."[58]

In the absence of "proof" of Nixon's complicity in Watergate, the hearings had ended with no groundswell of opinion demanding his removal. Some small proportion of the general citizenry, of the press, and of the polity were convinced that the "truth" could be gotten at only by resort to the impeachment process, but the overwhelming majority believed that the facts would somehow be established without the need for so drastic a step.

Still, it is significant that the words "resignation" and "impeachment" should have entered the public dialogue only months after Nixon's overwhelming public mandate. The Gallup poll dared include a question about "impeachment" *only after* political representatives had dared utter the unutterable in the halls of Congress. Even after the Ervin Committee had gone public, the Senate Democratic Whip, Robert C. Byrd of West Virginia, was calling the idea of impeaching Nixon "at best premature and at worst reckless." [59] On June 3, when Representative Paul McCloskey Jr. of California, who in 1972 had campaigned against Nixon for the Republican nomination, invited his fellow Republicans in the House to join in a discussion of Presidential impeachment, he was prevented by parliamentary maneuvering from this public airing of the subject. Not until June 12 were several Congressmen able to gain the floor for a ninety-minute discussion of whether there were grounds for impeachment. They may have been emboldened by readings of public opinion. And they could not have been unmindful of the large audiences for the hearings; was it not likely that their constituents were as offended by the unfolding testimony as they themselves?

In sum, the telecasts of the hearings did catch and sustain people's attention; the parade of witnesses and their testimony fascinated the press, politicians, and public alike. Directly, the hearings changed some opinions, especially about the seriousness of Watergate and Nixon's involvement. The main immediate effect of the gavel-to-gavel coverage, however, was to hasten shifts in the public mood already under way before the hearings began. Yet, as a result of the hearings, there was also a change in the meaning of Watergate and the nature of public concern. It is this shift in sentiments, not necessarily articulated and difficult for researchers to pinpoint and substantiate with hard evidence at the time, that helps explain the overwhelmingly negative response to the subsequent firing of Archibald Cox as Special Watergate Prosecutor. The outpouring of outrage two months later can be seen as a delayed response to what was observed and learned by viewing the hearings. The connection was noted by Chief Counsel Dash in his account of the Senate Watergate investigation and hearings. Referring to the unprecedented half million telegrams delivered to Congressional offices the weekend of the Cox firing, Dash wrote that

In large part this public reaction resulted from the keen interest millions of Americans had developed in the Watergate facts during our committee's televised public hearings that summer. Ironically, Cox had tried to stop the hearings. Now he had reason to be glad he had failed. [60]

The hearings thus set the framework for subsequent events. This delayed response may, in the long run, have been the most important consequence of the full coverage of the hearings which had allowed people to "see for themselves." Communication researchers, failing to establish any dramatic shifts in opinion directly and immediately attributable to viewer exposure, nevertheless did detect subtle changes in public sentiments as the hearings proceeded. They could hardly have been expected to know how lasting these would be or what part they would play in fashioning a truly dramatic shift in opinion following the "Saturday Night Massacre."

CHAPTER 6

THE BATTLE OF THE POLLS
October 1973–May 1974

"During much of the last nine months of his presidency, Nixon was engaged in a losing battle for public opinion over Watergate" (*Congressional Quarterly*).[1]

"As I increasingly saw it . . . the main danger of being impeached would come precisely from the public's being conditioned to the idea that I was going to be impeached" (Richard M. Nixon).[2]

"There is no doubt in my mind that our polls on impeachment of Richard Nixon had a profound effect. I know they did" (Louis Harris).[3]

"Contrary to the conventional wisdom, public opinion polls did not hasten the resignation of Richard Nixon; rather they delayed it. Had it not been for other events, the polls might have kept him in office" (Michael Wheeler).[4]

Few people in the wake of Watergate doubted that the precipitous decline in Nixon's popularity, as judged by the polls, played a part in his decision to resign. Nixon himself believed that public opinion was the critical factor in the "overriding" of his landslide mandate. Especially from October 1973 on, the President saw himself in a "race for public support," engaged in a "last campaign," only this time it was not for political office but for his "political life." He believed that the "politics of the situation" would determine the outcome, whatever the substantive basis of any impeachment charges.[5] Congressional Democrats, he reasoned, would be constantly taking the political temperature to determine whether they stood a better chance in the 1974 Congressional elections and in the 1976 Presidential campaign with Nixon out of office. Impeachment, for Nixon, was a "strictly political question"; much as some Republicans might also want to be rid of him, they would have to recognize that others would be outraged by the very idea. The public at large might even consider their efforts toward impeachment as "self-interested and disloyal."[6]

In line with this reasoning, Nixon's media strategy was designed to win the battle of the polls even when he publicly insisted that a President cannot

resign just because he becomes unpopular. At a question-and-answer session at the Executives' Club in Chicago, on March 15, 1974, Nixon asked himself and the audience:

Why doesn't the President resign because his popularity is low? . . . . Because if the time comes in this country when a President makes decisions based on where he stands in the polls rather than what is right or wrong, we have a very weak President. . . . . Resignation simply because he happened to be low in the polls would forever change our form of government.

But, as he grew gloomier, he confided to his diary that, in spite of his accomplishments abroad, "it seems almost impossible to break through in the polls."[7] He felt himself losing the battle for public opinion and this defeat, as he saw it, would ultimately force him from office.

Many people share Nixon's opinion that he lost his office because he lost his battle for public opinion, but others hold an opposite view. Some critics of polls, like Michael Wheeler and Timothy Crouse, (and even some pollsters, like Peter Hart and Patrick Caddell) have argued that the polls and other assessments of public opinion exaggerated the opposition to impeachment and thereby acted as a restraining influence on Congress, whose members hesitated to support so drastic a move until they could be certain the public would back their action.[8] These critics contend that, either by inadvertence or design, the most influential polls were slow to register the proimpeachment groundswell during the crucial months after the Saturday Night Massacre (October 20) when the country appeared ready for impeachment. Some of these critics have accused the pollsters of persistently asking the wrong questions, of letting themselves be manipulated by the White House, and of playing up every sign of opposition to Nixon's departure from office while ignoring the contrary evidence, thereby prolonging the crisis and keeping Nixon in office longer than necessary.

A third viewpoint regards the "battle of the polls" as irrelevant. Not only did Nixon misdirect his energy by conceiving his problem as a struggle to win the battle for public support but the media, in following his lead, diverted attention from the absolutely crucial element in Nixon's fight to avoid impeachment: the accumulation of evidence against him.[9] The judgment on whether or not to impeach would have to be based on more stringent evidentiary standards than those which the public applies in responding to pollsters' questions. There was only one battle for public opinion with which the White House had to be concerned—the one over public confidence in the fairness and objectivity of the process by which the President would be

judged.[10] An extreme version of this third view accords no influence whatsoever to public opinion but sees Nixon as "done in" by events, mainly by the revelation of the recorded conversations, by the ill-advised dismissal of the Special Prosecutor Archibald Cox, by the unexplained disappearance of some tapes, by the "accidental" tape erasures, and finally by the "smoking gun" that surfaced in the June 23 tape. Accordingly, Nixon resigned only because he was about to be impeached and found guilty. He would have been forced out even had he not lost the battle of the polls.

We evaluate the merits of the three viewpoints by examining two critical phases during Nixon's "last campaign." The first was in October 1973, in the immediate aftermath of the Saturday Night Massacre, when the idea of impeachment first became widely respectable; the second was the period of the White House counteroffensive. It began with "Operation Candor" in November and ended with the release on April 30, 1974, of some transcripts of Presidential conversations. In tracing the battle for public opinion, we have recounted some events in considerable detail without, we hope, getting bogged down in them.

THE SATURDAY NIGHT MASSACRE

The televised Senate Watergate hearings had set the stage for the next act in the Watergate saga by uncovering the secret recording system in the White House. Here, in the President's own tapes, was evidence that could either exculpate Nixon or confirm his involvement in the break-in and coverup. Archibald Cox and his staff immediately set out to determine which conversations would be needed for presentation to the grand jury. Their initial subpoena to the White House sought only eight tapes, including that of a long meeting among Nixon, Haldeman, and Ehrlichman on June 20, 1972, three days after the burglary. This tape, it turned out, was the one with 18¼ minutes of conversation erased.

A Holiday Weekend in October

The White House refusal to honor the subpoena for the tapes pitted Cox against Nixon. The subpoena convinced Nixon, if he had not already been convinced, that he had to get rid of Cox. His memoirs are clear on two points: Nixon had from the first objected to the creation of an independent Watergate prosecutor as a "slap at the ability of the Justice Department to do the job"; and had Attorney General Elliot Richardson, who conducted

the search, tried to find the one person whom Nixon would have trusted least "to conduct so political and sensitive an investigation in an unbiased way, he could hardly have done better than choose Archibald Cox." Privately Nixon called Cox a "partisan viper" who, so Kissinger had told him, was fanatically anti-Nixon. As if to flaunt this, Senator Ted Kennedy and Ethel Kennedy (Robert Kennedy's widow) had been among the guests at Cox's swearing-in ceremony.[11]

Judge Sirica, preferring to sidestep the complex issues, ordered the disputed tapes turned over to him so he could examine them *in camera* to decide whether they were privileged, as Nixon's lawyer had argued.[12] Instead, the President appealed Sirica's order to the United States Court of Appeals for the District of Columbia. After an out-of-court compromise proved hopeless, the court on October 12 upheld Sirica. This was the same day, by a curious coincidence, on which Nixon announced his nomination of Gerald Ford to replace Spiro Agnew, who had been forced to resign as Vice President because of his involvement in a kickback scandal.

The court's ruling left Nixon with but three alternatives. He could deliver the tapes; he could carry his appeal to the Supreme Court and risk an adverse decision; or he could try to finesse the issue by seeming to turn over the tapes without really doing so. In opting for the third, Nixon and his advisors came up with a compromise that at least one constitutional lawyer saw as a variation of the old shell game.[13] The Special Prosecutor would get a *typed* summary of the tapes, whose accuracy was to be authenticated by a respected elder statesman of the Senate, John E. Stennis, a Democrat from Mississippi. This was a compromise that Cox, as he made clear to the Attorney General, could not accept. Such summaries were secondhand evidence whose admissibility in a criminal prosecution was questionable. It is also highly probable that Nixon did not expect Cox to accept but only meant to drive him into a corner by making his refusal appear unreasonable.

Meanwhile, the Senate Watergate Committee had also been seeking tapes for its investigation. In a meeting with the President on Friday, October 19, its chairman and its ranking minority member were said to have accepted the compromise, but there seems to have been a misunderstanding. Ervin, and probably Baker as well, had agreed only to present the Presidential proposal to the full Committee which, they believed, would get *verbatim* transcripts of conversations relating to Watergate while Stennis would get custody of the tapes from which the transcripts had been made.

Although not everyone was clear about what had been agreed to in private, the President was undeterred from immediately telling the nation that procedures in compliance with "the spirit of the decision of the Court of Appeals" had been accepted by all interested parties except Cox. In a statement, released at 8:15 P.M. EDT that same Friday, he warned that there were those "in the international community" who might be tempted by "our Watergate-related difficulties" to misread America's resolve then being tested in the Mideast (this was the period of the Egyptian-Israeli war of 1973). Nixon assured the public that the verified summaries would contain everything needed for indictments against anyone who might have committed a crime. He did not wish to intrude on the independence of the Special Prosecutor, but Cox was a member of the Executive Branch and, as such, was "to make no further attempts by judicial process to obtain tapes, notes, or memoranda of Presidential conversations." His instruction to Cox, in more pungent terms, was "to cease and desist from his Watergate fishing operation." [14] Thus began the extraordinary sequence of events that would climax with the Saturday Night Massacre.

The initial reaction to the Stennis compromise was favorable. Many key political leaders and press commentators described the elder statesman as the logical man for the job. But there were others who suspected that the timing of the announcement—on the first night of a three-day week-end (this was during the brief era that Veterans Day was observed, not on its traditional November 11, but on the fourth Monday in October)—had been shrewdly calculated to gain acceptance of the compromise as a *fait accompli* before any doubts could be raised:

The evening news shows were over and would not be back for two days. The morning newspapers were on deadline and would hardly have time to search for much reaction to the President's move. It would be days before we [Cox's staff] could catch up [in the propaganda war], if ever, unless we acted immediately. [15]

The President's action may also have been triggered by John Dean's plea that same day. The former Nixon aide pleaded guilty to a single count of conspiracy to conceal the truth about the Watergate break-in, in exchange for which he was granted immunity from prosecution on any other charges. This removed the final barrier to his testifying as a major prosecution witness in the upcoming Watergate trial.

Time was of the essence. On the advice of his public information officer, James Doyle, Cox immediately dictated a response to the President. As Doyle recalls it, there were no secretaries in the office that Friday evening, so he had to type the statement himself. He ran upstairs to the law library where a few reporters were waiting, got the Associated Press on one of the two telephones in the room, the United Press on the other, and read them Cox's statement. As soon as camera crews from the networks had arrived, Cox read his statement for television. Though nobody at that moment had any idea of where it might be held, a Cox news conference was announced for 1:00 P.M. the next day. By morning, Both CBS and NBC had decided to broadcast the meeting live. ABC was scheduled to carry a football game at that hour.[16]

The Cox press conference was to become the main object of interest in Washington during what would otherwise have been an uneventful holiday weekend. Staff members of the Special Prosecutor's office early Saturday morning were calling Congressmen to drum up support and Congressmen were calling them for information. So many phones were ringing that some calls went unanswered. A couple of hundred supportive messages were also being relayed on the Western Union Telex machine. The White House, too, was being bombarded by telephone calls and telegrams, most of them unfavorable.[17]

In almost everyone's estimation, Cox's meeting with the press was a smashing success. He began by reading a prepared statement. After indicating his respect for the President and for Senator Stennis, he painstakingly explained his dissatisfactions with the Nixon proposal: the legal difficulties of going to trial without the best evidence, the vagueness of the White House plans for editing the tapes, and so forth. Then he reviewed the White House's recalcitrance in releasing the required evidence. The climax was his statement, "Whether we shall continue to be a government of law and not of men is now for Congress to decide and, ultimately the American people."[18] Then, having apologized for "being so professorially long-winded," he opened the floor for questions.

What mattered on television was not so much what Cox said but how he said it—the kind of personal image he projected. Some of his staff had worried that he might come across as an arrogant Boston Brahmin, as a member of the eastern establishment trying to "do Nixon in." Instead, he appeared folksy, unpretentious, disarming, more like a country lawyer talking good sense than like a Harvard law professor. At one point he referred to a newspaper headline that proclaimed "COX DEFIANT," remarking "I don't feel defiant. . . . I am even worried, to put it in colloquial terms, that I am getting too big for my britches, that what I see as principle could be vanity." Nixon seems to have been among the minority who saw him disingenuously "adopting the air of a modest and even befuddled professor."[19]

What reporters most wanted to know was whether Cox would continue to seek the tapes. Would he be going to court on Tuesday to report that the court's order had not been obeyed? What would he do if he were fired, possibly by the end of the press conference? Cox assured them he meant to press ahead, since it was highly doubtful that anyone other than the Attorney General could give instructions he was legally obliged to obey. He emphasized his admiration, respect, and affection for Attorney General Richardson but surmised that

Eventually a President can always work his will. You remember when Andrew Jackson wanted to take the deposits from the Bank of the United States and his treasury secretary said that he could not do it, he fired him; then he appointed a new secretary of the treasury and he would not do it so he fired him; and finally he got a third who would. That is one way of proceeding.

The significance of the last query at the press conference (from Clark Mollenhoff) has been largely overlooked by chroniclers of the weekend's events:

Speaking about public reaction to this sort of thing, would you think that it would be helpful if there was an outpouring of telegrams, calls and mail on the subject, to let the President have some idea of what the public mood is on the subject? Would you agree with that?

This had been the way Richard Nixon had fought to save his political life some 20 years before. He had asked a television audience to let General Eisenhower know whether they wanted him on or off the Republican ticket.

This press conference made Cox's firing into a *cause célèbre*. The phalanx of cameras meant the Special Prosecutor was speaking not only to the assembled reporters, but also to the public (some of whom took time out from the football telecast). He was, in addition, speaking to the Representatives and Senators, in whose hands the crucial decisions lay, and the very people whose next steps depended on what he would do—Judge Sirica, Attorney General Richardson, Deputy Attorney General Ruckelshaus, the White House staff, and most likely the President himself.

The man to whom Cox felt directly accountable, Richardson, was with Deputy Attorney General Ruckelshaus and three others. They reportedly kept glancing at each other as they watched but said nothing.[20] The Attorney General had already dispatched a letter to the President about the "serious difficulty" he was having with the instructions he was supposed to give Cox. His letter contained several proposals designed to rescue the compromise.

The President's men were likewise watching. Asked if Nixon, too, was viewing, they declined to say. Nixon never admitted he had watched the press conference, but his memoirs leave little doubt that he had. He felt, he has written, that Cox was "trying to get me personally . . . and I wanted him out." [21]

Judge Sirica also saw the press conference on television.

Cox explained his refusal in *reasonable patient tones*. If the White House had been gambling that Cox would seem arrogant in not accepting the Stennis plan, they had lost. Cox's performance turned the tables on the White House and added further to the impression that Nixon was covering up the Watergate scandal. Since the President's ploy was already public, he could not turn back. [22] (italics ours)

Thus Nixon's "cease and desist" order had backfired. It was stirring a storm of protest, which he exacerbated by his next move. At 2:20 P.M., not long after the televised press conference, General Alexander Haig, Haldeman's successor as Nixon's White House chief of staff, phoned Richardson and asked him to fire Cox.

Any doubts that Richardson might have had seem to have been dispelled by Cox's television performance. He went to the White House firmly resolved to resign. Haig appealed to him to withhold his resignation at least until the Mideast crisis cleared. The President, too, appealed to Richardson's patriotism. As Nixon was to put it to his White House counsel, though not to Richardson, "If I can't get an order carried out by my Attorney General, how can I get arms to Israel?" [23]

Richardson resigned shortly after 4:30 P.M. Ruckelshaus, next in the line of command, never had any doubts about what he should do. When Haig telephoned to relay Nixon's order, he sent his resignation to the White House. Haig was to announce later that he had been fired. The last person who could act as Attorney General and fire Cox was the Solicitor General, Robert Bork. He was a constitutional scholar who believed the dismissal was the President's constitutional prerogative and carried out his order.

But matters did not stop there. At 8:22 P.M. that same Saturday when the Presidential press secretary Ron Ziegler made known the triple departure, he also announced that the Office of Special Prosecutor had been abolished and that the director of the Federal Bureau of Investigation would seal off the offices of the Watergate Special Prosecution Force.

If the White House had wittingly timed the confrontation with Cox to come at the beginning of a holiday weekend, it seriously miscalculated. The President, or his media advisors, had obviously not anticipated the stream of bulletins that constantly broke into regular TV programs and allowed millions to witness history in the making. Football fans had got the play-by-play description of the struggle between Cox and the White House during time-outs and half-time breaks in the game. CBS deemed Ziegler's announcement important enough to interrupt its evening of situation comedies, including the top-rated *All in the Family*. And all networks broadcast advance notice of late evening specials that would put the day's events into perspective. Thus, on NBC after the evening news, John Chancellor reported that not only the offices of the Special Prosecutor but also those of the Attorney General and the Deputy Attorney General had been sealed off. "This," he said,

is a stunning development and nothing even remotely like it has happened in all of our history. All of this adds up to . . . a grave and profound crisis in which the President has set himself against his own Attorney General and the Department of Justice. . . . What it means is that the worst dream of everybody who is worried about the President's secret tapes have become true.[24]

The occupation of offices and the sealing off of files seem to have been what most outraged public and politicians alike. The Cox staff was bitterly angry that FBI agents had actually been dispatched to enter their premises *before* Cox had even received official notice of his dismissal. They deliberately used the presence of the news media to put their case before the public. Henry Ruth, in charge once Cox was dismissed, told reporters how the guards had tried to keep him from entering the premises even though there had been no departmental order or other legal move—just the announcement from the White House. On camera, Ruth said he had asked the guards about removing his personal belongings. Suppose, he had wondered out loud, he had love letters from his wife in his desk? The guards had answered no. Doyle, when asked about his plans, answered, "I'm going home to read about the Reichstag fire." Ruth agonized that "one thinks in a democracy maybe this would not happen. . . . I was thinking . . . that perhaps it wasn't *Seven Days in May* [alluding to a popular novel about an attempted *coup d'état* by American generals]. Maybe this is *One Day in October*."[25] Wihin 24 hours the whole series of episodes came to be known as the "Saturday Night Massacre."[26]

These and other televised remarks made in the heat of emotion alarmed not only the public but also Judge Sirica and others following developments on television. To Sirica "it began to look as if some colonels in a Latin American country had staged a coup. . . . As far as I was concerned, the president was breaking the law." [27] Sirica's reaction counted far more than the opinion of just one ordinary viewer, but his response was not atypical.

With an intentional assist from the Watergate prosecution staff, television played an important role throughout the weekend. Doyle, as press relations officer, saw to it that the camera caught vivid glimpses of the takeover that would convey its threatening arrogance. When he arrived on Sunday after church at the building housing the staff offices, there were network camera crews standing outside and an FBI agent just inside the lobby. Doyle made certain that his conversation with the agent who tried to block his entrance was recorded on videotape. Later in the day, after the FBI men had been replaced by Federal marshals, he held a meeting with the press, where he announced that the staff, by a unanimous vote, had agreed to ignore the White House claim that the Office was abolished. All of them would report for work on Tuesday after the holiday.

That same Sunday the late Oliver Quayle conducted a national telephone poll for NBC. But even before his finding that fully three-fourths of the nation sided with Cox was reported on Monday evening network news (October 23), other available measures made the depth of public indignation apparent. Most publicized were the counts of mail, telegrams, and telephone calls descending on official Washington. Richardson was later to speak of "three million messages" to Congress as "the greatest outpouring of its kind that has ever taken place." [28] We have come across other estimates of a half million telegrams to Congressional offices that weekend and a million calls and telegrams overwhelming the White House. While such "unofficial" counts are notoriously unreliable—the one to two million letters Nixon's 1952 "Checkers Speech" supposedly had elicited turned out, upon a more careful count, to be nearer 300,000[29]—other measures attest to the magnitude of the response. For instance, Western Union reported a tenfold increase in messages to all government offices. Accustomed to handling about 3000 on an average day (of which about 6000 a week go to Congress), on Sunday, October 22, it transmitted some 30,000 messages, a tenfold increase. By Tuesday the Western Union president for public affairs was reporting the "heaviest concentrated volume on record," with 150,000 telegrams to the District of Columbia—10,000 of them to the White House.

The traffic forced the company to bring in extra workers, set up special high-speed printers, and reprogram its computer. Another estimate had 300,000 telegrams arriving in Washington during the ten days following the massacre.[30] No one knows, of course, how many thousands tried but failed to get through to Western Union or to reach Washington by telephone.

The exact number matters less than the image of a deluge. In late November the Gallup Poll asked: "Have you happened to have written a congressman, senator, newspaper editor, or television station urging that President Nixon be impeached or that he resign, or have you signed a petition in this regard?" What made news when the results were released on December 16 was that 94 percent had done none of these things. Yet even a rough calculation tells us that the other 6 percent of some 140 million adults who felt moved to go on record amounted to a staggering 8.5 million.[31]

Most messages, even those to Republican leaders, were anti-Nixon. Senator Javits of New York had received 1150 telegrams by the time he returned from the long weekend, of which only a handful supported the President. The flood of anti-Nixon messages so concerned multimillionaire Republican Representative H. John Heinz from Pennsylvania (later a Senator) that he paid for a poll on the dismissal among the 174,000 households in his district.[32] No statistics were released from the White House, where everyone was "taken by surprise by the ferocious intensity of the reaction," and by "how badly frayed the nerves of the American public had become."[33] Haig branded the reaction a veritable "firestorm" that threatened to engulf the White House and everybody in it.

The swiftness with which the public reacted is evident in the results of a Gallup Poll in the field and three-quarters completed when Ziegler announced that Cox had been fired. On two standard questions, there was a sizable difference between the responses of those interviewed before and after this news broke. Approval of Nixon's performance in office during the first two days of interviewing was about the same (31%) as in earlier surveys; after the announcement it was down to an extraordinary low 17 percent, while support for impeachment was up from 30 to 45 percent.[34] Though there were too few interviews after the announcement to assure statistical reliability, the drift of opinion was unmistakable and validated by other surveys. The *Sindlinger Economic Report*, which continuously records Presidential approval ratings for periods ranging from two to nine days, reported a drop from a 40.1 average approval rating October 17–19 to 23.5 percent October 20–23. The NBC poll on October 21 found 44 percent of those queried favoring impeachment, a statistic remarkably close to that found by Gallup on October 21–22 after Cox was fired.

An October 23 survey of House members by the *Congressional Quarterly*[35] indicated that Democrats felt under enormous public pressure to begin impeachment proceedings while Republicans said their constituents, though concerned by Nixon's actions, were not yet ready for such a drastic move. Some members of Congress may, when questioned, have been aware of poll results but mainly, we assume, their impression of a strong negative reaction came through phone calls, telegrams, and the news reports. It is hard to tell how much the legislators were responding to misgivings conveyed by their constituents or, following their own impulses, projecting their own sense of outrage onto them. For official Washington had been informed of events in the same way—and at the same time—as the general public. It was one of those rare occasions when Washington "insiders" reacted to a political event much as the general public did. The mood had definitely changed:

Inside the government or near it, in the watchful circle of the Washington community, reactions against Nixon seemed to have so much in common with the popular impressions outside government. Citizens at large were swept into a "firestorm" of protest and suspicion. But so were commentators, congressmen, and civil servants. Apparently the President's behavior planted the same question in all minds.[36]

Politicians and public felt equally deceived. Yet if Nixon's action had only affected his standing with the public, bringing approval to a new low, he probably could have survived; but after October 20 his reputation in the government was irrevocably damaged.

The impeachment process was set in motion on October 23. House Speaker Carl Albert, in a late morning press conference, said that he would refer all impeachment resolutions to the Judiciary Committee. Within two days, 84 representatives, including one Republican, had introduced a total of 22 bills and resolutions calling at the least for an investigation to look into the possibility of impeaching the President. Eight of these were referred to the Committee. Though similar resolutions had previously been introduced against five Presidents, including one against Nixon himself in 1972, none since 1868 had gotten this far. The idea that a President might be compelled to leave office was no longer unthinkable. Yet, so far as the public was concerned, this represented no more than a vague sentiment—a "gut feeling"—that had not yet crystallized into a firm resolve. But this round in the battle for public opinion had clearly gone against Nixon.

To Stem the Tide

The White House, in firing Cox or, at least, in the manner of his firing, had obviously made a serious misjudgment. Facing facts, the President quickly, though unexpectedly, reversed himself on the tapes. On October 23, Charles Alan White, acting as the President's counsel, agreed to surrender the tapes. In an appearance before Judge Sirica, Wright declared flatly that, "This President does not defy the law." Two hours later, Alexander Haig said Nixon had responded not just to the threat of impeachment but to a "whole milieu" of concerns—including the need for national unity. Haig himself was certain that this threat would subside as soon as the confusion of the people, of the press, and of Congress had been cleared up and the truth allowed to emerge.

If the reversal was meant to appease impeachment sentiment in Congress, it did not succeed. When news of Nixon's compliance reached the House, the *Congressional Quarterly* had already polled 132 Representatives; those who had indicated their support for impeachment were re-questioned. The news, it turned out, had not changed many minds.[37] Next day Representative Peter Rodino, Democrat of New Jersey, chairman of the House Judiciary Committee, said that his committee would "proceed full steam ahead" despite Nixon's decision to surrender the tapes. There was also an appeal by Senate Republican leaders to Nixon that, as a move toward restoring public confidence, he name a new special prosecutor.

Events took a new turn early on the morning of October 25, when the President, as commander-in-chief, placed American military forces around the world on a high alert. He explained this extraordinary action, taken just after a second Mideast ceasefire had gone into effect, as a response to a Soviet alert reported by American intelligence. He meant to put Brezhnev on notice that the United States was resolved to stop any Russian intervention in the Mideast. Next day Nixon prefaced a twice-postponed press conference with a long statement in defense of the worldwide alert and in celebration of his having achieved the ceasefire. He also announced that arrangements for the actual delivery of the tapes were being made and that a new special prosecutor would be named the following week. Then, responding to a reporter's question, he attacked the press for "such outrageous, vicious, distorted reporting" as he had ever seen or heard in 27 years of public life. Challenged for particulars, he gave none but drew attention to the unstated suspicion that the military crisis had been manufactured as a diversion from his Watergate troubles:

I know for example, in your [CBS] head office in New York, some thought that it was simply a blown-up exercise; there wasn't a real crisis. It was the most difficult crisis we have had since the Cuban confrontation of 1962. . . . We not only avoided a confrontation but we moved a great step toward real peace in the Mideast.

The adage "a crisis a day keeps impeachment away" was making the rounds and Nixon was desperately trying to scotch it.

Given the fast moving chain of events, it is difficult to sort out the impact on public sentiment of any specific development—Nixon's decision to comply with the court order, the worldwide alert, the press conference, or news of Congressional intent to move ahead with impeachment. We can only track the public response as best we can from available evidence.

An ORC telephone poll, taken the day after Nixon agreed to comply with the court order, was reported by CBS evening news on October 25. Support for impeachment and/or resignation appeared to have been unaffected; 43 percent still wanted him impeached and 48 percent wished him to resign. Opinion remained solidly behind Cox, though the 69 percent disapproval of the dismissal was less than the 75 percent recorded by Quayle just after Cox was fired. Sindlinger's two-day Presidential approval rating for October 23–24 showed Nixon with a marginal gain, up by 3.2 points from 23.5 to 26.7 percent.

As for the alert and the October 26 press conference, these seem to have had a slight dampening effect on anti-Nixon attitudes. Yet Nixon hardly helped himself by attacking the press, as indicated by a special Gallup telephone poll following the press conference on October 26 and a White House–commissioned ORC poll on October 27–28. Three out of every five persons reached by Gallup said they had "seen or heard" the broadcast. ORC found 66 percent having "seen or heard *or* read about" it—an impressive, though hardly unprecedented, number of people. Although 31 percent of Gallup respondents who had watched or listened thought Nixon's responses on Watergate "convincing," 54 percent found them "not convincing," while the rest didn't know what to think or didn't care to say. ORC results show a similar imbalance toward the negative: Nixon's announcement that he would appoint a replacement for Cox had done nothing to convince the public that the firing was right to begin with; 70 percent still believed Cox was "just trying to do his job" and only 11 percent believed he had been "out to get Nixon."

Yet, in spite of this generally negative response to the press conference, Nixon's positive rating as President, according to Sindlinger, showed a remarkable recovery—to a 39.9 percent average in the five days that followed.

More important, impeachment sentiment had fallen considerably. According to the special Gallup poll, this had fallen from around 45 percent a few days before Nixon's televised appearance to a mere 28 percent just after the broadcast. Generalizations from special national polls like this one, conducted on short notice and based on a small sample, are chancy, but the falloff was a real one; even allowing for error, the proportion now favoring impeachment was down by at least 10 points.[38] ORC measured support for impeachment at 31 percent.

How to explain this surge in Presidential support following the broadcast? Other polls taken about this time indicate that the public was prepared to give Nixon higher marks for his handling of foreign affairs than for the way he was attending to domestic matters.[39] The difference is sufficiently striking to suggest that some of the public had indeed rallied to the President's side as he acted in the nation's defense in a military crisis. This seems to be the only valid explanation in the absence of firm evidence that he had gained sympathy by depicting himself as the victim of a hostile press.

In California, Nixon's home state, two thirds of those polled on October 27, 29, and 30 by the Field Research Corporation disagreed completely with his characterization of media reporting as "outrageous, vicious, and distorted." In the interim between August and October, the study also noted, more people had come to consider the news coverage of Watergate "fair and unbiased" and fewer to believe it "unfair and biased." There had also been a decrease in the proportion believing there was "too much coverage" and a sizable increase in the percentage thinking there was "too little coverage"— up from 4 to 22 percent.[40]

Nixon in lashing out at TV had singled out a CBS reporter for censure, thereby provoking a new crisis in his relations with the media. Not that everyone who witnessed the interchange thought the press unduly put upon; phone calls to CBS following the press conference were critical of the network by a ratio of 2 to 1. The network, in fact, was sufficiently concerned to commission its own survey from a firm not likely to be considered anti-administration.[41] By 57 to 30 percent, the public was found to disagree with Nixon's evaluation of television news as outrageous. People polled by ORC favored tough and probing questions even at the expense of discourtesy by 76 to 19. And, however much the journalists' skeptical questions about the need for the military alert may have vexed the President, only 23 percent agreed that the news media had been "out to get the President," as Nixon had suggested. Even before the results of its survey were known, CBS revoked a policy barring "instant analysis" of Presidential broadcasts, put into effect only on June 23 to assure what its chairman, William Paley, called a "better, fairer, more balanced, and more thorough coverage." Two weeks after the press conference CBS went back to furnishing commentary after Presidential appearances, since the new policy, Paley now said, "wasn't working." [42]

Television news staffs may also have found some satisfaction in a Minnesota poll: asked to rank various well-known public personalities on a scale ranging from "trust wholeheartedly" to "don't trust at all," Minnesotans trusted Walter Cronkite of CBS most of all, closely followed by Harry Reasoner, then of ABC, and John Chancellor of NBC. Least trusted of all was Spiro Agnew, the ex-Vice President; runnerup as "least trusted" was Richard Nixon. [43]

The News Distortion Charge

There is no denying that adverse reaction to the Saturday Night Massacre pervaded the news and editorials. The *Chicago Tribune*, up to now a faithful supporter of the President, termed his attempted compromise on the tapes "possibly the worst blunder in presidential history"; the *New Orleans States Item* called Nixon a "dictator" and the *Charlotte Observer* thought his actions "ruthless and dictatorial." Network evening news on Monday, October 22, the first day of regular programming after the memorable weekend, carried items about calls for impeachment or resignation by George Meany of the AFL-CIO, Leonard Woodcock of the UAW, and Senator Daniel Inouye, Democrat of Hawaii, of the Watergate Committee. Representative Jerome Waldie of California, a member of the Judiciary Committee, said he would introduce an impeachment resolution. Big play was also given the public reaction to Cox's firing, as measured by polls, the flood of telegrams to the White House, and such displays of displeasure as motorists honking for impeachment as they passed the White House.

What the President considered "offensive" about network coverage is recorded in his memoirs: "Monday evening [October 22] the network news shows ran nineteen different attacks on me by various congressmen; these were balanced by only five defenses, three of these by Bork." [44] Summaries prepared by aides may have omitted, or he chose to ignore, such items as those (on NBC) that "despite the surge of impeachment talk, Democratic senators would like to give the President one last chance to prove that he is not trying to hold back important evidence" and that 15 Republican state leaders it had interviewed still supported the President "to a man."

Richard Salant, then president of CBS Television News, was moved to defend its coverage in an internal memorandum. Balance, it pointed out, was not the strictly numerical issue the White House chose to make it, particularly in a running story with reactions as lopsided as they were: "We reported that Tip O'Neill, the Democratic leader, said that the House wouldn't support impeachment. We had a portion of a pro-Nixon, anti-impeachment speech by Senator Gurney in Nashville. And perhaps more persuasive to the ordinary viewer is the fact that we even reached out to Las Vegas to Jimmy the Greek [the professional oddsmaker], who was quoted as predicting a thousand to one against impeachment and two hundred to one against resignation." [45]

Then, when President Nixon agreed to turn over the tapes, eight of nine reactions shown on CBS Evening News were either pro-Nixon or neutral. Only one comment was outspokenly anti-Nixon.

A study of network news over ten weekdays, beginning Monday, October 15, and ending twelve days later on Friday, October 26, climaxed by Nixon's denunciation of television reporting, demonstrates that coverage was hardly the kind of unbalanced reporting the White House made it out to be. [46] Graduate students at American University, under the supervision of their journalism professor, watched 518 Watergate news stories but questioned the "objectivity" of just a few: Considered possibly "unfair" or based on questionable editorial judgment were five out of 134 screened on ABC, two out of 175 on NBC, and only one out of 209 on CBS, the network that had been the chief target of Presidential criticism. Singled out as most controversial was a story by ABC's Bill Gill, who quoted "informed" sources about testimony concerning a secret million-dollar investment portfolio involving Nixon's closest friend, Bebe Rebozo. Cox was alleged to have received information about these transactions just hours before he was dismissed. While Gill had made it clear that the information came from a government source, he did not report that Ronald Ziegler had already called it "flatly false."

This story does not, however, appear to be the one that triggered Nixon's bitter denunciation of TV: "When a commentator takes a bit of news and then, with knowledge of what the facts are, distorts it viciously," he had told both the assembled White House press corps and the American public, "I have no respect for the individual." It was believed, although never confirmed, that the President's ire had been aroused by a ten-minute interview Walter Cronkite had with the dismissed Special Prosecutor on the October 24 evening news, in which he asked Cox, "There's been a story, a news story, that not only concerns the question of investigating sources of campaign funds but the possible diverting of them into a private investment trust for the President. Do you know anything about that case?"

Cronkite's sin, in Nixon's eyes, was to have asked about the supposed portfolio without mentioning that the White House had already denied the charge. The American University study does not question the appropriateness of Cronkite interviewing Cox without someone there to defend the President's actions. However, when Bruce Herschensohn, an ardent Nixon loyalist, later spelled out the charges of bias against the networks, he pointed to the Cronkite interview as a prime example.[47] The eleven minutes (actually only 10) of airtime given to Cox, he wrote, amounted to the longest interview ever included in a regular news program. CBS had actually held other equally long interviews and Walter Cronkite later devoted airtime to an in-depth talk with Bebe Rebozo. CBS claims to have carried these interviews, including the one with Cox, as part of the news only because it judged them newsworthy.

The White House cited other examples to justify charges of bias. Staffers took exception to the use of apocalyptic language by correspondents who spoke of an administration *coup d'état* or who "in a tasteless or inflammatory way" had called the Cox-Richardson-Ruckelshaus episode the "Night of the Long Knives," comparing it with Hitler's murderous purge of his opposition in 1934.[48] The label "Saturday Night Massacre" was also considered prejudicial. Why, if the press was impartial, had reporters not dubbed the April 30 dismissal of Haldeman, Ehrlichman, Dean, and Kleindienst as the "Monday Night Massacre"?[49]

Equally prejudicial, according to the White House, was the title of a CBS January report on the Middle East, *The Mysterious Alert*. Had CBS treated the October alert as a contrived crisis, as charged? On his show, Cronkite referred to questions being asked in Washington: "Given the explanation of the provocation leading to the military alert, and given the timing of it in relation to the domestic political events of recent days, it was perhaps inevitable that the news was received with considerable skepticism" (Oct. 25). Thereafter, CBS correspondent Marvin Kalb gave Henry Kissinger ample chance to make his denial and put all doubts to rest. Cronkite even reported that the White House was furious at the very suggestion. Eric Sevareid commented authoritatively that "only far-out cynics think the crisis was manu-factured as an escape from Watergate."

A count of film stories on network news during the period from October 8 through November 2 does not bear out the charge that CBS, or the other networks, failed to feature or otherwise downgraded Kissinger's effort to ne-gotiate a Middle East ceasefire. In the three weeks before the alert, there had been five film stories about the Mideast situation for every three about Watergate. That period had included the week of October 8 to 12, when Agnew had resigned and Ford had been appointed to succeed him. It also included the fateful week when the "alert" had to compete for attention against the "massacre." Only during the last of the four weeks, the one that followed Nixon's press conference, did Watergate get more attention than the Mideast peace effort.[50]

Even if the news media were not irresponsible in distorting the news, as Nixon claimed, they nevertheless thrive on conflict and controversy, as they did in the wake of the Saturday Night Massacre. News interest and exposure to television news rose perceptibly during the entire Watergate period and not just during television blockbusters—like the Senate hearings and the impeachment debate. Even more important, the media refused to act simply as an adjunct to the establishment, as if their main obligation was to carry the official administration view. The conflict was after all *within* the estab-lishment, and each side was entitled to a full public hearing. The effort to achieve "balanced coverage" was, in the last analysis, bound to hurt Nixon, since it constantly put into question and undermined the version of Water-gate that the White House sought to convey.

The Tapes That Never Were

In his effort to stem the tide of negative opinion after the Cox firing, the President may have revived some flagging loyalties by his three-pronged strategy: dramatizing himself as a peacemaker, demonstrating his willingness to cooperate with investigators by promising to appoint a new special prose-cutor, and depicting himself as the victim of a vindictive press. But any modest advance in this "battle of the polls" turned out to be short-lived.

One week after the court had been assured that all nine tapes sought would be forthcoming, J. Fred Buzhardt Jr., a White House attorney, told Judge Sirica *in camera* that two of the subpoenaed tapes simply did not exist. For many, this was the last straw. Sirica recalls how astonished he was. The original subpoena had been issued in July; yet, "here it was the end of

October, and the White House was making the first public admission that the two critical tapes didn't exist." He acted quickly to make their nonexistence a matter of public knowledge.[51]

The two "missing tapes"—as they were described by Sirica and most of the press—should have contained a June 20, 1972, telephone conversation with John Mitchell, Nixon's campaign manager, and a meeting in the Executive Office Building on April 15, 1973, in which Howard Hunt's request for executive clemency, relayed by John Dean, was said to have been flatly rejected. The White House now claimed that neither conversation had been recorded: the first, because the President had telephoned Mitchell from the family quarters where there was no taping capability; the second, because the tape had run out and not been replenished. Nixon recalled that he wrote at the top of a briefing paper November 1 the following "frustrated note":

There were no missing tapes.
There never were any.
The conversations in question were not taped.
Why couldn't we get that across to people?[52]

The "missing tapes" could only increase a growing skepticism about any statement from the White House. An ABC poll, reported on its November 11 evening newscast, found that two thirds of a national sample considered unbelievable the explanation that the tapes never existed,[53] and decisive majorities responding to a Harris survey (November 12–15) endorsed the following propositions:

- the two missing tapes were ordered destroyed because they would have proved Nixon knew about the Watergate coverup (by 47–27%);
- the tapes turned over to the court would be found to have been altered beforehand to remove incriminating evidence (by 58–28%);
- so far as the missing tapes were concerned, Nixon was trying to cover up his personal involvement in Watergate (by 55–25%); and
- Nixon was not telling the truth when he said two of nine conversations were never recorded (by 55–23%).

Where the Saturday Night Massacre had triggered the first serious move toward impeachment, now the debacle of the "missing tapes" brought demands that Nixon resign. By November 4, one Republican Senator, Edward Brooke of Massachusetts, had joined some Democrats in demanding that Nixon leave office for the common good. Three major newspapers—the *New York Times*, the *Detroit News*, and the *Denver Post*—were also calling for resignation, along with some once staunch Nixon supporters. Howard K. Smith (ABC), considered by the President "an old friend," suggested on October 31 that "either Congress or the President, by his own patriotic decision, should relieve the nation of a burden that's grown too heavy to carry any longer." *Time*, in its first editorial (November 12) in 50 years, observed that Nixon had "irredeemably lost his moral authority, the confidence of the country and therefore his ability to govern effectively." The Conservative *National Review* had already taken a similar editorial position.

Barry Goldwater, a spokesman for Republican conservatism, urged the President to appear before the Senate Watergate Committee to answer questions about the circumstances under which the tapes were *not* made as the "only way" to restore his credibility. On November 7, Nixon used television time for what he later called a "desperate, strong measure." [54] Concluding an address on energy policy, he said that he wanted to close with a "personal note." More than one viewer must have gasped, recalling how Lyndon Johnson had unexpectedly announced his irrevocable decision to neither seek nor accept nomination for another term at the end of a speech on Vietnam. This time no such surprise was in store. The President ended by assuring the American people "I have no intention whatever of walking away from the job I was elected to do."

As to the popular response, however distrustful most people might have been and however much they wanted Watergate to end, there was as yet no firm majority favoring Nixon's resignation. The Harris and Yankelovich polls in mid-November showed a very considerable gap between the proportion convinced that Nixon was involved in Watergate or knew more than he was telling and the proportion wanting him to resign.

A Broad View of Shifting Opinion

The rise and fall in "approval" of the President's performance in office has been used as a fever chart to trace the impact of Watergate developments. It shows Nixon's popularity gradually falling after the summer of televised hearings, then suddenly dipping after the Cox firing, followed by a partial recovery. The fact that Gallup took the nation's pulse midway into the massacre weekend probably exaggerated the depth of the dip giving the impression that the damage from the aborted tapes compromise was most ephemeral. But even though Nixon's approval rating went up again in November, never again did it return to its pre-massacre level.

What seems obvious is that the long, steady decline in Nixon's popularity was a response to his handling of Watergate, on which the public gave him generally poor marks, while any temporary recovery was the result of activities not related to Watergate, such as his handling of the energy crisis and of the Mideast war. The permanent damage caused by the Cox firing is revealed by responses to a question in the Harris Survey, "Do you tend to agree or disagree that President Nixon has lost so much credibility that it will be hard for him to be accepted as President again?" When this question was asked for the first time, just before the massacre, 60 percent agreed. Next month this proportion was up to 73 percent, even though at this time (between October 26–29 and November 12–15) Nixon's handling of foreign affairs was gaining in approval.

The real payoff, of course, was in what people felt they could do about Watergate or what they were willing to have their representatives do. Impeachment sentiment had risen considerably—from 26 percent in August to 37 percent in early November (Gallup)—but the majority were still resisting the idea. Support for resignation followed the same pattern. After November, all through Winter and Spring 1974, polls indicate little movement in either sentiment (See Table 6.1). Harris stopped asking about resignation and Gallup reworded the questions it had been asking. Roper polls that began in November consistently showed more support for impeachment or resignation than either Harris or Gallup, but none of these recorded much change.

When, just after Nixon's resignation, we asked people in a telephone poll in strongly Republican Suffolk County, New York, to recollect at what point they had begun to accept the idea, if at all, that the President would either have to resign or face impeachment, many identified the Cox firing as the decisive turning point. It had convinced them that there must be evidence proving Nixon's involvement. Why, otherwise, would he not hand over the tapes? Yet there were among them a good many who kept on wavering anytime the President showed himself cooperative or signalled a national crisis. These reactions reflected political loyalties. After October 20, most Democrats or Independents, including many who had voted for Nixon in 1972, ceased to have doubts. But Republicans, who took Watergate seriously and did not regard it as "just politics," found it more difficult to sustain the idea of Nixon's having to leave office. They naturally wanted to believe the best of a Republican President of whose foreign policy achievements they were so often reminded. It was precisely this benevolence that was so severely taxed by the disclosure that two subpoenaed tapes did not

TABLE 6.1 Proportions Favoring Resignation or Impeachment in Selected National Polls

Question	August 1973	November 1973	April 1974	June 1974
Harris (A) Resignation	28	43	40	
Gallup (A) Impeachment	26	35/37 [a]		
Harris (B) Impeachment (conditional)	39	53		64
Yankelovich: Resignation	20 [b]	29 [b]	38 [b]	
Impeachment	10 [c]	10 [c]	17 [c]	
Total removal	30	39	55	
Roper: Impeachment (with charges)		(42) [d]		
(without charges)		(47) [d]		
Both versions		44	53	
Gallup (B) Impeachment			52	50
Gallup (C) Conviction			46	44
Harris (C) Impeachment			42	52
Range on Impeachment	10–39	10–53	17–53	44–64

* See below for exact text of questions.
[a] Gallup took an early and a late November poll.
[b] Resignation responses
[c] Impeachment responses
[d] The difference is not statistically reliable but may be real.

Versions of Impeachment Question

Harris (A): "In view of what happened in the Watergate affair, do you think President Nixon should resign or not?" (June 1973–April 1974—asked 11 times)

Gallup (A): "Do you think President Nixon should be impeached and compelled to leave office or not?" (June 1973–February 1974—asked eight times)

Harris (B): "If the Senate Watergate Committee decides that President Nixon was involved in the coverup, do you think Congress should impeach him, or not?" (August 1973–July 1974—asked seven times)

Yankelovich: "Would you like to see Nixon continue in office, decide to resign, or be impeached?" (August 1973–April 1974—asked three times)

Roper: (Following a list of possible criticisms or charges against Nixon about which the respondent was asked if "you think it is a serious offense and . . . . think he may be personally responsible for it"; the other half of the sample was not given such a list.) "Because of the various charges that have recently been made against Nixon, do you think impeachment proceedings should be brought against him or not?" (November 1973–May 1974—asked three times)

Gallup (B): (Following an explanation of the impeachment process similar to Ropers's.) "Now let me ask you first of all if you think there is enough evidence of possible wrongdoing in the case of President Nixon to bring him to trial before the Senate, or not? (April–August 1974—asked five times)

Gallup (C): "Just from the way you feel now, do you think his actions are serious enough to warrant his being removed from the Presidency, or not?" (April–August 1974—asked five times)

Harris (C): "All in all, do you think President Nixon should or should not be impeached by Congress and removed from office?" (March–June 1974—asked four times) exist and, subsequently, by the news of an 18¼ minute gap in one of the tapes. An interviewer catching them in a moment of anger or despair might find them endorsing the move to impeach. Yet these same people would have second thoughts when Nixon launched Operation Candor or pleaded in a State of the Union speech that "one year of Watergate is enough." What finally convinced these "waverers," as we shall see, was his release of edited transcripts in place of the subpoenaed tapes of the Presidential conversations.

Attitudes toward impeachment and resignation were also affected by political developments, such as the Agnew resignation on October 10, which made Nixon's removal more acceptable to some Democrats. The nomination two days later of Gerald Ford to be Vice President reassured some Republicans but delayed the impeachment inquiry because the staff of the Judiciary Committee found it difficult to complete action on his confirmation and work on the impeachment inquiry at the same time. As long as some Republicans remained suspicious of a Democratic power grab in the absence of a Vice President, there was little the Committee could accomplish before a Republican succession was a constitutional certainty. (In the absence of a Vice President, Speaker of the House Carl Albert, an Oklahoma Democrat, would have succeeded.) Ford was sworn in December 6.

NIXON'S LAST HURRAH

Richard Nixon continued to react to Watergate in political terms. In his bid to turn public opinion around, he centered his strategy on holding the following he still had, ignoring those who had already turned against him the previous summer and were by now *definitely* beyond his reach. But he might yet salvage some support among those whose faith had been sorely tried by the Dean testimony and then further shaken by the events of October. Nixon had tried to assuage them when he agreed to hand over the subpoenaed tapes and once again he would seek to convince them with his promise in the April 29 "tapes" speech that "the materials I make public tomorrow will provide all the additional evidence needed to get Watergate behind us."

End of the year polls in 1973 showed only one quarter of Independents and just over half the Republicans approving his handling of his job. But 56 percent of these Independents and 79 percent of the Republicans still opposed impeachment.[55] Nixon could not afford to lose them, because, as he saw it, the main danger of his being impeached came from having the idea of impeachment become acceptable to a majority.

Nixon had targeted three groups. The first consisted of self-styled Independents with Republican leanings, who hoped that whatever Nixon might have done did not amount to an impeachable offense, because they feared the acrimony and trauma that would come with impeachment. A second group, the Republican identifiers, did not really care how deeply Nixon had been implicated in the Watergate coverup. To them the whole affair continued to smack of the usual politics. The legal and political means by which he sought to stave off impeachment rallied their spirits but only as long as they seemed to work. Finally, there was Nixon's natural constituency, the Republican stalwarts who would remain unreconciled to the end and ultimately find comfort in the manner of his leaving.

This, then, was the target audience Nixon sought to rally in his "last campaign." His aim was not to convert but to sustain their confidence until people would weary of Watergate. His attacks on the news media were not meant just to pressure the media but to reinforce the opposition of Republicans and conservative Independents to impeachment.

Counterattack: Operation Candor

Overall, Nixon's several media-orchestrated counterattacks caused no significant movement of public opinion. This is not to say that these efforts to reinforce the image of Watergate as a partisan political issue had no effect. Each produced a brief rally of support, which then fizzled.

Operation Candor was a catch phrase invented by *Newsweek*. Quickly picked up, it was to gain currency as a shorthand for the President's attempt to turn opinion around after the twofold disaster of Cox and the missing tapes. It began in early November with a series of meetings with almost all Republicans and 46 Democratic Congressmen. Two months later it ended, without much fanfare.

In private meetings the President told the congressmen that he was as worried as they about "why in the hell the president can't clear up Watergate." [56] Some of those present suggested a dramatic gesture to win back the confidence of the American people, such as going before a joint session of Congress for cross-examination—a kind of voluntary impeachment proceeding without legal duress—to give the President a national rostrum, which he could use to clear up Watergate once and for all.

Nixon rejected this advice. Rather than face Congress as a defendant, he preferred the strategy that had served him so well in the 1972 campaign. Then he had managed, for the most part, to avoid showdowns with unfriendly questioners while dominating the news through carefully staged public appearances. Now, in Operation Candor, he sought to implement the same game plan with press conferences before groups known to be supportive and sufficiently important to assure film footage on the national news. Thus, he could appear to be facing the press while actually avoiding sharp questions from an increasingly hostile White House press corps, an ingenious and, he assumed, a foolproof way of calling attention to what his administration had achieved and what it still hoped to achieve.

The first appearances were scheduled in the South. This was Nixon country, where polls showed him doing best. A number of influential congressmen were from that section. If he could mobilize his constituency there, this would translate into a solid bloc of Congressional support. The crowd scenes, shown on local television, were a repeat of the election campaign, though on a smaller scale. Nixon must have been able to reassure some of his followers. He made small gains in both the Harris and Gallup polls, but in the South, where he had concentrated his efforts, his gains were just about double the national average.

Success, however, was brief. Operation Candor soon began faltering. Its gains were offset by events beyond the control of the White House. Several local appearances produced the intended national stories, but without the desired favorable copy. One incident stands out. This was on November 17, when the President appeared before the Associated Press Managing Editors Association in Orlando, Florida. Carried live on radio and television in the early evening, the question-and-answer session contributed yet another classic phrase to the Watergate vocabulary.

Answering a question about his personal finance and tax payments, Nixon addressed the nation at large: "I want to say this to the television audience. . . . People have got to know whether or not their President is a crook. Well, I am not a crook. I have earned everything I have got." This was an unhappy choice of words. With them the President had undone much that this carefully managed appearance could have achieved. He later insisted that the remark was no "spur-of-the-moment statement" but a calculated answer in "down-to-earth, understandable language" to past attacks on his personal integrity.[57] But from the mouth of a President, charged with setting standards for moral conduct, the phrase was hardly a felicitous one. By this highly personal disclaimer on national television, the President made himself an object of ridicule. Few people remembered much that he said there, but they did remember, "I am not a crook."[58]

A November 20 meeting with 19 Republican governors also backfired. Only the day before George Gallup Sr. had told them that the proportion of Americans identifying themselves as Republicans continued to shrink. This dismal tiding was disseminated on ABC and NBC evening news. Nixon, subject to pressure from Republican leaders whose sagging spirits needed a lift, promised the governors detailed answers to various charges such as would lay to rest any lingering doubts. When one governor asked, "Are we going to be blindsided by any more bombshells?," Nixon assured him there would be none. Headlines in the press read: NO MORE BOMBSHELLS.

The bombshell that burst the next day made a mockery of this pledge. The press had a field day with the revelation that a shrill buzz had blocked out some 18 minutes of a crucial conversation on one of the subpoenaed tapes. Republican leaders were angry and resentful. The disclosure fed the distrust of an already suspicious public. Even before the discovery of the gap, three of every five Americans suspected that the tapes, when handed over to Judge Sirica, would already have been altered to remove any evidence of Nixon's involvement in the planning or coverup of Watergate. After its existence had become general knowledge, they suspected Nixon by a three to one majority. Moreover, this suspicion was shared by over half those calling themselves Republicans![59]

Rose Mary Woods, the President's loyal secretary, was called on to explain in court how she had accidentally erased the tape. She said it had happened when, while transcribing the tapes, she answered the telephone with one hand while stretching to keep her other hand on the keyboard of her typewriter. The networks reenacted the scene to show the absurdity of her claim and the "Rose Mary stretch" became a national joke.

Yet another illustration of how an initially favorable response was soon dissipated is provided by Nixon's release, on December 8, 1973, of documents on his financial standing, including his Federal tax returns for 1969–72. Nixon said he hoped thereby to "lay to rest" allegations about his personal wealth. He also sought to still public comment on the low amount of income tax he had paid in three of the last four years with a promise to abide by the decision of a Joint Congressional Committee on whether he owed a capital gains tax on the sale of land adjoining his San Clemente home and on whether he was entitled to a deduction for having donated his Vice Presidential papers to the National Archives. Rumors about the misuse of campaign and Federal funds on his residences in California and Florida were also rife. Nixon alluded to these when he announced that the San Clemente estate would be given to the nation after he and his wife died. This was an offer on which he was to renege when, five years after his resignation, he sold the estate at a hefty profit to a consortium of Orange County businessmen.

Each of these gestures elicited an initially positive response. The press and public officials noted that this was the fullest disclosure ever by a President of his personal finances. Still, the Harris Survey (January 7–10) found that, in releasing the documents, Nixon had raised more doubts than he had erased. Fewer people (26%) now thought he was being honest about the financing of his homes than thought (56%) he was being dishonest about it. And apparently the size of the income tax payments spoke louder than any words. Three quarters of the people—including most Republicans—thought it was "wrong for President Nixon to have paid less taxes than a person with an income of $8,000 a year, when he is paid a salary and expense account totalling $250,000 a year." Press comment also focused on the ethical standards Nixon had apparently set for himself. As President he had to set an example and be "holier-than-thou" in filing a tax return.

Nixon's gamble that, with Operation Candor, he could go over the heads of Congress and appeal directly to the American people had failed. Tired and impatient as Nixon's constituency may have been over Watergate, most had not actively opposed impeachment. Nor had Operation Candor halted the impeachment process in its tracks, as the President had hoped. A poll of House members in early November on how they would vote *if* asked to impeach the President, showed that of every ten two were ready to vote "yes," nearly four prepared to vote "no," and the rest yet undecided.[60] By January 1974 the belief that the country might be better off in the next few years were Nixon to leave office was no longer confined to Democratic legislators. Nearly one fourth of Republican voters and two fifths of Independents subscribed to this view. Fewer and fewer of them still believed that Nixon was altogether innocent, but Congress as a body still feared that impeachment might be more destructive than the ill it was meant to cure. The pressure on Congressional Republicans was in some ways even greater than on Democrats. If there was to be a vote on impeachment, Republicans had reason to want it over quickly; they did not wish to have it close to the off-year elections in November 1974.

THE PRESIDENTIAL TRANSCRIPTS

Nixon's campaign to save his political life now turned more and more to painting the investigations of Watergate as partisan politics. On January 31, he ended his State of the Union speech with a call to end all investigations, emphasizing that he had "no intention whatever" of resigning. With these remarks, he set off an ovation well orchestrated to impress the television audience with the strength of his support in Congress. A television viewer could not have detected how partisan was the response compared to that traditionally greeting this ceremonial occasion. Most Democrats and some Republicans sat on their hands; there were even some hisses and boos which some radio and television commentators did mention after the speech.

Meanwhile, the House Judiciary Committee had also become involved in a deep struggle with the White House over access to evidence—in particular over the tape recordings of Presidential conversations. By April 1974 the conflict came to a head when the Committee, by a near-unanimous vote of 33–3, decided to subpoena, not nine but, 42 tapes and set April 25 as the deadline for compliance. In typical fashion, the President proposed a compromise. Finding it unacceptable, the Committee gave the President five more days to comply.

On April 29, just before the deadline, Nixon, in yet another surprise move to unbalance the opposition, went on national television to announce that he was complying by turning over to the Judiciary Committee and making public not the subpoenaed tapes but *edited* transcripts of the relevant conversations. The drama of this most unexpected maneuver nearly matched that of the "Saturday Night Massacre." But this time there was no immediate firestorm, only the same delayed negative response that had greeted so much of Operation Candor. Both the initial swing toward Nixon and the subsequent recoil were wilder than the previous shifts, like that in response to the disclosure of Nixon's financial records. At first, the speech had kindled hope, elicited surprise and even elation. Nixon, it appeared, had finally decided to cooperate, but by the time Gallup conducted a special telephone poll on May 2, opinion had firmed up against the President. Congress was equally condemnatory. Even Nixon's long-time supporter, *New York Times* columnist William Safire, found him "guilty of conduct unbecoming a President."[61]

Given the ultimate failure of the speech to turn opinion around, it is easy to forget how well conceived it was to do just that. It was superbly planned and skilfully delivered. More than half of the adult population heard the President say that "in these folders that you see over here on my left are more than 1,200 pages of transcript of private conversations I participated in between September 15, 1972, and April 27th of 1973, with my principal aides and associates with regard to Watergate." As usual, he moved to anticipate the opposition by granting their argument. His effort to protect the confidentiality of Presidential conversations had "heightened the sense of mystery about Watergate" and "increased suspicions of the President." His reluctance to release the tapes was out of different considerations. The "uninhibited discussion" in these recordings, he confided, would show people in the White House speaking with the "same brutal candor . . . necessary to bring warring factions to the peace table or to move necessary legislation through the Congress." Further, the tapes would tell an ambiguous story; they would even encourage sensational news stories likely to embarrass him and others. But he was willing to take that risk. The transcribed portions of the conversations included *everything relevant* to Watergate—the "rough and the smooth."

Making these transcripts public was to demonstrate that the President had "nothing to hide" and to make it absolutely clear that this was the limit to which he would contribute to the investigation. Chairman Rodino was invited, along with Edward Hutchinson of Michigan (the ranking Republican), to listen to the full tapes so that they could determine for themselves whether the transcripts were accurate and included all relevant information.

Instant analysis focused on how the Judiciary Committee would react. The consensus was that most members, including some Republicans, wanted the tapes, not edited transcripts. As for the speech itself, Howard K. Smith who had earlier called on Nixon to resign, called it rather impressive—if only the President had made it earlier. John Chancellor found it one of the most extraordinary Presidential addresses ever given. Next morning (April 30) the reactions reported on the front pages of the *New York Times* and the *Washington Post* were at least grudgingly admiring and sometimes ecstatic. William Greider, in a front page *Post* story, noted that Nixon had neither sweated nor stammered as he had in other recent television appearances. He was "self-controlled and deliberate . . . speaking with a slow and patient sternness, the coolness of a defense lawyer, summing up his own case." In a long career of bold gambles, it was by far his most daring. The embattled

President had offered up the one "defense most difficult for him to surrender—his private self, the unvarnished Nixon who operates in the privacy of the Oval Office, the man whom few have ever known."

R. W. Apple, of the *Times*, [62] conceded that "the President had made his most powerful Watergate defense since the scandal broke." The main reason Mr. Nixon had so long resisted the idea of releasing the tapes, he thought, was to be found in his pride. "Nixon," Apple wrote, "is not a man who will enjoy having his 'brutal candor' and private musings spread on the public record; he is not a man who enjoys being ridiculed. But in the end he clearly decided that his survival required no less." Many reporters thought, as did many members of the public, that the President, at long last, had pulled the rug out from under his detractors. How clever of the President to have baited the trap, to have let Dean hang himself at the witness table! Now he would produce the secret weapon to show him for the liar he was. Similar hopes had been voiced just after the existence of the tapes was first divulged, but these, too, had proved wishful thinking.

Nixon's speech had been stage-managed to establish so firmly in the public mind the President's version of what the tapes showed that it would withstand later reports based on a reading of the transcripts. Deliberately, no advance text had been supplied, but the press was given an account of "what the transcripts showed" so this could be reported before their release the following day. The height and bulk of the volumes of transcripts shown on television (later discovered to be half-empty) were meant to convey an image of compliance, to show the public just how much had been demanded of the President and how far he had gone to accede to these demands.

Mainly, the White House had reckoned that most people would not read the transcripts or certainly not read much of them. This is where they miscalculated. They certainly did not count on the interest the copies of the edited transcripts and commentary were about to stir up. The *New York Times* not only serialized them but rushed a paperback into print, as did the *Washington Post*. They became bestsellers. The White House had also underestimated the ingenuity with which television news staffs would get the evidence out. The problem with the transcript story, so far as TV was concerned, was the lack of pictures. In a CBS special aired in prime time May 1, reporters read from the transcripts, "starring" as Dean, Nixon and Haldeman. On May 4, after the evening news, NBC broadcast a similar 90-

minute reading with professional actors in the White House roles. In this way a mass audience was exposed to the content of the conversations. No social science study of the effect of this handling of the "tapes story" exists, but one surmises that the attention television drew to the content goes a long way toward explaining why the initially favorable response to the release of the transcripts was so quickly dissipated.

A number of Republican leaders reversed themselves upon seeing what was in the edited documents. John Rhodes of Arizona, the House Republican leader, who had first said the transcripts showed the President to be "in substantial compliance" with the Committee's subpoena, soon changed his mind. A few days later, he said he would accept the President's resignation if offered. Hugh Scott, Republican minority leader of the Senate, likewise denounced what the transcripts revealed as a "deplorable, shabby, disgusting, and immoral performance by all." At a House Judiciary Committee meeting on the evening of May 1, called to consider Nixon's response to its subpoena, some Southern Democrats expressed concern with the forum he had chosen. James Mann of South Carolina spoke of the President's mounting an "electronic throne" to tell the American people what is or is not to be made available. Republicans were still arguing for another try at a compromise before finding the President in noncompliance."[63]

Public opinion also entered the internal debate. Joshua Eilberg, a Democrat from Pennsylvania, invoked a constituent poll he had taken two weeks earlier. Almost eight out of ten wanted the President to give the Committee all the information it desired. If that was the mood of the people, the Committee should listen. Not everyone agreed on just where the public stood or that the grave decisions facing the Committee should be "based upon the shifting sands of public opinion." Representative William Cohen, a Republican from Maine, said the portions of the transcripts he had been able to read thus far struck him with "how much that had been done in this long year of Watergate" had been "directed to the PR factor, whether it be public relations or public reaction." The public might perceive the "President's tender to us" as substantial compliance, but Cohen believed his duty as a member of the Committee to rest on much higher grounds.

How much influence did concern over constituent reaction have on the Committee vote on whether or not to accept the edited transcripts as compliance with its subpoena? The decision to reject was by a narrow margin— 20 to 18. Two Democratic members voted with the Republican minority and Cohen opted for rejection despite some doubts that the public would fully understand why the transcripts were inadequate as legal evidence. The debate suggests that members wanted to be fair as well as to appear fair.

And how did the public react to Nixon's offer of compromise? A special May 2 telephone survey by Gallup showed that the "developments of the last few days" had caused many (42%) to lower their opinion of Nixon; 36 percent felt as before, while only 17 percent were more favorably disposed. People who had read or listened to the reading of the transcripts were distinctly more negative than those who had not. They were also somewhat more likely to back the Committee in its refusal to accept the transcripts in lieu of the tapes. More people were now inclined to believe Dean's version rather than Nixon's and a plurality now thought there was enough evidence for the House to vote impeachment. It was among the 38 percent who both watched the speech *and* read the transcripts or heard them read that Nixon suffered the greatest loss of credibility.[64]

As a backlash of negative opinion built up, Nixon loyalists took their cue from a theme in his speech which stressed the need to separate the legal from the image component. Joseph Alsop (May 3) judged that the release of the transcripts, with their many "expletives deleted," had hurt Nixon "image-wise"; the language was "repellent" but this was not an impeachable offense—even in the Presidency. In the long run, Alsop prophesied, the evidence in the transcripts would help exonerate and the average House member, knowing more about courtroom gangs than the average man in the street, would not be quite so repelled. But as people read or heard about the transcribed conversations, and then about the discrepancies between them and the text of conversations that had already surfaced, it became harder to sustain the position that the public would object to impeachment. A Harris survey (May 7–8) indicated that the public, by a 2–1 margin, rejected Nixon's (and Alsop's) version of what the transcripts showed. By this time, a plurality was for "impeachment and removal." A Roper poll in mid-May also showed impeachment sentiment on the rise—up from 53 percent before the release of the transcripts to 58 percent after exposure to their content.

Nixon's "bold gamble" had backfired, and left him more vulnerable than before. While only some of his natural constituency had come to favor impeachment proceedings, many had, as Nixon feared, by now become conditioned to the possibility. Trends charted by Roper show that as understanding of the impeachment process rose, so did the belief that it should occur.[65] More accurately, as the idea became more familiar, it became less frightening. The process was no longer viewed as inevitably destructive. The roughly one third who remained firmly opposed to bringing impeachment proceedings were mainly older, less educated, white, white collar workers— and Republican. Insofar as the Watergate affair was the battle for public opinion, which Nixon considered it to the very end, it had been effectively lost with the release of the edited tapes.

POLLS AND PUBLIC OPINION

Pollsters have been accused of asking wrong questions, thus delaying the resignation of Richard Nixon. This raises the question: was public support for impeachment really stronger than recorded by the polls? Our examination of questions and our interviews with some of those responsible for drafting them turned up nothing to convince us that public pollsters during this period deliberately slanted their questions or even that their findings grossly distorted the actual speed with which the tide was turning against Nixon.

As to just where the public actually stood at any point, much depends on what questions one selects from the many that were asked. Thus, throughout the seven months in which the House Judiciary Committee was looking into the possibility of impeachment, polls indicated that the public supported its mission and approved its quest for the tapes.[66] Perhaps questions about the impeachment inquiry provided a more valid measure of public sentiment for impeachment than more direct questions about impeaching Nixon. Nevertheless, the news media tracked impeachment sentiment by focusing on the changing percentage who favored Nixon's impeachment, mainly because the question reappeared in the same standardized form in more polls and more often than questions about executive privilege, who should have control over the evidence, and so forth.

The strength of impeachment sentiment obtained through various questions did indeed depend on how the questions were phrased. Table 6.1 charts the responses to eight questions on the issue of Nixon's removal from office during four key months, all from respected national polls. The range of variation during any one month is quite considerable. It averages close to 35 percentage points.

This only underlines something well recognized by survey researchers: Any ambiguities in a question, the alternatives provided the respondent, and the context in which a question is asked have some effect on the response.

As for ambiguity, the question that drew most fire from critics of the polls was Gallup's, "Do you think President Nixon should be impeached and compelled to leave office or not?"[67] This phrasing called on the respondent to make two judgments at once: Should Nixon be forced out? Should this be accomplished through the constitutional impeachment procedure? The question, first introduced in June 1973, was repeated in seven subsequent Gallup polls until February 1974 and then changed. In April, Gallup asked people, quite directly, whether they thought there was enough evidence to bring the President to trial before the Senate. The consequence was a considerable jump in support for impeachment between the February poll, when the old version of the question was last asked, and the one two months later, when the revised version was introduced.

The alternatives in a question can also influence the response. There is an obvious difference between resignation (Harris A) and removal by impeachment (Gallup A). To the extent that these two polls are truly comparable, they show a slight but hardly overwhelming preference for resignation over impeachment. But when the two are posed as alternatives, resignation gains, as in the Yankelovich question: "Would you like to see Nixon continue in office, decide to resign, or be impeached?" Late in November 1973,[68] given these choices, the public opted for resignation; the 10 percent favoring impeachment is far below what any of the other polls were then registering and surely the one statistic that might have bolstered the sagging spirits of pro-Administration forces. The alternatives, as offered, were made to appear less ambiguous than they were in fact. A President remains in office while he is impeached; he is removed only after the Senate has convicted. Given the wording of the question, most respondents were not ready for an impeachment they probably understood as "forced removal from office." Those aware of the tedious nature of the impeachment process might have been content to have him resign immediately.

Questions about impeachment or removal from office as conditional on some finding of guilt also drew quite different responses from those that sought simply to elicit what persons thought "now." This is evidenced by responses to two questions asked in the same 1973 poll before the Cox firing. One was the Harris B version, with impeachment conditional on an adverse finding by the Ervin Committee: the other simply read, "Considering all the developments of the Watergate case, do you think Congress should begin impeachment proceedings against President Nixon, or not?" The two questions brought vastly divergent results. The distribution was just about reversed, from a majority for the conditional version to a majority against the unconditional one.

How the context of questioning further affects response was demonstrated by the Roper Organization. An impeachment question in its November survey was prefaced by this explanation: "Actually impeachment of a president begins with an investigation of charges against him by the House of Representatives and if they think the charges have sufficient basis, a later trial by the Senate." People, once so informed, were found to be less leery of impeachment than other polls, particularly the one that Yankelovich, with its triple alternatives, were indicating at the time. The public, when given this preface, was "evenly divided on whether President Nixon should be impeached because of the charges against him."[69] Only the conditional question (Harris B) yielded a higher reading on impeachment.

That different polls give different readings of public opinion at any given time is probably less surprising and less serious than the different readings of trends over time, as shown in our table. The April and June 1974 Gallup responses suggest a decline in impeachment sentiment, albeit of only two points and possibly due to sampling error, but the Harris Poll recorded a 10-point rise during the same two-month period. Harris also showed support for impeachment finally passing the 50 percent point.

The wording of some questions leads one to believe that some pollsters may, to begin with, have been as confused as the public about the impeachment process. Answers obtained were in good part reactions to a word that, for some, stirred images of the ultimate punishment (removal from office) and, for others, the initiation of a legal process that could as readily exonerate the President as prove him guilty. The Gallup A question, which clearly led to an unduly low estimate of impeachment sentiment, should have been changed and clarified. But once asked, it provided a month-by-month record of change of whatever it was that the question was recording. Since trend data are valued, Gallup was, quite understandably, reluctant to reword the question until the need to do so became painfully evident. Some of the rise recorded in April reflects the change in the question (Gallup B) rather than in public sentiment.

Since the Harris Poll as a rule asks more political questions than Gallup, it also included more questions on Watergate. Initially, questions about Nixon's leaving office most often posed the issue in terms either of resignation or of removal from office under certain conditions. It was not until

March 1974 that Harris first asked such a question without any "ifs" attached. The new question (Harris C) was almost the exact equivalent of the one Gallup was about to abandon because of growing doubts about its validity as a measure of impeachment attitudes. The timing lent some substance to suspicions about the motive behind the change. Did Harris intend to show less support for impeachment than there actually was? This is doubtful in view of the many other questions asked concurrently with this one. Thus, if one looks at responses to the conditional question (Harris A), a case can be made that the Harris Poll had called attention to wide support for impeachment early on. Indeed, one of the questions used by Harris showed a plurality favoring impeachment as early as September 1973. This had turned into a majority by mid-October, even before the firing of Archibald Cox. Let us cite the example of a Harris release dated February 25, 1974. It began: "By nearly 3 to 1 the American people want impeachment proceedings against Nixon carried forward, but they are in no rush. . . ."

That no national pollster should have followed Roper's lead in pursuing the matter of knowledgability is unfortunate. When his interviewers asked people early in November what they understood by "impeachment," the results were somewhat startling. Presented with a choice between the "correct" meaning—trial by Congress—and the widely accepted but inaccurate interpretation—removal from office—half claimed to know it meant a trial and two out of five chose the wrong alternative. On the highly probable assumption that many people were guessing correctly between the two alternatives, Roper estimated that knowledge of what impeachment was could be well below the 50 percent level. Even among the group most knowledgeable about impeachment, the college-educated, the number who knew (or correctly guessed) the meaning, was no higher than two out of three.[70]

There is reason to believe that in the months after Roper found such a low level of information the American people became more knowledgeable. To some extent the press, which took on the role of educating them about impeachment by reviewing the trial of Andrew Johnson and other precedents, helped. And, as people came to "understand" the impeachment process, so the Roper data indicate, it also became more acceptable.

Polls as News

Given the many disparate measures, no one can say with any certainty just how the public divided on impeachment or how much support there would have been for such a move had the House Judiciary Committee moved more rapidly. If polls did in any way misrepresent support for impeachment, it was in large part because of the significance the news media assigned to certain statistics that were singled out. The publicity given any measurement helps define the climate of opinion. It does make a difference whether a headline reads ONLY A SLIM MAJORITY OPPOSED TO IMPEACHMENT or LESS THAN HALF THE U.S. FAVORS NIXON'S EXIT. Even syndicated columnists like Harris and Gallup are at the mercy of headline writers and editors who make cuts to conserve space. And they have even less control over interpretations given their findings—by Congress, the White House, commentators, pressure groups—once these have entered the public domain.

What the debate about polling effects often overlooks is that polls do not speak for themselves but are subject to journalistic judgment. News values help determine both what questions are asked by pollsters and what findings are reported and when and how they are reported. The main customers of the public polls are, after all, the newspapers, news magazines, and television networks. Gallup and Harris are syndicated, Yankelovich linked to *Time* magazine. After Watergate, the networks strengthened their own polling operation, usually by joining with a newspaper, for example, the *New York Times*/CBS News Poll, the NBC/Associated Press Poll, and the ABC/*Washington Post* Poll. Hence, their questions deal with issues considered timely and newsworthy. Mainly, they reflect what the news has emphasized. Sometimes they make news of their own.

Only a small proportion of the polls on Watergate ever became national news. For example, of 38 Gallup press releases between September 2, 1973, and July 28, 1974, just ten, or about one in four, made the television evening news on at least one network. The biggest month for poll items was January 1974, followed by November 1973, when the effects of the massacre were being tracked, and April 1974, when Watergate became a legal battlefield and the big question became where people stood on impeachment. Networks varied in the emphasis they gave to polls of every kind. NBC spent the most time on tracking Watergate sentiment, with CBS second, and ABC a rather distant third. More precisely, NBC gave two-and-a-half times and CBS twice as much time to polls as did ABC. However, the time devoted to these items on all three networks amounted to much less than one percent of news time.

The one poll question most prominent on TV news was the Presidential popularity rating, which served as a kind of Dow-Jones average of the Watergate story: the barometer by which the press, politicians, and public judged Nixon's changing fortunes. Because these measures raised more questions than they answered, the play given them spurred Nixon supporters into accusing the press—or at least part of it—of being in cahoots with the Democratic left, of trying to undo a political mandate. For Nixon to resign, wrote one columnist,[71] would be unpatriotic because it would radically alter the American system of government. In its consequences, it would be a kind of 27th amendment to the Constitution, written or unwritten, that would have the President hold office for four years or "until such time as his rating in two national public opinion polls were to fall below 30 percent for three consecutive months"! On the assumption that he had lost his ability to govern, he would have to resign. This tongue-in-cheek argument which sees polls as acting to drive the President from office indirectly supports those who take the position that the polls delayed Nixon's departure.

Pollsters are not always innocent victims. In seeking to establish the relevance of their ratings, they may exaggerate their importance. One finds examples of this in syndicated columns by Louis Harris. During the Watergate months, he was partial to phrases such as, "Mr. Nixon has gone a long way toward losing his *trial by public opinion*" (Jan. 21, 1974) and "The key to Mr. Nixon's fate . . . over the . . . months . . . *he has been on trial*" (Jan. 31, 1974). The big play was reserved for the "majority" who believe, agree, have confidence in, approve, and so forth. Thus Harris could write as late as the end of January about the public as having "not entirely closed the door on possible ultimate Presidential exoneration" (Jan. 31, 1974). And how did he know this? Because the number who endorsed resignation or impeachment was still short of "the critical 51 percent." It was big news when Harris and Gallup found *majorities* in favor of impeachment—a barrier, incidentally, a Roper survey had crossed more than two months before.

Insofar as the news media, including the releases by the pollsters themselves, harped on the significance of the "magic majority" for all it was worth, they came close to imputing to it the binding force of the ballotbox. For his part, Harris, in an April 18 release, tried to right any wrong impression he might have given readers about the role of public opinion in the impeachment process. Though public reactions were an important part of the process, he told them, "in a 'representative' form of government a great deal must be left to the considered judgment of those elected to make the crucial decisions on public policy."

THE ROLE OF OPINION ASSESSMENT

What can be said then about the role of public opinion in these long eight months from the Cox firing until the House Judiciary Committee began hearing evidence? This was a period during which the adversaries maneuvered for mass support that neither side could take for granted but each felt it needed to put an end to Watergate. On one side were Nixon and the White House; arrayed against them, a growing number of establishment figures who, for one reason or another, felt victimized by Presidential caprice. Some had been antagonized early by the high-handed use of administration resources to win political battles, especially during the 1972 election; others, with no obvious axe to grind, believed passionately that even a President was subject to the law and obliged, like any ordinary citizen, to cooperate in the investigation of suspected wrongdoing.

Much of this maneuvering took place in public, a forum that gave Nixon, as President, all the media attention he wanted at times of his own choosing. This advantage was reduced by Watergate and the issues related to it, which caused his appearances to become controversial and turned them into two-sided affairs. Since the news media thrive on conflict, nothing suits them better than a confrontation. During the months under examination, the opposition to Nixon was sufficiently prestigious and powerful to enjoy a degree of recognition the media normally accord only the Chief Executive. While the Senate Watergate Committee, the Watergate Special Prosecution Force, and the House Judiciary Committee pursued the case, the media kept it before the public, acting as if the people were the real judges. The publicity given even the legal aspects of the dispute remains one of the more unusual aspects of Watergate.

Moreover, it is this public airing of matters normally left to the legal process or to political bargaining that lends importance to the distinction between the immediate reaction to an event and the more general climate of opinion. This is a distinction that published polls, geared as they are to journalistic immediacy, often blur, and yet it remains critical to an understanding of the political process. What counts in the long run are not the immediate reactions to specific events, no matter how intemperate these may be. Storms of indignation, as we have seen, dissipate; they are too volatile to be taken as the basis for political decisions. In this respect the polls probably depicted public opinion as firmer and less movable than it actually was. Lack of attention to what the public might settle for if given decisive leadership tended to exaggerate the hardness of the opposition to impeachment. Reluctance to endorse the idea was was interpreted as opposition, especially since, as the evidence shows, what impeachment was was not very well understood. This illusory picture of the public will makes polls a potentially powerful deterrent whenever decisive action is called for, but the mythical man in the street is not yet sufficiently informed to weigh all relevant implications.

Although the polls undoubtedly forced attention to the groundswell of anti-Nixon sentiment, there is another way in which "precision journalists," acting as pollsters and playing the numbers game, might also have played the White House game. In putting the emphasis on whether more people agreed than disagreed, reports of poll results probably reinforced the idea of Watergate as a purely political and partisan issue. To make it appear this way was an essential ingredient of the Nixon strategy, based on the expectation that the public would tire of a political fight and put pressure on Congress and on the media to direct their attention to other, more pressing matters.[72] Their preoccupation with the upcoming Congressional elections was not lost on the President.

What of the other view, that the polls hastened Nixon's departure? First, Congress, understandably wary about the 1974 elections, did not want to be too far out of step with public opinion. Most of its members did take the pulse of their districts through trips home and other contacts by mail and telephone. Lacking adequate resources for scientific polling, they incorporated questionnaires into their letters to constituents, relying on questions in published polls tailored to their needs; for example, would people vote for a Congressman who voted for impeachment? did they think Watergate would have an impact on the Republican party's chances in 1974? Nor did anyone, one assumes, fail to note that every effort by Nixon to turn the polls around—in Operation Candor, in his State of the Union message, through the release of the transcripts—ended in failure. Nixon, the most avid poll watcher of them all, went out of his way, publicly and in private, to assure Congress that he knew they were worried by what they read.[73] He confided to his Diary early in 1973: "I don't give one damn what the polls say insofar as affecting my decisions. I only care about them because they affect my ability to lead, since politicians do pay attention to them."[74]

Second, whatever their effect on Congress, the publicity given the polls, along with other reporting of Watergate, helped the public to understand impeachment and to accept it as a real possibility. Furthermore, the rise in support for impeachment that followed the April release of the transcripts reflected mainly a decrease in the proportion who had seen the process as "too destructive for the country," while "the percentages opposing impeachment because of a belief that the charges [against Nixon were]either not true or not serious enough remained constant."[75] We further suggest that the continuous publicity about polling results on impeachment gave the idea extra currency and thus made it more familiar and less threatening.

Third, polls documented the extent of suspicion about Nixon whenever he withheld evidence or sought to explain himself by going on television, as he did time after time. The polls could have demonstrated, to anyone inclined to read them that way, that a majority was quite prepared to accept the judgment of an impartial body, provided the judges proved themselves fair and to be acting on the basis of evidence. As early as Fall 1973, polling responses should have made it clear that the public wanted a full investigation of Watergate. Thereafter there was too much distrust of major institutions[76] for the controversy to be resolved on faith alone.

The manifest concern of the various actors and institutional agents, including Nixon himself, with polling results casts serious doubt on the third view, namely, that public opinion played no role whatsoever in the outcome of Watergate. The view is nevertheless popular among the Washington press corps and the legal fraternity. It is reinforced by members of the House Judiciary Committee, who later were to insist that their decision was based solely on the evidence. Yet the public record of the proceedings contains many references to the public demand for a full investigation. As we shall see later, it mattered to everyone intimately involved in the impeachment decision that their actions appear "just"—including the Supreme Court Justices, who finally decided the tapes issue. In view of Nixon's challenge that he would only obey a "definitive" opinion, the justices felt impelled to speak with unanimity. Justice Lewis F. Powell, according to Woodward and Armstrong's insiders' account,[77] recommended a delay until after the vote of the House Judiciary Committee because, so Powell is said to have argued, those "opposed to impeaching could make the point that without the tapes they would be now authorized to have, the Committee would be acting prematurely in judging Nixon." Other justices believed that any postponement would be playing into Nixon's strategy of delay, but also insisted that the Court should never adjust its timetable to promote whatever secondary political effects the justices might prefer.

The news media in any political controversy have the ability to create a bystander public, to involve the onlookers in the dispute. This period surely documents that strategic role. The media also provided the political actors on both sides with a looking glass image of how they appeared to the public. The polls and the way they were reported in the press were an important element, yet by no means the only one, in creating this image. They became crucial insofar as certain selected "opinions" were communicated to the politicians and assimilated into their view of possible reactions to be taken into account.

There has been much discussion, especially during campaigns, about the possible influence of public opinion polling on the political process. Much of the debate has centered on whether or not the polls change voting decisions and voting behavior and thus have an effect on election outcomes. This remains an intriguing and significant problem for research, but the more basic question, it seems to us, concerns how scientific polls and their reporting have become an integral part of the political process through which decisions are made and issues resolved. Our analysis in this chapter is a mini-case-study intended to clarify the direct and indirect impact of polls on that process.

CHAPTER 7

TELEVISION AS AN AGENT
OF LEGITIMATION
The House Judiciary Committee

With the nation watching on television, the House Judiciary Committee began its final impeachment deliberations on the evening of Wednesday, July 24, 1974. By the time these ended, on July 30, the committee had approved three articles of impeachment against Richard M. Nixon. Developments the following week made it evident to nearly everyone, including the President, that the House would follow the Committee recommendations and that conviction by the Senate on one or more counts was a near certainty. Rather than face such an ordeal, Nixon chose to resign.

Without the live coverage of the impeachment proceedings, would the Watergate controversy have ended as it did and when it did? Would the same groundswell of pro-impeachment sentiment have developed both in Washington and in the rest of the country? Would there have been the same quiet, unchallenged acceptance of resignation had not the debate over the impeachment articles been televised in full?

The answer to all these questions must be "no." Without the televised debates, the political scenario could have been quite different. The evidence shows that, as the debate began, many members of the public and of Congress had yet to be convinced that there were any but political grounds for impeachment. The telecasts changed few opinions about the extent of Nixon's complicity in Watergate or whether he was guilty of offenses sufficient to warrant his removal from office. Yet there was a perceptible increase in the number of people who accepted the need for impeachment proceedings. This was because impeachment had come to be defined by more and more people as derived from a legal mandate, with the outcome determined by the inexorable logic of the facts. Consequently, when the "smoking gun," buried in the June 23 tape, gave proof of the President's guilt only days after the debate ended, even those who had remained confident that a Senate trial would exonerate him could accept Nixon's resignation as mandated by legal necessity.

What the hearings had done was to legitimate the *process* by which Nixon was ousted from the Presidency. Though the President was never actually impeached or tried by the Senate, the results were as if impeachment had run its full course. It had become more difficult for anyone to make a convincing case that Nixon had been denied due process and was being ousted from office in a political coup d'état.

The question is: what was it about the proceedings, and the way they came across on television, that convinced public and polity alike that impeachment was a fair and judicial, rather than a partisan political process?

TELEVISED EVENTS AS RHETORIC

The televised debate, spread over six days, lasted nearly 36 hours. It was broadcast live and in full by the networks. In addition, there were about seven and a half hours of network commentary before and after sessions and during the breaks taken by the Committee.[1] Responsibility for the telecasting was shared, with the three major commercial networks alternating days, as they had during the Senate Watergate hearings. Each network, in this rotation scheme, had two turns, but ABC, by the luck of the draw, had the best of it (Appendix, table 6). It was on the air the fewest hours, thus suffering the least financial loss, while covering the two most dramatic of the sessions—opening night on July 24 and the crucial vote July 27 on the first impeachment article.[2] CBS got the long hours, nearly twice as many as ABC. Public television had cameras rolling an average of 13 hours a day. But only eleven affiliates of the Eastern Educational Network carried the debate live from morning to late evening; most (118) public television stations did not begin their coverage until 7:30P.M., cutting in on the proceedings if they were still going on and then, after they ended, replaying a tape of the earlier debate.[3]

Compared with that of previous events, the television coverage of the House Committee proceedings was hardly unique in terms of either time or resources allocated. And yet there was something extraordinary about it. First of all, everyone was aware of the importance of the deliberations. Also, the televised event involved a unique mixture of rhetorical situations. It was more than a ceremony performed before millions of witnesses. Despite some elements of pageantry, it cannot be described as a spectacle without distorting its intrinsic character as a serious debate among the 38 men and women charged with making a recommendation to the full House. By inviting the television audience in, the scope of the conflict was extended beyond the Committee membership to involve the usually excluded public. They became, in Schattschneider's words, "as much a part of the over-all situation as . . . the overt combatants"[4] whose arguments they were following.

We can best indicate what kind of an occasion this was by considering its rhetorical aspects in the context of other televised political events. Such a perspective strikes us as fitting since, after all, the art of politics is essentially the art of persuasion,[5] even though more forceful measures are also used, sometimes with great effect, to reinforce the power of the word.

Leaving out such unanticipated crises as assassinations, riots, or demonstrations run amok, one can classify major televised political events as either *unifying occasions*, where the rhetoric stresses commonalities and the need to ignore differences in pursuit of the common good, or as *controversies*, in which the elements of contest and conflict are explicitly recognized and people are expected to take sides. Many events fall between these extremes, but the distinction is nevertheless fundamental.

An equally basic distinction concerns the audience to whom the rhetoric is mainly addressed. Inasmuch as any political event, if televised, becomes a public event, it always has two audiences. One consists of political insiders who, whether or not they are "on stage," are participants. The second consists of bystanders and onlookers, of people who read newspapers and watch television. Both audiences are important to the political actors, but each type of event differs depending on whether the action (or rhetoric) is directed primarily toward other insiders or toward the public, which is only peripherally involved.

Any televised event fits one of four types depending, first, on the dominant rhetoric, which may be *unifying* or *controversial*, and second, on the audience addressed, whether *exclusive* or *nonexclusive*, as illustrated in the following schema:

	Unifying Event	*Controversy*
Exclusive	Ceremony	Esoteric debate
Nonexclusive	Spectacle	Adversary Proceeding

The ceremony and the spectacle, though both unifying events, are geared toward different audiences. If the rhetoric is addressed primarily toward those on the television "stage," who share the spotlight, the television audience is witness to a ceremony. When a ceremony is staged expressly for the public, it becomes a spectacle. Television has the power to transform an event by giving it wide publicity. Awareness of the larger audience can introduce pageantry into what is intended as a solemn ceremony, so that the line between ceremony and spectacle becomes blurred.

The unifying ceremony is defined, above all, by participation in a common symbolic order. The category includes a broad range of events routinely covered by television, such as the swearing in of a new President or the official reception given a visiting head of state, as well as such "human interest" items as negotiators shown shaking hands or initialing an agreement after a grueling session of bargaining. Theirs is a symbolic gesture by which the parties signal that the agreement reached means more than the issues that once divided them. A President taking the oath of office is making a symbolic commitment of a similar nature. The "third parties" are there, as they are in a wedding ceremony, but they only reinforce a commitment that would have been made even without television cameras to record it.

In the pageant or spectacle, the participants no longer express what they necessarily feel. Instead they have become performers acting on behalf of "everyone" within an integrated structure of motives. Televised political events in this category include the homecoming of heroes—like that of General Douglas MacArthur in 1951, of the POWs from Vietnam in 1973, or of the American hostages released by Iran in 1981. Also included would be the official mourning following the assassination of President John F. Kennedy. The symbols employed in these events reaffirm the historic unity of America at times when it seems to need reaffirmation. Similarly, Presidential trips, such as Nixon's state visit to China in 1971, can serve as spectacles. Both communicators and their audiences recognize them as occasions in which unity and common purpose are to be played up. The rhetoric is usually demonstrative, with much self-praise and with vilification reserved for those outside the circle of common identity.

At times the element of spectacle is deliberately injected into events that are partisan in both origin and intent. What is controversial can be packaged in the unifying disguise of pageantry, as in certain Presidential addresses and press conferences (or even in state visits). News organizations sometimes pierce this veil of "deception" by treating what appears to be a noncontroversial occasion as controversial. They can inject some balance by scheduling their own analyses right after these events or by giving time to opponents to present their dissenting views.

Typically, the media have become the forum for extended political controversies. But there is still a difference, marked by the audience addressed, between the esoteric debate, which the public can observe from television's front row seat, and the adversary proceeding, arranged so as to afford partisan spokesmen the opportunity to compete for public support. In the esoteric debate, each side seeks to persuade members of the other camp by appealing to some common interest and to win converts with whom to form a dominant coalition. This differs from the adversary proceeding, where the two sides are not really addressing one another but vying for the approval of a public that serves as jury, referee, or judge.

The coverage of an esoteric debate should give the public some insight into how policy questions are thrashed out. The most familiar events in this category are national nominating conventions. Also, most Congressional hearings fit this mode. Like conventions, they are bona fide episodes in the political process. Although no political actor can be oblivious of the probable viewer response to his or her appearance, the television audience—at least in theory—has no part to play, and news organizations covering these events are supposed to act only as clarifiers, to supply a context to what is shown on the screen. Yet they feel compelled to keep viewers interested and even entertained. Interviews, offsite or behind-scenes coverage, and other media-generated activity that enliven the proceedings become as much a part of the event viewers witness as the official proceedings. Consequently, an event known through television affords an experience different from direct participation. How far television, by its coverage, should or can intrude on what it covers becomes a matter of news judgment and often a subject of controversy.

The adversary proceeding is different. The public acts as a third party toward whom the adversaries mainly direct their remarks. Its presence is an essential part of the event. As in the televised political debates, which have become an institution on the American political scene, each performer is openly partisan, though within a framework of rules carefully crafted to deny either contestant unfair advantage. In this sense the proceeding is genuinely bipartisan. Audience members cannot judge which contestant is superior in deliberative or forensic skill without exposing themselves to the opposing viewpoint. Television provides the transmission facilities but otherwise is not expected to intrude.

With this typology in mind, let us consider the Judiciary Committee meeting that convened on July 24 to decide which, if any, articles of impeachment to present to the full House for its consideration. Its televising transformed what was meant to be an esoteric debate hitherto conducted behind closed doors into an adversary proceeding: the audience was expanded to include the nation at large; both sides shared equal access to the viewing audience under rules intended to assure the judicial character of the debate and speakers addressed the onlookers as much as they did their colleagues.

The debate itself became a debate as much about whether or not there was a legitimate basis for impeachment as over the specific articles. Yet at certain points the debaters, by evoking symbols of national unity—the Constitution, the office of President, and the sacred nature of the duty thrust upon them—endowed the proceedings with the solemnity of a unifying ceremony. This was especially true of their opening remarks and the formal vote on the first impeachment amendment. Television, merely by its presence, introduced some element of spectacle but its low profile kept this to a minimum. The account that follows shows how committee members sought to cope with these ambiguities in the rhetorical situation, both before and while they were on camera.

THE IMAGE OF FAIRNESS

The closer the Judiciary Committee came to the opening of its public debate, the greater was the concern of all members with the appearance of fairness. Chairman Peter Rodino had repeatedly warned that it would be a national disaster if the Committee's inquiry were to degenerate into a partisan confrontation. Although it would have been unrealistic to expect a total absence of partisanship, he intended to keep name-calling and the usual kind of political invective at the lowest possible level. From the beginning of the inquiry, all members of the Committee, members of Congress, and even the general public had been made aware by Rodino that the appearance of fairness was at least as important as the actuality.[6]

This appearance of fairness is central to understanding the impact of the televised coverage on both the public and the legislative response. Whatever highlighted the partisan aspects of the impeachment inquiry would undermine the picture of judiciousness Rodino and others were trying to disseminate; whatever deemphasized these aspects would help make the Committee and its work appear "fair." To appear fair, it was essential that the Committee not be seen as engaged in a tug-of-war between Republicans trying to save the President and Democrats out to destroy him. A decision that split along strict party lines would convey the impression that impeachment was really nothing but politics.

In guiding the Committee's work and guarding its reputation, Rodino and his staff used the Senate Watergate Committee as a model of what not to do. Unlike that inquiry, this one was to avoid the partisan bickering and constant leaks to the press that could only demean its image as a substantial body. Rodino had, at all crucial points, both to produce a bipartisan consensus and overcome the kind of internal dissension that inevitably erupts onto the front page and to assure the public that he was not conducting a partisan witch hunt.

Projecting an image of fairness depended in large part on how the main actors in this political drama chose to present themselves, both before and after the cameras were allowed in. Along with the Chairman, these main characters included the committee's legal staff, especially John Doar and Albert Jenner, and the 37 other committee members. First, we take a look at the part each played in promoting and protecting this image.

Chairman Peter Rodino. As chairman of the House Judiciary Committee, Peter Rodino's reputation for fairness was at once critical and highly vulnerable. It was vulnerable, first, because he was new to the job of chairman; second, he bore the onus not just of being a politician but of being an Italian politician; and, finally, it was only natural that, as chairman, he would become the main target of attacks against the Committee. The chairmanship was his by reason of seniority. A 63-year old lawyer from Newark, New Jersey, he had become chairman only as Nixon began his second term in January 1973. He was hardly a national figure. From a district populated mainly by ethnics and increasingly by blacks, Rodino's main preoccupation in the House had been with immigration and civil rights. The first the public had seen of Rodino in a national role was during the hearings on the confirmation of Gerald Ford as Vice President which, it was generally agreed, he had conducted with dignity, diplomacy, and with consummate fairness.[7]

Throughout the impeachment investigation rumors kept surfacing that some skeleton in Rodino's closet was affecting his zeal for moving ahead. The suspicion that every Italian politician is a Mafioso dies hard. Speculation that the White House was trying, and would continue to try, to get the press working on a Rodino-Mafia connection was given considerable credence by some members of the Committee.[8] One of John Dean's lawyers had alerted Edward Mezvinsky, a committee Democrat from Iowa, to a somewhat sinister scenario that he believed Nixon would follow: At some crucial point in the inquiry—probably on a day when the Committee released damaging information—the White House would release some document from the files it maintained on its "enemies" to make sure the headlines were "balanced." Mezvinsky acknowledged that his own thinking had been even more paranoid: he had worried about the possibility that the White House might fabricate documents damaging to Rodino and other members of the Committee just as the White House "plumbers" had fabricated a cable implicating President Kennedy in the 1963 assassination of South Vietnam President Ngo Dinh Diem.[9]

So far as anyone has yet determined, there was no concerted White House effort to sully Rodino's honor.[10] If not, it may have been because Rodino took such care to be and to appear fair. He allowed would-be detractors few opportunities to mount attacks on his character. Certainly, the White House quickly seized the one opening he gave them. This involved an off-the-record remark during an informal discussion, in which Rodino said he "thought" that all 21 committee Democrats would vote for impeachment. The *Los Angeles Times* reported this as a prediction, in response to which the White House, through Kenneth Clawson, demanded that Rodino be discharged. This remark, he claimed, revealed the chairman's clear bias and it was time for his replacement by a "fair-minded Democrat."[11] Rodino and his close staff despaired that the careful orchestration of their show of responsibility and substantiality might have gone for naught.[12] So concerned were they that Rodino felt it necessary to deny, from the House floor, that he had ever made, or could have made, such a statement. He told his colleagues that he had never asked any member of the Committee how he or she would vote and hence could not know how anyone would vote.

From the very beginning, Rodino's main goal was to avoid partisanship. A review of the Committee's deliberations, all of which are in the public domain, reveals quite clearly how Rodino practiced patience and compromise to take the steam out of all issues that might appear as partisan squabbles. His job, as he saw it, was to pacify the extremes and allow the middle to emerge.[13] This is well illustrated by the manner in which he resolved the first crucial division within the Committee, over the speed at which the inquiry should move. Republicans wished to move quickly. Too much delay could only work against them. As Hamilton Fish Jr., a New York Republican, pointed out, the closer the 1974 Congressional elections came "the more likely whatever we do will be described as partisan." He said this without imputing a partisan motive to anyone. But it was equally clear that the Committee needed time to collect and evaluate the evidence. Impeachment, if voted with undue haste, could have the look of a political lynching. When in December 1973 the Republicans began to press for an early-March deadline, Rodino was able to defuse the issue by "hoping," without promising, that the Committee could finish its work by the latter part of April.[14] This deadline was foreclosed by Nixon's refusal to comply with the Committee's request for tapes and documents, but Nixon's continued recalcitrance, as the months rolled on, helped even more than Rodino's conciliatory skills to forge the kind of bipartisan consensus sought by the chairman.

In promoting a bipartisan image, Rodino and his staff were keenly aware of the need to make effective use of the media to educate the public about the nature of the impeachment process. At the same time, they could not allow the need for publicity to create an omnipresent bystander public. That would only cause the press to blow up the inevitable clashes of opinion and convert them into public controversies before they could be internally resolved. It was therefore decided to control the flow of official information to the press through briefings by Francis O'Brien, Rodino's administrative assistant, held every morning at nine o'clock. As the sole link between the staff and the world outside, O'Brien acted as the "sources close to the inquiry" whom reporters cited. The press, at first hostile to this arrangement, soon accepted these ground rules and no concerted attempt was ever made to break them. At least one reporter had great praise for O'Brien, whom she described as having performed his trying job "with good humor, unpretentiousness, and a surprising amount of candor."[15]

Aware that the image of fairness was fragile, Rodino had, at certain strategic points, sacrificed publicity for the sake of harmony. His biggest gamble was to close to the public the evidentiary sessions beginning in May as final witnesses were being heard. In this important decision the Democratic majority was joined by two Republicans. Rodino had been concerned—as had John Doar, his chief counsel—about the possible effect of testimony on a public unfamiliar with what other witnesses had already presented. At issue was the public's right to know versus the likelihood of their getting a distorted picture of the established facts. Yet in closing the sessions, Rodino, perhaps inevitably, contributed to a short-lived upswing in Nixon's fortunes. Closed doors invited leaks, and reports of partisan "squabbling" over the number of witnesses were inconsistent with the image of a bipartisan inquiry. For a time it seemed that Rodino might be forced to let the press come in, but the doors were to remain closed. Instead, to balance the distorted picture being created by news leaks, the Committee on July 11, while witnesses were still being heard and depositions taken, released 4133 pages of evidence. The eight-volume compilation gave the press all the copy it needed.

Rodino had never doubted that the final decision-making phase of the proceedings would have to be open and televised. Educating the public about the impeachment process was, after all, imperative. But he was also concerned that the televising not distract from the substance of the debate. Having watched the televised Senate hearings, Rodino believed that cameras pointing at the witnesses (and spectators) from behind the backs of committee members had detracted from the dignity of the occasion. In May, before the question of televising had been officially settled, he had a special room built outside the caucus room windows just to house the television cameras and to make them "invisible" to those inside.

What perhaps mattered most was that Rodino had managed to emerge from the months of intra-committee negotiations with his own reputation for fairness untarnished. He had earned the trust of committee members, Republicans and Democrats alike. No last-minute broadsides from anti-impeachment forces could undo that. The evident confidence the Committee had in its chairman was to count for a good deal as the public debate on the articles of impeachment began.

John Doar and the Legal Staff. Late in May John Doar had publicly stated his concern over the appearance of fairness: "What is important is that the American people believe that the [impeachment] process was fair, straightforward, clean, open, thorough—with an analysis and study of the best evidence possible." [16] The legal staff could not afford to be perceived as a prosecuting force, already certain as it began its work that Nixon was guilty of impeachable offenses and that its only mission was to build the strongest possible case. With his choice of staff, Rodino had already begun to promote the bipartisan image. Neither Doar, special counsel to the Committee, nor Albert Jenner, the special counsel for the minority, fitted a neat party label, while the rest of the legal staff was carefully selected to screen out partisan advocates.

The selection process had some of its intended effect. Press notices stressed

Doar's Republican credentials while noting his liberal leanings. He was a registered Republican who had served both in the Eisenhower and Kennedy administrations, after which he had worked in Brooklyn, as head of the Bedford-Stuyvesant Development and Services Corporation, founded by Robert Kennedy. At the press conference announcing Doar's appointment, Edward Hutchinson of Michigan, the ranking Republican committee member, managed to express his suspicions about Doar's ability to act impartially but without disrupting the image of a bipartisan consensus. By moving out of camera range to the end of the table he shared with Rodino and Doar, Hutchinson tried to make it clear that he was only an onlooker, not a participant in the announcement, but he did nothing more.[17]

Jenner's introduction to the public proved equally harmonious. He had been billed as a well-known trial lawyer who had practiced in Chicago. A lifelong Republican, he had also been a longstanding friend of Adlai Stevenson's family and had served as senior counsel to the Warren Commission, which investigated the death of John F. Kennedy. But Jenner soon got himself into trouble. In a television interview not long after his appointment, Jenner said, in response to a direct question, that the President should be held responsible for certain actions of his aides even if they had acted without his knowledge or explicit consent.[18] Two weeks later, to appease committee Republicans, he backtracked, explaining that a President should be held responsible only for those actions he had specifically authorized.[19] His original statement nevertheless drew a sharp rebuke from Charles Wiggins, a California Republican, who warned that no member of the staff should be making pronouncements on impeachment.

John Doar could not have agreed more. It was said that he used only two "ironclad admonitions" by which to guide his staff: they were to maintain absolute confidentiality and to be "fair."[20] At the very least, Doar was concerned over appearances. Both Jenner and Doar were mindful of the value of symbolic gestures.[21] Renata Adler, who served with the impeachment inquiry staff, later claimed that Doar did not go about his work with an open mind but had been convinced from the start that "the President must be, under conditions of exemplary fairness, *removed* from office" (italics ours).[22] If Doar really did take on the assignment with the closed mind that Adler attributes to him, he gave no signs of it. The image that came through to insiders and the attentive public was that of an unemotional, cautious, cool professional. No one had been able to discern his conclusions about

the case until less than a week before the public debate was to begin. Mezvinsky recalls John Doar as he prepared to sum up the evidence for committee members:

Looking at him, seeing that comfortable, rumpled presence waiting so casually, made
me nervous. For months, I had waited to see when and if the fire would flash out,
to see if the man would take a hard position one way or the other. . . . [He] was
barely started when it became clear that he had not just taken a stand. He had taken
a strong stand. . . . This was not the John Doar we were used to.[23]

The John Doar they had become used to had, by all accounts, been presenting the facts of the case to the Committee for the past several weeks in
a "characteristically deliberate and undramatic manner. . . . In a mono-
tone—intentionally monotonous . . . calculated to have its cumulative impact on the committee members. . . . also . . . to convince them of his
fairness, against the day when he [might] have to sum up the case for
them."[24] So convincing had he been that years later some staff members
still believed that Doar had not decided what to recommend until pressed
to do so by an impatient Rodino the day before he began summing up the
evidence for the Committee.[25]

The unanticipated forcefulness of this summary, together with his recommendation for a Senate trial on one or more of five articles of impeachment evidently had a stunning effect on those present; so did what happened
next. Jenner not only agreed with Doar but expressed this in a passionate
statement and without reservations. It was left to Samuel Garrison III, Jenner's assistant and a lawyer with impeccable pro-Nixon credentials, to rebut
Doar's recommendation. He argued that members of the Committee were
under an obligation, in arriving at their decision, to make a *political* judgment, to consider along with the evidence whether the interests of the country would be better served by Nixon's removal or by having him serve out
his full term.[26]

Chairman Rodino, in seeking to avoid the appearance of a partisan inquiry, had been determined that there *not* be two separate counsels, one
representing the Democratic majority and arguing for impeachment and another representing the Republican minority and arguing the case against.
Yet, by the time of the televised debate, Doar and Jenner were on one side,
and Garrison on the other. Yet the fruits of Rodino's efforts had survived.
Republicans on the Committee had come to believe that Doar and Jenner
were men of integrity who had prepared and presented the case for impeach-

ment in an appropriately judicious manner. Doar, it must be added, did not become a public celebrity during Watergate mainly because he played his big scene mostly off-camera. He had wanted to lay out the case without the interruptions and distractions that the cameras would introduce. Some committee members had feared that, with the press and public already familiar with much of the evidence, television coverage of the evidentiary phase might only bore them; others that Doar, with his low-key style, would come across as dull.[27] In any event, the decision to exclude the media from the evidentiary sessions expressed the concern of both Doar and committee members. What we shall never know, of course, is whether Doar's reputation would have remained so unsullied had the cameras been permitted in or whether his presentation would have proved so effective.

The Congress. Equally concerned, but for slightly different reasons, that the House Judiciary Committee act and appear judicious were the members of the 93d Congress, the great majority of whom would be seeking reelection that November. This concern would increase as the election drew nearer. Especially, those on the Judiciary Committee were painfully aware that their reputations, and in some cases their political futures, would be heavily dependent on how their behavior and actions were judged by their constituents.

Congressmen's long-standing practice of soliciting from their constituents views and "advice" on current issues has been supplemented by the increasingly routine use of polls to assess opinion.[28] In 1961–62, only 95 Congressmen—almost all without professional guidance—sent out some kind of questionnaire to constituents. The median response rate to these mailings was about 17 percent.[29] By 1974, about 70 percent were sending out such solicitations at least once a year.[30] The high rate of response they obtained was unusual. In the *Congressional Record*, as well as letters to constituents, Congressmen expressed their astonishment at the flood of responses. Since over three fourths of the questionnaires sent out between August 1973 and July 1974 included direct questions about Watergate-related matters, it seems logical to conclude that this was a subject on which people wanted to be heard. The timing of the polls and the questions they contained demonstrate that members of Congress were concerned that they appear to be acting judiciously.

We have examined polls taken by 163 congressmen (67 Democrats and 96 Republicans) during this time period.[31] They probably represent over half those sending out questionnaires. From this sample it appears that Republicans made the greater use of polls, although not all polls were available for our analysis. The proportion of Democrats and Republicans asking about impeachment was exactly the same, but there is a striking difference with regard to the time they took their polls. As impeachment neared, Republicans were more apt to be taking the pulse of their public: 59 percent of the Republicans sent out questionnaires *after* February 1974, compared with 39 percent of the Democrats. This is not hard to understand: Republicans would have been more uneasy over Watergate and felt more keenly the need to touch base with the folks back home on this troublesome problem.[32]

Congressmen often used letters enclosing poll questions or reporting results to inform constituents about impeachment or to advance their own views on the issue. They were likely to explain that the impeachment issue had to be resolved on "legal," not "political," grounds. The House, as they typically explained, would serve only as a grand jury and not as a trial jury. Only when and if it reached the Senate would the case be tried. While declaring themselves interested in the views of their constituents, they also made it clear that they would make up their own minds about impeachment, but only after all the evidence was in. Their decisions, they repeatedly emphasized, were to be made not on partisan grounds but on the evidence. Some used the occasion to defend their fellow members on the Judiciary Committee from unfair attacks.

A "Report from Washington," sent out June 1974 by William Stanton, a Republican from Ohio, illustrates the general approach. He found that 54.4 percent in his district opposed bringing President Nixon to trial before the Senate and 41.7 percent were in favor. In reporting this result, Stanton told his constituents that the response to his annual questionnaire ran ahead of what it had been in other years. Many people who had never before bothered to respond wrote that they thought it more important than ever to let him know how they felt. Defending the House Judiciary Committee and Congress, he put the blame where he thought it belonged:

No one is sadder than I am that twelve long months [since I last discussed Watergate with you], this subject is still very much with us. In all fairness, the Congress cannot be blamed for "dragging their feet on Watergate." If the President had acted decisively and expeditiously in meeting this problem head-on as he has so many others, Watergate would be history today. As it is, his resistance to Judiciary Committee requests for information pertinent to its investigation may prolong this agony until the end of the year or longer.

Whatever decision he might ultimately make, Stanton insisted that it would be a judicious one: he had been spending a few hours each week reading the transcripts of the Presidential conversations and it had been a shocking and disillusioning experience:

The picture that emerges is not one of moral leadership of the highest standard that we have every right to expect from whoever holds the office of President of the United States.

The question, so constantly asked him, of how he would vote on impeachment when the matter "reaches the House floor sometime in July" seemed "improper" at this point:

I see my current obligation as that of a member of a Grand Jury awaiting the presentation of the evidence and the arguments. As much as I deplore the content and tone of the transcribed Presidential conversations, I do not know that the President has committed any impeachable offenses as described in the Constitution. Nor will I until the impeachment inquiry is completed and I have the opportunity to carefully study the Judiciary Committee report. I cannot and will not reach a final decision on impeachment before that time.

A congressional poll could also seek a mandate to vote one's own conscience, irrespective of home sentiment, as when Representative Elford Cederberg, Republican of Michigan, asked (June 4) his constituents to choose among three alternatives:

(1) the President should definitely be impeached based on present evidence;
(2) the President should definitely *not* be impeached based on present evidence;
(3) you, as my Congressman, should weigh the legal evidence and render your decision on the facts presented.

Some Congressmen declined on principle to poll their district on Watergate. One of these, Rob Huber, a Republican from Michigan, in a newsletter sent out in the late spring of 1974, stated flatly that "on the question of impeachment, I will make my own decision based solely on the evidence of the House Judiciary Committee."

In other words, members of the Congress on both sides of the aisle, but Republicans especially, went out of their way to test the waters while assuring their constituents that this was not the usual politics and they would not be subject to pressure.

The House Judiciary Committee. Members of the Committee were more likely than the rest of the House to have polled their districts during this last year of Watergate. The Republicans among them were nearly twice as likely as Democrats to have done so,[33] especially the Republican hardliners who had been "seeking any rationale to excuse Nixon of anything but bad judgment."[34] Almost as likely to have sent out questionnaires were the Republicans who had been "trying for different reasons and with varying amounts of success to remain neutral." Democratic neutrals, while less apt than their Republican think-alikes to solicit their constituents' opinions, were still more likely to do so than the impeachment zealots, all Democrats, who "would very much like to find grounds to indict the President for high crimes and misdemeanors."[35]

One Republican hardliner, Lawrence Hogan of Maryland, found himself clearly at odds with the people he represented. A majority of respondents to his questionnaire favored impeachment; 39 percent were opposed. On resignation, the division was about even, split 46–45 in favor. Explaining his inclusion of the questionnaire, Hogan wrote in his March newsletter that the news media had continuously been seeking such information from him. He made clear that he would not be swayed by the results of the poll, and was "keeping an open mind until the evidence was in." Yet Hogan was to become the only Republican to make his position known in advance of the televised debate. On July 23, one day before it was to begin, he called a press conference where he announced, to the surprise of other committee members, that he would vote *for* impeachment because, he charged, the President had "lied repeatedly" to the American people.

Charles Wiggins, from Nixon's old district in California, another hardliner, who was to emerge in the debate as the most eloquent spokesman against impeachment, changed his mind about polling. To begin with, he had scoffed at colleagues who used the month-long January intersession to mingle with the voters at home or take straw votes to sound out impeachment sentiment. Later he explained the questionnaire he distributed as an effort to involve his constituents "more personally in the making of governmental decisions."[36] Recipients were invited to agree or disagree with a series of statements that ran the full gamut from "President Nixon should be impeached and removed from office as quickly as possible" to "Richard Nixon is guilty of no more misconduct than was tolerated in the case of Presidents Johnson and Kennedy." Like others, Wiggins made clear that, although he valued the opinions of his constituents and looked to them for guidance, he did not feel bound to follow their wishes blindly. To clarify his position, he distributed copies of a news item, in which he had quoted the British statesman Edmund Burke lecturing to his constituents in 1774: "Your representative owes you not his industry only, but his judgment; and he betrays, instead of serving you, if he sacrifices it to your opinion."[37]

This same care to let constituents know that their votes must, in the end, depend on how they judged the evidence can be observed in newsletters, press releases, and remarks entered into the *Congressional Record* by neutrals on the Committee. Among the exceptions were the three Southern neutrals, all conservative, who later would vote for articles of impeachment. They apparently thought it unnecessary to poll since they knew their constituents to be solidly opposed to impeachment, as were most Southerners. Walter Flowers, Democrat from Alabama, spoke for all three when he noted, for the record, that his people had voted for Nixon 2 to 1 but that he did not feel at all pressured to vote against impeachment: "It's too important and too long-term to do anything but vote my conscience."[38]

Of five Republican neutrals who later became key figures in the bipartisan pro-impeachment vote, both Robert McClory of Illinois and William Cohen of Maine, neither of whom had sent out a questionnaire, spoke up in closed session against the invocation of opinion polls in support of some proposed procedure or to justify a stand. During committee debate over whether or not to open the evidentiary phase, McClory had chided Wayne Owens, a Democrat from Utah, for using the increasing polarization of opinion as an argument for going public with their deliberations: "I would hesitate to have us take some action now because of what the polls may indicate or that we project what the limited polls have indicated, and respond to that." Cohen had similarly rebuked a Democrat for opposing acceptance of edited tape transcripts in deference to the mood of the people.

M. Caldwell Butler, Hamilton Fish Jr., and Tom Railsback, three other Republican neutrals, who later were to become part of the bipartisan coalition, had polled their districts on impeachment but then, like others, issued disclaimers that they would simply follow the majority. In fact, Butler's response to his poll was to question its validity. Fully 80 percent had answered "no" to the question "In your opinion, should a President of the United States be impeached and removed from office for the misconduct of his subordinates, even if it were established that the President had no personal knowledge of their misconduct and had not consented to it?" This apparently strong rejection of impeachment caused a bit of a stir. Some respondents pointed to the somewhat confusing way the question had been worded. Butler himself said he was skeptical about whether a finding of such strong opposition to impeachment accurately reflected the sentiment in his district. Still, this did not keep him from releasing the figure because, as he said, he lacked a more up-to-date reading of the public mood.

Butler, although a strong backer of Nixon's policies, had been of great help in disseminating, by what he said and what he did, the impression that the impeachment inquiry was being conducted judiciously and not as a strictly partisan vendetta. In April he had been the one Republican to go along with the Democrats on the first subpoena of a President ever to emanate from the House. He had taken seriously the Committee's vows of silence, as laid down by the chairman and his staff, by steadfastly refusing to answer questions put to him by reporters from local papers as to his judgment of Presidential involvement or how his view of the President might have changed. "My feelings toward the President," he told Jack Betts of the *Roanoke Times*, "are what the impeachment inquiry is all about." To those who interviewed him, he described the majority of the committee members as reasonable and open-minded. Rodino was singled out as especially deserving of praise for his fairness and the wise restraint he had shown in conducting the inquiry. "People are listening to each other," he told Charles McDowell of the *Richmond Times-Dispatch*, "I believe the destiny of the President is in good hands."[39] But while the members of the Committee, as they listened to the tapes and responded to the presentation of evidence, were increasing their respect for one another, the real problem, Butler believed, continued to be the President, who was prejudicing his own case by refusing to cooperate.

The recognition Butler received in the national press for his key role could only have enhanced his status in the eyes of his home district. Again, according to McDowell:

His willingness to desert the other Republicans on the [subpoena] issue had a considerable impact on observers of the grim drama of the impeachment inquiry. They began seeking out Virginians and asking what kind of congressman is this fellow Butler. . . . [He] has been in the papers a lot lately, not just in Virginia but all over. Television and radio stations are interviewing him and inviting him to be on panels. His colleagues have begun to ask his advice and treat him with a shade of deference that is not customary for freshman congressmen" (*Times-Dispatch*, April 14).

The attention given the activities of other neutrals also earned them standing and prestige which, as the moment of decision drew near, made it easier to transcend local and partisan considerations by keeping an eye on history.

Least likely to have polled their constituents were the so-called impeachment zealots convinced that the evidence in hand was sufficient to convict. Because most were equally certain that they had their districts behind them, their zeal could be damaging. Their premature announcements might impair the reputation for fairness the Committee was trying to cultivate as much as Republican charges of partisanship. They could also harden the line of division within it, and a straight partisan split on impeachment reduced the chance of acceptance by the full House.

Notwithstanding their freedom from constituency restraints, most zealots refrained from speaking out. As Don Edwards of California explained to a reporter: "We've had to change our behavior. We're members of a grand jury, and perhaps down the line we'll be judges or prosecutors, so we're not politicians any more. The chairman has reminded us, and we remind ourselves, we can't be swingers any more."[40] Occasional lapses, born of impatience at the slow-moving process, were indeed seized upon by the White House. Richard Nixon was to include a whole catalogue of partisan remarks by committee members in his memoirs, where he noted, with some scorn, that Rodino had said "we're going to proceed with decency and thoroughness and honor." As evidence of the true temper of the committee, Nixon cited New York Democrat Charles Rangel's description of his own role as making sure Rodino didn't get TOO damn fair. Nixon also mentioned a letter in which California Democrat Jerome Waldie began by thanking his constituents for supporting his efforts to impeach Nixon.[41] Waldie had been among those who, after the Saturday Night Massacre, had filed an impeachment resolution accusing the President of an obstruction of justice.

THE TELEVISED DEBATE

If impeachment was to have bipartisan support, the decision had to be made on "objectively" unassailable grounds. The question of how many Republicans would join with the Democratic majority in voting for one or more articles was crucial for the image of a bipartisan consensus.

To identify the limits of possible consensus within the Committee, some members had been meeting for some time to consider what points to include in the impeachment articles. This group of seven, identified in the press as the "fragile coalition," included the three Southern Democrats and four Republicans. To at least one committee member, they were "the big seven" while, among themselves, they were "the unholy alliance," "the magnificent seven," or "the terrible seven."[42] After several weeks, they had come to agree that they could vote for narrowly drawn articles on the Watergate coverup and the abuse of power. Nevertheless, there still remained the possibility that the Committee would in the end split along strictly partisan lines. Neither Rodino nor the legal staff felt certain how things would go once the public debate got under way. How firm the support for the articles would be depended on the final phrasing.[43] Mezvinsky, in his highly personalized account of his committee experience, mentions as "one of the many ironies of the situation . . . that the members of the committee did not know a whole lot more about the eventual outcome than did the members of the television audience."[44]

The Impeachment Vote

The vote on the first impeachment article, charging obstruction of justice, came at 7 P.M. EDT, on Saturday, July 27, the fourth day of debate. This was, without doubt, the dramatic high point in the proceedings. The mood, the words, the feeling that history was being made have been recorded on videotape as well as in print. The room was utterly still. Even some of those long prepared to vote "yes" responded somberly, quietly, and even inaudibly as their names were being called. Though all appeared anxious, no one appeared to take any joy in the occasion nor did anyone appear to be gloating.

The adoption of the article by a 27 to 11 vote was, as television and press commentators noted, more than an adequate show of bipartisanship. (See Appendix, table 7, for tabulations of vote.) ABC, responsible for that day's coverage, said the Committee had voted on the evidence. One reporter said he would never forget the words of Walter Flowers as he moved the amendment that brought the article to a vote. In a voice filled with emotion, he had told the audience: "There are many people in my district who will disagree with my vote here. Some will say that it hurts them deeply for me to vote for impeachment. I can assure them that I probably have enough pain for them and me." Flowers had not only been talking to the public; he was also talking to his friends, in and out of Congress, when he surmised that they would have done the same thing were they in his place on this unhappy day "confronted with all of the same facts that I had." His words were much replayed and cited as evidence of the agony of decision, as testimony that the members of the Committee had, for the most part, avoided "politics" and voted their conscience.

The timing of the vote, which could hardly have been more propitious had it been prescheduled, assured the Committee a larger audience than it might otherwise have had. It came while the early evening newscasts were on the air. Live shots of the Congressmen casting their vote were incorporated into the news and witnessed by many people who had not been following the proceedings or following them closely. The potential impact of the members' demeanor and words was thereby enhanced.

A dramatic and solemn occasion, this vote had a great potential for influencing judgments of committee fairness, but there had been other riveting occasions and there would be more. The first two articles of impeachment had been introduced on Wednesday evening, July 24, just after the opening statements by the Chairman and the ranking Republican. Setting the tone for the televised debate, Rodino had reminded the viewers that "our Constitution is being put to the test." Careful to strike a bipartisan chord, he explained how the Committee had investigated fully and completely the grounds for impeachment and provided a fair opportunity for the President's counsel to present his side. The Committee had been patient and fair and now the American people demanded that they make up their minds: "This inquiry is neither a court of law nor a partisan proceeding. It is an inquiry which must result in a decision—a judgment based on the facts."

Rodino had tried to keynote the proceedings by stressing the judicial basis underlying the Committee's charge. He was followed by Hutchinson, who as ranking Republican could be presumed to be speaking for his fellow Republicans on the Committee. Hutchinson conceded that "the people will have an unusual glimpse into the discussions of those charged with the decision-making in a unique judicial process" but then went on to point out that the proceedings were also part of a political process. By having opened the doors to the public—"judges and juries deliberate behind closed doors"— the Committee had determined that their function would be "more of a political than a judicial function after all."

Rodino was not about to be sidetracked and had the impeachment resolution introduced before any other member could speak. Article I dealt with the obstruction of justice, Article II with the abuse of power by the President. With the resolution on the floor, the "gentlemen" and the "gentleladies" would be recognized in turn but "for purpose of debate only." By this procedure, Rodino meant to signal that opening statements were not to be used for political rhetoric. Generally, members took the cue to discuss seriously the background, rationale, and evidence relating to the articles. But there was also a certain amount of posturing. Thus, members would open with a reference to the provisions of one or both articles and then pass over specifics to use the allotted time to address their constituents or to appeal to the public at large. Some remarks also appeared to be directed at colleagues in the House, who would make the ultimate decision on whether Nixon should stand trial in the Senate.

A striking contrast is provided by two Republicans speaking on opening night. Charles Sandman Jr. of New Jersey, a theatrical speaker, insinuated that the result of the debate was a foregone conclusion, saying, "There are sufficient votes here. . . . There is no use kidding anybody about that." He charged that three weeks ago the Committee had changed from a nonpartisan inquiry into a highly partisan prosecution. Until then, Doar had seemed one of the fairest lawyers Sandman ever had met, but no longer. In his view, Sandman explained, the Committee was more than a "grand jury"; to justify impeachment the evidence would have to be "clear and convincing." This initiated the theme that would be echoed by other hardliners to justify their vote against impeachment. Taking a completely opposite tack, Tom Railsback of Illinois, a leader of the "fragile coalition" who had helped formulate and refine the impeachment articles, emphasized the fairness and judiciousness of the proceedings and expressed great praise for Rodino. Then, addressing his constituents, he pledged that the Committee would seek the "truth," whence, speaking without notes, he launched into a detailed review of the evidence bearing on the Presidential abuse of power. In a phrase much repeated by the press, he said he found impeachment an "awesome responsibility." It is hard to believe that he failed to convey sincerity.

Opening statements lasted through Wednesday evening and the morning, afternoon, and evening of Thursday, July 25. Those delivered in prime television time had the best chance of reaching a large audience. If anyone starred on the second evening, it was Barbara Jordan, a black Congresswoman from Texas, who in a strong, clear voice, and speaking slowly for emphasis, declared that "my faith in the Constitution is whole, it is complete, it is total, and I am not going to sit here and be an idle spectator to the diminution, the subversion, the destruction of the Constitution." Journalist Elizabeth Drew wrote from Washington that "one senses that she believes it in her bones."[45] So impressive was she that one of us, monitoring the debate, jotted down this observation, "She'll be a national figure after this" and, indeed, she was.

With the one exception noted, no speaker went so far as to demean the work of the Committee or to question publicly the integrity of its staff. Those opposed to impeachment concentrated on the conclusiveness of the evidence. For instance, Wiley Mayne of Iowa characterized it as nothing but a "series of inferences piled upon other inferences." This alleged lack of "specifics" was to become the pivotal argument. In making "proof" of Nixon's guilt the focus of the debate, the Republican hardliners shared the Democrats' basic premise that this was no time to invoke loyalty to one's party or to its chief. In the context of the law, argued Charles Wiggins, "personalities are irrelevant." He had winced on hearing himself characterized on television as the President's "chief defender." Even more than others, he insisted that the case had to be decided according to the law, and the law, in this case especially, could be characterized in one word—fairness. This meant that the President, like everyone else, had to be presumed innocent until found guilty.

On at least two occasions, the debate took on a political coloration that threatened the reputation for "fairness" and "judiciousness" that Rodino and the staff had been so intent on nourishing. On Friday, July 26, the day on which the obstruction of justice article was originally to have come to a vote, several Republicans objected, as they had previously, that the nine counts contained in it were too vague, lacking the specifics on time and places and events needed to back up the allegations. This, they argued, was manifestly unfair to the President and perhaps even in violation of the constitution. The infighting and apparent impasse highlighted the fragility of the bipartisan coalition that had sought a common ground. These sharp exchanges between Democrats and Republicans on the issue of "specificity" were not only telecast live, they also, of course, made the evening network news, where those who had missed them heard them described as a "bitter fight."[46]

Again, on Tuesday, July 30, the last day of the debate, partisan infighting erupted. With three articles already passed, the issue concerned the introduction of still more articles of impeachment. The number had been left open, as Rodino was concerned about not pushing too hard and reluctant to go beyond the three that had been agreed upon.[47] Now there was disagreement on how many should be introduced and on the order in which to take up any additional articles. Tom Railsback, having voted for the first two articles, had voted against the third, objecting that anything beyond two was "political overkill." Actually, it had been a Republican, McClory, from Railsback's home state of Illinois, who had been the chief advocate of a third article, which charged the President with unconstitutional defiance of the Committee's subpoena. Now in allowing two further articles to be introduced, the Democratic leadership did act "politically." One charged Nixon with secretly bombing Cambodia and then falsifying information about this;

the other charged him with engaging in willful income tax evasion and the illegal use of government funds to improve his homes. Introduction of these articles was a concession to Democrats looking for a chance to air these issues in public. Yet, when it came to voting, the leadership maintained the bipartisan consensus by siding with the Republicans to defeat them. They did not want to embitter those "neutrals" whose support would be needed when the articles already accepted came up for debate in the full House.

It was the order in which the last two articles were debated that most clearly threatened the image of "fairness" the committee had been so careful to cultivate. Loathe to inject the still-lingering bitterness over the Vietnam War into the debate, the leadership was relieved to have the Cambodian bombing taken up in the afternoon, when fewer people would be watching. But they had no such objection to debating the tax article in prime evening time, even if they were not about to vote for its adoption. It was good ammunition for Democrats, as the public had shown itself highly incensed by Nixon's low income tax payments and the apparently unwarranted diversion of public funds for improvements to his private residences at Key Biscayne and San Clemente. Yet if the Democrats chose to make the order of debate a political decision, the Republicans were not prepared to let them get away unscathed. The following points, made in the thick of the evening debate, epitomize the thrust of the Republican attack and Democratic defense:

Mr. Sandman (R.,N.J.): Now let me tell you one other thing which I think is awfully important, and I want to see these people who are moving this resolution deny what I am about to say. This bunch of baloney was supposed to be taken up this afternoon and not tonight, but there is a bigger audience on TV tonight than there was this afternoon.

Mr. Lott (R., Miss.): This afternoon, quite to the surprise of some of us, we spent the better part of the afternoon working on an article dealing with the bombing of Cambodia which we, most of us, knew would be defeated. Why? For a very good reason, so that tonight we would have an opportunity to talk about the President's taxes. It is a good political issue.

Mr. Brooks (D., Texas) somewhat later: Mr. Lott from Mississippi was concerned about whether we had Cambodia or taxes tonight . . . or in the afternoon, and he reminds me of the story of the hard-working mother who gave her son two ties for his birthday. The next morning he came down with one of the ties on and she said, "Son, you didn't like the other tie."

That the order of debate should have generated debate indicates once more how continuously conscious of the television audience committee members were and how this, in turn, affected the conduct of the proceedings in many, sometimes subtle ways.

Content Analysis

For a more systematic analysis of how television content helped project an image of "fairness" or "unfairness," we first coded all references during the debate to: (1) Chairman Rodino, (b) the Committee and its individual members; and (c) the arguments for and against impeachment. (These tabulations should be seen as a supplement to the qualitative account.) We also analyzed television commentary before and after the debate to ascertain whether themes picked up in the commentary tended to reinforce or modify the impressions conveyed by the committee members.

Most of the coding was done directly from nearly 23 hours of videotapes of the coverage, but limited to three days: ABC on July 24, CBS on July 25, and NBC on July 30. This includes the opening sessions, when members would have been most keenly aware of the need to appear "judicious," and the last days, when they may have been less self-consciously aware of meanings being conveyed by words spoken in the "heat of battle." Also, it includes one day of coverage by each network.[48]

The most general finding: What committee members had to say about themselves, about the Committee as a group, and about the process in which they were engaged overshadowed any statements by television journalists about these same matters. Television focused on the actual proceedings and kept comment to a minimum. It helped convey an image of "fairness" and thereby advanced the Committee's purpose just by being available. In this sense, to use McLuhan's enigmatic phrase, the medium was the message.

But Rodino, too, was an important part of the message. His image as a fair and judicious chairman was established by the tributes his colleagues repeatedly paid him in the two days of opening statements and nothing was said thereafter to threaten it. Only a tiny proportion (about 5 percent) of the characterizations of Rodino were negative—for example, a reference by Sandman to the Chairman's "ruling with an iron hand"—and none of these was made during an acrimonious debate. Rodino's name was hardly mentioned during the heated infighting on July 30, in which he himself did not participate.

Nor did anything in the commentary draw attention away from his impartial role as a steady, low-keyed, undramatic chairman presiding over a potentially highly charged debate. In referring to Rodino, the news staff mainly employed neutral and bland descriptors. He was the "leader" or "chairman." The camera further underlined the centrality of his role by focusing on him whenever he pounded the gavel and whenever the Committee was dispersing or reassembling. In fact, Rodino's role appeared so pivotal to us when we monitored the live coverage that we were surprised to find that the content analysis had not turned up more references to his political beliefs, about where he stood on impeachment, about the role that he had played in guiding impeachment through the Committee, and about the key part he continued to play even as the deliberations were being televised.

Rodino himself was not always satisfied with the quality of the debate, even though opening night had drawn such rave notices. ABC anchormen had declared themselves "impressed" by the Committee's sense of "awesome responsibility," the patriotism, and the sincerity of the members. Nevertheless, off-camera Rodino felt compelled to caution speakers to be more specific, to begin their remarks by laying out just why they were taking one stand or another.[49] By the second day, those favoring impeachment were explaining at great length the reasoning that had led to their decisions. Yet reporters called no attention to the backstage influence exerted by the chairman, which had led to this subtle but significant shift in the mode of public presentation. Nor did the commentary note, to cite another example, Rodino's willingness, displayed on several occasions, to extend debating time so that those meeting off-camera could work out changes that were to make the articles more acceptable to the "neutrals."[50]

The Committee. Committee members made good use of the television opportunity to promote their individual and collective images. They depicted themselves as a body of lawyers, working on the constitutional and legal issues related to impeachment in a nonpartisan and objective fashion. Television journalists, although generally inclined to accept the members' self-flattering definitions, were ready to expose the partisan intent behind their maneuvering whenever the debate heated up.

The tone of the debate, as noted, was set during the two opening sessions, when very few (about 7%) of the members' remarks implied that partisan considerations might or could have entered into the Committee's decision. Even on July 30, when some Republicans openly questioned the motives of those proposing the last two articles of impeachment, the proportion of statements from members impugning the Committee did not rise. Yet the number of media references to the partisan aspects of the Committee's debate more than doubled—from about one third of all references to the committee on July 24–25 to over two thirds on July 30, the final day of the debate. There was a subtle change in "labeling." When, on the first two days, some Republicans had been considering joining the Democrats to vote for impeachment, this exemplified the bipartisanship Rodino, Doar, and others had so long labored to reach. But, on July 30, when the Democratic leadership, in the spirit of compromise, elected not to seem vindictive by pressing for a partisan victory, the commentary defined this as political infighting and dwelt on it at some length (Appendix, table 8).

The image of the Committee as a serious, hard-working, nonpartisan group was also sharpened by what was not shown. To begin with, television news was operating under a directive that limited camera choices. Nothing that could distract attention from the debate was to be allowed. And, by prior agreement, newscasters were not to cut away from the business at hand by going behind the scenes when the debate might prove routine, too technical, or otherwise likely to bore the audience. This still left cameramen with choices. They could have focused on the vacant seats of members temporarily absent; they could have tried to catch the passing of notes, the side conversations, and other signs of activity outside the formal arguments. Instead, such politicking and "human interest" touches went mostly unrecorded. They certainly were not publicized.[51]

If the coverage hewed closely to the formal debate, it was not without its moments of levity. Such moments were supplied largely by William Hungate, a Democrat from the Mark Twain country of Missouri. With his humor, he made his points, maintained a modicum of perspective, relieved the tension, and improved the atmosphere. Thus, with the Committee entangled in a seemingly endless argument about whether the President could be "proved" to have committed an obstruction of justice or whether his guilt could merely be "inferred" from the premise, itself unproven, that Watergate could not have taken place without his knowing about it and that therefore he must have participated in its coverup, Hungate came to the rescue. "I tell you," he said as the room exploded into laughter, "if a guy brought an elephant through the door and one of us said, 'That is an elephant,' some of the doubters would say, 'You know, that is an inference. That could be a mouse with a glandular condition.' " Much as those present (and probably most of the television audience) seemed to enjoy this light touch, enough people were offended to cause him to defend his levity later in the debate: "I would apologize to some if they have found occasional attempts at humor offensive but I have never thought a sense of humor needed to destroy your sense of responsibility and in my case I felt it better to have a sense of humor than no sense at all."

Actually, the kind of sharp exchanges that the press could label as "partisan infighting" and feature in the nightly news were few and far between. What was perhaps the most personal, though atypical, attack occurred as the televised drama was nearing its end. Despite constant interruptions from opponents of impeachment, Elizabeth Holtzman (D., N.Y.) finally managed to read into the record the fact that the Internal Revenue Service, contrary to what was being alleged, had *not* cleared President Nixon of tax fraud. As her time expired, Sandman tried to negate her argument by raising a point of parliamentary inquiry. In view of all these "false" accusations, he wanted to know, "Where do we stand upon what we say here tonight insofar as libel is concerned? Are we protected or immune from that?" In turn, Holtzman (later Brooklyn District Attorney) rose to a point of personal privilege:

I would like to state that I resent the remarks of Mr. Sandman because I have presented this as fairly as I could in terms of my reading of the Senate reports and materials before me. I certainly agree that we must be fair and honest and honorable, and I have tried to do that, and I think by casting aspersions on my integrity, Mr. Sandman is trying to undermine the integrity of the committee, and I personally, personally resent it, and I wish he had considered his remarks.

Sandman had begun to answer when Rodino, with uncharacteristic abruptness, cut him off by recognizing the next speaker.

What in the last analysis was most important to the image of the Committee was the distribution of votes on the articles of impeachment. Articles I and II were adopted by unambiguously bipartisan majorities, and on none of the others was the split along strict party lines. The vote on Article III, which charged the President with unconstitutional defiance of the Committee's subpoenas, was closest; it passed by 21 to 17, with only two Democrats and two Republicans crossing party lines. The last two articles were rejected by one-sided margins, with nine Democrats joining the Republican opposition to reinforce the image of judiciousness that the Committee sought to build. Yet the Democrats were, in fact, acting more out of political considerations than on the merits of the cases. For the debates over Cambodia and Nixon's willful tax evasion had a potential for repoliticizing the impeachment process. During the last vote, the office of Mezvinsky, sponsor of the tax evasion article, was flooded with calls accusing him of trying to kick the President while he was down.[52]

Arguments in the Debate over Impeachment. In debating the articles of impeachment, committee members could argue from several premises: they could argue politically, they could address the legality and constitutionality of the articles of impeachment, or they could treat this as an evidentiary proceeding where the only valid argument concerned the "facts" of the case. A "political" argument makes its point by seeking to establish an identification between the speaker and the audience. This can be accomplished by appealing to a common interest or communal bond rooted in sentiment, compassion, or just a sense of decency. The legal argument, by contrast, derives its validity from being in accord with some binding statute or precedent. The evidentiary argument seeks only to ascertain what happened.

An example of a political argument would be that, in bombing Cambodia, Nixon had not acted illegally, but just unwisely from a political point of view. Supporters of the impeachment article could be accused of seeking to capitalize on the current unpopularity of the course the President had chosen. As Congressman Wayne Dennis (R. Ohio) put it: "If the same thing were done tomorrow in a popular war, nobody would say anything about it." The members of the Committee, he implied, were courting popularity by playing up to their constituents rather than meeting their higher responsibility. The other two categories of arguments should be self-explanatory and require no further illustration.

Legal and evidentiary arguments clearly predominated over political ones. This is the main finding from a count of the frequency with which each type of argument was advanced during the debate (Appendix, table 9). Even on July 30, the most partisan of days, only about one fourth of the arguments advanced could be classified as "political" in our sense of the term.

Because our content analysis does not cover July 26, the day on which debate bogged down in disputes over lack of specificity, it may actually understate the preoccupation of committee members with the "evidence." Article I, then under consideration, though amended to meet such objections and now including nine separate areas of offenses, still did not satisfy those opposed to impeachment. The article still lacked, so they claimed, exact times and places and events to back the charges. In answer, the staff provided all members with memoranda summarizing the evidence. These came to be referred to privately as "scripts." On July 27, when these were available, those favoring Article I, took turns reading them." Faced with this avalanche of "specificity," their opponents capitulated. They stopped calling for more documentation.

But even on other days in the debate the hard-liners dwelled on the need for more "evidence," for the "smoking gun" that no one had yet been able to produce. Without this, they argued, the case against Richard M. Nixon would never hold up in the forthcoming Senate trial. Two thirds of all references to "evidence" referred to the taped records of Presidential conversations. The rest concerned testimony that had or should have been heard by the Committee or to specific documents, such as Nixon's tax records. By building their case around the alleged lack of evidence, impeachment foes helped define the proceedings as a legal, rather than political, debate and, paradoxically, laid the groundwork for the catastrophic erosion of political support just days later when the "smoking gun" found buried in the June 23 tape destroyed the premise of their argument.

Refraction

Both those favoring and those opposed to this first-time broadcast of a Congressional committee conducting a business meeting (rather than a hearing) had recognized that its televising might influence the proceedings. The cameras could be hidden and the commentators might refrain from expressing their personal views; nevertheless, the awareness of a huge bystander public could not but intrude into the proceedings. The official record is replete with references to the millions watching; their choice of words and arguments both show how mindful committee members were of the viewing audience. A round of "opening remarks" was eliminated because ten hours of speeches would only have turned the audience away. Similarly, the choice of persons to introduce the articles and to lead the debate was made with one eye on the audience. Or—yet another example—when Railsback, attempting to explain the agony of decision to his constituents, ran out of time, Democrats yielded so that he might finish. This was not just "good politics"; it was good television.

A more vital question concerns the influence of its televising on the outcome of the debate. Did it make it either easier or more difficult for the seven Republicans—McClory, Railsback, Fish, Hogan, Butler, Cohen, and Froehlich—to vote for impeachment on at least two articles? What was its effect on the three Southern Democrats—Mann, Flowers, and Thornton—who, in supporting impeachment, went against strong opposition from their heavily pro-Nixon constituencies? All but Froehlich and Hogan had been part of the "fragile coalition" working to formulate articles they could support. Although at certain critical moments in the debate, publicity appeared to be making the coalition even more fragile, television, in singling out these little-known Congressmen for special attention, conferred on them a status they had not enjoyed before. Television must have sustained, if not actually strengthened, their resolve to cut free from more mundane political considerations. It gave them a national, even historical, stature. The inferred approval of millions could only have made them feel less vulnerable; the publicity surrounding their decision-making provided a "sense of occasion" that encouraged the voting of one's conscience.

Members of the "fragile coalition" used television to appeal to the people back home, who then responded by encouraging them to continue what they were doing. Judging from mail they received, it was becoming more respectable to vote one's conscience than to bow to constituent opinion. This was especially evident to the Southerners, whose constituents seemed to be taking a special pride in the acclaim the media gave the eloquent words and lofty sentiments they expressed. There was another element in this feedback loop: committee members discovered, during brief recesses to vote on matters before the House, their performance was having an immediate and significant effect on Capitol Hill. "The Judiciary Committee proceedings," said John Anderson, chairman of the House Republican Conference,[53] "gave the Congress a much-needed lift. They restored to the Congress a sense of dignity. . . . Those televised proceedings were hung on very carefully by members of Congress. Members of Congress don't often listen to each other. Nothing is more boring. But this was different."

This attentiveness made it doubly necessary that a positive impression, once created, not be dissipated by an overly heated debate. One of the most trying moments for the "fragile coalition" came when anti-impeachment stalwarts, similarly attuned to the bystander public, were pressing hard for "specificity." James Mann, who had been strongly opposed to the televising of the debate, was moved to observe at one point that the cameras were moving events, exactly as he had predicted. "I do not think Mr. Sandman would be so strident, or even so partisan," he told his colleagues and the television audience, "if these proceedings were not being conducted to influence the opinions of the American people." Harold Froehlich, a freshman Representative who had won his seat by the narrowest of margins, directed a series of questions at Rodino and the staff, mainly to signal his uneasiness.

At what point in time, Froehlich wanted to know, could the President's attorney demand a bill of particulars on the impeachment articles? The camera briefly caught Railsback talking to Froehlich. Later, off-camera, Froehlich and Hogan would be asked to join the "fragile coalition" for dinner.[54] Next day, reassured, Froehlich voted for the first article of impeachment.

Only in one sense may television have had a dampening effect on the outcome. We refer again to the defeat of the fourth and fifth articles of impeachment, voted down with the help of Democrats who did not want to appear "vindictive." Had the deliberations not been televised, there is a good chance that at least one of these articles would have passed, yet not with the same show of bipartisan support that gave legitimacy to the passage of the first two articles and to the proceedings of the Judicary Committee.

THE PUBLIC RESPONSE

Who watched and how attentively? The pattern of viewing during the impeachment debate differed from that during the Senate hearings the year before. Fewer people watched at any one time and fewer stayed with the proceedings over long periods. The "impeachment junkie," unlike the "Watergate junkie," was a rare breed. Robert Laing and Robert Stevenson, studying response in Seattle, characterized most viewing as "casual surveillance," more like "viewing on the run" than sustained attention.[55] Typically, people would keep their radio or television on, follow with one ear while doing something else, but then pay close attention during the crucial votes.

Opening and closing nights drew the largest audiences, but on all six nights, entertainment programming on the two other networks attracted a large share of the audience.[56] Still, with only a 20 percent share of each evening's audience, the cumulative exposure over six days came to some 70 million Americans. This, *Broadcasting* reminded its readers, was "double the entire population of the U.S. in 1868 when Andrew Johnson became the first—and thus far the only—President to be impeached."[57] Surveys, based on respondent recall, provide similar estimates. Somewhat over one half the adult population had some exposure to the "live" TV broadcasts; another one third had seen at least some excerpts on the news. Only 10 percent of all adults had heard none of the proceedings on radio, nor gotten even a glimpse of them on television.[58]

Considering that the hearings came at the height of the summer vacation season and that the coverage was rotated, these audience statistics testify to a considerable amount of interest. This was no "captive audience." Nor was it as politically self-selected as was the audience for the Senate Watergate hearings or for most major political events on television. On the contrary, the audience included millions who were not at all antagonistic either to Nixon or to the Republican party.[59] A study by McLeod, Brown, and Becker of viewing during this period concluded that "interest in the outcome" and "interest in politics" were less determining for the amount of exposure than two other variables. One, which they call "high TV dependency," is indicative of a habitual turning to television for news about national and world events. The second is a matter of "availability"—that is, viewers have to be sufficiently free from other pressing commitments to avail themselves of the opportunity to watch.[60]

Again, as with the Senate Watergate hearings, the distinction between "being exposed" and "not being exposed" to the television coverage was blurred—so saturated were the media with news of the debate. Information quickly reached even those not following the live coverage. This spill-over is something to keep in mind in assessing the impact of the televised hearings on public opinion.

A second distinction is equally crucial to the study of television effects—that between the direct and immediate impact of a televised event on those exposed and its more long-term indirect effects. The public meaning of what has been witnessed on television tends to emerge gradually by further discussion. First impressions are often modified when checked against other information, including the reactions of significant others and credible mass media sources.[61] A common definition gradually builds up. In this instance events moved so swiftly that it is even harder than usual to distinguish between a direct response to the television coverage of the impeachment debate and more delayed and indirect response, as events followed. Three days after the proceedings had ended (August 2), the White House, in compliance with a Supreme Court ruling, delivered the first set of three Presidential tapes to Judge Sirica for inspection *in camera*. Then, on August 5, the *Washington Post* reported that the contents were highly incriminating. That same day, as Nixon, at the insistence of his staff, released transcripts of these tapes along with a public statement, the situation was drastically redefined. The transcripts clearly refuted the President's previous claim that, "At no time did I attempt, nor did I authorize others to attempt, to implicate the

CIA in the Watergate matter," a statement he had made on May 22, 1973, and reiterated many times. The conversation left no room for doubt that Nixon had known, as early as six days after the break-in, that the Watergate operation had been financed by the Committee for the Reelection of the President. From then on, for political rather than security reasons, he had participated in the coverup of the bungled burglary.

For Nixon, the consequences were absolutely disastrous. His support among Senators and Representatives simply evaporated. Even his most eloquent and vigorous defenders deserted him. Wiggins was one of them. In an emotional statement, he demanded before television cameras that Nixon resign even before he was impeached. Hutchinson, Lott, Latta, and other Republican stalwarts obviously spoke for many others when they said they felt deceived by the President whom they had tried to defend.

The rapidity with which these developments followed makes it difficult to sort out the influence of the televised debate from the devastating effect of the disclosure of the smoking gun. It was now virtually certain that the President would be found guilty in a trial by the Senate. Nixon, in resigning, was bowing to the inevitable and trying to cut his losses.

What we know about the immediate response to the debate comes from mail to committee members and comment in their local papers. Some were cheered by the expressions of support for their votes. After he voted for Article I, the majority of letters Butler received from his district approved; those from outside were even more in favor.[62] The *Roanoke Times*, Butler's home-town newspaper, editorialized: "We respect his decision and believe most of his constituents will also—even those who wish the evidence could have persuaded Mr. Butler differently." William Cohen, perhaps the most impressive debater among the "big seven," went home to find his constituents backing his right to vote his conscience; of 270 letters received that weekend, only one-third were negative in tone.[63]

Others took a good deal more heat. Two months after the vote, Walter Flowers was still answering constituents' angry letters.[64] Seven of every ten letters to Railsback during the hearings opposed impeachment, but most of these came from outside his district. The ones from home endorsed his stand by two to one. This contrasts with the telephone calls to his Rock Island office, which ran 43–25 against him and were "often vitriolic."[65] When Railsback next visited his district, he said, he had to face a number of quite angry people. Several years later, he still thought he would have been able to justify his support of impeachment to his constituents and allay their misgivings even if the evidence in the final tape had been less conclusive.

The impression of an immediate shift in the climate of opinion is bolstered by the findings of polls completed before the tape transcripts were released. First in the field was *Newsday* with its poll of the two Long Island counties. Respondents were contacted by telephone the night the debate ended. Louis Harris and Associates conducted its national poll on July 31 and August 1; interviewing by the Gallup Organization was spread over four days, beginning on August 2 and ending on August 5. Everyone of these polls shows a swing toward impeachment on questions asked both before the debate and afterward. The increase found in the different samples and over varying intervals, ranging from 9 to 15 percentage points, is large enough to signal an unmistakable trend (Appendix, table 10). But when *Newsday* asked those who said they had watched at least some part of the television coverage if this had changed their beliefs about impeachment, their collective answer was a resounding "no." The small proportion who said that the debate changed their minds account for part of the increase in impeachment sentiment.

Within the context of a longer trend in opinion, the influence of the televised proceedings appears as significant but subtle. In the late spring the White House had launched an intensive media offensive to counter the adverse reaction to the release of the transcripts. In June, after Henry Kissinger had arranged a disengagement settlement between Syria and Israel, the President took off for a "triumphal tour through the middle East," followed by a trip to the Soviet Union. With the Judiciary Committee meeting behind closed doors, Watergate had taken a momentary backseat in the press and on the networks.[66] In the absence of much "bad" news, Nixon's chances for surviving Watergate appeared to have improved. Ratings of the Presidential performance were registering slight gains. There were also signs of impeachment weariness. A Gallup reading, taken June 21–24, found a majority of Americans believing that the mass media were providing "too much coverage" of Watergate. Though polls continued to show that the public backed the Committee's quest for the release of the tapes and other evidence, the number doubting its ability to judge the case fairly was on the increase. Thus, opposition to impeachment *appeared* to be gaining some ground just before the debate began. Had the televised proceedings only reconvinced those who had momentarily lost faith? Or had they also won new converts among those hitherto not in favor of impeachment?

To begin with, how much lost ground was there to be regained? National polls supply no clear answer. In a post-mortem review of opinion trends, the Gallup report[67] called attention to findings from its May 31–June 3 poll. There had been a "slight decline [since late April] in the proportion favoring [impeachment], following a long upward trend" in support of such a course of action. The one-month decline, from 51 to 50, was reversed and back to 51 by July. On another Gallup question, asking whether there was enough evidence to bring Nixon to trial before the Senate, the same pattern was observed, a slight downturn—from 48 to 44 percent so believing—with a partial recovery by July to 46 percent. If there was a dip in pro-impeachment sentiment, it was certainly minute and not lasting. And there could have been no "dip" at all, with the "slight decline" a spurious product of statistical chance.

Other soundings suggest that the "dip" in impeachment sentiment was real. A "before" poll by *Newsday* was conducted on June 24, when the Committee was still meeting in closed session and, with the President capturing headlines, Watergate news was at a low ebb. Their finding that support for impeachment was down from its April level was so astounding that the paper commissioned a second poll on June 26—with identical results. Comparing opinion among the subgroups within the sample, however, showed that not all parts of the public were as likely to have lost faith in impeachment as the way to remove the President. Support for impeachment was increasing among college graduates even as it was decreasing among the less educated. Stephen Cole, a sociologist who analyzed the poll, speculated that, as the impeachment proceedings seemed to bog down and become increasingly complex, it took sophistication to understand what was happening. Those without the requisite educational background might be becoming fed up with the whole thing and no longer wanted to hear about it.[68]

Still, people wanted Watergate resolved one way or another. If the removal of Nixon was one solution, then there were at least two ways to achieve it. The alternative to extended impeachment proceedings was to have him resign. To many people it would not have mattered which way he was removed from the Presidency. Examination of trends in sentiment on removal—whether by resignation or impeachment—suggest that the televised committee decision did more than cancel out whatever gains Nixon had been making during the previous weeks. It also made impeachment the more popular of the alternatives. By the time the voting ended, support for removal by impeachment had increased considerably over the previous April figure (Appendix, table 10).

There was also an increase in the number who *expected* Nixon to be impeached—always a much smaller group than those who thought he *should* be impeached. After an early summer dip, polls recorded a sharp increase (Appendix table 11). In late May and in mid-July, most people still doubted that "President Nixon will be found guilty and impeached[sic] and removed from office." Within two weeks the doubters had become a clear minority. Impeachment now had official sanction; to expect it was realistic; to approve was no longer tantamount to taking a political position.

The post-debate study by Laing and Stevenson,[69] designed to pin down the influences of the proceedings on viewers, provides evidence that the televised debate helped to depoliticize and thus legitimate the impeachment decision. They found that most people regardless of whether they had followed the live coverage, talked about the impeachment controversy with considerable sophistication. Very few defined it in terms of a conspiracy, be it by Nixon's political enemies, the mass media, or some other sinister force. But there were differences in the perceptions of viewers and nonviewers: viewers were less likely to "see the impeachment controversy in terms of pressure from others in the political system or their own feelings toward Mr. Nixon." Viewers also had more information about the process and, in arguing for or against impeachment, were more able to specify and focus on arguments that had been put forth during the committee's deliberations.

The fate of this survey, launched on August 5, the day the transcripts were released, also documents how quickly the Judiciary Committee decision was overtaken by events. Interviewing was to extend over five days. By the third day, there were marked changes in people's expressions of desired and expected outcomes of Watergate. Support for impeachment rose steadily even while more and more people came to expect that the controversy would be resolved by Nixon's resignation. This movement of opinion reiterates our belief that the televised hearings, while they had little effect on perceptions of Nixon's guilt, had made impeachment more acceptable. It became the preferred solution once the clear and convincing "proof" had been produced.

THE DEBATE AS A MEDIA EVENT

Most published recaps of the Watergate saga have praised the television performance of the Rodino committee and assumed that the public responded favorably. These statements are typical:

By their conduct during these televised meetings members of the House Judiciary Committee displayed to millions of Americans a magnificent example of government in action.[70]
The country was able to observe by live television coverage. . . . a group of 38 Representatives, each of whom had an enormous command of the facts of the case. For the first time, the country was to be made aware in a systematic manner of the case against Richard Nixon, and in less than a week the Committee made that case an overwhelming one.[71]
As the Judiciary Committee completed its televised sessions, it was clear that its thorough and largely bipartisan efforts had made it difficult for most other members of Congress to vote against impeachment without appearing to discredit themselves.[72]

Hardly any responsible commentator agreed with the ex-President that "the Democrats postured shamefully, pretending that they had not made up their minds. My supporters were eloquent but they were fighting a lost battle."[73]

The public, too, in looking back, was generally favorable toward the Committee. In late August, after the resignation, Roper interviewers asked what individuals (or groups of individuals) "looked good in the whole [Watergate] affair." The House Judiciary Committee ranked third, behind Special Watergate Prosecutor Leon Jaworski and the Federal courts. Only nine per cent of those questioned said it looked "rather bad," and one out of five could not or would not judge the committee performance.[74] In November 1974, when the Center for Political Studies at the University of Michigan conducted its post-election survey, the Committee was still remembered for a job well done. Three fourths of this national sample felt the hearings had been fair and only slightly fewer (71% to be exact) approved the committee's impeachment decision.[75]

How much did the coverage of the debate by television, as distinct from the debate itself, contribute to the favorable public image? The coverage depicted the decision process as a genuine adversary proceeding designed to get at the truth and conducted fairly. Both those for impeachment and those against had had full opportunity to state their case. The bipartisan aspects of the proceedings were stressed. Overt partisan moves were noted but not allowed to become the dominant theme. Instead, those crucial moments when the assembled audience could become witness to history in the making were treated with appropriate solemnity. After Rodino's keynote address and, again, before, during, and after the vote on the first article, the commentary repeatedly called attention to the historic nature of the event. It also stressed that the proceedings were receiving "uninterrupted" gavel-to-gavel coverage. Except for some vague and off-hand reports of meetings at which strategy was being developed, off-screen activity received only minimal attention. The big story was in the committee room. This contrasts with network coverage of esoteric debates, particularly of political conventions, during which backstage events are introduced to provide the "real" excitement whenever proceedings are judged to be boring.

Television journalists refrained from creating news and seeking exclusives. But they kept trying, much as they would in covering a political convention or an election, to anticipate how the vote would go. How closely they stuck to the official event is evident in the small number of commentator references to Richard Nixon. His name surfaced only in the reading of impeachment articles or in charges read by members, which were then repeated for the television audience. Such matters as whether the President would comply with the Supreme Court ruling or his friendships with some members of the committee were referred to only in passing.

An adversary proceeding, just because it addresses a wide audience, must also provide for certain ceremonial elements. A downplaying of partisanship presumably facilitates the acceptance of whatever decision is ultimately reached. On their part, the television journalists must demonstrate their neutrality and the producers achieve a balance in the viewpoints of persons interviewed. In this case, the balance was skewed in favor of the "fragile coalition," most of whom were Republicans. Because their not-yet-confirmed intentions lent some element of tension and excitement to the developing story, these members of the Republican minority were more often interviewed than Democrats. In the number of times their names were mentioned, McClory and Railsback, both "swing voters," were second only to Rodino. Yet this "imbalance," if it can be considered such, served to underline the bipartisan nature of the outcome.

The Viewer's Point of View. To understand the public response to the televised proceedings, one has to take account of viewers' convictions about the necessity and or inevitability of impeachment, which in turn affected their expectations of the televised event. Were they about to be witness to a genuine contest, that is an adversary proceeding, or to a partisan spectacle staged with one objective in mind: to drum up support for what had already been decided? Depending on the viewer's frame of mind, the proceedings could be seen as a unifying event, as a reaffirmation of due process and of equality before the law, or they could be viewed as a degradation ceremony inflicted on an absentee President, who would have no opportunity for rebuttal. A large segment of the public had obviously made up its mind beforehand. That some of those who disliked the decision would displace their hostility on television was only natural. But a significant minority approached the event with an open mind—as they might had they been chosen as members of a jury.

Detailed interviews held within the week following Nixon's resignation illustrate how their mental set affected what viewers saw and how they evaluated it. The following summaries of responses, drawn from longer protocols, are divided between two categories of viewers: those whose minds, before the debate, were pretty much closed on the subject of impeachment and those still seeking clarification. The former group includes both those who had long been convinced that Richard Nixon was guilty of impeachable offenses and others who believed, and would continue to believe despite his resignation, that he had done nothing to warrant removal from office.

Persons who had long felt the need for Nixon's removal were most apt to stress the historical occasion and to look at the proceedings as a unifying event.

A teacher, he had been convinced by the Dean testimony during the Senate hearings. He hoped Nixon would not only be convicted but given a prison sentence. Once he realized the debate would be televised, he looked forward to it. The highlight, for him, was the point at which they voted for Article I. The time of reckoning seemed very profound to him. It was like watching, he said, "man take his first step on the moon." It was great to view a historical occasion at first hand. He had expected the Judiciary Committee members to be a very select group, very knowledgeable about the law, with no superstars, but had anticipated a more heated debate. They seemed restrained to a degree but he guessed that "it's hard to blow up in front of 40 million people." What he saw of the debate bolstered his confidence in the political system. Impeachment, he concluded, is a good way to resolve such matters—very fair and yet lenient.

This young man and others like him declared themselves delighted that the Committee had treated the "President like any other man on trial and were really looking for the facts of the case." For them, the experience had been a stimulating one. They had learned that the President was not beyond the law, that "skeletons in political closets are always dragged out." They also sounded the "whole world is watching" theme, noting that millions could get their information first-hand and then draw their own conclusions. Viewing the event was a unifying experience. It made them feel part of the "system" more than they had before.

Equally impervious to persuasion were those who wholeheartedly opposed

Nixon's removal and who had approached the hearings as a partisan event, responding much as they might have responded to a half-hour presentation on election eve by a candidate whom they opposed.

Most outspoken was a middle-aged Republican who thought the Committee had made up its mind to impeach the President even before the debate. TV, in his opinion, was slanted and biased against Nixon and the Republicans were in the minority. He had nevertheless been impressed by the strong attempt of the minority group—particularly Sandman and Wiggins—to defeat impeachment. He also learned how vicious some people can be, though their behavior was no different from what he had expected. Otherwise he learned nothing from watching. After the Committee voted to impeach, he hoped that the House would vote to impeach because he was sure the Senate would not convict the President. The tapes would be exculpatory or not so damaging as they proved to be. There also would be a trial where the President could defend himself. He was pleased when he heard the three tapes would be released and hoped they would exonerate Nixon. Even though they did not, he understood what Nixon had been trying to achieve in covering-up and so he approved of these actions. Viewing only validated this viewer's expectations. He had remained steadfastly opposed to everything the Committee was doing. Now what he had seen made him hope the process would run its full course and lead to what he considered its logical conclusion: the exoneration of Richard Nixon.

Others who, like him, never lost faith in Nixon's innocence, questioned the legitimacy of the impeachment proceedings for resolving the Watergate controversy, as expressed by a retired man who, according to his own admission, had paid little attention to the hearings:

He had not been eager to watch. He thought Nixon was being railroaded. The committee members weren't fairminded but playing partisan politics. Still, he thought it would all blow over: the House would impeach but the Senate would vote in Nixon's favor. The only one on the Committee he could remember by name was Rodino. His first thought when the tapes were released was, "Why did the damn fool keep them instead of destroying them?" Even after their release he hoped that Nixon would still be found innocent as he had lied only for "the good of the country."

Among those who had approached the telecasts with minds perhaps not exactly open but not completely closed were those who had at some point in the last eight months decided that impeachment was the only answer to the crisis facing the country. These persons were most eager to talk about the proceedings. They had followed them much as they might have followed a debate between Presidential candidates and, as a rule, were better able than others to articulate their impressions of committee members and to detail their reactions:

One man, who had watched almost all of the debate said he had wanted to see our government in operation over this critical issue. What stood out was opening night and the addresses by Democrats and the conservative Republicans, mostly the young people. It completely renewed his faith in elected officials. Several of the Republicans had disgusted him. They were "hard-assed politicians and liars," who blatantly had disregarded the facts. Still, he had found some of the young Congressmen very appealing and described himself as happy that the issue was big enough so as not to become a partisan issue.

Another man had praise for the media and the "wonderful, wonderful system." What had impressed him in particular was that the committee members should have been both so sad and sincere. A third man was pleased to discover that his mind had not been so closed that it could not be changed:

He found this more interesting than the Senate hearings because this hadn't been affected by "overkill." Thus, for him the highlight in watching had been the discussion and vote on tax evasion. He was swayed by Sandman's defense of Nixon. He was relieved because he had changed his mind about Nixon's guilt on this one count. It had made him think that he was still open-minded about Nixon and that facts could change his opinion. In line with this, he reported that he had first been pleased at the news that the tapes were finally being released and yet had felt "personally weird" about the man's personal comments being exposed to the world.

In addition to affirming some attitudes already held, the viewing experience gave these viewers a "sense of fair play." Both sides had had their way in the debate at one point or other. More than before, they now allowed themselves to believe that they could be persuaded by a reasonable argument. Viewing had given them a sense of gratification.

The last group had watched the most avidly. While they had no longer accepted Nixon's protestations of total innocence, before the debate, they had yet to be convinced that impeachment and removal from office were justified. The group included a number of "backsliders" who, in the weeks before the hearings, had come to doubt the "fairness" of the Judiciary Committee. They were the most prone to define the event within a bipartisan framework. Having watched to obtain information, they found the experience an edifying one. They enjoyed talking about how much they had learned—about the Constitution, about the workings of the committee, and about what an impeachable offense was. As one middle-aged man put it, impeachment was "like a trial except no one is in custody." We summarize the remarks of one woman, who was persuaded by watching the hearings that impeachment was necessary.

She was far more impressed by the Committee than she had expected. The Congressmen were fairer than she had thought they would be. The Committee impressed her more than the Senate Committee because there wasn't as much showmanship. They were well prepared and she didn't think all of them had arrived at a decision on how to vote before hand. They were evidently split in their views and trying to convince each other—or maybe the TV audience. She found herself watching more closely than she had anticipated and couldn't turn the set off. It was very educational and she found out a lot. Among the things that stood out in her memory: when Republican Representative McClory decided to vote *for* Article II after *not* voting for Article I. He gave lengthy reasons. She also learned things she hadn't known before; for instance, that the failure to hand over the tapes could be a "high crime" or "misuse of office." Later, after hearing about the three tapes, she thought Nixon had had a lot of nerve to lie that long and wondered why he had given them up after lying so long. She hadn't thought his supporters would react so strongly against him—they must have had their eyes closed the whole time.

Another woman also approved the way the Committee had conducted itself but remained unconvinced about the necessity for impeachment until after the release of the final incriminating evidence:

She had hoped that the Committee would be impartial, have integrity, give Nixon a fair shake, a hope that was bolstered by her satisfaction with the way the Ervin committee had conducted itself. She thought the House Judiciary Committee proved to be very open-minded. Its members were looking for clues and evidence either way. Being a staunch Nixon supporter, she had never believed that the committee would actually go through with impeachment. This is what made her disbelieve that the final decision had been made beforehand, a view that was confirmed by the televised interviews with committee members during the hearings. She remained optimistic that the full House would not support impeachment because, if they did so, the Senate would go along. Her first reaction to the news about the three tapes was curiosity about what might be in them. Then, as she watched "people on the street" being interviewed by CBS, she found them stunned and shocked. She also explained that she had been impressed by Dean during the Senate hearings but then became dubious because, as a loyal Nixonite, she couldn't get herself to believe that Nixon was personally involved. For that reason, too, she had been anxious when Nixon delayed handing over the tapes, since that implied guilt. Now she knew.

Seeing people in Nixon's home town telling TV that Nixon should resign and finding so many people anxious for the "mess to be resolved" by a quick ouster was also persuasive. Several respondents singled out Railsback as the Congressman who had "had to vote for impeachment though he didn't want to and . . . worried about the effect on young people if Nixon was not impeached and that it would be dangerous if he got away as if not guilty."

Not everyone who had been suspicious of the Committee was reassured in

the end. As a representative of this minority, we mention a young conservative, who found that the Committee had conducted a witchhunt, just as he
had expected. He, like many others, had learned something from viewing
the proceedings but more, he said, from watching ABC's local news. He
had come to accept that Nixon's involvement in Watergate went beyond
that of a chief responsible for acts his subordinates had perpetrated. Hearing
that the tapes were about to be released, he was pleased because they would
prove Nixon innocent. Even the defection of Nixon's backers failed to sway
his belief that impeachment could not be justified. But he was ready to
acknowledge that the President was not so much the victim of persecution
as he had thought.

In sum, the reactions to the televised impeachment debate were by no
means uniform; there was a broad range of responses. Mainly, the public
had learned a lot about the charges against the President and how the process would have worked. Though Nixon was never actually impeached by
the House nor tried by the Senate, the televised debate served as a substi-
tute. Despite the repeated disclaimers by committee members that theirs was
not a trial nor even a grand jury hearing, this was not the impression of
many viewers. On the contrary, they would say, time and again, that it was
"like watching a trial" or that it was "like the members of a jury finding him
guilty." In the words of one respondent, "the committee proved that he was
guilty—he was a bad apple." It took the evidence that Nixon's supporters
had so persistently called for as the only adequate "proof" of sufficient malfeasance to warrant impeachment. Some remained unreconciled and believed he should have served out his full term. Yet whatever the specific
reaction, it was *as if* Nixon had been impeached. It had become hard for
anyone to maintain that resignation was forced on Nixon by his old enemies, that it was part of a political vendetta rather than the impersonal
working of the law. Not everyone was fully convinced, but the opposition
was at least temporarily silenced. It is in this sense that the televising, by
extending the scope of the contest and debate beyond the Committee, helped
to legitimate and gain public approval for the end of the Nixon Presidency.

CHAPTER 8

CEREMONIES OF TRANSITION
TV As a Unifying Agent

In a sixteen-minute address to the nation, Richard Nixon announced on Thursday evening August 8, 1974, that he would resign the Presidency effective at noon next day. At 11:35 A.M. EDT the following morning, White House aide Alexander Haig delivered a one-sentence letter to Secretary of State Henry Kissinger. It read:

Dear Mr. Secretary:
I hereby resign the Office of President of the United States.

Sincerely,
Richard Nixon

Less than a half hour later, in the East Room of the White House, Chief Justice Warren Burger administered the oath by which Gerald Ford succeeded to the Presidency.

There were none of the customary celebrations, inaugural parades and festive balls to signal the end of one administration and the beginning of another. Only a brief low-keyed swearing-in ritual followed by a brief and equally low-keyed acceptance speech marked the passage of power. The circumstances through which Ford had come to office were unprecedented. He had no electoral mandate and he was the hand-picked Vice President of the man now so clearly repudiated. His inaugural statement acknowledged the potential weakness of his position, but reminded his audience that the oath he had just sworn was the same that had been "taken by George Washington and by every President under the Constitution." Now that he was assuming the Presidency

under extraordinary circumstances never before experienced by Americans. . . . I am acutely aware that you have not elected me as your President by your ballots. So I ask you to confirm me as your President with your prayers. . . . If you have not chosen me by secret ballot, neither have I gained office by any secret promises. I am indebted to no man and only to one woman, my dear wife. . . .

Ford hardly needed to plead for acceptance. There may not have been much celebration in the streets, but neither was there much open display of displeasure at the changeover. The legitimacy of his succession did not become the subject of serious controversy. The public response was muted largely because the ground for changeover had been prepared in advance. Nixon's resignation, however sudden, had not been entirely unanticipated. The bipartisan endorsement of three impeachment articles, swiftly followed by the release of the incriminating tapes, had made inevitable what hitherto had seemed only a likelihood. Nixon's departure from office, by one means or another, was simply a matter of time. The public was ready.

Still, things might have been different. The Nixon era could as easily have ended with a bang and not a whimper. Without the opportunity the media, and mainly television, provided the public—particularly those not yet reconciled to the need for impeachment—to witness the manner of transition and to judge its legitimacy, the long controversy might not have ended so uncontentiously. The televising of Nixon's resignation speech, together with the extended before and after coverage, helped in two ways to assure the almost unchallenged acceptance of the unprecedented transfer of power: by treating Resignation Night as a ceremonial occasion, deemphasizing partisanship and stressing themes of unity, and by cloaking the unusual in the routines of the usual, thus making the occasion seem familiar and less problematic than it actually was. So it was that television served as a unifying agent by muting dissent and discouraging celebration.

Events and Pseudo-Events

Was there really a ceremony of Presidential transition? Or was it a "pseudo-event" invented for television? The question is whether the events witnessed via video would have existed had there been no media to cover them.

The neologism pseudo-event, first introduced by the historian Daniel Boorstin,[1] sets up what appears to be a simple, clear, and sharp distinction between two kinds of events to which the media may respond. There are "spontaneous events," which do happen and would happen even without the media reporting them; the news media can, in reporting what happened, do no more than render as authentic an account as possible. Other events, the so-called pseudo-events, are artificial in that they are *made* to happen so as to serve some interest or purpose. They may or may not involve outright deception, but the way they are planned, or planted, in order to be reported makes their relation to "reality" ambiguous. Often the news reported becomes the event, as happens whenever a "newsworthy" statement by a public figure elicits reactions from other public figures that then spawn more statements (events) of a similar character. The original statement becomes an important event because of the attention it has attracted from the news media.

Much effort goes into manipulating the media to cover the "right" events. According to Boorstin, it is the absence of spontaneity, the fact that an event is specifically planned for the convenience of the news media, that makes it a pseudo-event. Not only is there a buildup to its occurrence, but editors are specifically alerted, through press releases or handouts, to where and when it will take place. Press agentry or, to use the more modern term, news management plays an integral role throughout. Boorstin, in inventing the term, clearly implied that there was something fraudulent about planning events so as to take advantage of available news media.

To believe, as some do, that the press created Watergate is to regard it as one big pseudo-event. Certainly, following Boorstin's definition, it could be considered mainly as a series of pseudo-events. These would include not only the crucial Cox press conference and most of the Nixon appearances during Operation Candor but also Ford's televised appearance outside his home shortly after Nixon resigned and, perhaps, even Nixon's resignation speech. The last, no less than the others, was produced as a television event. Compared with "spontaneous" happenings, such as a Presidential illness, the signing of a peace treaty, or a Presidential swearing-in ceremony, which would occur whether or not the media were present, they are, by definition, less "real."

This much-used distinction between pseudo-events and real events strikes us as too sharp to be analytically useful. Much of politics is nothing but communication, and even a Presidential illness will be dramatized by the media and can be exploited for political gain. Publicity is always a potential resource. The revelation that a supposedly spontaneous event has actually been stage-managed can be as much a pseudo-event as the initial fakery. Interpreted in this literal fashion, the category of pseudo-events would become so all-embracing as to make it include nearly all communication by elites to the public.

A more meaningful distinction is between events that are public and those that remain privileged. What the availability of mass media has done is to shift the boundary between the two spheres. While much of the real give-and-take of political bargaining continues to take place off-stage, political figures are now forced into a posture of openness, into putting on their best possible face, and into an effort to manage their image, all by way of legitimating themselves and their actions to their constituents. This imperative is hardly new; it precedes the advent of the modern media. Yet, the ubiquitous presence of the mass media at parliamentary debates, in the court room, and so forth has added a new dimension. The opening of esoteric decision-making to a wider public tends to blur the line between the privileged and the public and change the symbolic significance of once privileged events.

Since time immemorial, rallies, parades, pageants, coronations, and other ceremonies have involved a degree of make-believe. They serve as occasions for the expression of individual loyalties and the collective rededication to a common purpose. In the mass society, media coverage makes it possible for the entire citizenry to participate. The images conveyed can become the focus of collective sentiments, and it is to assure a proper unifying response that they are carefully stage-managed by those responsible for their production. The plans news staffs have for covering these events likewise incorporate assumptions about what is appropriate and what viewers expect. Thus, the depiction of dissent, which is part and parcel of partisan events, would be considered inappropriate for an inauguration ceremony, where patriotic symbols inevitably crowd out those apt to be divisive.

In preparing for the President's speech and his expected resignation, the media had evidently to shift gears. Hitherto they had been a battleground for the various Watergate skirmishes, but now, with the situation about to change, they felt under some compulsion to depict the office of President as one to be revered and its incumbent as worthy of respect. The fact that Nixon had demeaned the office by exploiting its inherent power for clearly partisan purposes introduced some ambiguity into the journalistic role. Their sense of civic responsibility was an inducement to play down anything that could potentially mar the solemnity of the occasion, yet they were also reluctant, as journalists, to transmit only that which political managers believed to be in the public interest. The media event that evolved was a compromise between the two contradictory impulses, but it became the "reality" to which everyone—political elites, the public, and the press—responded.

Rumors of Resignation

When Richard Nixon did announce that he would resign, hardly anyone could have been totally shocked. That he would have to leave voluntarily or face a losing battle in Congress had become progressively clearer once even his staunchest defenders turned against him. Ford, too, reluctantly made ready to abandon the sinking ship. Reiterating his belief in Nixon's innocence, he nevertheless said he would no longer involve himself in the debate over resignation and impeachment. Political and press pundits were already speculating about who would become Vice President and whether Congress would grant Nixon immunity from prosecution. Senator Byrd, assistant majority leader, reportedly opposed any such deal, saying that all men were equal before the law. The House, unsure of what Nixon would do, went ahead with its preparations for impeachment; its rules committee approved full television and radio coverage, and the Republican minority leader, John Rhodes of Arizona, announced that he, too, would vote to impeach.

Meanwhile, the White House continued to deny rumors of impending resignation. In the statement accompanying the release of the transcripts, the President strongly implied his faith that the Senate, upon examination of the full facts, would render a verdict of acquittal. Next day a cabinet officer quoted Nixon as saying, "For me to resign would be something outside the Constitution."[2] According to insiders' accounts, the White House staff had prepared for both eventualities: one speech writer drafted a resignation speech and another the text for a confession of his involvement in a coverup, in which Nixon would apologize, and appeal to the American people for forgiveness.[3] Nixon's decision to go on television, although made on August 7, was not announced until the next day. His speech was to be "brief, dignified, generous, and almost upbeat," wrote an aide, this "could be one of his shining hours, and the way he departs will have a tremendous impact on the country's future."[4] Ford, too, had asked his top aide to draft a speech "just in case."

Some of the resignation rumors sweeping the country originated in newspaper accounts. On August 7, the *Providence Journal-Bulletin* reported that an "irrevocable" decision had been reached. Its suspected source was Rabbi Baruch Korff, whose National Citizens Committee for Fairness to the President was Providence-based. Further feeding this rumor was the *Phoenix Gazette*, which cited a "highly reliable source," presumably Senator Barry Goldwater, that resignation was imminent and set for that afternoon. Several radio bulletins actually mentioned the Senator by name, provoking an angry denial from the floor of the Senate, where Goldwater referred to the "damn lies that have appeared on NBC this morning and ABC this afternoon." But the story had not been fabricated out of thin air. An ABC reporter, who apologized, had been told by another Senator that Nixon had given these indications to Goldwater but this same Senator, who had asked that he not be identified, now said that he had been mistaken about the source.[5]

The *Washington Post* that same morning left the impression that the only question yet unanswered was the matter of "when." A Woodward and Bernstein item told of dismay among the White House staff. A source with first-hand knowledge was quoted, "I don't mean to be alarmist, and it has to be said delicately, but the President will not listen to anyone, not really listen. He's serene, I'd say serene, but not in touch with reality." The President was reported to be secluded with his family, including his sons-in-law, all of whom had joined him in the White House.

Later in the day there were other rumors flying about: the networks were setting up for a formal Presidential address; high-ranking Republicans in both houses were telling other members of their party to expect a resignation. These rumors were reported but remained unconfirmed. The major event of the afternoon was Nixon's meeting with Goldwater, Senator William Scott of Virginia, and Rhodes. Upon leaving the White House, these three were surrounded by reporters to whom Goldwater announced, facing the cameras, that "there had been no decision made." They had merely reported to the President what support they thought he could count on. Rabbi Korff, also interviewed by TV as he left the White House, said that Nixon might resign unless there was a flood of support from Americans of all persuasions.

Such a response was not in the cards. By the morning of August 8, it was generally taken for granted that resignation was imminent. The morning papers were full of the plans for the Ford takeover though, officially, the many meetings going on out of camera range were nothing more than an "exchange of views about the current situation." This became a day of waiting, for both public and press, and a long wait it was. Sally Quinn has described the press room at the White House at 9:30 A.M. as:

already beginning to fill up with reporters who were to keep the day-long vigil waiting for President Nixon's resignation. . . . Around 10:30 the place was getting crowded. . . . Reporters were testing each other for that day's rumor quotient, comparing rumors, discounting them and by doing so they began to create an atmosphere of hysteria as they became worried over their deadlines.[6]

At 11:00 A.M., Gerald Warren, acting as White House spokesman, told the press that Nixon was meeting with the Vice President. There would be more news in an hour. When word went out that the noon briefing was to be given by Ron Ziegler, Quinn heard a "murmur went up. This had to be it." Cameramen began pushing reporters out of the way. Finally, at 12:30 P.M., Ziegler appeared, looking as if he were stricken, sweating as he stepped up to the podium, hands shaking as he announced that, "Tonight, at nine o'clock Eastern Daylight Time, the President of the United States will address the nation on radio and television from his Oval Office."

Ziegler's statement received live coverage only on radio; TV carried it later on videotape. Throughout the rest of the day both radio and television bulletins kept the public apprised of new developments, yet continued to exercise caution, afraid, in the words of one network executive, "to go 'live' with a possibly untrue rumor in a matter of national concern." The kind of breaking news involved in the resignation story came from nonpublic sources and so was difficult to handle, requiring "special responsibility in a time of disquiet."[7]

The diary of journalist Elizabeth Drew describes these events from the audience perspective:

A bulletin on the radio shortly before 11 A.M.: Gerald Warren has announced that in about two minutes the President and the Vice-President will meet in the Oval Office. Warren is said to have made the announcement "in a grave manner." The radio, a few minutes later: Helen Thomas, the U.P.I. White House correspondent, has written that the President has decided to resign. One cannot reach the White House by telephone. The switchboard is overloaded. The last time, to my knowledge, that the White House switchboard was overloaded was on that Saturday night when Special Prosecutor Cox was fired.

When Drew turned on her radio shortly before 12:30, she suddenly heard Ron Ziegler's voice. To her, he sounded shaken and out of breath, barely able to speak.

Here is what an "ordinary viewer" learned about these developments from reporters in a special ten minute wrap-up on CBS television immediately following Ziegler's pronouncement:[8]

Walter Cronkite was shown talking to a breathless Dan Rather who had hurried across the street from the White House because no cameras had been allowed on its grounds. Rather reported that Ziegler gave a two-minute speech, telling reporters about Nixon's planned address. Nixon was said to have met with Ford for one hour and ten minutes this morning. Rather inferred from this that "at the very least, a decision to step aside or step down" had been reached. But he did not mention resignation but went out of his way to repeat the facts about what Ziegler had to say "so that there is no misunderstanding." Rather also mentioned that Ford had looked "grim" as he walked to his own office. Asked by Cronkite about Ziegler's mood, Rather described it as "matter of fact, drawn. He coughed at least twice as frequently as he does when the announcement has tension" and he had lost weight—about 30 pounds. There was considerable strain on him and on everyone around the President, to say nothing of the "unbearable" strain on the President himself. Cronkite next asked Rather about an Associated Press report according to which John Rhodes had said that "the President will resign late this afternoon." Rather said nothing definite about resignation had emerged yet but "we must be candid and direct with our viewers. The fact is that everyone will be stunned and shocked if the President does not announce his resignation. It is taken for granted, but may not be the case, by every Republican leader that I have spoken to during the past 24 hours that Nixon will resign."

This wrap-up between Cronkite and Rather was typical of broadcast coverage during the afternoon of August 8. There were reports that Vice President Ford was delaying a twelve-day trip to Hawaii, which had been scheduled to begin at 4 P.M., of a meeting between Ford and Secretary of State Kissinger; and of statements by political leaders as to when Ford would be inaugurated. NBC reported at 2 P.M. that Tip O'Neill had said Ford would probably take office between 4 and 6 P.M. Its 4 P.M. update by John Chancellor referred to Nixon's speech tonight "at which time it is expected he will resign" effective at 11 A.M. tomorrow. On CBS Cronkite was explaining the mechanics of the transition: Nixon would send a letter to the Secretary of State, upon receipt of which he would have relinquished his office. Ford would be sworn in as soon as possible. All agreed that the likely time was Friday noon.

Prelude to Resignation

By early evening, all networks were awaiting what they now took for granted would be a resignation speech. Virtually the entire evening news dealt with the upcoming event. In fact, the anticipated speech took up a higher proportion of newstime—in terms of the number of reporter stories—than any other major news event in several years.[9] Only passing attention was given to such other news as the very considerable July increase in the wholesale price index, to the fighting in Cyprus, and to Nixon's veto of an appropriations bill, an act that CBS characterized as probably his last official act. This was hardly a new emphasis. National news had been dominated by the probable changeover ever since the "smoking gun" was found.

After the newscasts, CBS and NBC continued with two hours of special coverage while waiting for the big event. ABC had moved up its regular newscast and had two-and-a-half hours before Nixon's appearance. During this long interim, the journalists dwelt on six aspects of the story: the steps taken to assure an orderly transition, Ford's background, the absence of signs that resignation was creating a major crisis, its legitimacy, the kind of speech Nixon would make, and the prospect that he would receive amnesty.

Orderly transition. Ziegler had said the President would meet with a bipartisan group before he spoke. An AP story told of Ford having impressed on his staff the need for a smooth and orderly changeover. Ford had also met with Kissinger and would ask him and the rest of the cabinet to stay on.

The profile of the incoming President. Ford was shown performing his official duties, such as honoring seven Medal of Honor winners. There were short items about his life in Grand Rapids, Michigan, his home town.

Limits on the dimension of the crisis. A number of stories indicated that there had been no earthshaking economic or political setbacks in response to the almost certain resignation. British television had reported a mixed but generally upbeat reaction in Europe. The dollar had gained in value. The New York stock market had declined after a rise following rumors of resignation, but market analysts remained cautiously optimistic.

Legitimacy of the succession. Howard K. Smith, on ABC, reflected that, with Nixon's resignation, the nation's two top officials would be unelected. The 25th Amendment had made possible a government imposed on the American public and abolished a part of our democracy. Eric Sevareid (CBS) pointed out the Nixon administration would be dying of self-inflicted wounds.

Likely tone of the resignation speech. Resignation with dignity was judged the only safe and sane way for Nixon to depart. Some people, interviewed by reporters, hoped that the speech would not be divisive. Concern was expressed that Nixon might use the occasion for yet another attack on the news media and other enemies. NBC explained that the "tone of the speech" would determine House members' attitudes concerning amnesty and documented this in interviews. ABC and CBS linked Nixon's willingness to "confess" to the likelihood of immunity from prosecution.

The possibility of amnesty. Amnesty was the one still unresolved issue. Earlier reports had hinted that Nixon might be granted immunity from prosecution under certain conditions. Senator Brooke of Massachusetts was ready to introduce a resolution that Nixon not be prosecuted in Federal or State courts if he resigned, but only if he first made a full confession of wrongdoing. CBS specifically linked the immunity issue to the White House visit of the Republican trio the day before. Their colleagues, according to a highly reliable confidential source, had urged them, should the subject of impeachment be raised, to show the President a "sense of Congress resolution" that they could get through to give him immunity. Goldwater claimed that the subject never even came up. But while some Senators were obviously reluctant to go through with a trial, they also feared a public uproar if Congress chose to grant Nixon immunity. As everyone waited for Nixon to speak, speculation continued on what kind of a bargain might have been struck. Meanwhile, telephone calls and telegrams against immunity were said to be approximating, in number and intensity of feeling, those which had followed the firing of Cox.[10]

All this recalls the atmosphere of an election night coverage, where no one seriously expects an upset, but everyone is held in suspense until the outcome is certain. The networks set the tone first with their expectations, then with their predictions from early and very incomplete returns, and finally with their interpretations of what the outcome implies. There is also the same "sense of occasion" that one finds in the reporting of any major turn of events. As time passes and the outcome becomes more certain, other issues relating to party unity, the ability of the winner to govern, the political mood of the nation, and the direction in which it is moving become an increasingly important part of the story and take over from the reporting of returns. In other words, the election-night broadcast is more than a vote count; it is also a ritual. Awaiting the verdict, then watching the loser concede and the winner accept the concession helps to convert what began as a highly partisan political campaign into a symbolic affirmation of the democratic process.

In covering the resignation, television followed the ceremonial model of election night. The networks had preempted all prime time entertainment programs. CBS ended its coverage at midnight EDT, but NBC went on for another hour, then followed with an hour of *Tomorrow* entirely devoted to resignation and the changeover. ABC concluded at 2 A.M., after an hour of film documentary on Nixon's life.

The speech itself took only 16 minutes. Then why so much broadcast time devoted to the event? Nothing startling was expected to happen until Nixon had spoken, and neither the reporters nor the persons they interviewed had much to add in the way of new information or interpretations. To the contrary, a media critic, Alexander Cockburn, who reviewed the entire 148-page CBS transcript from 7 P.M. to midnight, wrote that "the news and interesting commentary could. . . . be boiled down to Nixon's actual speech and maybe three or four pages besides."[11] But, we would contend, the long broadcast served to frame the main event, with the continuous replays of high points in the speech and the controversy leading to resignation establishing the reality and irreversibility of what had happened. The event was inherently momentous, but would the same short speech, squeezed in between *Just For Laughs* and *King Fu* (ABC programs which were cancelled), have seemed quite the historic occasion that it was?

THE SPEECH

As the long broadcast began, what remained in doubt was only what Nixon would say and how he would say it. How would he explain his decision to resign? Would he, as some feared, attack the media or the "liberals" for having engineered his downfall? Or would he confess and acknowledge some guilt in connection with Watergate? The tone the President would strike is what injected an element of suspense.

The speech's 57 sentences dealt with four themes: the resignation and the reasons for it; the need for a smooth transition; the extent of Nixon's "guilt"; and a defense of himself and of his administration. A sentence-by-sentence analysis shows that the first three topics were touched on only in the first half of the speech. The President's rationale for resigning was dealt with in 11 of the first 25 sentences. He did not claim that he was driven from office. He did state that he was leaving reluctantly, against his own personal preferences and instincts ("I have never been a quitter") and contrary to the urgings of his "entire family." The compelling reason was that he no longer had "a strong enough political base to justify continuing" the effort to complete the term of office to which he had been elected. He was putting the "interests of the nation" before "personal considerations." Nixon repeated this "personal sacrifice" theme six times, stressing that the country needed a full-time President and a full-time Congress.

Some of this explanation was coupled with pleas that people be understanding and patient and cooperate with the new President. This need for a tranquil transition was the second main theme of the speech. Ten sentences assured the public that with Ford the leadership of America would be in good hands. The first essential was "to begin healing the wounds of the nation, to put the bitterness and divisions of the bitter past behind us. . . ." The imagery—"healing the nation"—seems to have been borrowed from

Johnson's inaugural speech after the assassination of John F. Kennedy. The tone struck was certainly what many had hoped for. Yet he abandoned this theme after the 21st sentence.

Another ten sentences, including the first five, made reference to his "guilt." Nixon admitted no crimes, only "wrong judgments." Apologies? There were none. He gave thanks to those who had supported his cause but disavowed any "bitterness" toward others who had opposed him. "Our *judgments* might differ," he said of these opponents who, he conceded, were like himself concerned with the good of the country. In his decisions, so many of which had shaped the history of the Nation, he had always tried, he insisted, "to do what was best for the country."

Hereafter the tone of the speech changed. The second half contained a predominance of statements that can only be called "self-serving"; they can be found in 22 of the last 31 sentences. Here Richard Nixon spoke of his accomplishments and extolled his own character, citing Theodore Roosevelt's preference for the man "who at the worst, if he fails, at least fails daring greatly." He also defended himself, by indirection, against the charge that he had abused the power of his office. "When I first took the oath of office as President, 5½ years ago, I made this sacred commitment: 'to consecrate my office, my energies, and all the wisdom I can summon to the cause of peace among nations.' I have done my best in all the days since to be true to that pledge."

Self-serving statements also occur in the first part of the speech in conjunction with the three other themes. When all statements relating to "self-sacrifice," to Nixon's honorable motives, and to his Presidential acts and accomplishments are counted—and we count only explicit mentions—36 of the 57 sentences (63% of the speech) were devoted to self-justification of one sort or another. It was as if the President, having chosen not to go on trial, was now appearing as his own character witness in a television defense. With the "jury" assembled, who now would appear before the cameras to rebut or affirm his testimony?

RESIGNATION NIGHT COVERAGE

The television audience for this speech was somewhere between 90 and 110 million; most news magazines and newspapers settled on the higher figure as the "official" count.[12] This was not a record audience for a television event—130 million people had watched Neil Armstrong step onto the surface of the moon. But it was probably a record for a single quarter hour, inasmuch as more people probably heard Nixon's "I shall resign" than heard Armstrong's "one small step for a man, one giant step for mankind." The moon landing was almost exclusively a video spectacular, while the Nixon speech is estimated to have had another 40 million listening on radio.

Certainly this was the largest live audience ever assembled for a televised political speech. And most stayed on to watch at least some of the coverage that followed. Between 9:30 and 10:00 P.M. EDT, the network share of the television audience was a full 90 percent. Our Long Island telephone survey found that nine of every ten adults had heard Nixon's words either as they were spoken or when they were replayed later in the evening as the speech and the coverage merged into one event.[13]

Network Analysis

No strong criticism of network "instant analysis" was to emerge from the White House where those watching reported the commentary to be "gentle. . . . with the exception of Roger Mudd, then of CBS, who had said that the President had evaded the issue and had not admitted his complicity in the coverup."[14] This impression was apparently shared by Nixon's family, who also told him that most initial reactions were "favorable," with "many of the television commentators and newspaper columnists" calling it a speech aimed at bringing the country together.[15] Outside the White House the networks also received good marks. A front–page article in the *Washington Post* (August 9) praised them for their "thoroughness [in] descending on the story with force, both in terms of personnel and in time allotted"; for the tone they had set—"it caught the spirit of the day and the general lack of anger in the country"; for "fairness" as evident in "the network correspondents' air of circumspection and avoidance of editorialization on the subject of Mr. Nixon's presidency."

Others, however, voiced misgivings; the networks had been "too fair" in their appraisal of the speech. To the *Time* media critic, the TV newsmen "appeared to be straining for evenhandedness."[16] *Newsweek*, too, noted the "somber magnanimity toward the speech itself on the part of most newsmen."[17] CBS, whose news staff had long been a major source of irritation in the White House, was chastised for "going soft" on Nixon. Dan Rather, then its White House correspondent, was singled out by *Broadcasting* as having sounded "perhaps the strangest note. [As] the CBS newsman highest on the White House enemies list, [he was] downright mournful, saying Nixon went out with a 'touch of class,' even 'nobility.' "[18] Not everyone who alleged "over-fairness" was this charitable. The media critic for the liberal *Village Voice* wrote of "Dan Rather's fall from grace among his liberal admirers when he lauded Nixon's speech."[19] The strongly liberal *Nation*, editorialized that the speech was "essentially the same kind [Nixon] . . . had made in the same setting . . . on thirty-seven prior occasions." It was "dishonest, self-serving, and evasive." In spite of this, three of the ablest TV newsmen—Cronkite, Rather, and Sevareid—had "discussed it on the CBS network in terms grotesquely at variance with the speech. 'If not his finest hour,' [Rather had said], 'it was close to it.' (Was this meant to be ironic?). . . . It was left to Roger Mudd to inject a few realistic comments."[20] Mudd had sharply criticized Richard Nixon for attributing his forced exit to Congress rather than to his own misdeeds. Although many reporters had apparently shared the feeling that Nixon should have candidly discussed his role in the coverup, Mudd "was in a clear minority during the Thursday night broadcasts."[21] Though CBS was the main target of criticism, the other networks did not go unscathed. John Chancellor (NBC) was rebuked for describing the speech as "unrestrained and statesmanlike"[22] and Howard K. Smith (ABC) for mentioning the flaws of the 25th Amendment. This reminder, wrote a critic, was hardly "urgent" at "such an emotional moment."[23]

In the opinion of most media critics, the networks had performed well. Yet some felt they had tried too hard to be fair and to cultivate an air of extreme solemnity, even of tragedy, which the speech did not warrant. Was this criticism justified?

An Evaluation

Intrigued by this novel charge that the media had been "too fair," Larry Levine, at the University of Wisconsin, undertook a systematic content analysis of network commentary.[24] Every evaluative statement concerning the President, his record in office, his behavior with regard to Watergate, his speech, and his motives for resigning was classified as either favorable or unfavorable. Aware that repetitive evaluations by a single newsman or spokesperson would influence the conclusions, he also compared the number of segments (i.e., interviews or commentaries) which included at least one favorable statement with the number containing at least one unfavorable statement—no matter how often anyone repeated his opinion, it was counted but once.

The picture that emerged, whichever measure was used, was one of reasonable quantitative balance of favorable and unfavorable comments. All networks were certainly "fair" insofar as they maintained a near-balance in statements. Overall, NBC turned out to be the least favorable in its coverage and CBS the most. Yet NBC was the one network whose news staff made more statements favorable than unfavorable to Nixon. On both ABC and CBS the balance of staff comments was unfavorable. (Appendix, table 12)

If CBS was on balance slightly more positive in its treatment of Nixon, it was not because its reporters were overly kind but because the people they interviewed were kinder in judging Nixon than those interviewed by NBC. While news personnel evidently took care—probably, as we shall see, excessive care—to give both sides of the story, they either could not, or did not try to, assure the usual balance of opinion among guests brought on camera. How to achieve this was problematic. No one could know for sure whether Republican or Democratic leaders would judge the President more kindly now that he was leaving. Yet, TV journalists are not completely at the mercy of those they interrogate; by the phrasing and tone of questions they can influence both the content and direction of responses. ABC alone seems to have been able to elicit a parity of favorable-unfavorable statements from its guests.

Post-speech coverage on all networks focused on two aspects of the event: first, what Nixon had been expected to say, what he did say, how he said it, and the reactions to it; second, the likely effects of the resignation announcement on other countries, on domestic stability, and on the November election. Yet, by exercising different options—for example, reviewing the past or stressing the future—each news team framed the event in a unique way and gave it a subtly different meaning. Thus, ABC devoted nearly one-third of its air time to non-live origination, far more than did either NBC or CBS. More than half of this consisted of film, much of it devoted to a biography of his political career, and his Presidency. There were also documentaries on Ford and on the Nixon family. This large infusion of specially prepared background material was the result of advance planning begun a year before after Elmer Lower,[25] then President of ABC news, had recommended that the network prepare for such an eventuality. ABC, which in those days often lacked the resources to provide coverage as comprehensive as that of the other networks, earned praise for its well-prepared documentary, which allowed it to stay on the air after NBC and CBS had long signed off. This advance preparation also helps explain the balanced character of its coverage. Though its coverage was by far the longest, the number of statements, by commentators or interviewees classified as "evaluations" was by far the smallest.

CBS led in the amount of live coverage, whether in form of commentary on events, studio interviews, or remote pick-ups. Its commentary, more than that of ABC or NBC, came in discussion among its reporters. CBS had also prepared special material as background, yet its "political obituary" —a videotape history of the Watergate developments that had led up to the resignation—was never shown. Instead the coverage centered on the events of the long day and the likely impact of the resignation. About 11:45P.M., four newsmen joined Cronkite for a wrap-up: they concluded that one set of institutions—the judicial-legal—had worked well but that another—the electoral system—had worked badly. As a result, the American people would have, for the first time, a President and Vice President not selected by popular vote.

NBC relied most heavily on interviews but it, too, made considerable use of its videotapes and film. These became vehicles for discussion of the future Ford administration—his stated intention to retain Kissinger as Secretary of State, the good relations he had enjoyed with Congress, his likely choice for Vice President, his noninvolvement in any of the Watergate scandals, and the prospect that he would be able to govern effectively. Although NBC balanced interviews (there were eight Democrats and two well-known critics of the Nixon administration against eleven Republicans), Levine's analysis shows that what they had to say was, on balance, unfavorable to Nixon.

Whatever their differences, all three networks treated resignation night as a ceremonial occasion, with ABC stressing the past, CBS the present, and NBC the future. ABC signaled the end of an era; CBS concentrated on the immediate political significance of the day's events. While NBC also paid a good deal of attention to the effects of the resignation, it went out of its way to invite viewers to pay attention to the new Presidency. Thus, on NBC about half the segments mentioned Ford, compared to only about a quarter on either CBS or ABC.

If some newsmen had been generous in their praise of a speech containing no admission of complicity in the coverup, this was partly because their worst fears had not been realized. For one thing, they had worried that the President might be irrational. They had heard of a highly emotional meeting with Congressional representatives an hour before the speech. The President and some of his visitors were said to be weeping openly. No one could be certain that Nixon might not lose control of himself in front of the camera.

Two years after the event, a colleague reported that Dan Rather had attributed his "over-fairness" to a sense of "relief." Earlier he had feared that "Nixon might throw away his prepared speech and do something irrational."[26]

Also, journalists (along with Congress and the public) feared that Nixon might prove a "spoiler." It was, after all, the President himself who would decide whether his speech would be part of a unifying ceremony. He could concede in the style of a gracious loser on election night and thereby invite an equally magnanimous return gesture. Or, he could treat the airtime commanded as President as yet another chance for a political maneuver. When Nixon, in their judgment, acted with a "sense of occasion," news staffs reacted with relief. Eric Sevareid, just minutes after, called it "on the whole as effective and magnanimous a speech as Mr. Nixon has ever made"; there had been no attacks on his enemies, such as those Vice-President Agnew had made after his resignation. Cronkite agreed that it had been a "conciliatory" speech "as certainly hasn't always been the case." On ABC, Harry Reasoner said the speech could not have failed to be impressive— "certainly in terms of some of the speeches Richard Nixon has made, it was not divisive."[27] It was not so much that the speech was all they might have hoped for, but rather that it had not confirmed their worst fears.

CBS management, especially, had worried that Nixon might attack the news media and accuse the press of hounding him out of office. In 1962, he had directed his anger at losing the gubernatorial race in California against those who had covered his campaign, as he told the assembled press, "You won't have Richard Nixon to kick around any more." Would he repeat this performance? Arthur Taylor, then corporate president of CBS, had shared with Daniel Schorr his concern that Nixon "might make a vicious attack on the news media—especially CBS, which he regarded as his most implacable foe." Hearing that a crowd was gathered outside the White House, Taylor's concern extended to the safety of the CBS personnel:

He believed that 10 percent of the crowd was capable, under certain circumstances, of cruelty and violence, and he told Socolow [the Washington bureau chief], "Keep an eye on security—we're responsible for the safety of our CBS News people." His longer range worry was that Nixon might polarize the nation on the subject of television, precipitating the long-feared uprising against the news media. I agreed that everything we knew about Nixon justified such a fear.[28]

Schorr further contends that once CBS learned—by means unknown to him—that there would be a "kind of tacit truce,"[29] reporters were cautioned by management not to be too vindictive. Taylor has publicly denied this charge, first made at Duke University in response to a question about "CBS going soft on Nixon" (January 17, 1975). It was "absolutely preposterous" that any expression of concern by him could have led to an order to tone down the resignation coverage. Both Cronkite and Rather denied receiving any such instruction. There are different views, but one thing is clear: CBS producers and newsmen that evening agreed among themselves that "This is not a night for recrimination."[30] Later, Richard Salant, then president of CBS News, said he had killed the "political obituary" and also given instructions to Bill Leonard, a CBS News vice president (later president), to "emphasize continuity in government, not to jump up and down in glee on Nixon's body, but to concentrate on the transition." He should have known that on this rare occasion when he had issued instructions for covering a news event, Salant reportedly told Schorr, people would go further than he intended.[31]

No explicit suggestions to put a damper on critical commentary would really have been needed. Most journalists made an assumption about the mood of the country. There was some feeling that most people wanted to be done with the whole affair. They were tired of Watergate, and this could create a potential for anger against the media as the bearer of bad tidings. In covering resignation, television saw itself almost as much on trial as the President himself. As long as Nixon remained mindful of the national interest and left the White House in a dignified way, without seeking to play on partisan passions, it would be incumbent upon television not to do anything to detract from that performance.

Once it was clear that Nixon would play the gracious loser, the news organizations could respond with the magnanimous gesture of a winner and stress the unity theme, treating the event as part of a ceremony of transition. Because CBS had been so much a part of the Watergate controversy, some of its best-known newsmen felt under particular scrutiny. It would surely have been difficult for Dan Rather, who had been so visible a target of Nixon's hostility, not to be conscious of his personal feelings in responding to the speech. In his book on the adventures of a TV journalist, Rather makes no mention of his controversially non-controversial comments during the coverage.[32] According to a second-hand account, he arrived at the CBS studio shortly before Nixon went on the air and had no time to think about what he wanted to say. But his friends thought he "was acutely aware that night of everyone looking at him as if somehow his finger were on the gun—what will Dan Rather be like, will he be gloating—and that he had very simply bent over backward."[33]

Public Response

The common focus of attention provided by the long evening of television coverage may have had more effect on the public response to resignation than what commentators said or what fill-ins were used. So continuous and riveting was the drama, that it was made to appear as the last act in a national tragedy. In staying with the resignation story for so many hours, television was reenacting its own performance after the assassination of President Kennedy in 1963. Then, the networks had been praised for the role they played. By supplying information, they had scotched rumors and averted panic, allowing the whole nation to mourn together. Television had assumed that same function in helping the nation through the tragic loss of Robert Kennedy and Martin Luther King, both in 1968. By providing a focus for the expression of indignation and grief, as viewers participated vicariously in the rituals of leavetaking, television had provided a vehicle for beginning the process of "nation-healing."

The resignation of a President under threat of impeachment was obviously different from the undeserved tragedy that had befallen another President. Yet, the tragedy in the evening's developments was touched on by a number of those who appeared on camera. It was incoming President Ford himself who, in his brief televised remarks after the speech, defined the official mood by calling the resignation "one of the saddest incidents in U.S. history." Both Edmund Brown, former Democratic Governor of California, and Herbert Klein, once in the Nixon White House, also spoke of the "sense of tragedy." For Carl Albert, Speaker of the House, the element of tragedy lay in Nixon's desperate effort "not to say he was framed." "Sad" also became a favorite description of the mood in the nation's capital, used by both Democrats (such as Senator Henry Jackson) and Republicans (such as George Bush). In calling this a "sad" occasion, Bush hastened to say he did not mean to leave the impression of being "relieved."

We lack an adequate record of the immediate public response to the resignation. With so many people remaining at home to watch TV, reporters assigned to tap this response had to grasp at straws. The main "response story," both on TV and in the print media, focused on a crowd estimated at anywhere from one to three thousand people gathered along Pennsylvania Avenue and in Lafayette Park across from the White House. *Newsweek* (August 19) described this as a "mostly young and hirsute crowd [that] danced in the night . . . whooping 'Jail to the Chief' and 'Executive Deleted.' " *Time* (August 19) termed it "exuberant." Yet on the air, Robert Schieffer of

CBS was "a bit surprised" and possibly, given the apprehensions of CBS management, relieved that it was "as good-spirited a crowd as it is." When TV viewers, watching the scene outside the White House, pondered the significance of loud honking from cars they could hear yet not see, they were soon informed that this came not from a caravan of celebrants but from impatient drivers delayed by a traffic accident. Another crowd, in San Francisco, was "not happy" and "not jubilant." The response of a crowd at a baseball game between the Minnesota Twins and the Kansas City Royals was described in an Associated Press report: the cheer that followed an announcement of Nixon's resignation "carried the same volume as that accompanying a double play by the home team." Some people had been listening to the speech on their portable radios. One couple who had been camping at Yosemite National Park told us that the news brought out people from all over the campsite. In this instance, one of the few cases of spontaneous public celebration we have heard of, the campers had no television coverage to divert them.

But what of those watching? In Springfield, Missouri, reporters sampled the reactions of people who had watched the speech on television screens at a local shopping center and at the Ozark Empire Fairgrounds. They summed the responses of 56 people, most of whom, presumably, had voted for Nixon (as had 73 percent of voters in the Ozarks), as: no weeping, no real glee; sadness, a little delight, a lot of acceptance. More than half articulated the "personal tragedy" theme, indicating that they felt "sorry" for the President or "sad" after the speech. Typical was the response of one man who spoke of his "very mixed emotions. This is a sad day—a tragic day. [The President] did the right thing. The country, for the biggest part, was against him and he couldn't function to the extent he should have. It would have been better if it had never happened." [34]

Nixon's resignation, judging by these reports, had saddened but not angered those who supported him. Was there also resentment? Reporters had to work hard to come by examples of anger, despair, or organized protest. One instance, dug up by *Time* (August 19), concerned angry calls to a television station in Grand Rapids, the home town of Gerald Ford, after it had shown people celebrating at a local bar. On the Op-Ed page of the *New York Times* (August 13) a Burlington, Vermont, newspaper editor referred to the transition of power as an unconstitutional and immoral "bloodless revolution." A Nixon supporter made news on August 18 by putting up in her front picture window a four-foot color poster of the President that she said she might keep there "forever." Not to be outdone, Rabbi Korff of the National Committee for Fairness to the President and George Dumas, head of another anti-impeachment group, vowed to keep up their fight against the "giants of the media" which had done such a "hatchet job" and now were "fearful of history judging them as assassins." [35]

Most descriptions of the mood on resignation night emphasized relief. The public response was curiously muted. The anticipated flood of post-speech phone calls simply did not materialize. In at least one Western city extra long-distance telephone operators had been hired to handle the overload but were said to have had nothing to do. By the time most public opinion surveys, including our own, were in the field, the responses tapped were no longer uncontaminated reactions. Not only had there been considerable commentary in the press but three other televised events could have influenced attitudes towards the resignation and the President himself.

On Friday morning Nixon had bade a televised personal farewell to his Cabinet and the White House staff in the East Room of the White House. Although a "public event," it might more appropriately have remained a "privileged event." It was the most emotionally charged appearance Richard Nixon had ever made and one could only wonder that he got through it without breaking down. In a rambling talk, he reminisced about his father and especially his mother. As tears welled in his eyes, he depicted her as a saint about whom no books would ever be written. And, moralizing, he ended with this advice, "Always remember, others may hate you, but those who hate you don't win unless you hate them—and then you destroy yourself." On the screen the family could be seen fighting back tears; others in the room were openly weeping.

The second major television event was the swearing-in of President Ford at noon. In a brief speech, he sought to assure his large national audience that he would be President of all the people. He asked all to purge their hearts of suspicion and of hate, and invited their sympathy for the departing President:

I ask again your prayers for Richard Nixon and his family. May our former President, who brought peace to millions find it for himself. May God bless and comfort his wonderful wife and daughters whose love and loyalty will forever be a shining legacy to all who bear the lonely burdens of the White House.

In the third of these events, a televised appearance before Congress on the evening of August 12, Ford moved to make it clear that a new leader was at the helm. He announced several opening moves against inflation, pledged to have an open administration with regard to both domestic and foreign policy, and emphasized his belief in "the absolute necessity of a free press." He insisted that there would be no illegal wiretapping, eavesdropping, bugging, or break-ins. And, assuring that the days of confrontation and controversy were over, he pledged to be President "of the black, brown, red and white Americans, of old and young, of women's liberationists and male chauvinists and all the rest of us in between . . ."

It is our estimate, based on a reading of available polls, that by the time Ford had moved to establish the authenticity of his own Presidency, about eight out of every ten adults applauded the outcome of "two years of Watergate." More than one, but certainly no more than two, out of ten were distinctly unhappy. A special telephone poll by Gallup (for *Newsweek*)[36] immediately after the speech showed 79 percent believing that Nixon did the "best thing" by resigning while just 13 percent thought he should have stayed. Our survey in heavily Republican Suffolk County, New York, which began August 12, indicated an identical 79 percent believing that he was "right to resign" and 11 percent believing he had done the wrong thing. Support for resignation was overwhelming, even among Republicans.

A Range of Emotions

To the overwhelming majority of people, the resignation did not come as a complete surprise. The expectation of a premature end to the Nixon Presidency absorbed much of the shock and tempered the response. But some people had been expecting it longer than others. Accordingly, we hypothesized that individual responses would reflect the amount of time they had had to grow accustomed to the possibility. With this in mind, we classified our sample of adults in Suffolk County according to the point in time when they had come to accept the idea that Nixon would either have to resign or face impeachment.

20 percent were *early deciders* who had reached this conclusion by the time the Ervin hearings adjourned in August 1973

25 percent were *late deciders* who so concluded at some point after Cox's dismissal in October 1973 but before the impeachment hearings began

41 percent were only lately *reconciled* to the idea, swayed directly by the impeachment hearings or, indirectly, later as the "smoking gun" surfaced

14 percent were as yet *unreconciled* to the need for Nixon's resignation

This distribution, though based on only one locality, is in reasonable accord with what we know about the movement of opinion on impeachment from June 1972 through August 1974.

Now looking at the four groups, we found, not unexpectedly, that they differed politically. All of the unreconciled, except for some acknowledged nonvoters, had voted Republican in 1972 and were strongly conservative in their orientation. Among those lately reconciled the proportion of Nixon voters, though a strong majority, was much smaller; as many as a third either had not voted in the last election or had voted for McGovern. The late deciders had divided their vote rather evenly between Nixon and McGovern. Only the group of early deciders consisted entirely of McGovern supporters.

Though all groups found some satisfaction in Nixon's resignation, each responded differently. What follows is a brief profile by way of explaining the reactions that characterized each group.

The Early Deciders. Those who, for a year or more, had believed the President would be compelled to leave office were mainly young adults with at least some college education. Now they refused to countenance the idea that in resigning Nixon had given any thought whatsoever to what was good for the country. Almost all thought his only motive was to escape impeachment and half wanted the impeachment to go forward nevertheless. What most distinguished this group from the others was their attitude toward Nixon. They simply could not comprehend why others had not also opted for impeachment as early as they. They suspected that these others had either avoided the facts or had an absolutely "blind faith in Nixon." Generally cynical about the level of morality in government, they had been fascinated by the Senate Watergate hearings, which they could still recall in vivid detail. How could anyone not have recognized then that Nixon was "at least a liar?" One person opined that some people had been against impeachment because they were "too patriotic and [therefore] gullible while others felt guilty because they voted for McGovern and didn't want to appear prejudiced against the President."

Most early deciders had continued, when the Senate hearings ended, to follow Watergate news but some, having grown increasingly pessimistic that Nixon might get away with it after all, had "given up" on Watergate. Now, however, all were generally pleased at the outcome—not ecstatic or triumphant—but *pleased* that what they had long considered the only real alternative to a trial by the Senate had finally come to pass. The degree of pleasure was related to how involved the interviewee had become in the controversy over the tapes and over impeachment. Still, few felt inclined to celebrate, since they did not view resignation as a complete victory nor did they regard it as the ultimate end to the Watergate controversy. The need for Nixon to remove himself from office was not sufficient punishment. Their common feeling, as one inelegantly expressed it: "He should have been convicted with a five-year sentence. Any private citizen would have been thrown in the can."

The Late Deciders. Almost all late deciders believed that Nixon had been right to resign but they doubted that, in doing so, his concern had been mainly for the country. Despite widespread skepticism on this point, three out of four felt more optimistic about the future than they had a year ago. Beyond this core of agreement, the late deciders divided in their specific responses to the resignation, depending on how closely they had been following the impeachment controversy via the mass media.

There was, on the one hand, a majority who were Watergate "freaks." They had been insatiable followers of events, knew a good deal more about Watergate than the average respondent, had frequently talked to others about the issue, and described themselves as very much preoccupied with it. They were far more likely than the early deciders to stress the importance of having all the facts brought out in public. They also were by far the most vocal group in their praise of the news media for bringing the scandal into the open. Television came in for their special praise. Their response to Watergate fell into a pattern. The seeds of suspicion about Nixon's veracity had been planted by the Senate hearings, especially by the Dean testimony. Yet most continued to give the President the benefit of the doubt until the investigation had run its course and all the facts had been brought out. Finally, they had become convinced by events—mainly by Nixon's obstructionist tactics—that there was sufficient cause to compel Nixon to leave office. They responded to resignation with renewed faith in elected politicians. They were *proud* that the system worked. Some "thanked God that the truth was out." Now Nixon, they believed, should not be immune from prosecution because "no man is above the law."

On the other hand, there was a minority of late deciders who had "tuned out" once Nixon's persistent refusal to release the information on the tapes convinced them that his claim of noncomplicity in Watergate would not stand up. Hence, they were surprisingly uninformed about the developments that had led to the resignation. They responded with *relief* to Nixon's speech, having experienced the continuation of the man they considered "guilty of everything from the word 'go' " as an almost intolerable burden. Some of these late deciders were Democrats who had voted for Nixon and then felt personally betrayed. Having him resign helped to rectify things, but they were quite uncharitable in their references to the fallen President. Epithets like "crook" and "liar" flowed easily from their lips.

The Reconciled. The whole atmosphere created by the impeachment hearings and the surfacing of the incriminating tapes had made it difficult for the lately reconciled to sustain their belief in Nixon's innocence of impeachable crimes. This was true even of those who had watched very little of the live hearings and were exposed only to excerpts on television news or in the newspapers. All reacted with relief to the resignation but for different reasons.

First, some were relieved because they had grown weary of the continued national preoccupation with Watergate. They had long hoped that the President could prove himself innocent, and clutched at every straw to sustain this belief. At the end, they had become convinced that Nixon was indeed guilty of an impeachable offense—at least of obstructing justice and most probably of "abuse of power." Half judged him guilty of at least one other charge—income tax evasion, the illegal use of public monies, or having waged war illegally. Consequently, they did not regard the resignation as an act of altruism, as did the unreconciled. The outcome satisfied them because it meant that impeachment proceedings would now be cut short. Relieved that Watergate was over, and with their long uncertainty at an end, they now felt optimistic about the future.

A second, and altogether different ground for relief, was that Nixon had avoided a trial. These people had been less concerned over the question of Nixon's guilt or innocence than about his ability to win out in the coming trial. Even after the passage of the articles of impeachment, they had been counting on him to "grandstand" it. Now, with the evidence out, this was no longer a viable prospect. Resignation, as they saw it, was the only way to avoid a trial in which he stood little chance of acquittal. "His only guilt," said one 54-year old mechanic, a political conservative, "was lying about his knowledge in the coverup. . . . The man was an idiot, a nut. When the tapes were first revealed, he should have said, 'They're secret. I'll destroy them.' What could they do besides impeach him? They're not going to shoot the man. I'd have destroyed the tapes and said, 'You take it from there.' " This man and others lately reconciled felt Nixon's only crime was having been caught. The media and the House Judiciary Committee had been out to get him, wanting to impeach him for what everyone else does. Still, they had thought he would weather the storm. The surfacing of the tapes had demolished their faith in Nixon's ability to "hack it." The "smoking gun" had gotten too much publicity, and they preferred to have Nixon resign rather than be removed by the impeachment process. So they, too, were relieved.

The Unreconciled. The common judgment of those yet unreconciled was that Nixon—to quote one respondent—was "guilty of nothing except, perhaps, tax evasion," which hardly was sufficient ground for impeachment. They thought Nixon was wrong to have resigned. He should have stuck it out, but they were ready to believe the President when he said that, in resigning, his main thought had been for his country. Asked whether he had resigned to escape impeachment or because, as Nixon put it, he had "lost his base of political support in Congress," five out of every six accepted the President's explanation. But since they thought he should not have been so hard pressed to resign, they were by far the least optimistic about the future of the country.

They were unanimous in regarding Nixon not as the perpetrator of any crime but as a "victim," whom a full investigation would eventually have exonerated. If he had lied, as some acknowledged, he had lied for the "good of the country," out of a concern about the possibility that, as Nixon had put it, the "FBI investigation might lead to the exposure either of unrelated covert activities of the CIA, or of sensitive national security matters that the so-called plumbers unit at the White House had been working on. . . ."[37] Thus, they believed the President when he explained his behavior and resignation as governed by "higher motives" of this sort. Yet, in one man's own words, "we forced a President out of office without knowing all the details" and this made him unhappy about the resignation. If only Nixon had gone through with impeachment, the true story would have been revealed, with a full impeachment hearing serving as a corrective to the slanted and biased reporting of Watergate.

In the opinion of those yet unreconciled, the House Judiciary Committee probe had been unfair. So, too, the Senate hearings. The Senators had asked silly questions and John Dean had been a liar. Yet they expressed surprisingly little anger at the way things had turned out, precisely because they accepted Nixon's act as the purest form of altruism. Their admiration for their elected leader and the satisfaction they felt in the style with which he took his leave was coupled with pride that "our country can wash its dirty linen in public." To this extent Nixon's insistence in his televised speech that "as President I must put the interests of America first" apparently had helped his loyal-to-the-end supporters to define the situation as he did. One, who had been an activist in Rabbi Korff's movement, told an interviewer, "We can make the transition calmly. I still feel we have more freedoms than any other country. Let's face it—in how many countries could something like this happen and you'd even hear about it?"

To recapitulate the mood that marked the resignation of Richard Nixon and the change in administrations: it was a mix of satisfaction, pride, relief, and some sadness; but almost no anger. The early deciders were *pleased* to have been proved right all along but not quite sure what resignation would imply: would Nixon escape all further punishment for his indictable acts, all perpetrated in the name of patriotism? The late deciders were *proud* of the system; it had evidently worked as it should have in dispensing justice but with "due process." Those only lately reconciled to the need for impeachment were *relieved* that Nixon had chosen to resign rather than forcing them to face the agony of impeachment, which the "smoking gun" had made inevitable. Those yet unreconciled were somewhat *disillusioned and unhappy* but not bitter or vengeful.

If some media critics were offended by what they saw as the networks' bending over backwards to be fair in their treatment of Nixon on resignation night, not a single person we interviewed was ready to fault their coverage— and certainly not those unreconciled to the need for his departure. One of these viewers explained that, as she watched on resignation night, she could tell that the sympathy she felt for the President was being shared by the reporters. "The media," she said, "had pressed the case too hard." Then, when he resigned, they were "shocked" because it was "like they opened Pandora's box."

Once debate over Watergate had ceased, media treatment of the resignation and, therefore, of the transition with its focus on Ford, adhered to the format of a unifying ceremony. Open dissent had no place in the surface display of good will to everyone. Not only the incoming President but Nixon as well was treated gingerly, at least until Ford's unconditional pardon revived the old animosities. Post-resignation commentary gave scant recognition to rumors of some kind of a deal. Instead, the cameras and reporters immediately sought out Ford, much as they would any President-elect. Coverage was built around unifying events and common concerns rather than behind-the-scenes activities with their potentially divisive effects. This is not to say that the specific events that marked the transition—the inauguration of Gerald Ford, and his first address to Congress—took place only because the press was there to report them. It was that the presence of the news media added a necessary dimension by enlarging the circle of participants. Watching television, everyone could join in ceremonies that were familiar and uplifting occasions for looking forward and forgetting, if not forgiving, the past. By performing its ceremonial function, television not only made the transition of power a "reality," but made it seem less extraordinary than it actually was.

CHAPTER 9

PUBLIC OPINION AND THE PARDON

On September 8, 1974, exactly one month after the resignation, Gerald Ford granted ex-President Richard M. Nixon a "full, free and absolute pardon . . . for all offenses against the United States which he had committed or may have committed or taken part in" during his tenure as President of the United States. Nixon accepted, expressing his hope that this "compassionate act will contribute to lifting the burden of Watergate from our country." Neither he nor Ford specifically mentioned what was being forgiven. Again, Nixon admitted to nothing more than "mistakes and misjudgments," which had caused many people to see his "motivations and actions in the Watergate affair [as] intentionally self-serving and illegal."

Under the agreement between the ex-President and the General Services Administration Nixon was to retain possession of his Presidential papers and of the controversial White House tapes which, for at least three years, were to be held in a government facility near San Clemente where he could control access to them. All tapes were to be destroyed by September 1, 1984—or earlier should Nixon die before that date.

REACTIONS TO THE PARDON

Restrained as the response to resignation had been, just so unrestrained were the expressions of indignation that swept the country after the pardon. On Capitol Hill some prestigious Republicans joined Democrats in deploring Ford's action: Senator Brooke labelled the blanket pardon without a full confession a "serious mistake"; Senator Packwood of Oregon declared that "no man is literally above the law." Some House members called for a revival of impeachment proceedings. Jerald ter Horst, the newly appointed White House press secretary, immediately resigned in protest and as a matter of conscience.[1] Phillip Lacovara, a Republican and top member of the Watergate Special Prosecution Force, also resigned; the ground had been cut out from under it. Members of the Watergate grand jury were quoted

(NBC Nightly News, September 9) as feeling betrayed. Wives and lawyers of convicted Nixon associates said they would press for similar pardons or reduced sentences. Most outspoken was Martha Mitchell, the estranged wife of the former Attorney General, who charged in a television interview that the whole thing had been arranged before Nixon left office, a suspicion other public figures dared whisper only in private.[2]

The pardon once more made Watergate the major news story. Network news highlighted the cynical reactions of the ordinary citizen. A CBS reporter (CBS Evening News, September 10) talked with four persons just convicted by the San Francisco municipal court, one for public drunkenness, another on a drug possession charge, a third for driving a car with a faulty muffler, and the fourth for overtime parking. All complained about unequal treatment before the law—little guys aren't treated like big guys. A North Dakota judge made national news on two networks (September 9) when he dismissed two traffic offenders whom he ordinarily would have sent to jail because they would only be pardoned by the President.

These reactions reported by the news media were not, however, isolated instances. In the first few days after the pardon, some 110,000 telegrams, mailgrams, and personal messages reached Washington, according to Western Union. Telegrams being received by the President and on Capitol Hill were overwhelmingly negative. According to Deputy Press Secretary John Hushen, opinion ran about 5 to 1 against the pardon. Senator Howard Baker's mail was against Ford's action by 9 to 1. For the first time in his short tenure in office Ford became the target of hostile feelings. He was publicly booed as he arrived in Pittsburgh to address a transportation conference. The White House acknowledged calls running at least 2 to 1 and telegrams 5 to 1 against the pardon.[3]

The Public Response

CBS was the first with a poll on reaction to the pardon (September 10); this showed the public disapproving by 2 to 1. Two days later the *New York Times* front-paged the results of a specially commissioned telephone poll conducted by Gallup on September 10, in which 62 percent disapproved. A third poll, by NBC, also reported on September 12, painted a similar picture: some 60 percent disapproved.

Much of the objection, it appeared, was not so much to a pardon for Nixon as to a pardon without either a trial or a full confession by the ex-President. Of every ten persons who expressed disapproval, four would have been opposed under any circumstances but six disapproved on the ground that they wanted a trial before any pardon was issued. If one assumes that the latter were objecting not on principle but to the timing of the pardon, then this group, together with those who approved Ford's action, add up to a better than two-thirds majority who, at a later date or under different circumstances, might not have been so opposed.[4] This accords with the finding of a Harris poll (September 22–27) where people were asked whether they would have felt better about the pardon had Nixon beforehand made a full confession of his guilt or been brought to trial. A majority said they would have felt better.

After the pardon, these questions about a confession or a trial were, of course, hypothetical. Yet, just before the pardon (Gallup, September 6–9) 55 percent of all Americans had favored a trial and been less than enthusiastic about pardoning the ex-President should he be found guilty. A Roper survey in late August had posed the question this way:

Some people feel that former President Nixon should be vigorously prosecuted on the charges against him just as many citizens would be, and sent to jail if convicted or it will mean we have two standards of justice in this country. Others feel he has paid an extremely high penalty already by leaving the Presidency and no further action should be taken against him. Still others feel he should be prosecuted on at least some charges to establish his guilt or innocence and given a light or suspended sentence if he is found guilty. Do you think he should be prosecuted *fully*, prosecuted *lightly*, or *not* prosecuted at all?[5]

The responses (in percent) were as follows:

43, fully
19, lightly
32, not at all
6, don't know

These are clear indications that most Americans had not wanted the ex-President to get off scot-free. A *Newsday* poll (September 3) found an even split: asked whether "former President Nixon should be prosecuted for his role in Watergate," 46 percent said "yes" and 46 percent said "no." Respondents were then asked to choose among three statements the one that coincided most closely with their own feelings toward the former President:

(1) He already had suffered enough and should be left alone
(2) He should be prosecuted but, if convicted, not sent to prison
(3) He should be prosecuted and, if convicted, treated like any other citizen

With the question so refined, 59 percent now expressed their approval of prosecution, 24 percent conditionally *only* if the former President would not have to go to jail.

None of this explains why people felt as they did about immunity or punishment. Our post-resignation survey, also on Long Island, asked those favoring immunity to choose between justifications: the potentially divisive effect on the country versus the belief that resignation was punishment enough. Two thirds found both reasons important and could not choose between them. On the other hand, two thirds of those opposing immunity from prosecution pointed to the need for "equality before the law" as their overriding concern; a minority thought a trial was needed as the "only way to get the full story out."[6] Ford's justification of the pardon had echoed the views of those opposed to further prosecution but had not addressed the objections of those who believed that Nixon should be brought to justice like any other citizen.

These findings, taken together, suggest that after the resignation, there had been general agreement on Nixon's guilt but considerable disagreement about the appropriate penalty for his transgressions. Most important, the punishment issue had become for most citizens a matter to be settled through the appropriate courts and not through political bargaining. Most people would have been ready to accept a jury verdict, whatever it might be, but with Ford's granting of the unconditional pardon, the question of appropriate punishment had become repoliticized. Approving the pardon were mainly those who remained unreconciled to the need for Nixon's resignation and those who had accepted it out of relief that the long struggle had come to an end. On the other side were some who were upset by the pardon and were searching for more than abstract justice; they resented Nixon's being the beneficiary of a pardon denied to others, including his closest aides, Haldeman and Ehrlichman. Others feared that, as long as the exact extent of Nixon's culpability remained buried, people would soon forget why he had had to resign.

There was almost as much anger over the tapes agreement as over the pardon. A mid-August NBC survey[7] indicated that 74 percent of the public wanted all Presidential tapes and papers turned over to the special prosecutor and courts. No doubt, some were moved by a concern for justice, as these documents might be needed for evidence in the trials of Watergate defendants. And there was also the concern, real to many, that the tapes be preserved for history so that one day the truth might come out. But there had also been deep resentment at the "President's men" making money off

Watergate. Letters to *Time* (August 19), for example, denounced book publishers for allowing "Watergate criminals" to profit from their crimes. Now
there was the prospect that Nixon might do the same. Newspapers were
reporting that the ex-President was to retire to San Clemente, where with a
generous pension and a paid staff, he could work on his memoirs, aided by
the tapes now to be placed in his custody. People feared that, when finished,
he could destroy the tapes and, since he would never be subject to cross-
examination in a court, have the final word on Watergate. He also stood to
make a fortune on his memoirs; the advance offered by a book company
was reported to be in excess of two million dollars.[8] The record of the Nixon
Presidency preserved in the tapes—carefully edited, of course—could not be
worth much less.

While the pardon could not be undone, the tapes agreement was revok-
able. On September 11, a U.S. district judge issued a temporary stay barring
the White House from going ahead with the transfer of the tapes. (The
government was already planning to spend $110,000 to install and guard a
vault for the records near Nixon's San Clemente home.) Three days later
the White House capitulated. No transfer was to take place without prior
discussion with the special prosecution task force. By September 24, a Senate committee had voted to repeal the agreement through which Nixon was
to retain custody and control of the tapes and of Watergate-related papers.
Although Nixon would have access to the tapes, they were forever to remain
under government control. Their destruction would require a specific legislative act.

Whether responding to the vindictive mood of the country or their own
indignation, members of Congress quickly acted to restrict some of the privileges that Nixon was enjoying as an ex-President. Senators on an appropriations subcommittee balked at a request for $850,000 to cover Nixon's
pension and expenses through June 1975, calling this an "unprecedented
amount." Noting that a staff of 13 persons assigned to Nixon full-time was
costing the taxpayers $340,000 per annum, Congress voted to discontinue
payment for a maid and a butler and to cut in half the funds requested for
transition money.

Public Opinion as a Factor in the Pardon Decision

The emotional reaction to the pardon should have been anticipated. But
did Gerald Ford have any reason to believe controversy over this decision
would be short-lived?

One poll, just after Nixon resigned, indicated a great deal of sympathy for the ex-President's plight. Asked in a special telephone poll Gallup conducted for *Newsweek* on August 11, "Do you think it should be agreed not to press an investigation of possible criminal charges against [Nixon]?" the public by 55 to 37 percent favored letting bygones be bygones.

This was the only poll to indicate so charitable a reaction. In Suffolk County, on August 12, people were opposed to immunity by a ratio of 47 to 45. On August 16, NBC, in a nationwide telephone poll, reported the same rather even split, 48 to 46 against further punishment and 47 to 45 against requiring the ex-President to stand trial. The regular Gallup poll taken August 16–19 found well over half the public believing that "Nixon should be brought to trial for possible criminal charges arising from Watergate." And when the same question was repeated on September 6–9 there was almost no change. Two other national polls taken in early September showed similar support for continued prosecution (Appendix, table 13).

The *Newsweek* poll with the first news of public response to the resignation may have left a deeper impression than later polls, which showed less sympathy for Nixon's plight. The findings made news on NBC August 12 and in newspapers throughout the country. Most significantly, the poll caught the attention of those who had to decide whether or not to prosecute. "Just about this time," wrote two staff attorneys in the office of the Special Prosecutor, "the press reported that a Gallup poll taken shortly after Nixon's resignation disclosed that 55% of those interviewed thought Mr. Nixon should now be 'left alone' rather than brought to trial."[9] Jaworski himself, pondering whether Nixon could receive a fair trial, found the polls "indefinite.
. . . Shortly before the resignation, a majority polled was opposed to special consideration for Nixon [probably a reference to a California poll]; several days after the resignation a majority polled opposed further investigation of him"—undoubtedly a reference to the Gallup/*Newsweek* poll.[10] And what concrete evidence, other than the *Newsweek* poll, could have led Gerald Ford to believe, in Nelson Rockefeller's words, that the public now that "Nixon had been hung" didn't believe "he should be drawn and quartered?"[11]

Why should the findings of this one poll have belied the evidence coming not only from other polls but also from the flood of letters, mailgrams, telegrams, and telephone calls? First, was the poll—given the small sample size—in error? The larger the sample, the more confidence one can have that the observed proportion holding any attitude approximates that in the entire population. The sample was 550, compared to 1500 reached in the later NBC poll. A second source of potential error lies in the wording of the question. Respondents, in the Gallup/*Newsweek* poll, were being asked over the telephone whether "it should be *agreed not* to press an investigation of possible criminal charges." A "yes" answer meant agreement *not* to press charges; a "no" answer that charges *should* be pressed. This may have caused some confusion. Beyond that, an "agree" option always enjoys a mild advantage, as much as five percentage points over the "disagree" option.[12] In the next special *Newsweek* poll on September 5, the question was, in fact, revised considerably, and the opinion division on immunity was the exact opposite to that found on August 11.

Taken at face value, the findings suggest that the early poll tapped a momentary groundswell of compassion, following Nixon's emotional farewell and Ford's expressions of sympathy for the family. A photograph of Julie Nixon Eisenhower and her father in tearful embrace, featured on many front pages, personalized the nature of the tragedy. But any swell of sympathy must have dissipated within days. The polls in early September, just before the pardon, indicated opinion was still polarized over immunity, but these findings were not published until after Ford acted. We have not been able to establish with any certainty that the results were furnished the White House prior to their release, though such requests are often made and honored.[13] But even if the returns from the September polls came too late to influence Ford, he and his advisors must have been aware of the strong opposition indicated in the mid-August readings. Therefore, the pardon must have been a calculated gamble to risk the public furor that did indeed follow. The new President took it despite prior assurances that he would be bound by the public will. During the hearings on his confirmation as Vice President, when asked whether, if it came down to it, he would pardon Nixon, Ford had replied that the public would not stand for it.[14] That was in October 1973. Now, in issuing the pardon, he said, "I cannot rely on public opinion to tell me what is right."

Although Ford, in later hearings before the House Judiciary Committee, denied that he had entered into an agreement of any sort with Nixon, this does not exclude some tacit understanding. Ford had repeatedly expressed his personal sympathy for Nixon. As a party loyalist, anxious to get Watergate off the Republican back, he was willing to risk the storm of protest, in the expectation that it would soon subside. He could not have counted on much help from Capitol Hill to weather it. There, a sense-of-Congress resolution against further prosecution had been circulating just before the resignation but Senator Brooke, an original sponsor of the idea, had withdrawn his support after Nixon's speech, which he considered an "arrogant affront" to the nation. Other prestigious leaders, in and outside Congress, had also stated their opposition to immunity; the president of the American Bar Association had publicly asked that Richard Nixon's name be added to the list of those already indicted for conspiracy in the Watergate case.

The White House had nevertheless been testing public response as its spokesmen, at intervals, insinuated that prosecution was neither desirable nor inevitable. Less than three weeks after taking office, Ford himself had responded to a reporter's question about whether he "would use [his] pardon authority," by letting it be known that he "was not ruling it out. It is an option and a proper option for any President." In the last ten days or two weeks, he said, he had been asking "for prayers and guidance on this very important point." [15] Here he was appealing to a charitable impulse that he apparently assumed to be more widespread than it actually was, at least according to the polls.

The President and his advisors were also hoping to cash in on Ford's popularity. According to press and polling assessments, Ford had won the confidence of the American people, who viewed him as honest and candid. Would they not then accept his decision as an "honest" one? *Washington Post* columnist David Broder was to say after the pardon that the public had been expecting too much of the new President; now they were disappointed. *Washington Star* columnist Mary McGrory thought his ecstatic press notices had led Ford to believe that a contented public would accept his explanation for the decision, however unpopular. [16] Perhaps, as the talk went, he had come to think of himself as Eisenhower, the great healer.

Yet another factor in deciding whether to pardon was the intention of the Special Watergate Prosecutor. With impeachment cut short and Nixon again an ordinary citizen, the responsibility for pressing the case against the former President fell into his hands. A decision by Jaworski not to prosecute would obviously have been welcomed by Ford. But Jaworski and the large majority of his staff were split on whose responsibility this was. Most of the staff saw the decision *not* to prosecute as strictly political and outside the legal domain. They were aware, as was Jaworski, that the public reaction would be a consideration. Would it be too divisive were Nixon to be indicted along with the other Watergate conspirators? If public sentiment was for indictment, would the decision *not* to prosecute be even more divisive? As they saw it, the decision not to prosecute had to be made by a body accountable to the electorate, while it was up to the Special Prosecutor to decide whether the case against Nixon was strong enough to warrant prosecution. This latter decision had to be made without regard to the potential divisiveness of proceeding.[17]

Many on the staff thought Jaworski was procrastinating because an indictment of the former President went against all his instincts. He was also under constant pressure from his many Texas friends not to prosecute.[18] On the other hand, the large number of letters, phone calls, and telegrams reaching Jaworski's office favored criminal action against Nixon by 3.5 to 1.[19] He also tended to rely on a few trusted journalists as sounding boards, especially on Anthony Lewis of the New York Times. Lewis was said to have written a column especially for Jaworski's eyes. The column argued against any immunity from prosecution, but was not ready until after the pardon, and hence never published.[20] Nixon's lawyers also invoked public opinion in trying to persuade Jaworski not to prosecute. Here is part of a letter Jaworski received from Herbert J. Miller Jr.:

Of all events prejudicial to Mr. Nixon's right to a fair trial, the most damaging have been the impeachment proceedings of the House Judiciary Committee. . . . All who watched were repeatedly made aware that a committee of their elected Representatives, all lawyers, had determined upon solemn reflection to render an overwhelming verdict against the President. . . . Not only has the media coverage of Watergate been pervasive and overwhelmingly adverse to Mr. Nixon, but nearly every member of Congress and political commentator has rendered a public opinion on his guilt or innocence. Indeed for nearly two years sophisticated public opinion polls have surveyed the people as to their opinion on Mr. Nixon's involvement in Watergate and whether he should be impeached. Now the polls ask whether Mr. Nixon should be indicted. Under such conditions, few Americans can have failed to have formed an opinion as to Mr. Nixon's guilt of the charges made against him. Few, if any, could—even under the most careful instructions from a court—expunge such an opinion from their minds so as to serve as fair and impartial jurors.[21]

That this letter (and others) weighed heavily on Jaworski can be gauged from his subsequent request for a complete file of press clippings for the week of Nixon's resignation and for all available data from the Gallup and Harris organizations bearing on the public's perception of Nixon's guilt.[22] When word of the contacts between the prosecutor's office and the pollsters was leaked, a rumor spread that the Special Prosecutor was about to commission a poll to decide whether or not to indict. In that case, the responsibility for the decision would have been the public's!

The rumor was probably unfounded. Yet there seems to have been an ongoing debate within the special prosecutor's office on whether Nixon was entitled to special consideration. The phrasing of arguments pro and con suggests that the polls were also being carefully watched by the staff. Phillip A. Lacovara, the special counsel to the prosecutor, argued that more "objective" factors should prevail over public consensus, whatever it might be. On the other hand, James A. Neal, who headed the Watergate prosecution task force, mentioned in a long memo that many people felt Nixon had been punished enough, that a trial of Nixon could lead to a "tragic event" and that "such a prosecution would divide the country for a considerable period of time." Two members of the staff, who themselves favored prosecution, nevertheless felt that "Neal's personal leaning" against prosecution reflected the views of a large segment of the American public.[23] It would seem that they, too, misread the strength of the opposition to indicting Nixon and proceeding with a trial.

During the first month of the Ford administration, the question of a pardon for Nixon came up for daily discussion in the White House but, according to ter Horst, "neither Ford nor his advisors were prepared for [the] fury of the reaction."[24] Nor does ter Horst believe that the pardon helped the healing process, as Ford had hoped. It only reopened the Watergate wound. We do not know all the calculations that led up to the gamble. Did Ford, aware that a storm was bound to come, choose to provoke it by moving quickly? Nixon's fate would then no longer be an issue in the Congressional elections so near at hand and there would be two years for people to forget Watergate before the Presidential election in 1976. Or, did Ford and his advisors judge—especially from the Gallup/*Newsweek* quickie immediately after the resignation—that the public was less vindictive than other polls made it appear?

THE EFFECT OF THE PARDON

Newly elected Presidents usually enjoy some kind of honeymoon period. For that time, however brief, the chief executive ceases to be a Republican or Democrat and becomes the President of "all the people." Vice Presidents who take over as Presidents begin their terms of office with even higher approval than those directly elected—at least as shown by Gallup ratings over four decades.[25] There is no bitterness left by a campaign, and the glitter of victory has not been worn off in the interval between election and inauguration. There is also a sense of crisis that leads the nation to rally around its leader: as Truman took over from Franklin Roosevelt with World War II not yet over, his approval rate was 87 percent; Lyndon Johnson, right after the assassination of John Kennedy, had the endorsement of 79 percent. In both instances, some of the halo from their charismatic predecessors may also have spilled over. Whatever the explanation, Dwight Eisenhower's approval rating (68%), at the start of his first term, was a full eleven points lower than that of Johnson, even though he was one of the most personally popular Presidents in the twentieth century.

Ford, like other Vice Presidents elevated to the Presidency, also did well. In the August 16–19 Gallup poll, 71 percent approved his performance in office and only three percent disapproved. The other 26 percent adopted a wait-and-see attitude. While most people were not very familiar with Ford's political views, hardly anyone considered him an extremist, and he was generally accepted as someone who would do little damage. Few people thought of him as more than an interim President who would hold things together until the national election two years ahead. On foreign affairs, he had already signaled continuity. He would keep Henry Kissinger. Nor was his accession to office expected to bring any significant changes in domestic policy. While his support was general, it was also shallow and short of enthusiasm. Even on the matter of Ford's much remarked "candor," there was reserve. Of the 85 percent who, before the pardon, thought him an "honest man," according to a mid-August Roper poll, half opted for the "reasonably honest" rather than the "very honest" alternative.[26] In other words, perceptions of this unfamiliar figure were somewhat more restrained than might be inferred from the overall approval rating and from reports in the press.

The pardon brought out into the open misgivings about Ford that had been submerged in the general atmosphere of good will. There was a precipitous drop in Ford's standing in the Gallup poll, from 71 percent approval in mid-August to 50 percent at the end of September, with the rise in disapproval even greater. On the day that the pardon was announced, Gallup interviewers were in the field. On the last two days of their polling (September 8 and 9), approval was down sharply from the first two days (September 6 and 7), a clear indicator of the pardon's impact. When Roper, late in August, asked respondents to describe themselves as strong or moderate supporters or strong or moderate critics of Ford, supporters had outnumbered critics by 73 to 13 percent. By October this ratio was down to 63 to 27 and then down again in November to 56 to 35. Also, where strong supporters had outnumbered strong critics in August by a ratio of 23 to 3, by November the balance was near even—12 to 11 percent. That Ford's losses were almost entirely among Democrats indicates the extent to which, with the pardon, the controversy over impeachment and Nixon's fate had been repoliticized.[27]

Though the pardon was widely regarded as an honest tactical mistake, there were those who questioned Ford's motives in granting it. There were even rumors that Ford had been blackmailed into promising a pardon. They found their way into the press and were explored in magazine articles.[28] In October, when the President appeared before a subcommittee of the House Judiciary Committee to answer questions about the pardon, he was asked whether there was any substance to these suspicions. Not even Ford's categorical denial, witnessed by millions over television, could satisfy the skeptics. An aggressive prosecutor would have asked more penetrating questions than the committee about Ford's meetings in the White House with Haig and Nixon.[29] But how many people, with one President forced to resign, would really have wanted to know that their new President was now himself covering up his role in a coverup, even if it could have been proved? The public wanted to give him the benefit of the doubt. They disagreed, but by only 47 to 45 percent, that "with the pardon of Nixon, President Ford has become involved in the Watergate mess" and discounted by a larger plurality—of 47 to 33 percent—the probability that Ford had actually "made a deal with Nixon to pardon him before he resigned" (Harris, September 22–27). Not unexpectedly, those most likely to suspect a prearranged deal were those who disapproved the pardon.[30]

Despite these suspicions, Ford's personal reputation was hardly tarnished. His greatest assets remained "his degree of frankness and openness in dealing with the American people" and "his attitude toward the press."[31] Paradoxically, Ford's willingness to assume responsibility for ending Nixon's prosecution did great damage to his image as a firm leader; whereaas 70 percent, in a Harris poll, agreed just before the pardon that he would be "a strong and decisive President," this was down to 52 percent three weeks later (September 22–27). Yet, during this same period, his rating as a "man of high integrity," dropped by only 12 points, to a still-high 75 percent agreement. As of mid-January 1975 it was 77.

The adverse reaction to the pardon may have been diluted by the stream of news stories in August and September, most originating in San Clemente, about Nixon's mental anguish and his deteriorating physical health. The former President was said to be suffering from a deep depression and in a near-suicidal mood. He was experiencing pain from a recurrence of the phlebitis, an inflammation of the leg vein, for which he had been previously hospitalized. Nixon's personal physician said it "was going to take a miracle for him to recover." These reports may have lent credibility to the concern for the suffering of "Nixon and his loved ones," which Ford cited as one reason for his decision. Later, in testifying before the Judiciary Committee, he played down Nixon's health as a factor in the pardon.

Many people could not believe that Nixon's illness was that serious. Polls document just how skeptical much of the public had become: among those who disapproved the pardon, few were willing to acknowledge that Ford had been moved mainly by compassion, misplaced or not. Overall, half agreed that the "health issue had been brought out to create sympathy" (Harris Survey, September 22–27). Since Nixon's testimony had been subpoenaed for the Watergate trial of his key aides, many thought he was not above faking illness to avoid having to testify. Suspicions grew when his attorney pleaded that Nixon's health would not allow him to testify in a civil suit in which 21 persons were charging violations of their civil liberties by White House security agents. Ziegler, still his press secretary, felt obliged to point out that pending court actions had "no bearing whatsoever" on Nixon's decision to enter the hospital two weeks after the pardon. When Nixon was discharged on October 4, the physician who had treated him in the hospital declared him medically unfit to travel to Washington for the Watergate trial for anywhere from one to three months. He might, however, be able to give a written deposition in about three weeks. A panel of three doctors, who later examined Nixon at the request of Judge Sirica, concluded that a deposition could not be taken before early January; a journey to Washington before mid-February was out. These developments made the idea that ill health had justified the pardon seem plausible. By November, 38 percent had come to accept this as grounds for a pardon where only 28 percent had done so in September, but the vast majority of the public still agreed that Nixon, in San Clemente, should be required to answer questions under oath.

Equal Treatment Before the Law

The compassion with which Ford treated Nixon brought two other issues to the fore: the extension of pardon to Watergate conspirators still facing trial and a similar amnesty for draft evaders and deserters from the armed forces during the Vietnam war.

The Watergate Conspirators. With the main unindicted co-conspirator already home free, "equal treatment before the law" had concrete implications for the prosecution of other Watergate defendants. As Phillip Lacovara, in resigning from the Special Prosecution Task Force, put it, he did not want to be part of a prosecution of Nixon subordinates whose guilt was subordinate to that of their pardoned chief. "Who could be enthusiastic about pursuing those who had done Nixon's bidding when the top man was never going to be held accountable?"[32]

Would the pardon be more acceptable to the American people if the same compassion were to be shown to Nixon's men? Just two days after the pardon, the White House let it be known that Ford was "studying" the matter of pardons for the other Watergate defendants. This statement, issued through his acting press secretary, was quickly amended the next day when a spokesman explained that no consideration was being given to a blanket amnesty. Then, the day after that Ford made his policy clear: he would not pardon any of the defendants before their trials. This day, September 12, was the same day the Senate, by a 55–24 vote, approved a resolution that urged exactly this policy. The original statement had obviously been a trial balloon, quickly deflated once it became clear that additional pardons would not make the pardoning of Nixon more palatable either to the public or to the Congress. An instant telephone poll (*Newsday* September 10) anticipated the Senate response, finding public opinion polarized around the issue of pardons for the Watergate defendants—45 percent thinking that, like Nixon, the other Watergate defendants should be pardoned and 44 percent opposed. But few who approved the pardon had any opinion on how hard other criminal prosecutions growing out of Watergate should be pressed.

There never was much enthusiasm for pardoning Nixon's men, either among those who approved the Nixon pardon or those who disapproved it. Despite the rhetoric about the blow to "equal justice," few seemed to believe that two "wrongs" could now make things "right." A Harris poll (September 23–27) found only 20 percent agreeing that "justice would be served" by dropping the case against Nixon's former aides. When asked directly whether the Watergate trial of former Nixon aides should be called off in view of the pardon, somewhat more (34%) responded positively.

Months later, after the Watergate trial had ended and four of the five men were found guilty, the public—by a margin of 5 to 1—expressed its agreement with the verdict. By an equally large margin, they also thought these men had received a fair trial. Was the public now ready to forgive

Nixon's men as Ford had forgiven Nixon? Opinion remained divided. Half said the men should go to jail; half thought that "because former President Richard Nixon was pardoned, other Watergate figures should also be pardoned." The majority of the public felt justice had been done by letting the judicial process continue and would not be better served by extending to others the "quality of mercy" shown their leader. At any rate, with the trial process completed, Ford granted no pardons to any of Nixon's co-conspirators.

Equal Justice and the Draft Evaders. The pardon issue also became entangled with the issue of amnesty or pardon for some 50,000 young Americans charged with (or imprisoned for) evading the draft or deserting from the armed forces. The idea of amnesty was not unprecedented. After the Civil War, Lincoln had offered to restore the civil rights of deserters prepared to swear allegiance to the Union. Nixon had not been so ready to forgive. In his judgment, the Vietnam-era draft evaders or deserters, whatever their motivation, had broken the law and had to be punished before being allowed to return to society. Mindful of the opportunity to put this emotionally charged and long-smoldering issue to rest, Ford, on August 19, signaled his intent to rectify the situation. In an address before the Veterans of Foreign Wars, he declared that "these young Americans should have a second chance. . . . So I am throwing the weight of my Presidency into the scales of justice on the side of leniency." He requested that the Attorney General report to him personally before September 1 on the status of all Vietnam draft dodgers and deserters. The next day, the White House let it be known that the President would have a proposal later that week. Ironically, it was the pardon for Nixon that Ford announced.

It was inevitable that people would link the two issues. There was open speculation that Ford, in the face of such strong reactions to his lenient treatment of Nixon, was now prepared to be more lenient to the military offenders than he had originally intended.[33] One columnist, William Safire of the *New York Times,* even proposed a "Vietgate" solution that would grant pardon and amnesty to both Vietnam offenders and Watergate defendants.[34]

Proclamation 4313, issued September 16, fell far short of such a "Vietgate" proposal. It set forth a program for the return to society of those "convicted, charged, investigated or still sought for violations of the Military Selective Service Act or of the Uniform Code of Military Justice [whose] status remains unresolved." Although a clear break with the vengeful, punitive stance of the Nixon years, it did not extend to the military offenders the same unconditional pardon granted the former President. There was to be a conditional amnesty, based on a case-by-case review. The offer was not "forgiveness" but a willingness to "forget" the past of those ready to commit themselves to some alternative service. This was exactly what Ford had had in mind when earlier he had told the VFW, "I want them to come home if they want to work their way home." [35]

During the televised press conference (September 16) in which Ford announced the amnesty program, he was sharply questioned, first on his motives for pardoning Nixon and turning the tapes over to him, and then about the proposed amnesty for the Vietnam-era offenders. Why, questioners wanted to know, had he been so much more lenient toward the former President?

Q. "If your intention was to heal the wounds of the nation, sir, why did you grant only a conditional amnesty to the Vietnam war draft evaders while granting a full pardon to President Nixon?"

A. "The only connection between those two cases is the effort that I made in the one to heal the wounds involving the charges against Mr. Nixon and my honest and conscientious effort to heal the wounds for those who had deserted military service or dodged the draft. That is the only connection between the two. In the one case, you have a President who was forced to resign because of circumstances involving his Administration, and he has been shamed and disgraced by that resignation. In the case of the draft dodgers and Army and military deserters, we are trying to heal the wounds by the action that I took with the signing of the proclamation this morning."

On the issue of amnesty for Vietnam-era offenders, the public had proved themselves no more compassionate than they now were toward Nixon. Over the years, the Gallup poll showed the overwhelming majority of Americans opposed to the return "without some form of punishment" of those who had fled the country to avoid the draft. The *Newsweek* poll on September 5— three days before the pardon and eleven before the amnesty proclamation— found only 12 percent of those questioned agreeing that Vietnam amnesty "should be linked to immunity for former President Nixon"; 77 percent were opposed to any linkage making one contingent on the other. There was apparently considerable public support for the kind of conditional amnesty later proclaimed by Ford: 69 percent favored the granting of amnesty "if the men were required to perform some alternate service, such as helping in hospitals or serving in the Peace Corps." [36]

Ford's program of conditional amnesty proved far less controversial than his pardon of Nixon. In early October, a Yankelovich survey for the *New York Times* found 61 percent of New York State voters still believing that Ford had done the "wrong thing" in granting Nixon an unconditional pardon compared with 43 percent still troubled about conditional amnesty, mostly because it was thought "too lenient." [37] Nor did the amnesty program serve, as Ford had hoped, to make the pardon of Nixon more acceptable. Attitudes toward deserters and draft dodgers were too closely tied to deeply felt convictions about honor and duty to one's country to be readily affected by what Ford might or might not do about further punishment for Nixon and his associates. Rather, the issue of the pardon quickly evolved into a debate over one man's political judgment and, as far as the press was concerned, on what this might mean for the upcoming elections.

For many, the pardon remained a blot on the American system of justice; it did seem that there were indeed two standards. As James Doyle wrote about the pardon: "Watergate justice was just as erratic as the criminal justice has always been: deferential to the mighty, blind to inequities. It is a system for elitists." [38] Much of the public apparently shared Doyle's point of view. What satisfaction people had derived from the resolution of Watergate was mitigated by anger or frustration or just plain disbelief that Richard Nixon was now beyond further punishment.

SENTIMENT AND OPINION

Sentiment differs from opinion. The former is not a reasoned view to be defended; it is rarely articulated completely or recorded. Much of what polls tap as opinion is rooted in sentiment. People just "feel that way" and can hardly say why. Often, people maintain opinions even when changes in their "gut feelings" cause them discomfort. If there was, as the Gallup/*Newsweek* poll implies, a surge of sympathy for Nixon right after his farewell speech, this was not so much a change in opinion as in sentiment, a matter of mood. Such quick changes in the public mood, triggered by objects or acts that appeal to human sentiments—whether expressed as sympathy or anger or despair or joy—are usually unrecorded by pollsters. Not only are such sentiments difficult to measure; but they come and go too quickly to be caught. The shift, sensed by keen observers, often goes undetected in opinion polls until unavoidably manifest in a surprise outcome—in the unexpected results of an election or the unforeseen emotional response to some public decision.

For the most part, the nation was, both before and after the pardon, in a strongly punitive mood according to all measures. This stands in marked contrast to the usual readiness of the American public to minimize political wrongdoing, to forget transgressions, and to forgive their perpetrators. Richard Nixon himself had exploited this tendency, most successfully in the 1952 campaign when, in his famous "Checkers" speech, he defended his use of a special fund set aside for him by supporters in the Southern California business community. What was there about Watergate and Nixon's role in it that provoked this uncharacteristically punitive response? There are no in-depth studies of the response to the pardon. We turn instead for explanation to a study of the moral and political values of two student generations.

In July 1973, when the extent of Nixon's complicity was still far from clear, we administered a questionnaire to students in seven colleges and universities.[39] Most of the 365 respondents were mobility-oriented, politically liberal (not radical), and ranged in age from 19 to 29. The 26 percent who had voted for Nixon in 1972 was disproportionately low, yet not so startlingly out of line considering the Nixon vote among college students in metropolitan New York. These young people, though hardly representative of all voters or even all young voters, were not untypical of persons everywhere who early decided that if Nixon were shown "to have participated in the Watergate coverup," he should "be compelled to leave office." At a time when the Gallup Poll was showing only a fourth of the public prepared to be so punitive, 67 percent of these young citizens felt this way. Understanding what made them so precociously punitive may help to understand the emotional response of so many people to the pardon.

When the Senate Watergate hearings were holding the American people in rapt attention, we wondered whether this generation of students was reacting to revelations of public scandal and confessions of public wrongdoing in the same way as a previous generation of students had reacted. We had as a base line for comparison information on student response to a television quiz-show hoax in 1959. Charles Van Doren, a young instructor of English at Columbia University and a member of a famous literary family, had won $129,000 by "defeating" other learned opponents on 21, a top-rated evening quiz show. He had become an intellectual hero, cheered on by millions who were not usually quiz-show fans. Unfortunately, this hero had feet of clay. He had been coached and given his answers in advance, as he subsequently admitted to a House subcommittee investigating fraud on a number of quiz and information shows.

Like Nixon, Van Doren had publicly proclaimed his innocence when charges were first leveled. He had lied before a grand jury. His confession, before the television cameras, came only after repeated claims to innocence could no longer be sustained against the testimony of others. Those who remember the quiz show scandal will also remember that the public pretty much absolved Van Doren from blame. Although he suffered some shame and an abrupt end to his academic career, he became something of a tragic figure, the object of pity and sympathy, depicted not as a villain but rather a victim of a television industry greedy for profits and of Congressional investigators bent on stirring up trouble in order to make names for themselves.

Participation in a TV entertainment scandal is not, of course, strictly comparable to Watergate. Dishonesty in quiz shows had fewer ramifications for the society. Certainly none of the perpetrators could compare in prestige and power with the President. Nor could anyone seriously claim that a conspiracy to rig a popular quiz show had thrown into question the legitimacy of the democratic process or that it posed a threat to civil liberties. But the essentially nonpolitical character of the quiz show hoax should not obscure the elements of comparability, including the unparalleled fame and acclaim Van Doren had enjoyed as a culture hero in the weeks before his unmasking, the deliberateness of the deception, the disclosure of how widespread such deceitful practice had been in the industry, and the extent to which such entertainment practices were at least tacitly condoned. The shock was great, especially among intellectuals who had been seduced into joining the mass audience. The world of television, so it seemed, would never again enjoy the same degree of trust. Who would ever again take what was witnessed at face value?

As Watergate came under scrutiny, we wondered whether the students of 1973 would react much as their counterparts had 14 years before. Would they judge acts of public wrongdoing as indulgently as students in 1959 had judged Van Doren's carefully staged deception? Would they justify their own reactions to his behavior in the same way? Or would they express a moral indignation that had been found so largely lacking in the 1950s?

To find out we used a research instrument almost identical to that used in 1959. Students received seven descriptions of cases in which "wrongdoing was publicly confessed to or otherwise exposed." They were then asked to say, in each case, whether they considered such wrongdoing "greater than," "less than," or "comparable" to Nixon's as yet unproven participation in the Watergate coverup and to explain the reasons for their judgments. Six of these descriptions were repeated verbatim from the earlier study; a seventh— a "San Clemente" type case was substituted for an item no longer judged meaningful; as an eighth item we added the "Van Doren" case.[40]

Four of the cases involved political chicanery. One was modeled on the acceptance of a gift by Sherman Adams, chief assistant to President Eisenhower, which ultimately led to his resignation. The other three summarized, but without naming him, controversies in which Nixon had been involved: the fund revealed during the 1952 campaign (whose legality he had defended in the "Checkers" speech); Nixon's first Congressional campaign in California, in which he lied about the support for and affiliation of his opponent, Jerry Voorhis, with radical causes; and—more obliquely—the then newly developing story about improvements made at taxpayers' expense to Nixon's San Clemente property. Though only a few students directly identified these "anonymous" wrongdoers as Nixon, many pointed out analogies with activities being revealed in connection with the Watergate case. Thus, one student wrote that "the Senator's fund [defended by Nixon in 1952] is like the funds secretly given to the Republican party." The case of "smear tactics" [against Voorhis] drew comments such as "Segretti [who directed a campaign of political sabotage against Democratic candidates in 1972] did the same thing for Nixon" and "like the 1972 election!" The use of "public funds for private property" item brought comments about current charges: "Nixon had the taxpayers pay for all his personal needs"; "The President doesn't give *me* money to fix my house" and "Almost like Dean's 'borrowing' office money to go on his honeymoon." The "unethical acceptance of a gift by a White House aide" brought this comment: "Things like this led up to Watergate. The purpose of the gift is obvious: the government official is expected to insure that the company [who gave the expensive gift] wins the bid [on a government contract]."

We have arranged these cases in table 9.1 in order of descending gravity. The numerals in brackets are summary measures representing the number of students who judged the particular wrongdoing as *more* serious than participation in the Watergate coverup minus the number who judged it *less* serious, so that any wrongdoing with a positive [+] gravity score was judged as more serious than Watergate and any with a negative [−] score less seri-

TABLE 9.1 Gravity of Wrongdoing[a]

1959 (N = 225)		1973 (N = 365)	
		Watergate Coverup (**0**)	
		San Clemente	(−24)
Campaign smear	(+152)	Campaign smear	(−59)
Exam theft	(+118)	Acceptance of gift	(−128)
Acceptance of gift	(+97)	Exam theft	(−136)
Art forgery	(+76)	Art forgery	(−178)
Nixon fund '52	(+36)	Van Doren Hoax	(−189)
Van Doren Hoax	(**0**)	Real estate tip	(−210)
Real estate tip	(−36)	Nixon fund '52	(−222)

[a] The values in parentheses are indicative of the relative gravity of the wrongdoing, as perceived by the students. While they indicate the relative ranking in each of the years, they cannot be used to compare the severity of judgment across the years, since both sample size and the zero point for the two years differ.

ous. The same information is reproduced from the 1959 study for the six items repeated in 1973; there Van Doren's participation in the quiz show hoax served as the zero point.

These students judged participation in the Watergate coverup far more harshly than participation in the quiz show hoax. In fact, these transgressions were at nearly opposite ends of the scale. The only delictum considered less serious than Van Doren's was profiting from a real estate tip, while helping to thwart the Watergate investigation was judged the most serious of all. Moreover, the two offenses that students ranked as second and third most serious were the ones they most often associated with the Watergate scandal. The severity with which they judged the San Clemente-type case points to its potentially explosive impact; charges that public monies had been used for improvements to Nixon's California and Florida hideouts were just beginning to surface at the time of the study.

The overall similarity in the gravity ranking of replicated items suggests that the two generations of students were using the same criteria in judging the seriousness of public wrongdoing. The moral calculus, as we described it in 1959, involved the clear visualization of some personal harm that the offense might inflict on people "like themselves." The greater the personal harm imagined, the more severe the judgment of the wrongdoing. Unless the offense could be envisioned as the direct cause of personal harm to potential victims who were readily identifiable, the seriousness of the "crime" tended to be downgraded—whether it was a white-collar or political wrong-doing that was involved.

Both the rank order and the explanations students gave for their judg-ments indicate that this was the main criterion used. "San Clemente" was judged harshly because students perceived the diversion of public funds for private benefit as taking money out of their *own* taxpaying pockets. The visibility of personal harm also accounts for the severity with which both generations judged the smearing of one's political opponent. Being a radical in 1973 no longer carried the risk or stigma that being a Communist did in the 1950s; yet, both groups were very sensitive to the way unwarranted ac-cusations could endanger the political career of the victim and ruin his life chances. The case readily evoked images of the "White House horrors," like the attempt to rifle the files of Daniel Ellsberg's psychiatrist or the forging of a State Department cable to make it appear that President Kennedy had wanted the South Vietnamese President Ngo Dinh Diem murdered. As one young voter phrased it, the "campaign smear" was "comparable to Water-gate because he [Nixon] also screwed the other candidate."

Judged least harshly were three wrongdoings which were perceived as harming almost nobody: the Van Doren hoax (everyone was entertained); the real estate tip (it did not drive up the price of land and the person with the inside track merely took advantage of the price rise "just as anyone else would have"); and the 1952 campaign fund was regarded by most as just another way in which political office holders could meet a variety of ex-penses. In 1959 this behavior had been judged more harshly.

When Watergate first surfaced, it appeared to be exactly the kind of im-personal wrong to which these students would readily accommodate. A break into the anonymous headquarters of the Democratic National Committee could be defined as affecting only the equally anonymous Committee. Only when these acts were divulged and testified to during the televised hearings was a new personal dimension added to Watergate. Individuals had been personally harmed, not only Ellsberg but major Democratic Presidential hopefuls, like Senators Jackson and Edmund Muskie, and television jour-nalists who were harassed by the Internal Revenue Service. Watergate was no longer simply a violation of some abstract rule, of some law or regula-tion, whose underlying rationale and significance were not immediately ev-ident. There were victims with whom one could sympathize, and this made participation in Watergate and its coverup a grave offense.

While there was considerable variation in the severity with which individual students judged participation in the Watergate coverup, political allegiances hardly explain it. The harshest judgments came from McGovern supporters, but overall there was little difference in the gravity with which Nixon or McGovern supporters judged Watergate.[41] Those who took the coverup most seriously were troubled by what they saw as its potentially far-reaching implications. Their explanations were replete with expressions of shock—at "Gestapo tactics," at evidence of how far the Administration was prepared to move against individuals to pursue its ends, and at what Watergate revealed about the morality of the government. What they were condemning was not just a coverup of the clumsy attempt at electronic eavesdropping but of the many similar White House activities that they feared as direct attacks on the well-being of the nation and their own personal liberties:

> Watergate affected the lives of millions of people by tampering with the election. . . . The threat is to the freedom of this nation.

> The activities of the Watergate conspirators have affected the lives of almost everyone in the country and probably a majority of the people on earth.

The alarm revealed in these quotes was not confined to young people like these. A poll just after the Senate hearings recessed in August showed 77 percent of an adult sample agreeing that "Watergate shows how even the privacy of the ordinary citizen is being threatened these days."[42] Yet, in judging Watergate harshly, the students at that point in time were more ready than most of their elders, to judge Nixon harshly and to want him punished by forcing him out of office if found to be involved. Why was this so? The answer lies in the crimes they thought he had committed.

To begin with, this was, for them, a coverup of a scandal that involved illegal, unethical, and dishonest behavior. Therefore, the President himself was—and these were the words most often used—corrupt, a swindler, a thief, a sham, a fraud, a cheat, and, especially, a liar. "The blatant use of public funds," wrote one, "pisses me off." According to another, "Nixon has the taxpayers pay for all his personal needs." Frequent references were made to "corruption" and to "ripping off the public." Some of the most bitter invective came from those who, though Democrats, had supported or voted for Nixon in 1972. They now felt betrayed. One Republican expressed the same sense of outrage in saying, "Cheating is cheating. That's no way to run a country with a President who's a liar."

Second, they sensed that Nixon had or would misuse his power. Underlying the many accusations that he had taken "unfair advantage of the public" or "denied the public the truth" was the concern that Nixon would not abide by the Constitution and "take care that the laws be faithfully executed." This sentiment is expressed in such comments as: "He has no respect for the Bill of Rights." "He thinks he's a King." "He's a bit of a power-hungry egomaniac." Some suspected that he might try to perpetuate himself in office: "We have three more years and by that time we won't be able to get rid of him." Another commented, "Nixon used unfair tactics to gain the election. He has misled the population and now one can only wonder how honest he can be in office and to what length he will go to remain there."

This last quote introduces what some saw as a third offense: he had gained power by unethical means and was not entitled to be President. As the beneficiary of dubious campaign practices revealed in connection with Watergate, he had been "illegally" or "fraudulently elected." He had acquired power by illegitimate means. Expressions ranged from dismay at campaign tactics (like the lament by a Republican who wrote, "It was dirty pool and *I* voted for him") to demands that the election be "nullified because Nixon had used unscrupulous means of getting to be President." The comparison that triggered the most comments about illegal power was that between coverup participation and the candidate lying about his opponent's political past. The "hypothetical case" inspired by Nixon's 1946 campaign was seen as the one "most parallel to Watergate. Here one sees a person committing a wrongdoing in order to gain power." Or, "Just as bad as Watergate. The candidate got elected while someone else deserved to."

Fourth, many contended, and this is the capstone, that by his acts *Nixon had failed to live up to the standards demanded of a President.* Whether Nixon was actually implicated in the coverup mattered less than his failure, evidenced by his behavior, to set the high moral tone required in leading a nation. Here are some ways in which this sentiment was verbalized:

An ordinary politician may cheat and lie and use dirty tricks against his opponents [but the President has] an obligation to set an example for us common folk by adhering to a high standard of moral conduct.

The White House, which is a symbolic American ideal, should be free of human failings which are prevalent elsewhere in society.

The President is supposed to be a paragon of trust and integrity.

If you can't trust the leader of the country, whom can you trust?

The last query sums up the undercurrent of feelings behind these lofty phrases. The harsh judgments of Nixon reflect something more than an ability to picture the specific harm inflicted on persons like oneself—the criterion used to judge the seriousness of other cases of public wrongdoing. Real power is incompatible with petty human motives. The cynicism that tolerates and even tacitly condones such corrupt practices as the rigging of quiz shows as long as they harm "nobody in particular" stops at the door of the White House. Students in 1973, like students in 1959, had some tolerance for real estate operators cashing in on inside tips and for politicians who accept money and gifts from supporters. Such acts were understandable: "It is human nature to look for an easy buck" or "Don't all politicians do this?" But a President is no ordinary person and the standards applying to the President are not ordinary standards. Once in the White House, more than routine honesty is expected of him, and the failings tolerated in politicians who are, after all, "mere mortals" become inconsistent with the Presidential role. A Van Doren can be seen as a victim corrupted by the system—so perhaps can a Jeb Magruder or a John Dean; but not a President. In a secular society, he plays a uniquely important symbolic role and it is a role that he cannot easily shed.

Trust was the other element that mediated between political preference and the demand for Nixon's removal. McGovern supporters had never trusted Nixon and were most ready to demand his removal at the slightest offense. But among those who had voted for Nixon in 1972, the most punitive were the Democratic crossovers, a clear majority of whom believed Nixon should be punished for "lying." They tended to feel personally betrayed, sensing that their suspicions of McGovern and their trust in Nixon had been misplaced. Regular Republicans were more sympathetic. If they were punitive, it was because they looked on Nixon's Watergate role as a betrayal of the public rather than of their personal trust. "What does this country stand for if he is not forced to leave?" Or, this more ambivalent way of expressing the same uneasiness: "My strong feeling is to allow the President to stay in office but I am concerned about the greater issues of trust and violation of honesty in government."

The self-styled independents who had voted for Nixon were by far the least punitive. Nearly all wanted him to continue in office or were unsure about the matter. It was within this group that distrust in government was indiscriminately diffuse, which led them to downgrade Watergate "wrongdoing": "To cover up is natural to anyone" or "Everybody does it" or "Politicians are always corrupt." Yet even those who thought Watergate a serious "crime" and were convinced that Nixon had participated from the start revealed their cynicism when they said that impeachment would make no difference:

The Nixon administration would still be in power and they are guiltier than he.

Since this thing happens all the time, I don't know if it would be practical to impeach all politicians who are corrupt and unethical.

Moreover, they argued, impeachment stood no chance. Nixon would halt the swift decline in his popularity with some dramatic counterattack:

Right or wrong, ever since his Checkers speech, he has been able to transform impending disaster into triumphant victory.

Thus, harsh judgments and calls for punishment were more than animosity against a Republican incumbent. The Presidency was still believed by most of these respondents to symbolize something higher than the dubious morality of political fund-raising and political patronage as the prerequisite for electoral success. The deep cynicism many expressed did not extend to the White House. Its occupant, just because he is the President, ceases being an ordinary politician. And this makes wrongdoing of the Watergate type altogether unacceptable. Some perceived Nixon's involvement as a betrayal of the personal trust they had placed in him; others saw it more as a breach of public trust. And yet a third reaction had its roots in a distrust so indiscriminate that the exposure of Nixon's participation in the Watergate coverup was only a convenient vehicle for confirming it.

Nixon could probably have diffused some of this by admitting his guilt, as Van Doren had done. Some of our most punitive respondents implied as much: The Senator who had accepted financial support from private sources and the Representative who had lied to win an election, they said, had "at least admitted their guilt." There were also more direct references to Nixon's failure to give a full accounting. "Something so serious should have been brought out immediately," said one. Another, with mixed feelings about the President's being compelled to leave office, said, "Nixon is not being honest with the American people. Even if he had no part in it, he should do his best to clear it up, which he is not doing. Rather he is hindering the investigation."

What many of the most punitive could not forgive was his failure to level with them. At what point a "full confession" could still have earned Nixon enough points to stave off impeachment is a matter for conjecture. Certainly, once the incrimininating tapes surfaced, Nixon could no longer convincingly portray himself as a victim entitled to public sympathy. Since his resignation speech showed no contrition, it could hardly diminish the demand for punishment, only mute it temporarily. However, our reading of the data leads us to suspect that Ford's unconditional pardon would have occasioned less of a storm and even gained wide acceptance if it had been accompanied by an admission of guilt. Ford's explanation that he wanted only "to heal the wounds" would have been more credible and the protest against an unconditional pardon as a violation of "equal treatment before the law" would have been less vehement.

Nixon, having failed to "confess," never became the focus of public sympathy; Ford never become the object of public vilification. It could have been different; unspent anger against Nixon could have been redirected at the new President. Yet, as the polls showed, Ford's reputation as a man of honor and integrity suffered remarkably little damage, despite a brief revival of charges that he had played some small role in Watergate and been party to a pardon deal. Neither charge became the subject of prolonged and bitter controversy. The media hardly pursued the subject and Congress certainly had no heart for doing so. When President Ford appeared before a House Judiciary Subcommittee on October 17, only one member, Elizabeth Holtzman, referred to the "very dark suspicions that have been created in the public's mind" and expressed her "dismay" that the format of the hearing would not provide the "full truth" to the American people. Ford, in his memoirs, called her a "cynical and highly partisan Democrat from Brooklyn, New York," whose "rudeness" in asking "nine accusatory questions" offended the other committee members—including her fellow Democrats.[43]

Perhaps the pardon had a cathartic effect, allowing pent-up anger to be dissipated in one brief outburst, thus clearing the air. That it would raise a storm should have been predictable. But why did it abate so quickly? The best explanation: Few people after the drawn-out battle of Watergate were in any mood to question the integrity and honor of yet another President—not most of the people, nor most of the press, and certainly not most of Congress. There was no disposition to open new wounds. The authority of the Presidency had survived the "wrongdoing" of one President but would it have survived a second "Watergate" investigation? There was a tacit agreement not to pry too hard.

CHAPTER 10

CONTINUITY AND CHANGE

Item (1974). Republican losses in the Congressional elections were nothing short of disastrous. The total net loss was the party's second largest since the Hoover–Roosevelt election in 1932.

Item (1974). Judged by survey responses, there was a tremendous erosion of trust in the *institution* of the Presidency between 1972 and this year. Its prestige, judged by ratings, declined by roughly 50 per cent.[1]

Item (1976). In the general election, candidates chose to run image, rather than issue, campaigns. The key question was, "Whom do you trust?"[2]

Item (1976). President Ford, the incumbent, lost the Presidential election by a narrow margin to the former Governor of Georgia, Jimmy Carter, almost unknown to the general public less than a year before.

Item (1976). In the 1960s, academic researchers were focusing on the causes of student unrest and protest; by the mid-1970s their focus was on the lack of interest in political issues on the college campus.

Item (1980). The ad agency handling Ronald Reagan's campaign targeted its efforts toward the "undecideds." To counter the "actor image," they projected him "as a *nice man* who ran a very complex state [California] very successfully."[3]

Item (1980). On the eve of the election, a political analyst wrote: "Whoever sits in the White House for the next four years will be debilitated by events, by his own speeches and actions. Most of all, he will be diminished by the nation's dissonant emotions. Yes, we must have a president; the Constitution requires it. He will be given all of the complex presidential powers and the theoretical freedom to make powerful decisions. But we will not grant him what he needs to be a leader: authority."[4]

Item. (1980). Reagan's pollster, Richard Wirthlin, described "the under-35 group [as] a sleeping giant in terms of its potential to transform politics.

But there's every indication that it will keep on sleeping this year."[5] Turnout among young voters reached a new low in the 1980 election.

Item. (1980). A banner crop of liberal Democrats, many first elected in the post-Watergate election of 1974, was swept out of office in the Reagan landslide.

Item. (1980–81). During the academic year Gordon Liddy, the most unrepentant of the original Watergate break-in defendants, now released from prison, had become the "hottest item" on the college lecture circuit. Paid $3500 for a performance, he drew large, enthusiastic, receptive audiences. Most of these audiences consisted of persons who were 11 to 14 years old during the last year of the Nixon Presidency.

What had Watergate to do with any of these developments? In the years following Nixon's resignation, there was a good deal of speculation about the "lessons" of Watergate and how it might affect the political process, particularly the "imperial Presidency," and about the constitutional issues it had raised.[6]

It would seem logical to infer a direct causal connection between the concerns aroused by Watergate and political reforms enacted shortly thereafter. Yet Watergate may only have accelerated changes already in the wind. Thus, the one area in which Congress clearly reasserted its power during the Ford administration was in foreign policy, an area in which pressure to limit Presidential initiative had been building for some time. Mounting opposition, in and outside Congress, to Lyndon Johnson's Vietnam policy was certainly one, and probably the most important, of the factors that dissuaded him from seeking a second term. Similarly, post-Watergate legislation (1974) on campaign finances, which established the Federal Elections Commission as an overseer, merely strengthened the provisions of an earlier bill (1971) intended to curb abuses stemming from mounting campaign costs and candidates' increasing dependence on large contributors. Some of the illicit operations, uncovered by Watergate investigators, were intended to circumvent disclosure provisions due to take effect April 7, 1972.

To establish a link between responses to a major political controversy and more basic changes in political orientation is less easy than many believe. With regard to the 1974 election, one is on reasonably sure ground, but the longer the timespan, the less certain the linkage. The bearing of Watergate on 1976 and later elections is more difficult to pin down. In considering its more basic and lasting effects we enter even more hazardous territory. We begin by proposing that long-term shifts in political attitudes, which amount to changes in the political climate, come about in any of three ways:

1. Attitudes formed in response to critical events can be generalized to other political events or objects.

2. A generation whose attitudes are particularly marked by these events in time replaces an older generation of voters and leaders, whose political mentality was predominantly shaped by a different set of events.

3. A controversy or complex of events comes to serve as a symbol that justifies or inhibits a broad range of politically relevant attitudes, actions and policies.

In this chapter, we have assembled some evidence bearing on each of these change-processes as related to Watergate.

THE GENERALIZATION OF ATTITUDES

Satisfaction with the political system is influenced by economic conditions and by how well people believe the government is performing on matters that directly affect their personal well-being. Watergate, which for a time became a major cause of dissatisfaction, focused on the Presidency, with the concern of most Americans never extending much beyond the personal fate of Richard Nixon. Once it was resolved, the concern over inflation, taxes, unemployment, and government spending once again regained their undisputed place as the pivotal factor in the citizenry's attitudes toward government. Judged in this light, the Watergate issue was a most ephemeral one, even though Nixon and Watergate remained "issues" in the 1974 Congressional election and cast their long shadow on the outcome of the Presidential race in 1976.

The 1974 Election. Too close an association with a clearly unpopular President is believed to be a political liability. Republicans had been worrying about the impact of the impeachment controversy on their chances in 1974, for polls that had shown the increased salience of the "honesty in government" issue also pointed to Watergate as one of the things that might make people less likely to vote Republican.

These forebodings proved justified. Overall electoral participation approached a new low and Republicans stayed away from the polls in disproportionately large numbers. Many others crossed party lines to vote for

Democrats. Although there is little to suggest that Watergate caused any significant number of people to change their party affiliation, the net loss of 48 Republican seats was devastating—on the average, 28 seats had been lost by either party in off-year congressional elections between 1934 and 1970.[7]

The televised impeachment debate contributed to this stunning Republican defeat. The heaviest losers were those Republicans who had remained visibly loyal to Richard Nixon to almost the end. In what Anthony Lewis of the *New York Times* called a "ritual cleansing," the voters "washed their hands of Richard Nixon by voting against Charles Sandman, Joseph Maraziti, David Dennis, Wiley Mayne . . . and Watergate."[8] While four of nine loyalists on the Judiciary Committee who had sought reelection went down to defeat, the pro-impeachment Republican members of the Committee, it seems, were better able to withstand the Democratic tide. Of the six who had voted for impeachment and were up for reelection, only Harold Froehlich, a Conservative freshman, lost his seat. Also unsuccessful was Hogan, who instead of seeking reelection had decided to run for Governor of Maryland.

A study by Gerald C. Wright Jr.,[9] in which he compared the proportion of the total vote each Republican Congressional candidate should have received with his actual vote, supports this conclusion. First he estimated the vote each Republican Congressional candidate should have received from past voting behavior in the district and from whether or not he was an incumbent and then compared this to the actual vote. From this he concluded that everyone of the loyalists on the Committee should have been reelected. Only Trent Lott of Mississippi exceeded Wright's estimate by a substantial amount. The vote for six others whose districts remained sufficiently unaltered to make comparison possible was an average of 7 percent below expectation, a shortfall large enough to cost four of them their seats. The 13.4 percent "loss" sustained by Sandman, whose campaign slogan, "When he speaks, the nation listens," dramatized his role in the proceedings, was the largest. By contrast, pro-impeachment Republicans gained 4.9 percent on the average, while the actual vote of Republican candidates who had *not* served on the Judiciary Committee matched closely that expected.

Having tested alternative explanations Wright concluded that the electorate in 1974 had reacted to the anti-impeachment votes of committee members. Their decision to defend Nixon had been a "major strategic miscalculation, at least from the standpoint of reelection." For the pro-impeachment

Republicans, "awesome responsibility" had its rewards: William Cohen's actual vote exceeded the expected level by 19.4 percent; in 1976, he was elected to the Senate.

The 1976 Election. Despite the opposition to Ford's pardon of Nixon and the likelihood that it contributed to his defeat, it is impossible to calculate the number of votes he lost because of it. To be sure, campaign surveys had asked potential voters how they felt about the pardon and whether this would affect their voting. Two thirds of Iowa voters questioned in late October said they were "less likely" to vote for Ford because of the pardon and only 2 percent said they were "more likely" to do so (Iowa Poll). Still, an affirmative answer to a survey question does not tell us whether or not the respondent actually voted against Ford and, if he or she did, whether this was *only* because of the pardon. The pardon could rationalize a preference based on quite different grounds. Some who disapproved Ford's decision could even see virtue in his "mistake"; the pardon revealed his overly generous and humane instinct.

That Watergate remained a strong undercurrent in the election cannot be disputed. Democrats did not openly introduce the pardon issue in the campaign but could hardly have been displeased by the publicity given the matter by the media in October. With election day near, the number of Watergate-related items on network evening news was higher than during any other month in 1975 or 1976. This increase in media attention was a journalistic response to newsworthy developments, such as the start of Ehrlichman's prison sentence, the overturning of the conviction of Robert Mardian, and a court ruling that Nixon's tapes could be sold, copied, and broadcast. They were coincidental to the campaign and in no way tied to Ford. But nearly half the items somehow linked Ford with Watergate, and two thirds were either part of a campaign report or directly preceded or followed such a report, thereby making it easy for viewers to associate the news item with Ford's candidacy.[10]

The key event that revived the newsworthiness of Ford's Watergate role was the appearance of John Dean on NBC's *Today* show on October 13. He alleged that Ford had met with a White House staff member for the express purpose of blocking the Watergate investigation. Dean's charge made the evening news on two networks, although the *New York Times* buried it on page 24 next day. But the story would not go away. The announcement, three days later, by the Special Watergate Prosecutor that he would *not* investigate the incident aroused the ire of some prominent Democrats, especially Wright Patman of Texas, chairman of the House Banking Committee, whose effort, during the 1972 campaign, to pursue the facts behind the break-in was alleged to have been stymied with Ford's assistance.[11] The media paid enough attention to the accusation to force Ford to address the issue in a televised news conference on October 20. When Senator Walter Mondale, the Democratic candidate for Vice President, raised it again less than a week before election day, his statement was also prominently featured on all three networks.

Nevertheless, the part Ford was alleged to have played in Watergate never became a major campaign issue. A national poll by Daniel Yankelovich in October found only 29.9 percent agreeing that they were "still worried that [Ford] may have been involved in the Watergate controversy." As to the pardon, opinion remained split, along the same partisan lines as two years before. In the ranking of 20 issues by potential voters the Nixon pardon proved "least important" of all in deciding how to vote. "Lack of trust in government" ranked seventh, just behind the energy issue.[12] Moreover, polls showed Ford gaining on Carter, who was still ahead, during the very period in which he had come under attack. Asked some months later why Jimmy Carter defeated Ford in last November's Presidential election, more Iowans cited the Nixon pardon and Watergate as "the main reason" than anything else.[13] It was, after all, in the Iowa caucus early in 1976 that Carter had first emerged as a viable Presidential nominee, offering himself as a new kind of open, honest, and moral politician—one not at all tainted by Watergate. However subtly, the revival of the Watergate issue through the media could only have helped Carter and hurt Ford, but no one will ever know how much better Ford might have done without the albatross of the pardon that kept some crucial number of citizens in some crucial state from voting for him. The narrow margin by which Carter won makes a plausible argument that had it not been for the pardon Ford could very well have won.

The Decline in Public Confidence. About the same time that Watergate began to be widely perceived as more than the usual politics, reports about a rise in political cynicism were making headlines. It was natural to infer a causal connection and for that inference to persist as "fact." That the cynicism was an effect of Watergate, however, is not established. For one thing, the scandal surfaced in a period when public disenchantment with political institutions and authorities was already rife. Trust and confidence in government, as measured by the University of Michigan Center for Political Studies, had been declining steadily since 1964; the tradition of loyalty to a political party had steadily eroded; ticket splitting had increased greatly. By 1972, electoral participation had already dipped to a post–World War II low,[14] though it was soon to drop further. A surprisingly large number of people appeared to have lost faith in America.

Some would attribute the start of this decline in public trust to the series of traumatic and violent events that began with the assassination of John Kennedy in 1963, followed by the confrontations over American military involvement in Vietnam, the murders of Robert Kennedy and Martin Luther King in 1968, and the near-assassination of Alabama Governor George Wallace while he was campaigning for the Presidency in 1972. One cannot doubt that these traumatic political events confirmed the atittudes of individuals inclined to be cynical and disillusioned and so contributed to voter malaise or a turn toward "unconventional politics."

Other explanations stress more basic changes in the economic and social system. One frequently hears the decline being attributed to the deterioration of general living conditions. Certainly, the effects of continuing inflation and rising rates of unemployment on an incumbent's popularity cannot be ignored. If prices rise sharply or people suffer prolonged joblessness, the legitimacy of a political regime may be seriously threatened. Yet economic factors hardly explain why the downward trend in public confidence should have begun in the 1960s, a period of sustained prosperity. They may explain the continuation of the trend into the 1970s when, during the Watergate years, there were serious price rises and the first gasoline shortages occurred.

A second structural explanation holds that grievances not negotiable through traditional political channels lead to an overwhelming sense of frustration that translates into diffuse and generalized distrust. From this point of view, the divisions of opinion on the great and burning issues of the 1960s and the early 1970s diverged from the cleavage between the major political parties. It was difficult for the aggrieved to find redress through the electoral system. Among the sources of dissatisfaction were the slow rate of progress toward racial equality; the perceived breakdown in law and order, marked by violence in the black ghettos of the inner cities; the steadily mounting casualties of a war with no apparent end in sight; the growing tax burden on residential property, especially in the suburbs of large metropolises; the evident ineffectiveness of many of Lyndon Johnson's Great Society programs; and—the source of deepest despair—the seeming unresponsiveness of official policy to the rising tide of anti-Vietnam War protest. The division of opinion on these other issues contrasts with that on impeachment, and later on pardon, which was pretty much along party lines, with both Congressmen and certain establishment figures acting as spokesmen for both sides. Insofar as there were established channels through which to voice dissatisfaction, Watergate—following this line of argument—should have reinforced public confidence rather than shaken it.

Following the reasoning of the German sociologist Karl Mannheim, as he probed a half century ago for the roots of societal irrationality,[15] we mention a third structural explanation for the erosion of confidence. Modern society, Mannheim pointed out, is characterized by a high degree of interdependence among its parts. Disturbances in any one sector have unavoidable ramifications for others. Negative spillover cannot be avoided but only minimized by conscious management and technical coordination. The growing complexity of society has also widened the gap between those in responsible positions, whose decisions have major technical components, and the public at large, whose members are motivated by competing group interests. The concurrent development toward "fundamental democratization" leads groups who previously accepted their allotted share of values to raise their demands, creating dissent over priorities. Any failure of the "system" to deliver is apt to raise questions about the competence and credibility of decision makers, all the more so when the nature of the problems they face is not too well understood. To the extent that the resignation of Richard Nixon could be seen as a personal abuse of power appropriately punished, the resolution of Watergate should then—in line with this reasoning—have helped to restore some of the faith that had been lost.

Finally, one cannot talk about the loss of public confidence in government and political institutions without recognizing that not all segments of society are equally disaffected. Some do not expect much from those in power while others, because of their higher expectations, are more vulnerable to disillusionment. The underclass of blacks and other minorities who benefit least from "the system" have exhibited a rather persistent anomie rather than an erosion of confidence. The young are most subject to disillusionment by political events. They have limited political experience and their ties to the political system as well as belief in the legitimacy of institutions are more tenuous. The young people born in the "baby boom" that followed World War II were highly visible critics of the society in the 1960s and 1970s. Their presence in unusually large numbers may explain the erosion of public confidence during those years; their volatile and skeptical attitudes spilled over to older cohorts who had been habituated to accepting, with less questioning, the authority of political leaders.[16] Whether or not the expansion in the youth population explains the decline in public confidence prior to Watergate, this line of reasoning calls attention to the need to give special attention to the reactions of children and young people in assessing the impact of Watergate on its further decline.

Clearly, a downward trend in public trust preceded the Watergate scandal. This can be seen in responses to questions, repeated at intervals from 1966 to 1980, by both Gallup and Harris. (Appendix, table 14). These attest to a progressive erosion of confidence in the executive branch and the White House only temporarily reversed when Carter replaced Ford as President. This resurgence of confidence in 1977, followed by swift decline, reflects a familiar process. It is at the beginning of a new administration that the media, by emphasizing the symbolic role of the President, reinforce the surge of good will that follows his inauguration and thus inflate his personal standing. Save for such symbolic peaks, including that right after Nixon's resignation, confidence throughout the 1970s remained at a level considerably below that of the mid-1960s, with the degree of public support closely related to judgments of the incumbent's personal characteristics and performance in office.

The decline in confidence in the White House and the executive branch must be viewed within the context of a more general decline that extended to Congress, the courts, and even the media. While Miller[17] has convincingly demonstrated that public confidence in both Congress and the Supreme Court is less clearly related to judgments of incumbents than is the Presidency, public confidence in these institutions seems actually to have increased, however temporarily, as a result of their performances during Watergate. The increase, as in the case of the Presidency, occurred when the media dramatized the symbolic functions of these institutions as well as their own role.

The few studies specifically designed to link institutional trust and Watergate attitudes failed to establish any significant pattern of co-variation. In 1974 Miller et al. found only a very low correlation (.14) between political cynicism—that is, a generalized disaffection from the system as measured by responses to five questions—and attitudes toward the pardon.[18] There was even less of a correlation between political cynicism and evaluations of the House Judiciary Committee, views on the impeachment vote, on Nixon's resignation and on the role of the media in Watergate. People who approved the Ford pardon were only slightly less disaffected from the system than those who disapproved. Other researchers who, earlier in the Watergate saga, had sought statistical proof of a direct linkage between political trust and Watergate-related attitudes or between trust and exposure to Watergate news[19] had also come up with negative findings. If Watergate was promoting disaffection, these studies in Michigan, San Francisco, and Madison, Wisconsin should have been able to detect it.

How can one account for this apparent lack of direct effect? Of several explanations advanced, one holds that the generalization of distrust is inhibited through a process of *personalization*, in which a distinction is drawn between the individual believed guilty of wrongdoing and the office or institution through which the wrongdoing is perpetrated. In blaming the White House incumbent or his close associates or advisors, one exculpates the system. Distrust is not generalized. As the paper by Miller et al. puts it, "Watergate was perceived predominantly in terms of personal failings rather than institutional flaws. Interpreting these events in terms of Nixon's personal integrity rather than system limitations apparently deterred the direct translation of reaction to Watergate into attitudes towards government in general, and resulted in a weak relationship between attitudes and political support."[20]

An alternative explanation holds that support for political institutions is generally greater among those who pay attention to public affairs through the news media. So it was during Watergate. The attentive public, though more negative toward Nixon and his entourage, was less critical of Congress, of the Presidency, and of the Supreme Court than were those who took little interest in day-to-day developments.[21]

Similarly, the better educated were less supportive of Nixon but more supportive of government institutions. These differences are seen as a function of political sophistication, even though the influence of political dispositions related to social class and hence education can hardly be ruled out. Be this as it may, the explanation assumes that it takes some sophistication to differentiate between the person and the office and to understand that an unsatisfactory political decision or solution can be the product of no one's doing but of a system of checks and balances that, in seeking to accommodate pluralistic interests, sometimes produces the most perverse results. A "more sophisticated view of politics retards the possible generalization of dissatisfaction with a single policy, incumbent or institution to disaffection from the political system as a whole."[22] This more sophisticated outlook bred among those most wrapped up in Watergate not contempt for the system but a concern for it. But even among those less attentive and less able to comprehend developments, a tendency to personalize issues kept them from generalizing Watergate to democratic institutions in general.

In sum, then, Watergate was not the main cause of the erosion of political trust but no doubt contributed, perhaps only by serving as a symptom of the times.

LONG-RANGE EFFECTS: THE THEORY OF GENERATIONS

According to the theory of generations[23] the political outlook characteristic of an age group is formed in response to significant events that occur as its members attain political maturity. Each generation then comes to view the world from its own specific historical perspective. Accordingly, one speaks of a depression generation or a World War II generation or a Vietnam generation as if each had a unique mentality. A change in the political climate occurs once members of a particular generation move into positions of visibility and influence and, presumably, put their own political stamp on the era.

In line with this theory, the key to the long-term effects of Watergate resides in the reactions of young people who experienced Watergate before their political atttitudes had crystallized. Did growing up during Watergate have basic and lasting effects on political orientations? Will it have produced a generation of adults who are political cynics, turned off from political participation of any kind? Or will it have motivated a generation of new voters to take a more active part in politics?

To look at Watergate in this way is to treat the events as a politically socializing experience. By political socialization we mean the process by which orientations relating to political objects (like regimes, parties, and policies) and political activities (like voting, participation in political campaigns, following political developments via the media, and even more "gladiatorial" activity like running for political office)[24] are established and internalized. Though socialization continues throughout life, childhood and adolescence are nevertheless the most formative. It is during these years that persons first become aware of the political universe that learning occurs in its most concentrated form.

Early studies on political socialization[25] tended to emphasize the transmission of specific political attitudes from parents to children. In the late

1950s and early 1960s, research followed a different line of inquiry. How was the political world perceived by children at different ages? How did their imagery change as they grew older? Greenstein's path-breaking study, based on a survey of New Haven, Connecticut, children in the fourth through eighth grades, demonstrated that "(1) children are at least as likely as adults to perceive high political roles as important; (2) they seem to be more sympathetic to individual political leaders (and, in general, to politics) than are adults; (3) in at least some cases their actual images of political leaders are qualitatively different from the images one would expect adults to hold, especially in the emphasis on benignness; and (4) most important, the widespread adult political cynicism and distrust do not seem to have developed by eighth grade (age 13)."[26]

The Greenstein study called attention to the symbolic importance of the President as a cognitive and affective stimulus for elementary school children. In their eyes the man in the White House *is* "the government." The significance of the Presidential image was also explored by Easton and Dennis who, in 1962, surveyed school children in eight cities.[27] For young children, they hypothesized, the President is a "benevolent leader" whose idealized image functions as a reservoir of "diffuse support" that later carries over to other elements of the political system. It allows adults to sustain their beliefs in the fundamental legitimacy of the political system, however strong may be their dissatisfactions with an incumbent or their grievances against particular governmental policies.

For pre-adult experiences to cultivate attitudes that defend against disillusionment and alienation from government, two conditions have to be met: First, young children must somehow be shielded from potentially negative influences until the idealized image of President as the "benevolent leader" has had a chance to form. If the process is interrupted, the child may come of political age without the firm basis of support that sustains confidence in government even when it is sorely tried by events. Insulating children from "bad news" via the media hardly helps, because children also experience the political environment through their parents, teachers, and other adults. Second, the experience of adolescents has to be sufficiently consistent with their image of the "benevolent leader" to sustain that imagery and certainly not so disconfirmatory as to undermine it.

The accumulation of research findings since shows idealization of the President to be not nearly so universal as implied by these earlier studies. Jaros et al.,[28] for instance, showed that children of poor whites in Appalachia saw the President more nearly as a "malevolent" than a "benevolent" leader. The basic hypothesis that links adult trust in political institutions to the cultivation of a positive Presidential image during childhood is also open to challenge. The causal connection between the two remains to be demonstrated: for instance, do those children of Appalachia, now adults, continue to perceive all government as malevolent?

In line with the theory of generations, the long-range effects of Watergate would depend not only on whether it destroyed the common childhood image of the President as a "benevolent leader" but also on how much it undermined the yet-untested faith of older children and adolescents in the integrity of the system. The specific reactions of the young to events like Watergate may be quite similar to those of their elders, but without the reservoir of idealism that usually inhibits the adult's generalization of dissatisfaction to the system, the political responses of these children, as adults, may turn out to be quite different. In that case Watergate's most lasting impact on the political process will be felt only as the Watergate generation becomes a dominant force in politics.

Now for a look at the evidence. How did children and adolescents respond to Watergate?

The Child's View of Watergate

Even first and second graders were very much aware of Watergate. Avid television watchers that they were, they could hardly have avoided it. Children, including the very young, are aware of major political events—at least in broad outline—though their knowledge may not extend to details. Also, they may fail to grasp their full import.[29] Moreover, their impressions of these events come largely from the news media and not from their parents, and Watergate was no exception. This meant that they knew only the main cast of characters—the personae who attracted continuous coverage and, of course, the President. Others who, like Archibald Cox and even Sam Ervin, played major roles but were on the screen for only a limited period, were quickly forgotten, especially by children in the lowest grades.

Most of what is known about what Watergate meant to children comes from surveys. We have nothing comparable in richness of description to the Wolfenstein volume on children's reactions to the Kennedy assassination.[30] But data culled from published studies[31] do present a consistent picture: children's image of the President in the Watergate years (March 1973–March 1975) had become distinctively less positive. To be precise, their imagery at any given age was less positive than that of children the same age in previous decades. In 1974, Dennis and Webster replicated, in Tacoma, Washington, the 1962 study of elementary school children Easton and Dennis had conducted in Chicago.[32] They found that the President was judged less *benign* ("would he help me if I needed help?"), less *knowledgable* ("knowing more than anyone" or "almost anyone"), less *reliable* ("keeping his promises"), and less *influential* ("the one who does most to run the country"). Judged by the much smaller number still agreeing that the President is "my favorite of all" or "almost my favorite of all," Presidential popularity had taken a nosedive (Appendix, table 15). The drop in "idealization" was greater among the fourth, fifth, and sixth graders than among younger children. Skepticism about corruption and dishonesty in government, which adults so readily verbalize, had surfaced precociously. These children of the Watergate era had abandoned their idealism for more "realistic" assessments earlier than the children of the Kennedy generation, as most directly evidenced by their views about Presidential trustworthiness. In 1962, seven of every ten sixth graders believed that the President "always or almost always" kept his promises. In 1974, only four of every ten children felt they could so "rely" on him. This skepticism showed up as early as the fourth grade, an age when separation of the office and its incumbent usually exists in the child's mind only in the most rudimentary form.

This decline roughly paralleled the trend so clearly documented among adults. Children's faith in the "honesty and intelligence of politicians" and in the "benevolence and competence of government" had also diminished. What we do not know is how much such changes reflected the long-term erosion of trust noted among adults and how much they were reactions to what children themselves were learning of Watergate.

After Watergate, there appears to have been a slight reversion toward pre-Watergate levels of Presidential idealization. One study in the Greater Boston area[33] found that attitudes of second through sixth graders, while still negative, had moderated by January 1975 from the extreme assessments of the previous fall, but attitudes toward other aspects of the political system, such as the "policeman" as a symbol of government, had continued their downward slide. Most compelling is the evidence from a longitudinal study by Bailey of children in the third through sixth grades in Arkansas schools.[34] He was able to reinterview twice the children he had first queried in March 1973 as third graders; they were questioned again, as fourth graders in 1974 and then as fifth graders the following March. Asked who did the "most to run the United States—the President, Congress, or the Supreme Court," the President had been named by 85 percent in 1973 but by only 60 percent in 1974; then, in 1975, when Ford had been in office for just half a year, the percentage went back up to 81. The pattern of responses on other Presidential attributes, reproduced below, indicates that by March 1975 these children had recovered some of their lost confidence and trust in the President as the head of the government and as responsible for their liberty and freedom. However, lost faith in the Presidential character—in his honesty and willingness to help poor people—was not so readily restored.

	1973	1974	1975
Percent agreeing that a President . . .			
gives us liberty and freedom	73	71	81
helps keep the government running	79	66	74
tries to help the poor people	82	65	61
is honest compared to most men	—	48	48

The Bailey study also hints at a more significant and, perhaps, more permanent loss of faith in the Presidency among a slightly older cohort. Responses to these same questions by children who were in the third and sixth grades in March 1973 were compared with those of children in those grades in March 1975. The 1975 cohort of sixth graders was consistently *less* positive toward the President than both their predecessors in the sixth grade and their contemporaries in the third grade (Appendix, table 16). No such difference between the third and sixth grades shows up in the 1973 data. Especially marked was the decline in the belief of sixth graders that the President "tries to help the poor people."

There can be no question that for children, even more than for their parents, Watergate revolved around the person of the President. The youngest may have understood little more than that the President was in some kind of trouble and perhaps guilty of serious wrongdoing. Their distrust, being so clearly focused on the President, may have readily dissipated once—Nixon having resigned—the question of Presidential guilt ceased to be news. It is nevertheless difficult to dismiss the suspicion of a residue of disbelief, fed by the precocious recognition of Presidential fallibility, that can affect a political generation.

A Study of Adolescent Responses

Further evidence on the likely fate of the idealized image of the President nurtured in childhood and of the early onset of political cynicism comes from two studies: a survey of Connecticut 14-year-olds by Greenstein and from a questionnaire administered by social science teachers to over 900 seventh to twelfth graders in seven Long Island schools (April 1974).[35] Greenstein's interesting findings on Watergate were coincidental to his cross-national study of adolescent definitions of national leaders. His interviewers did not introduce the subject of Watergate but were struck by the frequency and spontaneity with which children brought it up. Half the adolescents introduced the matter on their own in response to various questions, usually to express cynicism and disgust. The Long Island teachers, on the other hand, were keen to find out what students, with whom they were in daily contact, knew about Watergate, what information sources they used, the meanings they attached to Watergate, and their beliefs about its probable impact on the country and themselves. They were deeply concerned over the cynical attitudes they had heard students expressing in and out of the classroom and felt that they, as teachers, should be doing something to counter what they felt were the insidious effects of Watergate on their charges.

To obtain more than the usual trite written answers to open-ended questions, they devised two "games" to be incorporated into the questionnaire. Students were to write captions for each of four cartoon sketches, which unmistakably portrayed (1) the White House, (2) the Presidential seal, (3) the Statue of Liberty, and (4) the Capitol building. Not everyone chose to "play"; of those who did, over 60 percent wrote one or more Watergate captions. Although most of these students' parents were Republicans, their captions were anti-Nixon by a ratio of 5 to 1, a clear confirmation of similar findings by Greenstein. There was another game by which to gauge the students' familiarity with Watergate "facts." They were asked to write down from a matrix of letters—29 across by 31 down—"all the words you find in this puzzle that have anything to do with Watergate." The information measure consisted of the number of relevant words minus the number of irrelevant ones. Knowledgeable students had little difficulty in spotting such names as "Daniel Ellsberg" and "Jaworski" within the matrix. None, not even those least informed, singled out "Mary Poppins" as a Watergate character.

The level of interest in Watergate was also surprisingly high among this ordinarily politically indifferent population. Overall, only 6 percent said they had not been at all exposed to media coverage of the Ervin Committee the previous summer. Nearly 60 percent said they had watched at least some of the hearings on television or listened to them on radio, and that this had stirred their interest in the "facts." High school students were not only more knowledgeable than their juniors but also more likely still to be following

Watergate (mainly on television), while at the middle school level the main media source was radio. Only about one in ten reported informal conversations about Watergate within the last week with either friends or family. This contrasts with five out of six who reported that the subject had come up in some class. Most said that this discussion had concerned "facts" about the case—the hearings and trials and the break-in or "whether Nixon is guilty or not guilty" and going to resign or not—but not any basic issues facing the country. A few wrote that teachers had helped them put Watergate into context, pointing to "the similarities between Watergate and the Teapot Dome scandal" or discussing such issues as "how the job of the press [was] to keep a neutral stand," the effects of Watergate including "the amount of taxpayers' dollars being spent on investigations," "how it will affect our diplomatic relations with other countries" and the "moral issue of Watergate and constitutionality."

For the majority Watergate had come to stand for widespread political corruption. But where tenth, eleventh, and twelfth graders most often located the corruption in *government*, the younger ones tended to place it within the *White House*. What most concerned them was whether Nixon was to blame. Their disillusionment remained more personal and pretty much confined to the present incumbent. In the irreverent words of one student, "I hate Watergate because it could have been avoided by not electing that shit-head in the first place." "Crook" was the generally favored epithet—borrowed, of course, from Nixon's denial that he was one.

High school students were more likely than middle school students to assume that Nixon was directly implicated in Watergate and more concerned about what this implied about the extent of corruption in the political system. The eleventh and twelfth graders especially worried about the possible abuse of power, the threat to civil liberties (mainly the invasion of privacy), and what a few saw as the attempt by Republicans to steal the election. For them corruption in the White House was less a personal failing than a symptom of corruption in government, as illustrated by some of their comments: "Watergate shows how unfair our country can be"; "the question is how innocent our government is of criminal acts—whether or not our judicial system is based on how wealthy you are"; or, "Watergate means a weakening of the republican system—government is to be elected without the people's choice." But not everyone took Watergate to be a Republican plot. A few believed Watergate was a "tool being used by the left in order to gain a foothold in '76" or "a Communist movement to try to break up a democratic country so it will be open to easy access."

Nearly half who answered the question agreed that "it is impossible for a man to stay honest if he goes into politics." More ominously, cynicism about politics was greatest among those best informed about Watergate. They also expressed the least interest in taking on citizen obligations and were more likely to feel that Watergate had intruded directly into their "personal lives." Among eleventh and twelfth graders, 48 percent saw themselves so affected as compared with 30 percent of the seventh through ninth graders. The gap between the most and the least informed was even greater—57 percent of those scoring highest on the information game and only 19 percent of those scoring lowest feeling they had been personally affected (Appendix, table 17). Interestingly, as many positive as negative influences were mentioned by those specifying how the controversy had entered their lives. Even negative influences cited could be quite personal:

My parents get upset about it [Watergate]. Then they are mad and then they don't talk for the night. They get mad at me if I do something little.

Some references, like the following, were to one's sense of civic duty:

I'm going to think twice about even wasting my time voting.

People will be more careful in their ways and in voting if they do at all. I don't think I really want to vote. It's not really any privilege to wait for.

Others were more likely to look for a silver lining:

It will make me more conscious of political events, and also more wary when it comes to making political decisions (such as when I reach voting age).

Comments on political participation by high school juniors and seniors were substantially more upbeat than those of others. The following self-revelation by a twelfth grader was the most positive:

I have strongly decided to go into politics next year, because I think our country should be run honestly—fairly. I hope people will clean out dirty politicians and find a way to help finance campaigns without it always being "the richest man wins." . . . I don't have much of a chance unless I join the system.

This student, like some others, was persuaded—possibly by class discussion—that, in the long run, Watergate could be a good influence. But this position remained a minority viewpoint, even among the students in the upper grades.

What can one then predict about long-range effects as the Watergate generation becomes a force in politics? Is there really such a generation—one whose mentality is marked by the controversy that exercised the nation during their politically formative years? It does seem that there was a residue of disbelief, fed by the precocious recognition of Presidential fallibility, that may have led to the early onset of political cynicism among prepubescents. Ten or eleven years of age in 1974, they would cast their first vote for President in 1984. As for those who experienced Watergate as adolescents, some of these came of political age by 1976, some by 1980, years in which the turnout among young voters reached new lows. A Watergate effect? And the college students who crowded the lectures by Gordon Liddy in the academic year 1980–81 were the ones who had generalized their adolescent disgust with the President over Watergate to disgust with the political system. Was their interest in Liddy symptomatic of their cynicism or merely curiosity, or even possibly nostalgia? There does not seem to be a Watergate generation in the sense that there was a depression generation or a World War II generation, but it is also difficult to believe that the premature loss of political idealization will not have rubbed off on the impressionable young in some way somewhere along the line.

Long-Range Effects: Watergate as Symbol

Events can become symbols that justify or inhibit a broad range of politically relevant attitudes and behaviors. Cataclysmic events, such as the resignation of Richard Nixon and the controversy that led up to it, survive as images that change with time. As the details fade from individual memory, a public image evolves through a pooling of ideas that are then reaffirmed by the media. The resultant legend incorporates the lessons relevant to the present. Though still based on the actual incidents, the legend is a reconstruction of reality that can overshadow what really happened. Even personal recollections are influenced by legend-building.

One such legend, later exposed for what it was, grew out of accounts of the activities of Belgian *franc-tireurs* [partisans] harassing German troops during their march to France in 1914. Authentic incidents were exaggerated by fearful German soldiers whose stories were then picked up by the press, appropriately embellished, and used to justify a harsh policy in occupied territory.[36] A similar legend developed in World War II around the subversive activities of traitorous "fifth columns," whose strategic contribution to the early Nazi victories was greatly magnified in official Allied versions of the war, which were then echoed by the press. In fact, these infamous fifth column activities amounted mainly to spying for the Germans and a willingness by some people in nations overrun by Hitler's armies to collaborate with their occupiers.[37] But the legend explained the unexpected defeats and could be used to promote vigilance against the enemy and support for the military effort.

Legends have a way of surviving as symbols, in defiance of every effort by historians to set things right. In calling attention to the legendary aspects of Watergate, we do not mean to deny that there was a break-in or that the "White House horrors" ever occurred, or even that people blinded themselves to facts (as they occasionally do in wartime). But for many Americans, Watergate had become a symbol with multiple meanings. The symbol gave form to a host of dissatisfactions and grievances. If there is to be a long-term effect, this will depend very much on what Watergate comes to stand for, on the legend that will have grown up around it, on the meanings that will be read into this legend, and on the "lessons" to be drawn from it.

No one can predict with any assurance what version of Watergate will survive as political folklore or, for that matter, which actions and legal pronouncements will set a precedent. However, Watergate quickly became a political codeword. In Washington, every incipient scandal involving higher-ups in the government was symbolically linked to it. Thus, when President Carter's brother, Billy, appeared to be in trouble over his Libyan connection, the press spoke of a "Billygate." In 1981, when David Stockman, head of the Office of Management and Budget in President Reagan's cabinet, was accused of duplicity in pushing for budget cuts he himself apparently did not believe in, George Danielson, who had served on Rodino's committee, referred to this as "OMBigate."

The Image of Watergate in Collective Memory. In the immediate aftermath of Nixon's resignation, there was at least a temporary moratorium on political controversy. This pulling together was somewhat akin to what has often been observed among survivors of a disaster, when people are swept up in a sudden unexplainable wave of good feeling, a new-found comradeship accompanied by unusual displays of generosity and altruism. Some psychologists have referred to this as a post-disaster utopia;[38] it grows out of the discovery that the community is not so dead as many have feared when disaster strikes. Watergate had some of the elements of a disaster, albeit a political one. It did not jeopardize the public's physical well-being but shook their faith in the political world. The people at the top, in and out of government, no longer looked as stable or dependable as one had assumed. Things had happened that many believed could never happen; things long taken for granted could not be any longer. People were shocked, though not always by the same aspect of Watergate. For some, it was the intentional obstruction of justice by a President; for others, the widespread practice of electronic surveillance against private citizens and governmental officials or the political sabotage during the electoral campaign. Most perturbing of all perhaps was the reality of a duly elected President having to resign for reasons other than health or personal incapacity. Thus, when President Ford spoke of wounds to be healed, he did not necessarily refer to those inflicted by partisan debate. The injury was to the abiding faith that a President, whatever his party or political conviction, can be counted on to honor his constitutional oath, that neither he nor anyone else is above the law, that ours is a government of laws and not of men, that there is order and continuity built into the American system of government in spite of all imperfections and failings.

Immediately after Watergate, "survival" was the main theme stressed by the press: the country had pulled through, even if only by the skin of its teeth, but nevertheless fundamentally unscathed. The Constitution had worked, and the nation could take pride in its courts, Congress, and the integrity of the American press. Because of this outcome, Watergate was used to symbolize above all the survival capacity of the political system. From here on, the transformation of Watergate as a collective representation or shared image can be traced through the way the press looked back on Watergate. This examination is less than all-encompassing and covers references to Watergate in the editorials and columns of only the *Washington Post*, *Newsday*, the *New Orleans Times-Picayune*, and the *New York Times* from October to December of 1974 (the three-month period after the pardon), then during the same three months in 1976 (the time of the Carter–Ford Presidential campaign), and again in 1978 during the Carter years. This was supplemented by a selective monitoring of television commentary.[39]

By the last three months of 1974, "post-Watergate" had, without fanfare, entered the vocabulary of the press. The Congress elected that year become the post-Watergate Congress, the era the post-Watergate era. There were references to a post-Watergate mentality, and especially a post-Watergate morality, as exemplified by the caption of an editorial in the November 26 *Times-Picayune*. The initial euphoria had vanished. Too many questions remained and, in view of the pardon, were unlikely ever to be resolved satisfactorily. Ford's appearance before the House Judiciary Committee to explain why he had removed Nixon from all criminal liability just as other

Watergate cases were about to come to trial was used to justify a cynical attitude toward everything. Had justice really been served by Watergate or had it not demonstrated that there were two sets of laws, one for the President and one for the rest of the country? The tone by now was more often pessimistic than optimistic. The resignation of Jaworski as special prosecutor, the continuing controversy over the possession of Presidential tapes and documents, and particularly the November election evoked much comment related to Watergate and what it meant.

Of the four papers examined, the *Times-Picayune*, which had been most steadfast in its support of Richard Nixon, was also the most upbeat in its valuation of the Watergate "lessons." Three of thirteen commentaries sought to persuade readers that Watergate was over and done with, that the nation should forgo further discussion of it and turn attention to the many pressing problems neglected during the controversy. An editorial on October 20, "Watergate Is Taken Care Of," advised that "we shouldn't make Watergate eternal and that Ford should be believed on the pardon and left alone." Another editorial hoped that the "political scandal would eventually help politics and create a morality of public service for political candidates." Yet the tone was not unreservedly optimistic. The hope expressed for a moral rejuvenation was coupled with a warning that campaigns were still very dirty and that not much had been learned, considering the price that had been paid. One of the paper's columnists was moved on October 20 to warn that there were "no final victories." Watergate had discredited both parties and would affect the viability of the party system.

The more politically liberal *Newsday* also voiced some optimism but of a qualified nature. Its end-of-the-year editorial ventured to hope that the Watergate disclosures might be used to strengthen governmental institutions, "since there is only a slight prospect of the bitter memories leaving the people's minds" (December 28). There was little to indicate any desire to close the books on the Watergate scandal.

In general, the more specific the comment on Watergate, the more pessimistic the evaluation of its consequences. The concerns expressed by columnists featured in the *Washington Post* extended in several directions. Paul Duke (October 19) professed that "Watergate had been very shattering to children and to their beliefs in the honesty and goodness of politics and politicians"; it might lead to "political change and revolt due to the uniform cynicism and rejection that children now feel for politics." Tom Braden (October 26) bemoaned the "post-Watergate feeling of suspicion being created by press accusations without evidence"; the practice, if continued, could lead to a revival of "McCarthyism." George Will (December 27) worried about the euphoria in the aftermath of Watergate. Amid congratulations on having "survived," he pointed out, the truth was unwelcome. He quoted Yale law professor Alexander Bickel's depiction of Watergate as a manifestation of the radicalism of the past fifteen years that had applauded anti-institutional impulses and challenged the premise of legal order.

These comments illustrate how little consensus there was even at that time on either the significance or the probable consequences of Watergate. Columnists and editorial writers drew whatever lessons they wanted. The only common assumption was that "post-Watergate" was somehow different from what had gone before.

Two years later, in the last quarter of 1976, Watergate had ceased to provide daily political fare for journalists to feed on. Editorial writers and columnists rarely mentioned Watergate, except in connection with the Presidential race. Though the Democrats did not make Ford's role in Watergate a major campaign issue, the editorialists were not about to shroud it in silence. Mainly they emphasized its irrelevance but could not refrain from speculating: had Ford and the Republican Party succeeded in escaping the "shadow of Watergate?" Some political analysts who, in 1974, had urged that the Republicans must be punished at the polls, had reversed themselves. Conservatives, like George Will, bewailed the spectre of Watergate haunting the campaign. But there was also the fear that making "trust in government" the main issue would divert attention from the real policy options that the public should be considering, like energy and the economy. Thus, in a *Post* column that appeared on November 2, Joseph Kraft expressed dismay at the possibility that the "ghost of Nixon" might have "shaped" (deformed) the character of the campaign, the choice of the candidates, the attitudes of the journalists, and the underlying opinion. On the other hand, Pat Owens of *Newsday*, who had been conducting a one-man vendetta against Ford, wrote (October 19) that voters could separate Watergate from the Presidency only by defeating Gerald Ford, the "Son of Watergate."

So, by 1976, the press was treating Watergate as an unhappy reminder that government could not always be trusted, that those in power were not always honest. The reminder was probably unnecessary and all too often unwelcome. Not until 1978 were those who had hoped to exorcise the ghost of Richard Nixon finally granted their wish. By October of that year, the mentions in these newspapers of a Watergate spectre hovering over the nation's politics had ceased and there were only scattered references to the effect of the "trust in government" issue. According to one *New York Times* editorial, "The Congressional elections were not conclusive on any Watergate effect involving the righteousness of candidates." But the *Washington Post* (October 11) still divined a more direct effect of Watergate in the dearth of young Republican talent. David Broder saw the decimation of the 27 to 35 year old group of aspirants as a legacy of the Nixon years; they had either refused to run or had been swept aside by the Democratic tide of 1974. Most often Watergate, by 1978, had become little more than a symbol for "personal immorality." The epithet was invoked for new cases of public wrongdoing, even if there was no similarity.

On the level of institutional reform, the backlash against Watergate had likewise brought only paltry results. The various investigations had revealed at least five areas in which institutions needed strengthening:

• inadequate control over campaign financing that allowed the buying and stealing of elections;
• investigations of suspected wrongdoing by high government officials being subject to undue political pressure;
• the concentration of power in persons serving the executive branch without accountability to the electorate or Congress;
• the general ineffectiveness of Congressional controls vis-a-vis the executive branch;
• the routine and widespread use of illegal surveillance.[40]

The matter of campaign finance was the one area in which there had been real movement toward reform. Even here the new election laws had not been the direct result of Watergate disclosures. Indeed, the provision for publicly financed election campaigns passed by Congress went against the recommendation of the Senate Select Committee on Presidential Campaign Activities (the Ervin Committee). Several other provisions of the bill—the joint Congressional-Executive appointment of a Federal Election Commission and limitations on personal campaign expenditures—were later struck down by the courts. By 1981, the powers of the commission were in danger of being scuttled.

A proposal, also from the Ervin Committee, for an office to represent Congress in any litigation and to take on some functions of a special prosecution force, did not muster sufficient support for passage. Steps to institutionalize the office of special prosecutor were taken by Edward H. Levi, the Attorney General under Ford. As part of the Public Integrity Section of the Criminal Division in the Department of Justice, the office lacked legal status, but it did figure in several investigations during the Carter administration. Under the Ethics in Government Act of 1978, the Attorney General was required to make such an appointment unless allegations of serious Federal crimes, such as bribery, turned out to be completely without foundation.

The effort to reverse the concentration of power within the White House fared not much better. Already in June of 1974, Congress had passed the Budget and Impoundment Control Act. The House voted by 401 to 6 and the Senate by 75 to 0 to curb Presidential authority to impound authorized funds without full prior consultation, thereby putting an end to a practice many had considered as beyond constitutionally legitimate Presidential power. The Act, one of the last Nixon was to sign into law, made Congress an actual participant in the Federal budget-making process. Whether the Act would have passed without the atmosphere created by Watergate is not clear. Certainly, that atmosphere helped to produce majorities lopsided enough to have overridden a Presidential veto.

Furthermore, under both Presidents Ford and Carter, the number of advisors and assistants appointed without Senatorial confirmation and personally responsible to the President continued to grow in number and in influence. Nor was the apparent imbalance between the legislative and the executive branches of government redressed in any significant way. Congress, as always, could obstruct, but its so-called new assertiveness in the post-Watergate period was pretty much confined to the foreign policy area, where it insisted on certain consultations. As for Congressional supervision of intelligence surveillance activities, this remained open to debate. The need for disclosure and accountability had to be weighed against the requirement of secrecy, without which no legitimate intelligence activities can be effective. New events moved new considerations to the forefront. With the end of détente, a move to grant the CIA more leeway in domestic surveillance was making headway, while the agency was successfully pressing charges against persons for unauthorized disclosure of secret aspects of its operations or the names of its operatives.

The image of Watergate is still being reworked, but the lesson taught about the importance of a free press remains one of its most resilient elements. This importance was recognized in the Freedom of Information Act, amended by Congress in 1974 over the veto of President Ford. Much of what has been written on the subject attests to the wisdom of the founding fathers in appending a First Amendment to the Constitution. Without the free, unfettered press that amendment assured, the coverup would never have come unraveled. Beyond that, Watergate has given a new authenticity to the conception of the journalist as hero. Basically inaccurate—few reporters ever have the chance to act as sleuths—the conception has nevertheless had considerable resonance, largely because of Woodward and Bernstein's book, *All The President's Men*, and the prizewinning movie based on it but also through the almost daily cultivation of this image in the press. After Watergate, it sometimes seemed that every child dreamed of growing up to be an investigative reporter. What may be a harmless fantasy in children must be taken more seriously when ambitious reporters envision themselves as sleuths in constant pursuit of hidden wrongdoing. The press can become obsessed with insignificant leads in the hope that they will develop into sensational exposés. These are not, however, the major part of a reporter's job. Good reporting generally involves quick footwork in covering routine sources backed by conscientious research. Except in rare instances, the payoff from the kind of detective work for which Woodward and Bernstein became famous has not been impressive. Yet the "heroic" orientation among Washington reporters has survived into the 1980s.

This preoccupation with exposing wrongdoing can be at the expense of reporting the more mundane but nevertheless important developments in and out of government as well as major policy options not so easily depicted as right or wrong. The two foci are often in competition and the second tends to lose out. A press intent only on digging up the most sensational news rarely provides the information most needed for intelligent involvement in politics. During the Carter Presidency, an administration not celebrated for its successful news management, the journalistic hunt was for "little Watergates" involving the "Georgia Mafia." Congress suffered some of the same treatment. Its legislative activity received far less attention than an individual Congressman accused of padding his payroll. The way for Congress to break into the headlines was to have a major investigation of its own or a head-on confrontation with the White House.

The appeal of the investigative model is reinforced by another credo of journalistic ideology: the conception of the news media as playing an adversary role vis-à-vis the government. Reporters must not allow themselves to become merely a channel through whom officials communicate messages they believe to be in their interest to disseminate. This notion of an adversary role may be an effective ideological defense against the manipulation of politicians, but it provides no assurance that the news will indeed concentrate on what is important.

The adversary concept glosses over another question: "adversary against whom?" the President? the Congress? dissident members of Congress with a specific axe to grind? or an official suspected of wrongdoing that legal investigators have been unable to document? It also fails to ask in whose interest the press acts as adversary. Is it for some disenfranchised grass roots constituency without any effective voice of its own? or the "national interest"? or what? The adversary role is no guarantee that the reporter's role is in fact neutral. The news media may be free to take the anti-establishment side, but someone's interest is inevitably served by what they choose to communicate, be it information about some act of government or malfeasance by officials.

According to the Watergate legend, it was the initiative of the press that made it possible to uncover the extent of Presidential complicity. Without withholding the credit Bernstein, Woodward, and others so richly deserve, people need to be reminded that the main source of Watergate news changed as the controversy developed. After the 1972 campaign, action on Watergate moved to the courts, the Senate Watergate Committee, the Special Watergate Prosecution Force, and the House Judiciary Committee, with the press sustaining itself on information developed by these official bodies. It made few new discoveries, but the publicity given to every bit of new evidence and to serious legal arguments helped thwart Nixon's efforts to put Watergate to rest. His opponents could count on media publicity to keep the issue alive and to support their quest for full disclosure. The full power of the media was similarly enlisted for the various televised spectaculars with all parties conscious of the need to manage appearances. Finally, the leaks by which those privy to information sought to advance their cause, no less than these media events, imply at least a tacit collaboration between representatives of the press and the sources on which they rely.

Members of the Senate Watergate Committee were neither the first nor the last politicians to avail themselves of the press when it suited them. The subtle manipulation of publicity was an integral part of the Washington scene before Watergate and will remain so. Reporters need their sources as much as their sources value a good press. The relationship of the one to the other is not so much adversarial as what has been aptly described as an exchange relationship.[41] Occasionally there is conflict—as there was during Watergate. A source refuses to yield information that the press judges newsworthy and which, it believes, the public has a "right to know." But mostly the relationship between press and the political establishment is one of mutual cultivation. Reporters seek to establish themselves as trustworthy to receive confidential information, and sources seek out journalists on whom they can depend as worthy recipients of their confidences.

Finally, let us mention one more Watergate myth, which the press itself did a good deal to promote. The myth is hardly a fabrication out of whole cloth. It has some basis in actuality, though not as much as most of us want to believe. It was reiterated in the opening words of a CBS television documentary, first broadcast in December 1979.[42] In the "scandal that was Watergate," viewers were told, "we found that our constitution worked." Slowly but inexorably, the script went on, the underground river of illegal acts was brought to the surface, among them the President's obstruction of justice, which in the long run turned out to be the hard core of Watergate and brought him down. He had used the great power of his office, first to control and limit the investigation of the break-in and then to prevent the tapes from becoming public and being used as evidence. The courts, backed by the pressure of public opinion, finally forced their release and produced the "smoking pistol that would shoot Nixon down."

The emphasis in this retelling of Watergate five years after was on the legal process, on the pursuit of an abstract standard of justice that made the outcome inevitable. So it was perhaps, but only in the end. Throughout most of the controversy just what precedents applied and whether a judge's pronouncements could be enforced against a recalcitrant President was not at all certain. Could one really have assumed that no one was above the law? or that Nixon lacked the power to force the Attorney General, who held office by Presidential appointment, to fire a special prosecutor who insisted on going his own way? It was the special prosecutor, not the House Judiciary Committee, who went to court to enforce the subpoena for the tapes, which the Supreme Court upheld in the end. Whether Congress could have made its own subpoena stick, except by political pressure, is doubted by constitutional scholars.[43] Nor was it inevitable that the case that forced Nixon's hand would have been heard by Judge Sirica rather than some other judge.

The myth of inevitability does not fit the facts. "Watergate," wrote two members of the Special Prosecution Task Force, "was a very close call. A more accurate lesson might be: 'The system nearly *didn't work.*' " [44] There were many times when things hung very much in the balance and things could have gone differently. For instance, after the Woodward and Bernstein exposé moved the Senate into action, it was the testimony of John Dean that struck the first really telling blow against the President's case. Yet was it inevitable that Dean would testify in public? He was compelled to testify by a grant of use-immunity, which two Republicans on the Senate Committee opposed because "they regarded him as the principal culprit defaming the president. Had they succeeded, history might have been afforded a different view of the Watergate affair." [45] Again, what if Cox and then Jaworski had not been so determined to see the criminal investigation to a proper conclusion? What if Nixon had not fired Cox, who then proved so adept at using television to state his case that he aroused the public and the Congress and so provoked the beginnings of the impeachment inquiry?

Many interpretations are possible and many different lessons can be drawn from Watergate. Yet since the facts are so quickly forgotten, the folklore is what survives. Will Watergate come to serve as a warning signal that the system can be abused unless the public exercises vigilance? Or, if the "system inevitably works," can the public take heart that there will be no second Watergate? In that case, Watergate can be readily forgotten as an aberration in which one man tried to beat the system and failed. In the long run the effect of Watergate will depend on what political groups, the press and the educational establishment choose to make of it.

CHAPTER 11

PUBLIC OPINION AND THE RESOLUTION OF CRISIS

To clarify the role of public opinion in the resolution of controversy, we now introduce a comparative perspective. Watergate is not entirely without precedent. The cases we use are broadly similar controversies, only some of which led to full-blown crises of confidence. Each began with the discovery of serious transgressions by persons of high prestige, at or near the top of government. Yet some cut more deeply than others, because the individual or institution "on trial" symbolized the nation and should have been beyond reproach. Through their derelictions, each in his own way put into jeopardy the legitimacy claims of the constitutional order, but in each case, the resultant crisis was decisively terminated without any basic institutional change. And, as with Watergate, the outcome was accepted with a calm that belied the acrimony of the controversy, though public acquiescence could hardly have been taken for granted beforehand.

RESIGNATIONS AT THE TOP

We begin by looking at several cases in which crisis was averted and potential political fallout quickly diffused by the uncontested resignation of the person at the center of the controversy.

Filbinger

First, there is the case of Karl Hans Filbinger, who was the Prime Minister of the West German state of Baden-Wuerttemberg. It illustrates how moral indignation, aroused by the news media, can force a popular and respected leader out of office.

Filbinger gave up his post on August 7, 1978, six months after an article by Rolf Hochhuth was published in *Der Spiegel*, a weekly news magazine with a reputation for muckraking journalism. It accused him of excessive severity, as a wartime judge for the German navy, in prosecuting and sentencing military deserters in the months just before and immediately following the defeat in 1945. The accusation, more than thirty years after these events, caught almost everyone by surprise. Not only was Filbinger a highly respected political leader and a likely contender for the presidency of the German Federal Republic, a post soon to be vacated, but he had depicted himself as part of the opposition to Hitler. While many other would-be politicians had had to go through denazification proceedings to be "rehabilitated," Filbinger had remained unencumbered by his past.

Filbinger not only categorically denied the allegation but counterattacked by instituting libel proceedings against his accuser. When investigative journalists came upon records of more death sentences beyond those cited in the original Hochhuth article, Filbinger claimed to have "forgotten" them because they had never been carried out. Yet there was documentary evidence that in at least one case, that of a young sailor who had deserted in April 1945 when German forces everywhere were crumbling before the Allied onslaught, Filbinger had personally supervised the punishment.

At first his own Christian Democratic Party backed Filbinger. After all, even if the story proved true, he was certainly not the only German political leader with a questionable Nazi background. Filbinger attributed the "slanderous attacks" against his good name, based on events thirty years past, to a left-wing-inspired vendetta. In the face of mounting evidence that the charges had some foundation, Filbinger displayed a lack of sensitivity that was to cost him dearly with the public and even within his own party. No longer claiming to have been a resister, he now argued that "what was right then cannot be wrong today." This remark plus his air of injured innocence did much to arouse the moral indignation that finally drove him out. Filbinger appears to have been unmindful of the passion for public order among the German people, including his followers. If others had had to follow legal procedures to clear themselves of their Nazi past, why should this not also be demanded of Filbinger? As he became the target of public resentment, he became a political liability and resigned just as his fellow Christian Democrats were preparing to drop him.

Elements similar to the Watergate case are not lacking. Publicity for a clandestine act like Filbinger's short-circuiting of the denazification process or Nixon's evasion of income taxes brings the standards of a broader public morality into play.[1] Many acts that are acceptable when private appear, when performed publicly, either indecent or offensive. At the very least, they are an embarrassment to the witness. Whether or not the breach of propriety is followed by a demand for sanctions depends on whether the onlookers view it as a dangerous precedent or feel personally threatened or victimized.

In Filbinger's case, public resentment was similar to the hostile reaction that greeted Ford's unconditional pardon of Nixon. This moral indignation, as the Danish sociologist Svend Ranulf described it, is something different from the outrage that is a response to personal victimization. It is a disinterested demand by third parties, not themselves injured, that the offender be punished. The third party has nothing to gain save satisfaction that a principle has been upheld or justice has been done. Ranulf considered this an attitude characteristic of the lower middle class everywhere because they live "under conditions which force its members to an extraordinarily high degree of self-restraint and subject them to much frustration of natural desires." [2] But moral indignation has an even more distinct social dimension; it expresses an identification with the dominant *norms* (customs and laws) as well as *ressentiment*—emotional outrage expressed in a desire for vengeance—at receiving less than equal treatment when equal treatment is the accepted principle. [3]

Tanaka

How coverage by the media both stirred public concern and kept an issue alive is apparent in the Filbinger case. *Der Spiegel* was to Filbinger what the *Washington Post* was to Nixon. In the case of Japanese Prime Minister Kakuei Tanaka, it was the press which first publicized the story of his financial dealings but did little to keep the issue alive thereafter. The downfall of the Japanese Prime Minister began with a special issue of the magazine *Bungei Shunju*, which appeared on newstands in September 1974. An article entitled, "A Study of Tanaka's Sources of Income," based on the work of a team of about ten journalists, accused him of having used inappropriate methods to raise campaign funds for his Liberal Democratic Party. Among other things, he had invested money from political contributions in corporate shares and in land which, he knew from information available to him as Prime Minister, was about to rise in value. Whether or not he had also personally enriched himself was not clear at the time, but malfeasance was at least strongly implied. Tanaka, it was pointed out, could draw on this fund whenever he pleased and, according to another article in this same issue, his long-time female secretary was in charge of disbursements.

Japanese newspapers kept the same low profile in the initial reporting of this scandal as they had in earlier scandals involving politicians in power. They had not reported these until they were exposed by the parties in opposition. Unlike the German press, which carried the Filbinger story in full, Japan's leading newspapers, with a combined circulation of more than 25 million, largely ignored the *Bungei Shunju* article. In the weeks following its appearance, not a single paper carried a follow-up story and no Japanese newsman is known to have questioned Tanaka or one of his deputies about the allegations.[4] Nor was it any clamor from the national press that caused the matter to be brought up in the Diet (Japanese parliament) more than a month later. Rather, foreign newsmen stationed in Japan, having read the *Bungei Shunju* article, had been asking whether the charges were valid. When an inquiry was addressed to Tanaka in the Diet, he admitted to some irregularities but insisted that never in the 27 years of his political career had he allowed his business activities to interfere with his obligations to party and government. The issue seemed closed. Soon after, to shore up his otherwise sagging political fortunes, the Prime Minister left on an official twelve-day trip abroad.

The silence of the press must be understood as a consequence of the close ties between Japanese politicians and journalists. A leading party figure will have an individual reporter (*ban*) assigned to him. A reporter in this position acts, more or less, as that politician's mouthpiece. If he submits unfavorable information, he is apt to lose his journalistic privileges; it may even cost him his job. Consequently, Tanaka's forced resignation, announced on November 19, 1974, just two months after the disclosure of the political fund, had little to do with pressure from the press. It resulted from the mounting political problems Tanaka faced within his own party, which had, since the July 1974 election, been able to keep control of parliament only with the support of two conservative independents. As the oil crisis and mounting inflation put a halt to Japan's years of stunning economic success, public confidence in Tanaka's performance was eroding. By the time he resigned, his standing in the polls was at a record low for any postwar Japanese prime minister.[5]

In January 1975, after he had left office, Tanaka was assessed an additional $140,300 in taxes on his personal income plus another $491,000 in back taxes and penalties for understating the income of his business concerns. No criminal charges were filed. A year later there were more disclosures growing out of a probe by the United States Senate into the activities of multinational corporations. The Vice-Chairman of Lockheed, an American corporation, had apparently enlisted the help of one of Tanaka's confidants and financial supporters to promote the company's sales of Tristar jets in Japan. The influence that Lockheed, through these payments, had had on certain government decisions would have come to light earlier, had the initial investigation of Tanaka's finances been more thorough.[6] Yet the news media had not pressured the legislators to pursue the allegations very far. Tanaka was finally arrested in July 1976 on charges that he had accepted $1.4 million (later increased to $2.2 million) from the Japanese trading company that acted as Lockheed's agent. One of his businessman-associates was finally convicted in November 1981, but Tanaka's trial was still pending. Meanwhile, he managed to remain the dominant political figure in the Liberal Democratic Party though forced, because of the indictment, to relinquish his party membership.

Profumo

There are ways to deter the press from a Watergate-type of exposé. Yet, even when constrained, the press can still exert influence on political negotiations. In Britain, where libel and national security laws are far more stringent than in the United States, the normally close ties between political leaders and an elite corps of correspondents, as well as their editors, have been effective in dissuading the press from pursuing certain kinds of information or, at least, from publishing what they learn. What is called "parliamentary privilege" is based on a relationship of mutual trust. The lobby correspondent who covers the political news in and around parliament is also an important purveyor of information among politicians.[7]

In the relatively few instances where the privilege has been breached through improper disclosure, official censure has had the desired effect on offenders. The system discourages leaks and thus enhances an inevitable division between insiders and outsiders. How the two tiers are linked can be illustrated by the events that caused the resignation, on June 5, 1963, of John Profumo as state secretary of war and as a member of Parliament. Profumo was part of the British establishment and had excellent career prospects.

The press entered by way of the trial of a West Indian in Bristol on March 14, in which a very attractive call girl named Christine Keeler was to have been a principal witness but instead "disappeared." British security and some other insiders knew that this was the same Christine Keeler who had once had simultaneous affairs with a suspected Soviet intelligence agent and with

John Profumo. Though this agent, attached to the Soviet Embassy, had tried unsuccessfully to use Keeler's liaison with Profumo to obtain state secrets, British security had decided, after investigation, to dismiss the matter "as social misbehavior by a minister" with which it had no machinery to deal.[8]

The connection between Keeler and Profumo, though known to the press, had been kept from their readers. Keeler had been trying to sell the story of her affair to the *Sunday Pictorial* and, as proof of its veracity, had submitted a love letter from Profumo. Not a word of all this had appeared in connection with press reports of the Bristol trial. What did arouse the curiosity of insiders was an intriguing juxtaposition of news items on the front page of the *Daily Express* the day after, when it ran a story about Profumo's having been unsuccessfully asked to resign for "personal reasons" next to another not very infomative item showing a picture of Christine Keeler captioned "VANISHED." Later it was said that the juxtaposition was pure happenstance. For those in the know, however, it sufficed as a hint at a possible connection. One other paper made a knowing reference to the number of "distinguished men in public life" whom Keeler had known, and the *Sunday Pictorial* speculated about a "loyal friend" who, perhaps fearing that he might be named, had spirited her away before she could testify.

That no paper should have mentioned her contact with Profumo did not prevent insiders from making the connection. So persistent were the rumors in and around parliament that a Labour MP called on the Tory government to explain. Exactly a week after the trial was reported, Profumo was moved to make a personal statement to the Commons, in which he denied being the unnamed person responsible for Keeler's disappearance. He also went out of his way to assure its members that there had been absolutely "no impropriety whatever" between them. This statement, having been made in Parliament, the press was now free to report, thereby giving publicity to allegations that had heretofore only circulated privately. In this way, according to Colin Seymour-Ure, "the Press ensured that, if they were found true in whole or in part, the damage to the government's reputation and morale might be substantial. . . . In this particular affair the Press felt inhibited by the law from publishing what it knew; it needed cooperation from politicians. This it got, apparently without difficulty."[9] Profumo's formal denial could not prevent the full story from gradually leaking out, despite the rearguard action he fought by bringing law suits against two foreign magazines, one of which actually won him an apology plus damages. Still the pressure would not let up. Too many people knew about the incriminating story on which the *Sunday Pictorial* was sitting.

Three months later (June 4) Profumo sent a letter to the Prime Minister saying he "could no longer go around with this terrible guilt in his mind." He reiterated his denial of complicity in Keeler's disappearance and of having let any secret information fall into Soviet hands, but acknowledged improprieties in his relationship with Keeler, indicating he had come to realize that his attempt at deceiving his colleagues in the House was a "grave misdemeanor and despite the fact that there is no truth in the other charges, I cannot remain a member of your administration, nor of the House of Commons."

The affair surely received its share of notoriety once it surfaced in the press. Yet it was not public indignation that forced Profumo's resignation. The large news-reading public was not apprised of the full facts until after the Establishment had moved to settle the affair privately. Since the media did not press the case, there was no aroused public to pressure the government to investigate. The resignation was forced by insiders in anticipation of a public backlash should the story gain currency. In the government's eyes, Profumo was guilty of having left it open to criticism for a lack of diligence in questioning him when the matter first came to its attention. Thus, the imagined response of a bystander public entered into negotiations despite the constraints under which the press operated.

The political news coverage is obviously the main link between the debate that goes on at the exoteric (public) level and that which takes place at the esoteric (private) level. The three scandals—involving Filbinger, Tanaka, and Profumo—differ in the degree to which the public was privy to the debate within the circle of insiders. In the case of Filbinger, his own close associates learned of the charges against him in the same way as the public, namely through the exposé in the news media. By contrast, the lack of publicity given Tanaka's questionable campaign finance operations kept the scandal from developing into the equivalent of a Japanese Watergate. Nevertheless, the lack of publicity did not prevent those challenging Tanaka's party leadership from using his poor electoral performance and low standing in the polls against him, even while the legal case over the bribery charge dragged on for so many years. The Profumo affair, notwithstanding the government's apparent success in negotiating a "private settlement," illustrates the permeability of the boundaries between the esoteric and exoteric levels of political debate. The separation of the two levels is less than complete, but the occasions on which the public intrudes directly, like a sleeping giant aroused, are really quite rare and usually limited to matters that immediately affect people's personal wellbeing. But even when the public is not morally indignant or has no axe to grind, there is always latent pressure. Political actors know this and act to anticipate it so as to deprive the opposition of arguments that may weigh heavily with the public. Such prolepsis is essential to the stability of representative government. Political moves, being largely preemptive, must be made before a crisis becomes unmanageable.

Prince Bernhard

A preemptive strategy is illustrated by the Dutch government's handling of the scandal around Prince Bernhard, husband of Queen Juliana. Leaks, from the same United States Senate probe that played a part in Japanese politics, pointed to the Prince as a recipient of under-the-table payments by Lockheed officials to promote export sales. Bernhard was the Queen's consort, Inspector General of the Dutch armed forces, and an official or patron of more than 300 organizations, including the World Wildlife Fund. When the Prince's name had first come up in December 1975, the Senate committee, recognizing that the testimony was based on hearsay, had tried to keep it secret but it nevertheless found its way into numerous press reports throughout Europe. By February 1975 the Dutch government had to acknowledge that he was indeed the "high official" mentioned in testimony as allegedly receiving a $1.1 million gift. After Bernhard denied the story and demanded an investigation to clear himself, Premier Joop den Uyl went on television to state that, after private talks, he believed the Prince was not implicated and cautioned that the case not be prejudged until the inquiry was complete. Other Dutch officials, at this time, remained silent on the question.

The issue, not unexpectedly, stirred public interest. Not only was the royal family possibly involved but anything related to the government's purchase of expensive Starfighter jets touched on sensitive political nerves. A commission of inquiry into Bernhard's role was formed and its scope soon broadened to include matters involving other military purchases. After six months of investigation, the commission criticized Bernhard for his "conviction that his position was unassailable," for having "entered far too lightly into transactions that were bound to create the impression that he was susceptible to favors," and for allowing "himself to be tempted to take initiatives that were . . . bound to place himself . . . in a dubious light."[10] Although, the report noted, the sums Bernhard was said to have received nowhere appeared in his accounts, this did not rule out the possibility that they had been received either by him or by someone acting on his behalf. The government, in accepting the commission's report, chose not to exercise its right of a criminal prosecution. This would have required Queen Juliana's consent and it was judged "highly uncertain whether . . . . a criminal and still prosecutable offense would emerge." The Dutch Premier further explained that "the government has given consideration, with a view to that very equality before the law, to the fact that through the publication of the report of the commission and the conclusions the government attaches to it, Prince Bernhard will already have suffered drastic consequences as a result of his behavior."[11]

This was another settlement among the elite, without an institutional confrontation, to which the public readily acquiesced. Three days before the Premier's announcement, the press had reported Queen Juliana ready to consider abdication should the commission's report be too hard on the Prince. Later that same week, Parliament by a vote of 148 to 2 rejected a left-wing motion for criminal prosecution. While the leaders of all five political parties disagreed with den Uyl's contention that the passage of time had made prosecution infeasible, they supported his effort to avoid the constitutional crisis certain to be provoked by the Queen's threatened abdication. Bernhard resigned as Inspector General and his Lockheed connection quickly ceased to be a public issue. Queen Juliana remained as popular as ever; an October poll showed only 6 percent of the people believing she should step down from the throne. Bernhard soon reappeared with her at many public functions.

"Muldergate"

The kind of institutional confrontation that played such an important part in Watergate was suppressed in a South African scandal—soon to be dubbed "Muldergate." The scandal began with the revelation, in April 1978, that money had been diverted from a fund established in 1972 (without the knowledge of Parliament) by the executive authority to serve a variety of political purposes. Cornelius Mulder was the minister with jurisdiction over the fund but John Vorster, President of the Union of South Africa, took full responsibility for having transferred the funds to a special Department of

Information when he was Prime Minister. It was to be used, he said, to shore up the image of South Africa abroad. A commission was set up to inquire into government corruption. Part of the money from the fund, it would later find out, had allowed government officials to live in high style, even to pay the expenses of the department head's female travel companion.

In this case, it was neither the press nor the opposition that first brought the possible misuse of secret funds into the open. The information came from a civil servant with responsibility for overseeing government operations. Not until six months later was the press to play a more active role in forcing the hand of the government. This happened over the weekend of October 29, when the *Sunday Express*, a Johannesburg news weekly, reported that the Department of Information had been allocated almost $14 million to launch a new English-language newspaper, the *Citizen*, to compete against the predominantly anti-government English-language press. Given the stringency of South Africa's libel laws, no paper would have dared print so serious a charge without documentary evidence to substantiate it. Almost immediately, the *Rand Daily Mail*, the most influential of South Africa's English-language dailies, followed with a report that another $15 million of the fund's money had disappeared into private corporate hands. The story led the judge who had been conducting the commission's inquiry into the affair to release details about a secret plan to take over the control of opposition papers by lending money for their purchase on exceptionally favorable terms to a fertilizer magnate. When that scheme failed, this magnate had been loaned even more money to launch the *Citizen*, which he then sold early in 1978, using the proceeds from the sale not to repay the loan but to expand his fertilizer business. Mulder resigned almost immediately after these charges were aired.

Pieter Botha, who had succeeded Vorster as Prime Minister, dismissed the judge for his unauthorized release of information and appointed a new three-judge panel. The official report by that panel was rendered the following June: Vorster, it concluded, had called the 1977 election with full knowledge of "gross irregularities" in the use of government funds, of which he had not even advised his cabinet. He had, as Prime Minister, taken part in a coverup and later, as President, lied about it to the panel. The publicity sufficed for Vorster to resign his Presidency before any public outcry could disrupt the unity of the governing party. The opposition was not apparently well enough organized to exploit "Muldergate" to bring about a party realignment.

A CRISIS OF CONFIDENCE: LYNDON B. JOHNSON

Everyone of the scandals so far reviewed was somehow defused before it mushroomed into a full-blown crisis of confidence that would have put the legitimacy of the political system into serious jeopardy. Then, why should an essentially esoteric controversy, such as that over Watergate, have produced such a crisis? Part of the answer lies in the decline in trust and confidence, discussed earlier, in major political institutions that set in during the activist 1960s. Expectations and demands were too high to be met even by Lyndon Johnson's Great Society programs. Polarization over race issues, especially voting rights and school integration, and over the Vietnam War had spawned violence and left a taste of bitterness on all sides. Given the all-too-apparent failures of those in charge, people had become more skeptical of authority based on expertise, and the investigative style of journalism popularized by Watergate had both reflected and contributed to this changing political climate.

Lyndon Johnson was the first American President to experience the full brunt of the political resentments that built up in this era. His political problems, unlike Nixon's, did not grow out of any personal improprieties or wrongdoing, real or alleged, but stemmed from policies he had pursued: his commitment to fighting at one and the same time a costly war on poverty and social injustice and an even more costly war in Southeast Asia. Yet Johnson, seeing himself headed for a confrontation that could tear the nation apart, chose not to do battle. Unexpectedly, at the end of a nationally televised speech announcing a new peace move, he declared (March 31, 1968) that he would not allow "the Presidency to become involved in the partisan divisions that are developing in this political year. . . . Accordingly, I shall not seek, and will not accept, the nomination of my party for another term as your president."

The announcement took all but Johnson's closest intimates by surprise. There had been no hint of it in the news media. Johnson had whopping Democratic majorities in both houses of Congress, and few Presidents could have known better than he how to use the political resources of his office to assure his renomination. In his memoirs, Johnson claimed that he had long considered not running and had repeatedly discussed this possibility with his family and several close advisors.[12] Yet his decision might have gone differently if North Vietnam by launching its Tet offensive (January 1968) had not "legitimized the Vietnam war as a political issue."[13] The apparent strength of the enemy offensive lent credibility to charges by Senator Eugene McCarthy, Johnson's main challenger in the New Hampshire primary, that the claims of military progress by the administration could not be taken at face value. McCarthy ran as the "peace candidate." In this conservative state, where he had not been expected to do well, he garnered 42 percent of the vote against 47 percent for the President, who had not made a personal appearance there. The news media hailed this as a resounding defeat for Johnson, Senator Robert Kennedy, now persuaded that the party was already split, felt his entry into the race would not further weaken its electoral prospects. He announced his candidacy. Two weeks later Johnson took himself out of the race.

A full crisis seems to have been averted at this time because Johnson had read the handwriting on the wall. One of his biographers reveals him as acutely sensitive to public opinion and to the reaction of the press. "Television and radio were his constant companions. . . . [He] was a presidential teenager, listening not for music but news."[14] After Tet, the press, which had allowed itself to be news-managed into reflecting the officially optimistic version of the military situation in Vietnam, expressed surprise that the North Vietnamese could still pack so much clout. Televised battle scenes featured on the nightly news had a special vividness, but in the absence of empirical studies, no one can be sure of their effect on those who watched.[15] Be this as it may, the coverage of the offensive and its aftermath are believed to have deeply affected many Americans who, up to Tet, had been supporting the war.[16] How could they not lose faith in an Administration that had assured them that improved tactics and massive American troop strength had put victory within sight?

Between January and March, when Johnson "resigned" as a candidate, CBS, NBC, *Life*, *Look*, *Time*, *Newsweek*, as well as seven major newspapers—among them the *Wall Street Journal*, the *New York Post*, and the *St. Louis Post-Dispatch*—had in one way or another come out against the war.[17] *The New York Times* on March 10 had revealed a request from General Westmoreland for 206,000 American troops in addition to the 510,000 already in Vietnam, which stirred a major debate within the administration. The call for new troops deeply shocked the Senate, whose Foreign Relations Committee was holding hearings, televised in part, on the authority of the administration to expand the war in Vietnam without the consent of Congress. It had also become clear that some of Johnson's closest advisors, including Clark Clifford, the newly appointed Secretary of Defense, were beginning to break with his policy. On March 26, five days before his "resignation," several advised the President of their changed views. With McGeorge Bundy as spokesman, they told Johnson that the objectives sought in Vietnam were beyond the present commitment of resources, that the President would be ill-advised to press the war without more public support.

The polls showed that the first news of the Tet attack caused a slight rallying behind the war effort followed by a sharp drop in support from February to March.[18] More important was the fall in Johnson's approval ratings. Gallup revealed a new low for Johnson: down to 36 percent in March from 48 percent in January. This vote of no confidence reflected more than the troubles from the military situation. Deficit financing of the war had brought mounting inflation. The devaluation of the British pound had triggered a collapse of the gold market. The Report of the National Advisory Commission on Civil Disorders, issued in March, predicted more rioting if social programs failed to bridge the gap between the two separate and unequal societies living within the large urban areas. Johnson might even be forced to call on Federal troops to deal with domestic turmoil.

Johnson knew he had expended his political capital. He faced trouble from his advisors, a more assertive Congress, an increasingly critical press, and a disillusioned public. By stepping down when he did, before his renomination campaign was in full swing, he could extricate himself as a statesman and depict himself as moved only by concern for the country. Had he persisted in stepping up the American military involvement, given the political climate, this would have provoked a bitter political controversy. Had the election not been only a half year away, his action would almost certainly have produced a crisis of confidence comparable to that which developed over Watergate. With the election so close, the passions would have been channeled into an electoral battle. With the media, the Congress, and an ever larger part of the public questioning the legitimacy of his actions, Johnson, unlike Nixon, chose not to risk the confrontation.

CRISES OF CONFIDENCE: CASE STUDIES

We turn now to the three crises most comparable to Watergate: the impeachment of Andrew Johnson in 1868; the Dreyfus affair, which shook France in the late 1890s; and the abdication of Edward VIII in 1936. All are public controversies pitting one powerful institution against another, but then resolved with unexpected quietude, leaving the institutional balance essentially undisturbed. That we should look for analogies and differences to the impeachment trial of Andrew Johnson in 1868 is only natural. Johnson was charged with deliberate circumvention of the will of Congress, as was Nixon for his secret bombing of Cambodia, and with not faithfully executing its laws. The parallel with two other crises is less obvious. At stake in the Dreyfus case was the honor of the French army, which was popularly perceived as the foundation of the nation's claim to greatness. The scandal that polarized France began with the conviction of an officer by a military court on evidence that later turned out to be fraudulent. Yet the military persisted in covering up its injustice, raising doubts as to whether the army was subject to the same laws that governed other institutions in the republic. The third crisis arose when the marriage plans of a yet uncrowned king threatened to devalue the monarchy as a major symbol of British sovereignty, from which successive governments derived their legitimacy and which remained practically the only cement that held the commonwealth countries together in a period of growing economic and international crisis.

The three crises have to be viewed in their historical setting. Just as Watergate was exacerbated by the earlier urban ghetto violence and the bitterness of the struggle over Vietnam, a legacy inherited by Nixon, so these crises also had roots deeper than the personal misdeeds of an institutional representative. The controversy over Andrew Johnson was related to issues left unresolved by the Civil War, especially the treatment of the former Confederate states. Likewise the Dreyfus affair has to be understood in the context of continuing insecurity over the Prussian army's decisive defeat of France in 1870 and the instability of the political regimes that followed. Great Britain in the 1930s was in the throes of an economic depression at the same time that its predominance as a world power was being threatened by Italian incursions into Africa and by Hitler's remilitarization of Germany.

Our focus is not, however, the specifically political context but rather the different media situations. The controversies surrounding Johnson and the French military occurred when the print media were still the main source through which the public learned about political issues. By the time Edward VIII abdicated, radio was beginning to compete with the newspaper. In the Watergate years, television joined in. Presumably, the changing media context made a difference both in the development and in the outcome of the individual controversies.

The Impeachment of Andrew Johnson

On February 24, 1868, the House of Representatives adopted impeachment articles against President Andrew Johnson. This action was precipitated by his discharge of Secretary of War Edwin M. Stanton. An earlier impeachment resolution had failed to carry because many representatives, though antagonized by Johnson's acts, did not believe they were clearly illegal. With this new move to oust Stanton from the Cabinet, members of the House now believed the President had clearly crossed a constitutional threshold. They saw it as a clear violation of the Tenure of Office Act, passed by Congress in 1867, which prohibited the President from discharging any civil officer of government appointed with the advice and consent of the Senate without that body's explicit permission. Johnson had thrown Congress a clear challenge. The House vote was nevertheless along strict partisan lines, with every Republican present, but not a single Democrat, in favor of bringing Johnson to trial before the Senate.

The vote had come after a period of continuous confrontation. Johnson had so incurred the wrath of the Republicans that removal from office seemed the only way out. Had this been otherwise, the attempt to be rid of a Cabinet officer, an accepted prerogative of a President, could not have incurred this drastic reaction. A contributing factor was Johnson's irascible temperament. Historians agree that a certain coarseness, carried over from his lowly social origins and never quite polished off, fed Congress' resentment and readiness to be rid of him, a response similar to that of some Congressmen who, on listening to the tapes, were upset by the "earthiness" of Nixon's language.

Congressional antagonism to Johnson ran deep. There were those who believed he shared too close a kinship with the vanquished South to be entrusted with the resolution of basic issues, indicative of even more basic social cleavage left unsettled by the war. For them, the abolition of both slavery and rebel domination of state governments were primary objectives. Johnson, who was from Tennessee, a Confederate state, saw it otherwise. A Union victory signified the "return of southern white masses to loyalty and the humiliation of the southern aristocracy that had led them into treason." [19] To this end, Johnson had vetoed a number of Reconstruction measures on the premise that Congress lacked the right to pass such laws without the participation of the eleven former Confederate states. These vetoes were unacceptable to hard-line (Radical) Republicans, all the more so as they came from a President not elected on his own but advanced from the Vice Presidency after Lincoln's assassination. Though promptly overridden, the vetoes, together with other acts of obstruction, earned Johnson the enmity of the Radicals.

In spite of this opposition from Republicans, Johnson had no particular love for his fellow Democrats either. To obtain backing for his policies, he had contested the Congressional election of 1866 by campaigning under the National Union Party label, so as to occupy the middle ground between the Radicals and die-hard former Confederates. Johnson's unprecedented swing around the country in support of the new party met with little success. Many Republicans countered by moderating their stand against the rebels and by mobilizing a vocal opposition. As news of his campaign tour spread, he was met by organized groups of hecklers. The result was a Republican sweep and a hardening of positions on both sides.

With the country so polarized politically, animosities were bound to run high. On one side were the Radicals, to whom the Johnson policies were anathema. They had come to view him as a clear threat bent on circumventing the will of Congress—if necessary, by a coup d'état—in order to govern with a coalition of the newly reconstituted Southern state governments dominated by Johnson appointees and Northern "Copperheads" (antiwar Democrats). Those on the other side feared what they saw as a Jacobin-type parliamentary government, achieved through an enfranchisement of former slaves as a means to extend Radical domination from the states of the ex-Confederacy to the whole nation.

Several bills pushed through Congress in 1867 had only one purpose: to curb Johnson. One bill put the United States Army in charge of the entire Confederacy. It set up five military districts, each under a commanding officer with ultimate power over the newly reconstituted civil governments. These military commanders were also to supervise the election of delegates to the constitutional conventions, to be held as soon as a state adopted the Fourteenth Amendment and extended suffrage to blacks. By a second act, Congress required that any order from the President as commander-in-chief to these officers be transmitted through the chief of the army, General Ulysses S. Grant; an order by a different route would not be legal. Then came the Tenure of Office Act, which wrested from Johnson the control over his own official family. No civilian appointee could be removed until *after* Congress had confirmed his replacement. And, finally, in January 1868, Congress transferred the power over the appointment and removal of the military commanders from the President to the army chief. Johnson had vetoed every one of these bills. When these vetoes were overridden, he used every legal and some questionable means to evade their constraints. Stanton, in particular, had been a major stumbling block. As Secretary of War, he could prevent the appointment of more conservative military commanders. He could also nullify Johnson's efforts to thwart the ratification of the new state constitutions drafted under the Reconstruction laws. In deliberately challenging the Tenure of Office Act by his dismissal of Stanton, Johnson evidently was hoping that a friendly Supreme Court would enable him "to win victory over a policy he had been unable to defeat by appealing to the popular voice."[20]

What was the influence of *vox populi* in the escalating conflict between the President and the Congress? To understand the role of public opinion, we have to recognize that the political world of the post–Civil War era was quite unlike that of the Watergate years. Hard though it may be to imagine, in that era the conduct of politics was more violently passionate than it is today. Political discourse was intemperate and unrestrained by niceties now taken for granted. Hence, "witnesses" called before the House Judiciary Committee made many wild charges. Accusations ranged from drunkenness and adultery to the selling of pardons to former rebel officers and illegal profit-taking from a railroad built while Johnson had been military governor of Tennessee. Some even sought to tie Johnson to the assassination of Lincoln. Nevertheless, in the impeachment resolution that ultimately carried, the charges were carefully framed in terms of specific legal infractions.

Second, press coverage during the impeachment and trial was intensely partisan and more given to passionate opinion than to reflection on the points of law. The harsh language strikes us today as out of keeping with the tone of a responsible newspaper. Editors made little effort to report issues objectively but conveyed only information favorable to their side.

Third, each party, and each faction within it, had its own newspaper, which served as its mouthpiece. Some papers had taken the lead in a drive for impeachment. This was a matter of open and direct advocacy with no holds barred. Smaller local papers with limited resources would often reprint opinions and information from the larger ones. Newspapers, whether large or small, were the major link between Congressmen and their constituencies. Since the population in most areas was, to begin with, more homogeneous, and since they had little "outside" information other than that which editors chose to print, one can assume that there was also more congruence between the opinions of elected representatives and the people they represented than there was in the 1970s.

All this could not but increase the power of the press as a molder of public opinion. During the Senate trial, editorial opinion, most of which favored conviction, was a force to contend with. Editors readily accused any Senator who showed himself less than determined to convict of duplicity or accepting a bribe. The Radicals especially used newspapers to conduct an appeal for letters, which began pouring into Senatorial offices even before the trial was convened. Waverers were brought under special pressure from local opinion through letters, telegrams, resolutions, and visiting delegations. For instance, the Republican Campaign Club of Chicago cautioned Senator Lyman Trumbull not to show himself on the streets of that city should he fail to vote for conviction. If he did, their letter threatened, he would be strung up on the nearest lamp post. When others, such as Senators William P. Fessenden of Maine and John B. Henderson of Missouri, gave signs that they might vote to acquit, they were bombarded with telegrams asking that they change their minds.[21]

While pro-Johnson forces also resorted to threats and promises, they lacked the visible support to make these effective. With the tide so clearly running against him, Johnson found it wise to give an assurance that, if allowed to continue in office, he would cease his obstruction. This was a decisive political move, since the unity of the pro-impeachment forces had been forged by Johnson's uncompromising stand. In late April, as the trial entered a critical phase, the President, at the behest of his defenders, submitted the name of John M. Schofield as his nominee for Secretary of War. Schofield was a conservative. As military governor of Virginia, he had enforced the Reconstruction Acts but not so as to aid the Radicals. Johnson made other conciliatory gestures and throughout the trial was on his best behavior. He ceased his interference with reconstruction. He even let it be known that he might reconstitute his cabinet to make himself more acceptable.

Despite the decisive electoral victory that had made it possible to override Johnson's vetoes, Republican unity was more fragile than these votes indicated. The Republican Party incorporated diverse interests, not all eager to remove Johnson since, there being no Vice President in those pre-25th Amendment days, Senator Benjamin F. Wade of Ohio would replace him. Wade's agrarian views—his support of high-tariff and soft-money policies— made him unpopular with more conservative Republicans. Only their belief that the President had failed to protect Northern and loyal Southern interests in the rehabilitation of the South had made all Republicans allies.

By his concessions, Johnson had so managed to narrow the impeachment issue that it could now be decided on technical legal rather than political grounds. For some conservatives, this had always been the only valid consideration. There had been some difference of opinion on Stanton's status in office and whether, as a Lincoln appointee, his continuation in office was exempted from the provisions of the Tenure of Office Act. Had Johnson deliberately acted to circumvent the law, as charged, or had he merely meant to force a Supreme Court test of its constitutionality? With the most grating political issues finally smoothed over, those reluctant to vote for impeachment felt less pressure to consider any but the purely legal aspects of the case. During some two and a half months of taking evidence, of hearing arguments, and of deliberation, the issue was largely converted into a matter of law, and the united Republican front gradually gave way. The margins by which Johnson's defenders lost on procedural questions became smaller with every vote. Finally, seven Republicans broke party solidarity and allowed Johnson to escape by one vote short of the two-thirds majority needed to convict. The seven based their decisions on narrowly legal grounds.

Was this change in any way a response to public opinion? There are no opinion surveys or referenda through which to trace its movement but only the results of the 1866 election and the record left by the press. These suggest that those who had voted to put Johnson on trial, while not directly responding to constituent pressure, could at least count on broad public support. Then, as the sense of crisis gradually eased, a guilty verdict became less and less certain. No longer did the future of the Republic seem to hang on the outcome. Finally, a new issue fractured the precarious Republican unity—the manner in which the trial was being conducted:

Even as the pressure [to convict] intensified, the dissident Republicans were fortified by demonstrations of support from within the party. Shocked by the sudden intrusion of overly partisan pressure into the trial, many Republicans were repelled. The leading conservative Republican journals of the nation—the New York *Times, Evening Post, Nation,* and *Sun,* the Cincinnati *Commercial,* the Boston *Daily Advertiser,* Senator Anthony's Providence (Rhode Island) *Journal,* and Moroton's Indianapolis *Daily Journal*—hastened to the defense of their long-time allies." [22]

There is every reason to believe that the newspapers, speaking for the politicians, also spoke for their readers. Though there was anger against the seven recusant Republicans, most of it was rather short-lived. A politically motivated attempt to unseat them at the Republican national convention a few days after the trial failed. On the other hand, none of the seven—for various reasons not necessarily connected with their vote to acquit—was ever reelected to the United States Senate.

The partisan press reflected existing political cleavages. It aggravated the impeachment conflict but did not play an independent investigative or advocacy role of its own. The close links between press and party made this unnecessary. Nor is there evidence that key political figures planned their moves with an eye mainly to how the press would react. What the press did was to serve as a conduit. Papers drummed up support for their own side. Johnson, boxed in by his opponents in Congress and having failed to swing public opinion in the Congressional campaign, resolved the issue politically. He compromised to win enough support to avoid impeachment. In pressuring waverers to "vote the party line," the Radicals made a fatal mistake. By fighting the battle on political rather than legal grounds, they gave the wavering Senators a chance to cry "foul" and to justify their desertion on judicial grounds.

The Dreyfus Affair

France in the Third Republic (1870–1940) had a parliamentary form of government. Loss of an effective majority in the legislature would lead to a change in the prime minister and cabinet without a constitutional confrontation. The Dreyfus affair took place in a period of political instability marked by a continuous reshuffling of cabinets. What makes it relevant here is the way it touched on the honor of the French army, an institution which, more than any other, symbolized national aspirations. To impugn the army, as the Dreyfusards appeared to, was to many Frenchmen, even the Republicans among them, tantamount to an attack on France.

The political drama that held France spellbound for some two years had its origins in the conviction, on December 22, 1894, of an officer of the French general staff, Captain Alfred Dreyfus, on spy charges. Scraps from a torn-up memo retrieved from the wastebasket of the German attaché in Paris, when pasted together, showed that someone had been passing him information on the state of French armaments. Dreyfus, the only Jewish officer on the general staff, was arrested on evidence amounting to nothing more than an alleged similarity between his handwriting and that in the incriminating memorandum. Found guilty by a military court, he was condemned to imprisonment on Devil's Island off the coast of what is now Guyana.

This penetration of French security, made evident by the memo, had been an obvious embarrassment to the government of a country still haunted by its humiliating defeat by Prussia in 1870. As news of the trial leaked out, the press had had a field day. It inflated the crime to monstrous proportions and engaged in the wildest conjecture about its possible international ramifications. The virulently anti-Semitic *Le Libre Parole* led the way. When it was officially stated that the information supposedly passed to Germans was of "slight" importance, the paper predicted that the case was about to be quashed because the culprit was Jewish. The entire anti-Republican press never doubted Dreyfus' guilt and proceeded to try him in its news columns. Only one paper, *L'Autorité*, insisted editorially that even a Jew had the right to a presumption of innocence.[23] In this atmosphere, the government could hardly help noting that a failure to convict would have serious political repercussions. Certainly, counterintelligence officers could expect dismissal for incompetence in failing to apprehend the actual traitor.

With Dreyfus convicted and out of the way, few people, certainly not the military, wanted to see the case ever opened again. To tie up the loose ends, the investigating officers proceeded to forge additional evidence. They also put pressure on handwriting experts to testify against Dreyfus and circulated the false story that he had confessed. Later, when this "evidence" came under challenge, the army manufactured a new version of the memo—this one with annotations said to be in the handwriting of the German Emperor.

The coverup came unraveled in two ways: through Colonel Georges Picquart, who took over as chief of the counterintelligence service, and through the ceaseless quest by the Dreyfus family to reverse the conviction. Picquart had accidentally come across a handwriting that matched that on the memo used to convict Dreyfus. He recognized it as that of Major Esterhazy, another French officer. Picquart's superiors remained unconvinced and did everything they could to dissuade him from following through on his suspicions. They even arranged his transfer out of Paris.

Meanwhile, to keep the case alive after his brother's banishment to Devil's Island, Mathieu Dreyfus planted a story in a British provincial newspaper that Alfred had escaped. His effort at news management worked. The patently false report found its way into the Paris press via the *London Daily Chronicle*. As a result, *L'Eclair* (September 15, 1896), which often functioned as the mouthpiece of the general staff, published an article expressly meant to put a final finish to all rumors, conjectures, and misstatements about the Dreyfus case. The article was widely reprinted, a common practice, since every editor paid close attention to what his colleagues were publishing. Any startling revelation, true or false, would immediately be picked up, magnified, and commented upon. So, too, with the L'Eclair article. Intended to make the case for Dreyfus' guilt, it came under challenge on two points related to the mention of a letter from the German officer to the Italian military attaché, in which a reference was made to a "Scroundrel D." The letter was cited as part of the incontrovertible evidence against Dreyfus. For one thing, the interception of such a privileged letter would normally have been a most closely guarded secret. Its release certainly was counter to the usual imperative to say as little as possible about one's sources of intelligence. This need to protect these sources had been given as the reason for not placing the letter in evidence during the court martial when it was secretly handed to the judge.[24] This raised a second question: had Dreyfus been granted due process? According to Article 101 of the French constitution, whatever evidence is used to convict must also be made available to the defense.

The plant by Mathieu had served its intended purpose: the L'Eclair article could now be used as a peg for a response. This took the form of a privately printed pamphlet that Mathieu commissioned from a young literary critic. Although its source made it suspect, the response it generated helped keep the issue in the limelight. The rising tenor of public debate now prompted Le Matin, the daily with the largest circulation in France, to publish a photographic facsimile of the infamous memo, obtained from one of the handwriting experts in the original trial. Frantic that this might point to the real traitor, counterintelligence produced still more "evidence," which the papers were only too happy to print.

During this phase the press was the main prod toward making the reopening of the Dreyfus case a political issue. Yet it did not so much act on its own initiative as respond to the efforts of others—the Dreyfus family and of a few highly placed individuals who had come to suspect a miscarriage of justice that was now being covered up. The following description by a historian of the affair, could, with the substitution of only a few words, be made to fit Watergate:

The very secrecy and obscurity of the Dreyfus affair meant that most people, including the vast majority of deputies, for example, knew only what they read in the newspapers. And because of this importance, every politician and every ministry even was anxious to cultivate its contacts with those near the centres of power. This double action became particularly important with the Dreyfus case. Each newspaper saw this as an affair to be exploited and was looking for information; each of the main protagonists of the affair, including officers of the Statistical Section [counterintelligence], realized the importance of the newspapers and was anxious to use them. . . . The more the affair was shrouded in mystery, the more everyone who had the remotest connection with it, whether minister or clerk or office-boy, demonstrated his importance by revealing, or half revealing, special information.[25]

There is, however, a significant difference between the sensationalism of the French press and the news coverage during Watergate. By the time information on the Dreyfus scandal reached the public, it had been processed so as to fit each paper's editorial stand.

Gradually, the evidence began to point to Major Esterhazy as the true culprit. In November 1897, a full year after the facsimile had been published in *Le Matin*, Mathieu Dreyfus once again used press publicity as a resource. He wrote an open letter to the minister of war and gave a copy to *Le Figaro*, which published it. The army responded with an inquest and then, at the request of Esterhazy, a full court martial, where much of the testimony was taken in secret and Esterhazy acquitted in a unanimous verdict. But despite the secrecy, both inquest and trial were accompanied by the most sensational publicity, some of it pure fiction. What mattered was that nearly all of it played on the general fear of conspiracy—be it of Jews, Protestants, foreigners, a plutocratic consortium, or an anti-Republican army acting in concert with remnants of the aristocracy. This was the kind of "information" on which the press thrived. When Emile Zola, in three articles for *Le Figaro*, took a more rational approach, even that esteemed writer soon found the paper closed to him.

Enough had happened by this time, however, to arouse suspicions of a political conspiracy to obstruct justice. Zola was to articulate this view publicly in his famous *J'accuse* letter after Esterhazy's acquittal. The special edition of *L'Aurore* in which it appeared sold 300,000 copies, far in excess of the paper's normal circulation; people are said to have fought for a copy. The day it appeared, the Socialist leader, Jean Jaurès, warned the Chamber of Deputies that France was in danger of being taken over by international financiers, that the Republic was about to fall into the hands of the generals. Zola was not just appealing to his allies and potential followers but inviting a trial for libel. His accusations had zeroed in on some of the most distinguished persons in the military hierarchy. Nor did he spare the war office.

The Dreyfus court martial, he charged, had "violated human rights in condemning a prisoner on testimony kept secret from him" while that of Esterhazy had then "covered this illegality by order, committing in turn the judicial crime of acquitting a guilty man with full knowledge of his guilt." [26]

The debate went beyond the question of the appropriate legal procedure. It had definitely become political. [27] Fearing that Zola would use his upcoming trial for libel to reopen the Dreyfus case, the government decided to limit its case to one single point: had the acquittal of Esterhazy been directed from above, as Zola said? Though evidence bearing on the Dreyfus case was declared inadmissible, Zola's lawyers tried, time after time, to provoke army witnesses into revealing the "newly uncovered" documentary evidence for the original guilty verdict. Yet the army chief of staff was not required to produce the document, only to testify that it existed. Addressing the jury as if they were the nation, he offered a simple alternative: accept the word of the army or have its leaders resign. Given this choice, the jury found against Zola. [28]

All this publicity had so thoroughly politicized the issue that Dreyfus' personal fate by now meant less than what his conviction had come to symbolize: the power of those forces that did not yet fully accept Republican principles. When a less moderate Republican government was formed in the summer of 1898, General Cavaignac became its minister of war. Though certainly no Dreyfusard, he sought to reopen the case simply to remove it once and for all from the public agenda. He developed a file on Dreyfus, but when he tried to use this to move for a Senate trial of some leading Dreyfusards, the Prime Minister balked, insisting an expert must first reexamine the documents to be absolutely certain they were genuine. It was thus that the "scoundrel D" letter was determined to be fraudulent. When soon after the counterintelligence officer responsible for the crude forgery committed suicide, that should have ended the case. Instead, anti-Dreyfusards responded by impugning the reliability of the French judiciary.

Finally, on June 3, 1899, the French high court voided the sentence imposed on Dreyfus and remanded the case for a new trial. The army continued to "stonewall." That Dreyfus' conviction should have been based on forged evidence did not shake its position. Its defenders simply argued that the forgery had been mandated by the national interest. Other genuine top-secret documents with conclusive proof of Dreyfus' guilt, they declared, were so sensitive that their release could cause an international incident. They even withheld them from the military court at Rennes, where Dreyfus was tried for the second time. When the prosecution introduced a surprise witness, a former Austrian officer, who swore that while in Vienna he had seen proof that Dreyfus was a master spy for the Triple Alliance, cross-examination by the defense was unable to shake his testimony. Later investigation suggested he had been bribed.

The military tribunal failed to hand down a verdict sufficiently definitive to lay the case to rest. The vote went 5 to 2 against Dreyfus, although the court recognized "extenuating circumstances." At least one historian has called the verdict a "transparent fraud,"[29] but others have pointed to a certain perhaps unavoidable weakness of the defense. While successful in discrediting the prosecution case, it could not conclusively demonstrate that Dreyfus was innocent, and only a bold military judge would have dared overturn the case. To do so would imply that General Mercier, the former minister of war who managed the prosecution at Rennes, had been guilty of fabricating a case.[30] Among French journalists opinion was divided, but foreign newsmen were almost unanimous in believing Dreyfus innocent.[31] The highly unfavorable reaction abroad throughout the affair only served as ammunition for those opposed to revision.

The trial nevertheless opened the way for a surprisingly pacific resolution of the controversy. The government now offered a pardon and rehabilitation, which Dreyfus accepted. Anxious to be done with the issue, the government next drafted amnesty legislation for all those concerned. But the Dreyfusards were not about to settle. For them, the case had become a symbol of arrogant power. They persisted until they managed to extract from the minister of war in the next cabinet a promise for a full investigation of the army files bearing on the case. This led to a third trial, before the French supreme court, which nearly seven years after the judgment at Rennes annulled the earlier decision and declared Dreyfus innocent of treason. But the affair really had ended long before.

Several things strike us about the Dreyfus case. First, had it not been for the press, the case could never have engaged the attention of France in the way it did. As in Watergate, the publicity forced action that the government was not about to take. Second, in the highly politicized atmosphere, newspapers played on the fears and emotions of their readers and so helped polarize France into two camps. The unusual violence marking debates in the Chamber of Deputies was a measure of just how badly the country was split. Third, we note that, apart from the press itself, there are few indicators of public opinion. We have no polls. Accounts of the period point to many duels said to have been fought, to the friendships ruptured, and to the practice of asking possible guests about their stand before making up the invitation list to a party. A cartoon from the period shows two frames, representing the state of mind or, what Lewis calls the mindless state, of the French people over the affair: In the first frame, "Assembled before dinner, a typical family of means hears the host decree sternly, 'And above all, no talk of the Dreyfus case!' The second frame shows a scene of mayhem: table cloth torn, dishes shattered and silverware scattered, the butler and the diners pummeling and throttling each other. The caption reads, 'They talked about it.' "[32]

It appears that the weight of sentiment was anti-Dreyfus. The majority of the papers, especially the mass circulation press, were solidly on the side of nationalism and for reasserting traditional values. To be sure, the Dreyfusards were a highly articulate minority that encompassed most of the intelligentsia. The "Manifesto of the Intellectuals," to cite one expression of opinion, was signed by 104 of the most promising young writers on *Le Revue Blanche*. Outstanding academicians, artists, and writers had come to associate themselves in one way or another with the Dreyfus cause. This elite support was as important to the Dreyfusard strategy as that from the press. Nevertheless, the Dreyfusards were to remain a minority within the Chamber of Deputies, even among the Socialists. Small wonder that the moderate coalition headed by Prime Minister Méline, which had held on to power longer than any government during the Third Republic, took a "hands-off" position on the affair. In the election of May 1898, which brought to power a new somewhat more conservative coalition, every single Dreyfus activist was defeated and when the new Senate met, it refused to retain the venerable Scheurer-Kestner, among the first to take up the Dreyfus cause, as its Vice President. For most of France, revision was beyond all consideration. Only after both Right and Left had wearied of the potential for a political explosion ever present in the Dreyfus case did they finally join in seeking some resolution.

For close to two years, the Dreyfus affair had dominated the news and the political life of France. Yet there was no "national" news medium to present a uniform picture of developments to the public everywhere. There were no live broadcasts against which to compare the objectivity with which the trials were reported nor any other readily available yardstick. Accounts of the military trial at Rennes in the Dreyfusard papers had only the faintest resemblance to those in the anti-revisionist press. Hence the verdict in the second trial, though greeted with cries of indignation throughout the world, was received with little display of concern one way or the other in Rennes, as in the rest of France. No mass demonstrations are recorded. And, after the trial, Dreyfus himself accepted a presidential pardon. Charles Péguy, a prominent Dreyfusard, summed it neatly, "We would have died for Dreyfus. But Dreyfus wasn't at all for dying for Dreyfus."[33]

If the Dreyfus affair effectively ended at Rennes, as it seems it did, it was because each side had been given its due. The verdict had left the institutional honor of the army unblemished; the pardon had set Dreyfus free. Only the intellectuals, aroused by the miscarriage of justice, wanted the injustice remembered. The Rennes verdict was for them a weapon with which to battle the reactionary forces of militarism and nationalism. As for the general public, there were signs of weariness in the first Senate election after the trial. In this return to normal politics, the Republicans won only 15 out of 99 seats and those candidates who had been vocal Dreyfusards lost, no matter which party they represented.[34] Their earlier publicity had enabled the Dreyfusards to force the issue and to build a temporary coalition with an articulate public outside of parliament but it was not sufficient to create a totally new political climate.

The Abdication Crisis

On December 12, 1936, Edward VIII, the yet uncrowned King of England, bade farewell to his people. In a radio speech heard round the world, he explained that he had given up his throne because he could not live without the help and the support of the woman he loved. Many who heard him wept. This crisis, which pitted the King against the government, was played out in a new media age. Both parties had recognized the potential of radio as a political resource, but neither side was prepared to exploit it or even the popular press to the fullest. There nevertheless was always the threat that the other side would take to the radio in maneuvering for an advantage.

The King came under pressure to abdicate once he made known to Prime Minister Stanley Baldwin his intention to marry Mrs. Wallis Simpson. The public had as yet no inkling of his relationship with the American-born commoner, whose divorce from her second husband was then still pending in a British court. While the King had still been Prince of Wales, there had been some tension between him and the conservative British establishment. As Prince, Edward had been distrusted for what were defined as unconventional views. In visits to economically distressed areas, he had publicly taken up the cause of the poor, in a manner some thought unsuitable for a reigning monarch. There was also the matter of his unconventional social behavior, thought unbefitting a king—his circle of trendy friends, his frequenting of nightclubs, and his casual religious observance. All his various indiscretions were capped in the late summer of 1936 by a Mediterranean cruise he took in the company of Mrs. Simpson. Only deft signals from the foreign office prevented Edward, whose carelessness of protocol was another sore point, from committing serious diplomatic gaffes. He was, in other words, both interfering and at the same time neglectful in the discharge of his obligations as King. That he had now chosen a woman of Mrs. Simpson's background to be his wife and, by past custom, his consort as well, with all the rights and prerogatives that went with that position, merely gave those concerned about his fitness a point on which they could focus their misgivings and unite.

The British press had kept remarkably silent on Edward and "Wally," even while the American and continental papers were full of stories and wild speculation. The establishment could always count on the "quality" papers to exercise restraint on such delicate matters, but the rest of the press had likewise refrained from any reference to Mrs. Simpson, even after word of her divorce suit, discreetly filed in Ipswich instead of London, had leaked out. The silence on the pending divorce had been engineered by Lord Beaverbrook, a British newspaper magnate who saw himself as a behind-the-scenes wheeler and dealer. He had responded to a direct request from Buckingham Palace that Mrs. Simpson be spared the anguish of publicity. This gentleman's agreement was joined in by Lord Rothermere, another press magnate. *Calvacade* (a weekly on the *Time* model) was the one British journal to report the stories circulating in America but it suggested that they amounted to nothing more than idle gossip.[35] As one of Prime Minister Baldwin's closest associates wrote in the diary he was keeping: "The silence of our press is extraordinary and not enforced by the Government but by a sense of shame."[36]

The "ban" on news about the liaison extended even to imports. Those purchasing foreign publications on newsstands found relevant passages deleted and even whole pages of material missing.[37] None of this could, however, prevent hints and rumors from reaching England. Obviously, the establishment was in the know and the attentive middle-class public was getting wind of things. Edward's secretary warned him that he could not count on this self-imposed silence of the press to last forever.

There was nothing in British law to bar a British king from marrying whomever he pleased, provided she was a Protestant. Yet Baldwin, the Conservative prime minister, was to signal his opposition to this marriage in several personal meetings with the King. This politician by his adroit maneuvering gradually "transformed an inherently moral issue into a political one" with serious constitutional implications.[38] He let Edward know that his government would resign in the event the King would not change his mind. Baldwin also demanded that a decision be made before Christmas, which was four months before the final divorce decree would free Wallis to remarry. Edward suggested a compromise: a "morganatic" marriage, whereby his wife would enjoy the legal right of a marriage bond but have no right to her husband's titles or other prerogatives that she could pass on to her children. This form of marriage would require special legislation and, since it would mean a change in the line of succession, the concurrence of the dominion governments tied to the Empire by their allegiance to the Crown. For Edward, a far less adroit politician than Baldwin, the proposed compromise proved a grievous tactical error. It delivered him into the hands of Parliament and made his fate dependent on the responses of the dominion prime ministers, whose opinions Baldwin now began to solicit. Had Edward waited until after May, when he was to be crowned monarch, to play his hand, he could have dealt from a far stronger position.

Baldwin himself could not afford to take many chances. His own position had been made precarious by the deception through which he had led his party to victory in the last election by concealing the need for more armaments. When the pre-World War II crisis intensified, Baldwin had not only to admit to the deception but couple this with a plea for an increased military budget. Along with other Conservatives and the Church of England, he was banking on the coronation as a pageant of national unity to help his government weather a difficult period. Baldwin had forced Edward to make his intentions clear, knowing that in this matter the Labour opposition would not side with the King, however strong his standing with the working class. To the leaders of Labour, the King's interest in the social question smacked of the kind of paternalism that they had to counter to win the coming election. Baldwin, by obtaining a pledge from the opposition that it would not try to form a government if this one were to resign over the marriage issue, had forged a solid front in Parliament against the King.

The question was: Could Edward count on the masses to support him in a confrontation over his marriage plans? Would their affection for him mute any doubts about his prospective wife's fitness to be his consort? No one could be certain whether they would rally to his side. Therefore, Baldwin, who wanted the King's resignation, deliberately kept a lid on publicity about the King and Mrs. Simpson. His strategy was to hold off until the issue had been so narrowed that even were Edward to renounce his marriage plans to save his throne, he would only lose face with the very people most sympathetic to his efforts to free himself from the "unfair" restrictions placed on the personal life of a king.

Not a word of all these negotiations had appeared in the British press or on radio. The story first broke on December 2, the day after the cabinet rejected the morganatic marriage proposal. The peg for the story was a speech by the Bishop of Bradford about the upcoming coronation, which the Church was eager to exploit for religious appeals. Several passages in the speech mildly critical of the King were given far more than the usual play in provincial journals and then enlarged upon in commentary. With the taboo on Edward and Wally's relationship effectively breached, there no longer was any reason for self-restraint. By Thursday, December 3, the full story was in every London newspaper.

The lines along which newspaper opinion divided had been drawn in advance. Geoffrey Dawson, editor of the *Times*, was an intimate of Baldwin. The two had repeatedly consulted about Edward, and there was no surprise when the *Times* came down strongly on the government side. The *Morning Post*, the *Daily Telegraph*, and even the Labour Party's *Daily Herald* also reflected more or less the government point of view. But newspapers owned by Beaverbrook and Rothermere were behind the King. This gave him the backing of the popular press, with a combined circulation of 21 million compared with the 8.5 million who read the papers supporting the government.

Significantly, the tone of the popular press changed within a week. Though still personally sympathetic to Edward, it had become less stridently anti-government. Along with this shift had come a shift in public opinion more favorable to Baldwin's position. From all indications, even as expressed in letters to the *Times*, popular sentiment was, to begin with, strongly against the government. Inglis cites a number of observers (among them a young conservative politician who had been systematically canvassing his working class district) as evidence that at first most people were fundamentally tolerant toward the King and inclined to accede to his wishes. But after a weekend of truly sensational publicity, in which the public learned a good deal about the prospective bride, attitudes became less tolerant. Where the first letters to editors had expressed sympathy for a king browbeaten by his ministers, none of whom was particularly popular, the later ones were more skeptical. Wallis Simpson simply did not seem the sort of person those most inclined to applaud royalty could cheer with any enthusiasm.[39]

The government had undoubtedly counted on the adverse reaction to this publicity to convince the King that his position was untenable. But by all accounts, his decision to abdicate was made on December 3, before it was clear that opinion was turning against him. By December 5, the Saturday of the critical weekend, he had communicated that decision to the government. Edged into a corner, the King had struck a private bargain. Parliament was to pass two bills: a bill of abdication together with a bill that would make Mrs. Simpson's divorce effective immediately. As it turned out, Baldwin could not or would not make good on the second part. Edward had also asked that he be allowed to address the nation via radio, evidently in the vain hope that the people might rally to his defense and allow him to retain his throne. The government, not eager to enter into a test of popularity it might well lose, refused. Though opinion was turning against Edward, his abdication was by no means forced by it.

Not until the day after he had formally abdicated did Edward address his people via radio. Now, instead of appealing for support in his contest with the cabinet, he pleaded for understanding in words recorded for posterity: "I have found it impossible to carry the burden of responsibility and to discharge my duties as King, as I wish to do, without the help and support of the woman I love." Despite his insistence that the decision had been "mine, and mine alone," it was clear that it was not.[40] The alternative of abdication or marriage had been forced upon him; he would rather have remained King.

This resolution, too, had come through an elite settlement. The agreement to hold back on publicity caused the public to be taken by surprise but it also deprived the King of a resource he could have used in private negotiation. He was delivered into Baldwin's hands when the latter shrewdly denied him the opportunity to talk directly to the people. The Prime Minister held back until a coverage favorable to the government could be assured. By the time Edward was prepared to cash in on his popularity and flush out support for a "king's party" on both sides of parliament, as Winston Churchill was urging, it was too late. The final outcome might have been the same had he moved earlier, but a timely plea for sympathy would have brought public opinion into play and brought a somewhat different resolution to the crisis. As it was, Edward quickly left England. People readily abandoned him for his brother who, five months later, was crowned in Edward's place with all due pomp and circumstance.

COMPARISON WITH WATERGATE

All three major crises share certain characteristics. For one thing, each involved a usurpation of "normal" politics by a conflict over a symbol that blurred the more basic cleavages over the distribution of wealth, equal civil and political rights, relations between communal groups, and so forth. This usurpation is least clear with regard to Andrew Johnson, who inherited all of the conflicts left unresolved by the Civil War. We have noted that the press coverage of the conflict between Johnson and the Radical Republicans played on highly partisan emotions and helped keep the issue political. Nevertheless, once Johnson began to show himself conciliatory, the coalition against him, hitherto solid, showed cracks as social and economic issues regained their salience and a slim majority for his acquittal emerged. There was perhaps some legal base to the charges against Johnson, but it was the reemergence of politics and not the strength of the legal case that changed over the course of the trial and led to his being acquitted. In France, Dreyfus had become a *cause célèbre*, mostly as the intellectuals mobilized against the conservative defenders of the old system, but the Republicans and the left generally had remained divided over revision. Only years later, after the Republicans had achieved firm control of the government, could the verdict against Dreyfus be overturned without causing serious splits in their ranks. In England, the opposition Labour Party went so far as to enter an agreement with its conservative rival not to form a new government should Edward prove obstinate. Watergate, too, illustrates just how fragile was the coalition against Nixon. Before impeachment could carry, it had to be purged of all partisan overtones. Although Watergate reactivated earlier suspicions of Nixon aroused by his Vietnam stand, the same Congressmen who voted to impeach him for participation in the break-in overwhelmingly rejected the article based on his conduct of a secret war in Cambodia.

All three crises were similarly resolved by what were essentially elite settlements, in the Johnson case facilitated by his retreat from his intransigeant stance, in Dreyfus' case by his acceptance of executive clemency years before the appeal to the highest court finally reversed the guilty verdict, and in Edward's case by his willingness to trade his throne in return for consent to his marriage. There was no battle for public opinion similar to the one over Watergate, especially in England, where the influence of public opinion on the course of the abdication crisis was mitigated by the silence of the press. In the end, having readily been persuaded that abdication was in the nation's best interest, public opinion did little more than ratify the elite settlement. The other cases likewise illustrate that, with the "right" facts at hand, the public will often acquiesce, even against its predilections.

The media situation in the 1970s was obviously different from that in the 1860s, the 1890s, or the 1930s. What was clearly unique about Watergate was the availability of television, so that the mass public was more clued into political and intellectual life at the "center" than fifty or hundred years earlier. People could hardly escape Watergate. They could scrutinize the main actors on the television and see them juxtaposed against their opponents. The television perspective had become the dominant one for the press, the public, and political actors. Stations all over the country lived off the same national news feed and the same film clips for their local newscasts. Network news had carried a step farther the severance of the alliance between newspapers and political parties begun when the metropolitan press gained an independent circulation base and a constant stream of news from the wire services.

The ubiquitous presence of television most directly affects the political actors themselves. It forces them to be responsive to norms binding on other members of society. Where the Radicals, the anti-Dreyfusards, and even Edward could count on some papers for an unambiguously favorable version of events, the more "factual" reporting standards give no such assurance. To commit larceny in front of television is like committing murder in broad daylight on a crowded street. It is difficult to imagine that Esterhazy could have gained an acquittal in an open proceeding had it been televised. And what about the Senate trial of Andrew Johnson: would the Radicals have been less intransigeant with the spotlight of TV upon them as they faced a national audience rather than a parochial constituency? Or, given the national mood, would the recusants have felt under more pressure? It is at least doubtful that the military tribunal at Rennes would have convicted Dreyfus a second time had the debate preceding the trial or the trial itself been played out on television. The transparency of the legal case was recognized in every report that appeared in a foreign newspaper. As for Edward VIII, how might the boyish-looking King have fared against the dour Baldwin if both had appeared on television? A major contributory factor to Nixon's undoing was his inability to use the news and television time he so easily commanded to convince the audience that he had been frank about Watergate. The impression he conveyed cost him a good deal of support even in the early stages of the controversy. More than any partisan account, several of his carefully contrived television appearances, for all the effort that went into them, were generally seen as graphic documentations of "evasiveness."

Yet, for all its ubiquitous presence, the production requirements of television still leave the tagging of news developments very much in the hands of print journalists. Except when a big event is scheduled and television wants to cover it, video news is content to take its cues from the newspaper and to dramatize what is already making headlines. The television image is nevertheless a shared point of reference for journalists, a "corrective" against the brazenly one-sided distortions noted in the earlier crises when papers unabashedly manufactured "reality" that conformed to the prejudices of established communities of sentiment.

As a whole, reporting has become less transparently partisan than in nineteenth-century America and France, when there was not even the pretense of objectivity. Along with this goes the imperative to differentiate between reporting the news and editorializing about it. The distinction is not as absolute as it may seem but, with television, even the parochial press is compelled at least to appear factual. Editors, indeed, thrive on disclosures where they can let the facts speak for themselves. Not even intelligence and traditionally clandestine security operations can count on immunity. There is constant pressure on government to be open. During Watergate even editors friendly to Nixon joined the clamor for an impartial investigation as the best way to put the issue to rest. The contrast with the other crises is marked. Although the media, in pressing the issue too far, sometimes themselves became a party to the Watergate controversy, this is something media management would rather have avoided. There were not the same kind of ties between the media and the establishment found in Britain, which keep so many matters privileged and facilitate quiet resolutions to what might otherwise mushroom into full-blown public controversy.

Nor was the mass public so directly involved in the earlier crises. In the post–Civil War period, American political parties were the principal conduits between the centers of decision and the public. In the United States, as in France and, to some extent, also in Britain, each party had a press on whose political support it could count. In the absence of records with reliable estimates, we have no way of knowing how large a public was involved in these earlier crises. However, it is highly unlikely that these issues, as hot as they were, intruded as much into the public's attention frame as Watergate. In the only other crisis where a principal protagonist could have used the broadcast media to plead his case Edward was allowed on the air only after the controversy had been settled.

The importance of media appearances during the impeachment controversy was enhanced by the explosion of opinion polling, which allowed for an immediate assessment of public reaction to every new move. A continuous record of what the public "thought" on every conceivable aspect of Watergate was now available. No one seriously contends that opinion polls determine or should determine the decisions of public bodies. Especially where a situation is volatile or where the wrong questions are asked, these data, despite the awe with which statistics are sometimes regarded, can provide a less than accurate picture of where people stand and what they are willing to accept. Notwithstanding these caveats, the polls during Watergate were a more objective guide to changing sentiment than the highly selective expressions of opinion in earlier eras. But what the people thought then may not have mattered to elite actors as much as during Watergate.

None of this suggests that the public's role in Watergate was anything other than that of a bystander, whose opinions entered the calculations of political actors, sensitive to any murmuring among the multitude. In former times, those in the government got their information on popular opinion through political parties with editors and writers serving as important relay points. With American parties in some disarray, polling institutions (sometimes in conjunction with the press) have taken over some of this monitoring function. The public still does little more than react, even if some of its members develop a false sense of participation. People are persuaded of the "mediated" version of events. With the intrusion of the language of show business into television news, they are offered a familiar, though questionable, format of what is a complex reality. The picture is highly convincing.

Much of what passes as politics consists of symbolic action, whose function is to manipulate the acquiescence of the public to elite decisions.[41] Ordinary citizens generally see little reason to concern themselves over such esoteric issues as the method of financing political campaigns, about the civil liberties of a few thousand persons the government sees fit to treat as security risks, or about the political pressure on news media to act "responsibly," and so forth. Yet people do get involved. All too frequently they become more agitated over the mere hint of scandal than over policies with potentially far-reaching effects.

The first reactions to the Watergate disclosures were filtered through partisan sentiment. Hints of wrongdoing by one's own party usually encounter more skepticism than hints about similar wrongdoing by the other side. But in a major scandal, which overrides at least temporarily the normal political divisions, the symbolic issue dominates. As the alleged offenses by Nixon and his entourage came to be perceived as inadmissible deviations from the public order, there arose a demand for some form of punishment, the desire to see justice done, expressed as an essentially disinterested concern for order.[42] The almost universal acceptance of Nixon's resignation signifies just such an identification with the rule of law to a point where it overrides normal political allegiances.

This sentiment can become a most powerful urge. To a greater or lesser degree, it was manifested in each of the crises. How much influence this sentiment has on the resolution of crises depends not only on the media but also on political factors, such as the stability of the governing coalition and how secure it is from external challenge and from internal factionalism. Political power can be used to narrow an issue, provided wrongdoing is of limited dimension. Here one cannot overlook the nature of the relationship between the news media and leaders of the government. A press as aggressively independent as that in the United States was needed to articulate the moral indignation against the President. Nevertheless, in doing so, the press may have inadvertently downplayed other more fundamental issues embedded in the Watergate controversy as well as others facing the polity.

EPILOGUE

Watergate began as a narrowly political issue, the kind that often surfaces during an election campaign. A crisis of confidence developed only after it came to stand for something much more serious, for Presidential complicity in a political scandal and a continuing effort to cover up that complicity. With Watergate now a symbolic issue involving the integrity of the Presidency and the democratic values of governance, it could no longer be settled to almost everyone's satisfaction through the usual political bargaining, without recourse to the authority on which legal decisions are presumably based.

In this book we have traced the changing perceptions of the issue: what was the "crime"? who was to blame? and what was the proper punishment? We have also considered the contribution of the media to these changes in public opinion and that of public opinion to the extraordinary outcome. Based on the evidence, we reject the paranoid version of Watergate propagated by the White House that the crisis was manufactured by a hostile press which finally drove Nixon from office. But we also reject the populist view that Nixon was forced to resign because he lost his battle for public opinion.

The moving force behind the effort to get to the bottom of Watergate came neither from the media nor public opinion but from political insiders. The conflict pitted the White House against those who, for whatever reason, wanted full disclosure of the facts behind the illegal attempt to plant wiretaps in the national headquarters of the Democratic Party. These opponents included the Democrats' chairman who, as the intended victim, sought publicity as well as redress through a civil suit; the Federal judge before whom the initial Watergate case was tried; the Senate which, prodded by the Democrats, set up a select committee to look into campaign practices; the special prosecutors appointed as political pressure mounted to clear up the case; and the House, which was about to act on the three articles of impeachment its Judiciary Committee had recommended when Nixon, by resigning, short-circuited the process.

The press was a prime mover in the controversy only in its early phase, when the Woodward and Bernstein tandem first linked the Watergate burglars to the Nixon campaign committee and, during the campaign, uncovered other stories that hinted at the politically explosive potential of the "bugging" incident. But with Nixon's decisive electoral victory, the press came close to abandoning Watergate. Then, as the issue revived and conflict over the scope of the investigation intensified, the press mainly lived off information insiders were happy to furnish it.

Conflict and bargaining are the lifeblood of politics. Constituencies clamor for recognition, parties compete for dominance, special interests insist on being heard, agencies of government maneuver for power, while political officeholders seek to protect or improve their own positions. Given the potential for conflict inherent in the diversity of demands, it is coalitions that keep the decision-making system from fragmenting. Without such coalitions the result would be political gridlock: no one could get anywhere and nothing could be accomplished. Consequently, much of what is called politics is aimed at winning allies and isolating opponents.

Media publicity can be a major resource in building a coalition, but when used to drum up support it may also stir people from indifference to opposition. For this reason, political appeals must suit the interests of one's own constituency and be targeted to an audience from which a favorable response can be expected. Such appeals can be broadened by exploiting either or both of two sentiments: moral indignation and the resentment of what is perceived as undue privilege. Moral indignation, rooted in middle-class psychology, is indicative of a deep-seated desire for public order that finds expression in the disinterested demand that wrongdoing be punished. Public outrage at wrongdoing by public officials is exacerbated by resentment. Groups that see themselves as losing status, as enjoying less respect than they feel is their due, or as victims of what others seem able to get away with are especially susceptible to moral appeals. But the potential effectiveness of moral appeals also puts politicians under constraint, for the media are ubiquitous. The larger and more heterogeneous the reading, listening, and viewing public, the greater the constraint on what they feel they can do or say. Their private acts come under scrutiny and are judged by the same standards that are binding on other members of society. Transgressions, if not avoidable, must at all costs be hidden without arousing even a suspicion that there is something to hide, a lesson Richard Nixon failed to master.

During Watergate, both parties to the controversy worked to build coalitions. Watergate was not a dispute over a particular policy or piece of legislation. Therefore, they could not win support by invoking individual self-interest and habit but by appealing to concerns that override normal political loyalties. For this was a controversy involving fundamental beliefs and arousing deep-rooted and "lofty" sentiments. These emotions derived less from the "facts" of Watergate than what they implied about the Presidency, the institutions of government, and even the state of the nation. It is in this sense that Watergate, over which the parties maneuvered for months, was a symbolic issue. Its resolution required that the usual politics be shelved, at least temporarily.

Had the news media, by their coverage of Watergate, directly persuaded the public of the seriousness of White House misdeeds, of Nixon's complicity, of a threat to basic values, and that impeachment might be warranted? Not directly, but by their reporting and their comments, by the way they highlighted some events, by the context within which they framed these events, by the language they used to track developments, by linking news they reported to symbols familiar to the audience, and by the persons they singled out (or who offered themselves) as spokesmen in the controversy, the media certainly influenced the way the public—and politicians as well—thought about and defined the underlying issue.

That so many of the struggles between Nixon and his opponents should have had such wide publicity, and even been played out on television, accounts for the impression that the news media and an aroused public opinion forced the downfall of Richard Nixon. Certainly, the way both parties used the media to enlist support inevitably enlarged the arena of conflict. An attentive public formed and people began to align themselves. But beyond that it is difficult to demonstrate, in the narrowly scientific way that has become the researcher's norm, that watching or listening to a particular Watergate speech, press conference, or televised testimony was what directly changed people's opinion. Many media effects remain elusive and can be understood only as the outcome of a cumulative process. Thus we have pointed to evidence that minor, incremental, and sometimes subtle changes sooner or later contributed to major shifts. For example, the most important effect of the televised Senate Watergate hearings was a "sleeper," not immediately noticeable. By subtly changing the issue, the televised hearings prepared the ground for the outburst that so instantaneously followed the firing of the Special Watergate Prosecutor. Similarly, it was the high regard in which the major spokesmen against impeachment were held as the result of the televised Judiciary Committee proceedings that made their subsequent defection so persuasive.

The charge that the Watergate coverage was unfair or somehow "distorted" remains basically unsubstantiated. Nixon was hardly at the mercy of the media. The same publicity that was effectively utilized by his opponents was available to Nixon whenever he chose to make use of it. And Watergate did yield the headlines to other news on several occasions—not only during the Middle East crisis in October 1973 but later when, shortly before the impeachment debate, Nixon traveled abroad in what he called his "search for peace." As President, it was easy for Nixon to command attention; as leader of his party, he was apt to be treated gingerly by Republican editors until his intransigence overtried their loyalties. There is no question that the media thrive on scandal, and they did thrive during Watergate; but by the yardstick of reporting during the impeachment and trial of Andrew Johnson or during the Dreyfus case, they more than adhered to the norms of journalistic objectivity.

The main contribution of the media to moving opinion along was their extensive and full coverage of critical events. The visibility of the controversy helped more than anything to legitimate the process by which Nixon was ousted. It forced the debate onto a higher level. The less parochial and less moralistic the coverage, the greater is its emphasis on facts. Moreover, rational judgments are encouraged when the public sees itself as a jury in a trial. This impression was fostered throughout the controversy by continuous polling and by the appeals for public understanding from Congress, the White House, and others, at times when the country appeared to be polarized over Watergate. Few expected the public to acquiesce to impeachment as readily as it usually does to other acts of Congress. A Congressional conflict with the President, who enjoys a national mandate, is always a touchy matter, and even more so with Nixon who had just won reelection by such an overwhelming majority. A move to impeach was even more risky inasmuch as Nixon had hand-picked his replacement, who had in turn been ratified by Congress.

The legitimacy of the succession was hardly questioned. But what if the public had had no opportunity to observe the movers of public opinion at first hand? What if elite events had remained privileged, as they so often are? The end to Watergate might well have been the same if the Senate hearings had not been televised in full, if the struggle over the tapes and, especially, the Cox-Nixon confrontation had not taken place on the television screen, if the House Judiciary Committee had not debated in public for all the world to see, and if the ceremonies of transition from Nixon to Ford had remained a private affair. But would the passage of power have found so nearly unanimous an acceptance? With the President persisting in his efforts to derail the investigation by appealing for public support, could those conducting the impeachment inquiry have convinced Nixon loyalists that they were not motivated by partisanship? Not very likely, without the opportunity the televising of critical events afforded the public to judge for themselves.

The ease with which the transition was accomplished is also explained by the rising irritation at Nixon's apparent betrayal of the public trust. More and more of his erstwhile supporters came to view his various subterfuges, if not as outright illegalities, then as a threat to the public order which a President is sworn to uphold. In addition, resentment built over Nixon's tax writeoffs, his use of public funds to improve his private residence, and the illegal contributions he had obtained in return for political favors. While ordinary politicians were widely believed to engage in such chicanery, Presidents were supposed to be above self-aggrandizement at the taxpayer's expense.

The influence of the news media goes beyond the building of pressure that "something" be done to prevent such misdeeds. In widening the scope of a controversy, they modify the rules of the game, forcing politicians to justify themselves to an ever larger public. We have documented how the continued presence of the media helped transform what began as a campaign issue into a legal-juridical issue. Because the deliberations of the House Judiciary Committee were televised, they were cast into the mold of an adversary proceeding, with most arguments couched in legal rather than political language. The decision was depicted as compelled by the evidence, with members—regardless of personal conviction—accepting the majority decision. They saw themselves, as they had told the nation, as representatives of the impersonal authority embodied in the Constitution, the highest law of the land.

Watergate turned out to be one of those symbolic issues through which the public and its representatives could express how they felt about the Presidency, the rule of law, and the general principles by which the country should be governed. Then, once the issue was resolved and the initial shock of Watergate had worn off, the political system could continue to operate much as it had before. The coalition that had formed over Watergate and should have been strengthened by the Congressional class of 1974 failed to produce meaningful reform. Few of the underlying conditions that made Watergate possible were dealt with in its immediate aftermath.

Watergate, as a symbolic issue, should not be viewed as a delayed reaction to frustration over Vietnam, with Nixon taking the blame as scapegoat. Nixon himself had been widely regarded as part of the Vietnam solution, not the problem. He, rather than McGovern, had been elected in part because more people trusted him to bring a quick end to hostilities. After the peace agreement was signed, public approval for his handling of the Vietnam war rose steadily. What could and should have been done remained in contention, but not the current policy in Southeast Asia. Through most of Watergate, the Vietnam issue was deliberately sidestepped. The Judiciary Committee acted as if the unlawful wiretapping of the opposing party and its coverup was a more damaging violation of constitutional government than the unlawful waging of a secret war against the sovereign nation of Cambodia. This latter ground for impeachment was rejected by the Judiciary Committee over the objections of its staunchest advocates. As one put it, members had voted to "impeach a President for concealing a burglary but not for concealing a massive bombing."[1] Nor was there any public outcry at their failure to charge Nixon with depriving Congress, as the representative of the people, of its warmaking and appropriation powers.

Yet the resolution of the Vietnam issue made Watergate possible. Calls for national unity lost much of their urgency, and Watergate no longer had to compete for attention. A symbolic issue is more likely to become a major issue when no fundamental social or economic issue, be it slavery, economic reform, or military conflict, is of overriding political concern. Watergate was no exception. It can almost be said that the controversy filled a certain void. News interest perked up. People stayed close by their radio and television sets, waiting for each new development.

Still another question is how much the public was reacting to the substance of the Watergate disclosures or to Nixon himself. After all, other Presidents had been guilty of acts whose constitutionality was questionable or of behavior that fell short of the expected high standards of personal or political propriety. Yet these others somehow managed to avoid Nixon's fate. They somehow managed to keep up appearances either by sacrificing subordinates, who took the blame, or making sure that nothing beyond unsubstantiated rumor ever got out. Why should Nixon have failed with a similar strategy, one that he had previously employed with striking success? For one

thing Nixon by his behavior throughout his political career had made enemies within the working press. As President, however, he commanded deference and respect and was treated with caution. Yet, once insiders put him
on the defensive, these reporters were astounded at how far Nixon had evidently been willing to go to assure his reelection and to punish his "enemies." Thereafter they were ready to resurrect the image of the "old Nixon"
and were less willing to declare sensitive areas out-of-bounds. Nixon was to
harm himself further with the press by a pretense of openness. When pressed
on Watergate, he repeatedly assured his questioners that he would cooperate
to clear up the scandal, yet always with a proviso that allowed him to renege
at a later date. As a result, Nixon was to appear less and less ingenuous even
to his own followers. It was not the abuse of power, revealed in the Senate
hearings, as much of his obstruction of the legal process that in the last
analysis cost him the most support. The constituency that in the early months
backed him on Watergate became increasingly impatient to have the issue
resolved. This included many people who were still confident that the evidence would show that Nixon had done nothing worse than had other Presidents.

In this climate the opposition to Nixon gradually gained strength. It became difficult to defend Nixon on any but the narrowly legal grounds staked
out by Republicans on the Judiciary Committee. What must be reempha-
sized, however, is that the coalition favoring impeachment stood together
on the weakest possible foundation. For many, impeachment served only as
a negative rallying point for whatever they believed was wrong with the
country. Watergate was as much a symptom as a cause of the general disenchantment with politics and political institutions that anticipated the controversy. How alienated many citizens had become from the process is clearly
documented by the inability of the system to translate the division over Vietnam, deep as it was, into an electoral choice between an anti-war and a
pro-war candidate.

Be all this as it may, there could have been no real public opinion on
Watergate without the media. They alone could have called into being the
mass audience of "bystanders" whose opinion had to be taken into account.
It was likewise the media which, by reporting and even sponsoring polls,
presented the cast of political actors in Watergate with a measure of public
response to their every move. Nevertheless, the public never was an active
participant in the campaign against Nixon. It did not direct the course of
events, except when the reaction to Cox's dismissal signaled those in power

that the time had come to do something. The impression of public support made it easier to move against Nixon simply because the bystander public withheld the vote of confidence the President had so eagerly sought in order to defeat impeachment politically. Only in this sense, and this sense alone, was Nixon "driven" from office by his loss of public support.

APPENDIX

TABLE 1 Network Television Coverage of Watergate During the 1972 Presidential Campaign

	ABC	CBS	NBC
Total Time (in minutes)			
7-week period[a]	42.26	71.09	41.21
11-week period[b]	77.60	140.60	88.10
Mean Time per Newscast (in minutes)[c]			
7-week period[a]	1.15	2.00	1.15
11-week period[b]	1.20	1.45	1.10
Proportion of Political News (in percent)[d]			
of political newstime (11 wks.)[b]	15	21	17
of political items (7 wks.)[e]	7	10	11
of political items (11 wks.)[b]	17	19	20

[a] Source: Diamond, *The Tin Kazoo.*
[b] Source: Lichty, "Network News Reporting."
[c] Rounded to nearest 5 seconds
[d] Exact definitions vary slightly but all exclude human interest stories, weather, sports, and similar items.
[e] Source: Patterson and McClure, *The Unseeing Eye.*

TABLE 2 Attitudes Toward the Tapes

	% Wanting Tapes Handed Over	% Satisfied With Explanations
Approving Nixon's handling of job	18	59
Republicans	27	48
Conservatives	35	46
Disapproving Nixon's handling of job	75	9
Democrats	63	17
Liberals	66	16

Source: Opinion Research Corporation, August 18–20, 1973, survey.

TABLE 3 Percent Defining Watergate as "Serious"

	Gallup		Harris[a]
April 6–9	31	May	40
June 1–4	47	June	47
July 6–9	48	July	48
August 3–6	53	August	49

[a] Based on Harris Survey Release, September 6, 1973.

TABLE 4 Percent Believing in Nixon's Complicity[a]

May 11–14	56
June 1–4	67
June 22–25	71
July 6–9	73
August 3–6	76

Source: Gallup Organization
[a] Some of the May to June increase may be due to changes in question wording.

TABLE 5 Attitudes Toward Removal of President Nixon from Office (in percent)[a]

	For	Against	No Opinion
Impeachment			
June 22–25	19	69	12
July 6–9	24	64	14
August 3–6	26	61	13
August 18–20	23	64	13
Resignation[b]			
May 1–3	14	75	11
June	22	62	16
July	22	66	12
August 18–19	28	63	9
August 18–20	17	66	17

[a] Based on Gallup, "Do you think President Nixon should be impeached and compelled to leave office, or not?" The August 18–20 figure from an ORC survey, "Do you believe that President Nixon should be impeached and compelled to leave office because of the Watergate matter, or should he continue in office?"
[b] Based on Harris, "In view of what happened in the Watergate affair, do you think President Nixon should resign as President or not?" The August 18–20 ORC survey, included for comparison, asked, "Do you believe that President Nixon should resign because of the Watergate matter, or should he continue in office?"

TABLE 6 Television Coverage of Impeachment Debate on Commercial Networks (hours)

	ABC	CBS	NBC
July 24—Opening Statements	4.0		
July 25—Opening Statements (cont'd)		9.1	
July 26—Debate on Article I			5.8
July 27—Vote on Article I	5.5		
July 28—Sunday			
July 29—Vote on Article II		9.3	
July 30—Vote on Articles III, IV, & V			9.6
	9.5	18.4	15.4
Total		43.3	

Source: Lawrence Lichty, unpublished monitoring notes. Monitors for the *Congressional Quarterly* gave a total of only 35 hours 46 minutes, which presumably counted only live coverage of committee proceedings and omitted introductions and recaps.

TABLE 7 Vote on Impeachment Articles

	For		Against		
Article	Dems.	Reps.	Dems.	Reps.	Total
I Obstruction of Justice	21	6	–	11	27–11
II Abuse of Power	21	7	–	10	28–10
III Contempt of Congress	19	2	2	15	21–17
IV Bombing of Cambodia	12	–	9	17	12–26
V Income Tax Evasion	12	–	9	17	12–26

TABLE 8 Characterization of Committee by Time and Source (in percent)

	July 24–25			July 30			Three-day Total		
	Committee Members	Commentary	Total	Committee Members	Commentary	Total	Committee Members	Commentary	Total
Partisan/Political	6.5	68.8	27.7	6.8	31.9	10.5	6.7	41.3	12.3
Legal/Constitutional	93.5	31.2	72.3	93.2	68.1	89.5	93.3	58.7	87.7
	100.0	100.0	100.0	100.0	100.0	100.0	100.0	100.0	100.0
	(31)	(16)	(47)	(296)	(47)	(343)	(327)	(63)	(390)

TABLE 9 Arguments on Impeachment* (in percent)

	July 24–25	July 30	Three-Day Total
Partisan/Political	12.9	17.6	13.6
Legal/Constitutional	50.7	52.9	51.0
Assessment of Evidence	36.4	29.4	35.4
	100.0	100[a]	100.0
Total	(209)	(134)	(243)

[a] Some columns do not add to exactly 100 percent due to rounding.

TABLE 10 Opinion on Impeachment, Guilt, and Removal

	April	May	May/June	June	July	After
For impeachment (Newsday)	47			39		54
For removal or resignation (Newsday)	64			52		65
For impeachment (Harris)					53	63
For conviction by Senate (Harris)					47	56
For impeachment & trial (Gallup)	52	51	50		51	65
For removal (Gallup)	46	48	44		46	57

TABLE 11 Will Nixon Be Impeached and Removed from Office?

	May	July	August
Will be found guilty	29	27	47
Will not happen	53	55	40
Not sure	18	18	13

Source: Louis Harris Associates

TABLE 12 Network Resignation Night Coverage

	Statements			
	ABC	**CBS**	**NBC**	**All**
Favorable				
By news staff	22	50	27	99
In interview	35	46	25	106
	57	96	52	205
Unfavorable				
By news staff	25	55	22	102
In interview	35	35	53	123
	60	90	75	225
Percent Favorable	(49)	(52)	(41)	(47)
	Segments			
With favorable statement(s)				
By news staff	16	18	11	45
In interview	18	18	16	52
	34	36	27	97
With unfavorable statement(s)				
By news staff	19	23	12	54
In interview	17	16	21	54
	36	39	33	108
Percent Favorable	(50)	(55)	(38)	(46)

TABLE 13 Sentiment for Prosecution or Pardon

	% Who	
	Agree	**Disagree**
Do you think that President Ford should pardon former President Nixon on the grounds that he has suffered enough, or do you think such a pardon would be wrong?		
Harris (September 1–6)	35	57
Do you think Nixon should or should not be tried for possible criminal charges arising from Watergate?		
Gallup (September 3–6)	36	58
There have been proposals to give former President Nixon some form of immunity from any criminal charges related to things he may have done while he was in office. Do you favor or oppose them?		
Newsweek (September 5)	33	58

TABLE 14 Percent Who Had a Great Deal or Quite a Lot of Confidence in Each[a]

	1966	1972	1973	1974	1975	1976	1977	1978	1979	1980
Executive branch (Harris)	41	27	19	28	13	11	23			
White House (Harris)			18	18	13	11	31		15	18
Congress (Harris)	42	21	29	18	13	9	17		18	11
Congress (Gallup)			42		40		4	34		
Supreme Court (Harris)	50	28	33	40	28	22	29			
Supreme Court (Gallup)			44		49	46	46	45		

Source: *Current Opinion* (April 1977) 5(4); *Gallup Opinion Index*, 166 (May 1979).

[a] Gallup offered four alternatives: a great deal, quite a lot, some, and very little. Harris gave three, eliminating "quite a lot." Also, the Gallup question inquired about confidence in the institution itself while Harris asked about confidence in "the people in charge of running. . . ." The difference in absolute levels of confidence, with Harris consistently lower than Gallup, is probably due to the difference in question wording with incremental change of 1 or 2 percentage points from one year to the next probably due to statistical chance.

TABLE 15 Percent Who Agreed President Is/ Is Almost My Favorite of All

Grade in School	1962 (%)	1974 (%)	Decline in "Popularity"
2	80	54	−26
3	72	42	−30
4	70	22	−48
5	60	15	−45
6	51	7	−44

Source: 1962 data from Easton and Dennis: 1974 from Dennis and Webster.

TABLE 16 Comparison of 3rd and 6th Graders' View of President

	Grade in School	1973	1975
Percent Believing the President			
Does the most to run the U.S.	3	85	72
	6	79	68
Gives us liberty and freedom	3	73	87
	6	82	71
Helps keep the government running	3	79	82
	6	77	67
Tries to help the poor people	3	82	78
	6	74	55

Source: Bailey, "Political Learning and Development," 1975.

TABLE 17 Percent of Students Perceiving Effect on Self

Grade	%
7–9	30
10	34
11–12	48

Information Score	%
1 (lowest)	19
2	30
3	38
4	43
5	57

Source: Student Project (see chapter 10 note 35).

NOTES

Presidential statements as well as some others by high officials and public figures that have no reference other than the date given in the text were taken from the Presidential Papers and similar public records. Many poll figures similarly identified in the text by date of survey only were obtained either directly from the polling organizations or from releases of polling organizations.

1. OVERTURNING A LANDSLIDE

1. George H. Gallup, *The Gallup Poll: Public Opinion 1935–1971* (New York: Random House, 1972); *ibid.*, *1972–1977* (Wilmington, Del.: Scholarly Resources, Inc., 1978).

2. Richard M. Nixon, *RN: The Memoirs of Richard Nixon* (New York: Grosset and Dunlap, 1978), pp. 971, 972.

3. W. Phillips Davison, *The Berlin Blockade: A Study in Cold-War Politics.* (Princeton: Princeton University Press, 1958).

4. Bernard J. Cohen, *The Political Process and Foreign Policy: The Making of the Japanese Peace Treaty* (Princeton: Princeton University Press, 1957); Leon Sigal, *Reporters and Officials: The Organization and Politics of Newsmaking* (Lexington, Mass.: D. C. Heath, 1973); Todd Gitlin, *The Whole World is Watching* (Berkeley: University of California Press, 1980).

5. Joseph T. Klapper, *The Effects of Mass Communications* (Glencoe, Ill.: Free Press, 1960).

6. For a critique of these studies, see Kurt Lang and Gladys Engel Lang, "Mass Media and Voting," in Eugene Burdick and Arthur J. Brodbeck, eds. *American Voting Behavior*, pp. 217–35 (Glencoe, Ill.: Free Press, 1959).

7. Elihu Katz, Jay Blumler, and Michael Gurevitch, "The Utilization of Mass Communication by the Individual," in Elihu Katz and Jay Blumler, eds. *The Uses of Mass Communication: Current Perspectives in Gratification Research*, pp. 35ff (Beverly Hills: Sage, 1974).

8. Maxwell McCombs and Donald Shaw, "The Agenda-Setting Function of Mass Media," *Public Opinion Quarterly* (1972) 36:176–87.

9. Herbert Gans, *Deciding What's News* (New York: Pantheon, 1979); Philip Schlesinger, *Putting Reality Together* (London: Constable, 1978); Gaye Tuchman, *Making News* (New York: Free Press, 1978); and David Altheide, *Creating Reality: How TV News Distorts Events* (Beverly Hills: Sage, 1976).

10. Kurt Lang and Gladys Engel Lang, *Collective Dynamics* (New York: T. Y. Crowell, 1961), ch. 14.

11. Fred Davis, "A Watergate Afterthought: Muted by the Media or the Anesthe-

tization of Chaos." Unpublished paper, University of California, San Diego, December 1974.

2. THE PUBLIC AS BYSTANDER

1. Carl J. Friedrich, *The New Belief in the Common Man* (Boston: Little, Brown, 1942).

2. David Hume, *A Treatise on Human Nature* (Oxford: The Clarendon Press, 1967).

3. Edward A. Ross, *Social Control: A Survey of the Social Foundations of Order.* New York: Macmillan, 1901).

4. Congressional Quarterly, Inc., *Watergate: Chronology of a Crisis* (Washington, D.C.: CQ, 1975), p. 786.

5. Richard Ben-Veniste and George Frampton Jr., *Stonewall: The Real Story of the Watergate Prosecution* (New York: Simon and Schuster, 1977).

6. J. M. Edelman, *The Symbolic Uses of Politics* (Urbana: University of Illinois Press, 1967).

7. A. Lawrence Lowell, *Public Opinion and Popular Government* (New York: Longman's, 1913).

8. Herbert Blumer, "Collective Behavior," in A. M. Lee, ed. *Principles of Sociology*, pp. 189–94. New York: Barnes and Noble, 1951.

9. Some pollsters specifically asked respondents how they would have voted if the election had been held at that time.

10. Henry Maine, *Popular Government* (New York: Henry Holt, 1886) p. 184.

11. Walter Lippmann, *The Phantom Public* (New York: Harcourt, Brace, 1925), p. 106.

12. *Ibid.*

13. See Albert E. Gollin, ed. "Polls and the News Media: A Symposium." *Public Opinion Quarterly* (Winter 1980) 44 (whole number).

14. Albert H. Cantril, "The Press and the Pollsters," *Annals of the American Academy of Political and Social Science* (September 1976) 247:50.

15. See Louis Harris and Associates, Inc., *The Harris Survey Yearbook of Public Opinion: A Compendium of Current American Attitudes, 1971* (New York: Author, 1974).

16. Lowell, *Public Opinion.*

17. Elisabeth Noelle-Neumann, *Die Schweigespirale* (Munich: R. Piper and Company, 1980).

18. E. E. Schattschneider, *The Semisovereign People: A Realist's View of Democracy* (New York: Holt, Rinehart and Winston, 1960).

19. Karl Mannheim, *Man and Society in an Age of Reconstruction* (New York: Harcourt, Brace, 1940).

20. Philip Converse, "The Nature of Belief Systems in Mass Publics," in D. E. Apter, ed. *Ideology and Discontent*, pp. 206–64 (New York: Free Press, 1964).

21. Hugh Heclo, "Issue Networks and the Executive Establishment," in A. King,

ed. *The New American Political System*, pp. 87–124 (Washington, D.C.: American Enterprise Institute, 1978).

22. Lippmann, *Phantom Public*.

23. Schattschneider, *The Semisovereign People*.

24. Gabriel A. Almond, "Comparative Study of Interest Groups and the Political Process," *American Political Science Review* (March 1958) 52:370–83.

25. Charles H. Cooley, *Human Nature* (New York: Scribner's, 1902) used this concept for how a person imagined himself appearing to others.

3. 1972: THE WATERGATE "CAPER"

1. Maxwell E. McCombs and Donald L. Shaw, "The Agenda-Setting Function of Mass Media," *Public Opinion Quarterly* (1972) 36:176–87.

2. Bernard C. Cohen, *The Press and Foreign Policy* (Princeton: Princeton University Press, 1963), p. 120. Or, as we formulated the proposition prior both to Cohen and to McCombs and Shaw: "The mass media force attention to certain issues by suggesting what individuals in the mass should think about, know about, and have feelings about." Kurt Lang and Gladys E. Lang, The Mass Media and Voting," in Eugene Burdick and Arthur J. Brodbeck Jr., eds. *American Voting Behavior*, p. 232 (New York: Free Press, 1959, p. 232).

3. James M. Perry, *Us & Them: How the Press Covered the 1972 Election* (New York: Clarkson N. Potter, 1973), p. 269.

4. James McCartney, "The Washington 'Post' and Watergate: How Two Davids Slew Goliath," *Columbia Journalism Review*, July–August, 1973, p. 8. See also Charles Peters, "Why the Press Didn't Get the Watergate Story," *Washington Monthly*, July–August, 1973, pp. 7–15.

5. Ben Bagdikian, The Fruits of "Agnewism," *Columbia Journalism Review*, Jan.– Feb. 1973, p. 12. David Broder cites a speech by Bagdikian, in which Bagdikian had put the figure at "no more than 14 out of 2,200" to support his claim that "the average Washington news bureau had no one working full time on the Watergate story." *Washington Post*, May 8, 1973.

6. *Editorial Research Reports*, (1976) 1:259.

7. Doris A. Graber, "Press and TV as Opinion Resources in Presidential Campaigns," *Public Opinion Quarterly* (1976) 40:286.

8. Bagdikian, Fruits of "Agnewism," pp. 15f.

9. Based on *Bell and Howell's Newspaper Index* and Josephine R. Holz, "Watergate and Mass Communication: A Case Study in Public Agenda-Setting," M. A. thesis, University of Pennsylvania, 1976. Holz likewise worked from the *New York Times Index* and not from the actual newspapers.

10. Lawrence W. Lichty, "Network News Reporting of Watergate During the Election Campaign." Manuscript, University of Wisconsin, 1974.

11. *Ibid.*

12. The most detailed study of network television coverage during the 1972 campaign is C. Richard Hofstetter, *Bias In The News* (Columbus: Ohio State University

Press, 1976). It is based on videotapes for all weekday network newsprograms from July 10 through November 6. Unfortunately for our purposes, Watergate items were not categorized separately but apparently subsumed under either "Republican party affairs" or "government functioning." Lichty, "Network News Reporting," monitored network evening news coverage on CBS and NBC every day and ABC on weekdays only from August 29 through November 7. Edwin Diamond, *The Tin Kazoo* (Cambridge: M.I.T. Press, 1975) covered weekday evenings from September 14 through November 1, the Wednesday before election day. Thomas Patterson and Robert McClure, *The Unseeing Eye* (New York: Putnam, 1976), looked at weekday content of network newscasts from September 18 through November 6. Several major Watergate stories broke before mid-September; they were covered by Lichty but not by the others. The definitions of Watergate news may also have differed somewhat, inasmuch as they could have included such items as Republicans charging Democrats with campaign finance violations or Common Cause suing to force the disclosure of funds Republicans collected before April 7, 1972, which had no direct relationship to the "bugging incident." Descriptions of what was and what was not included under Watergate by each investigator are not entirely clear.

13. Hofstetter, *Bias in the News*, pp. 34ff.

14. Diamond, *Tin Kazoo*, p. 213.

15. Kurt Lang and Gladys E. Lang, *Politics and Television* (New York: Quadrangle, 1968) pp. 109–49, on the national convention telecasts in 1952.

16. Graber, "Press and TV." The 20 newspapers selected with the help of editors included many smaller papers, like the *Raleigh News and Observer* and the *Salt Lake Tribune*.

17. *Ibid.*, Table 6. The article contains some discrepancies between statistics cited in the text that do not affect the basic thrust of the finding. Also, since the TV figure is a proportion of the "campaign coverage" on television devoted to Watergate, it is calculated to a smaller base than all "political news," which was used in the studies summarized in Appendix, table 1.

18. David H. Weaver, Doris A. Graber, Maxwell E. McCombs, and Chaim H. Eyal, *Media Agenda-Setting in a Presidential Election* (New York: Praeger, 1981), ch. 3, makes similar observations about the difference in the effect of television and newspapers.

19. Gary Paul Gates, *Air Time: The Inside Story of CBS News* (New York: Harper and Row, 1978), p. 305.

20. Marvin Barrett, *Moments of Truth* (New York: T. Y. Crowell, 1975), p. 3.

21. Based on examination of the *Bell and Howell's Newspaper Index* for the *Washington Post*, *New Orleans Times-Picayune*, the *Chicago Tribune*, and the *Los Angeles Times*.

22. G. H. Gallup, *The Gallup Poll: Public Opinion 1935–1971* (New York: Random House, 1972).

23. Harris Survey, mid-September 1972.

24. Harold Mendelsohn and Garrett J. O'Keefe, *The People Choose a President.* (New York: Praeger, 1976), p. 200.

25. According to a mid-September 1972 Harris Survey, 84 percent considered the "attempt to wiretap another party's headquarters" a "basic violation of individual freedom," but only 57 percent believed this kind of wiretapping to be a commonplace occurrence; another 15 percent were uncertain whether it was or not.

26. Opinion Research Corporation, survey on August 28–30, 1973.

27. Mendelsohn and O'Keefe, *The People Choose*, p. 203.

28. Opinion Research Corporation, August 18–20 survey.

29. Polls by both Harris and *Time*/Yankelovitch record some slippage on this attribute, but Nixon's overall approval rating in the September and October Harris Surveys remained at 50 and 51 percent respectively. Gallup did not ask this question during the campaign.

30. Arthur H. Miller and Warren E. Miller, "Issues, Candidates and Partisan Divisions in the 1972 American Presidential Election," *Journal of Political Science* (1975) 5:393–434.

31. David H. Weaver, Maxwell E. McCombs, and Charles Spellman, "Watergate and the Media: a Case Study of Agenda-Setting," *American Politics Quarterly* (1975) 3:452–72.

32. Roger W. Cobb and Charles D. Elder, "The Politics of Agenda-Building: an Alternative Perspective for Modern Democratic Theory," *Journal of Politics* (1971) 33:892–915.

33. Weaver et al., *Media Agenda-Setting*, have recently introduced a distinction between "obtrusive" and "unobtrusive" issues, similar to our threshold variable, to take account of whether or not a concern lies within people's experience.

34. Donald R. Kinder and D. Roderick Kiewiet, "Economic Discontent and Political Behavior: The Role of Personal Grievances and Collective Economic Judgments in Congressional Voting," *American Journal of Political Science* (1979) 23:495–523.

35. Hans-Mathias Kepplinger and Herbert Roth, "Creating a Crisis: German Mass Media and the Oil Supply in 1973–1974," *Public Opinion Quarterly* (1979) 43:285–96.

36. National Advisory Commission on Civil Disorder, *Report* (Washington, D. C.: Government Printing Office, 1968).

37. Tom W. Smith, "America's Most Important Problem—A Trend Analysis," *Public Opinion Quarterly* (1980) 44:164–80.

38. Bagdikian, Fruits of "Agnewism."

39. Altogether 7 out of 30 newspapers examined failed to carry this story.

40. Ernest R. May and Janet Fraser, eds. *Campaign '72: The Managers Speak.* (Cambridge: Harvard University Press, 1973), p. 207.

41. This criticism was much discussed in panels of a conference of journalists, politicians, public relations consultants, and communication researchers, sponsored jointly by the Newhouse School of Communication and the Maxwell School of Public Affairs, Syracuse University. The sessions were videotaped and widely reported in the press.

42. William S. Paley, *As It Happened.* New York: Doubleday, 1979, pp. 317–27. Richard Salant's letter to *Variety* (December 4, 1972) appears on pp. 324–27.

43. Daniel Schorr, *Clearing the Air* (New York: Berkley Books 1977), p. 34.

44. Marvin Barrett, *Moments of Truth*, p. 139f.

45. Samuel L. Popkin et al., "Toward an Investment Theory of Voting," *American Political Science Review* (1976) 70:779–805.

46. Louis Harris and Associates, Inc., *The Harris Yearbook of Public Opinion: A Compendium of Current American Attitudes 1972* (New York: Author, 1974), pp. 70, 72. In October, a majority believed that McGovern would get peace on the wrong terms and nearly as many thought that his election would slow down the return of American prisoners as thought that it would speed it up.

47. Miller and Miller, "Issues, Candidates and Partisan Divisions."

48. Alex S. Edelstein and Diane P. Tefft, "Media Credibility and Respondent Credulity with Respect to Watergate," *Communication Research* (1976) 4:426–39.

49. Gary Hart, *Right From the Start: A Chronicle of the McGovern Campaign* (New York: Quadrangle, 1973), p. 392.

4. HOW WATERGATE MADE THE PUBLIC AGENDA

1. Gallup Poll, April 6–9, 1973. Opinion Research Corporation in a survey conducted for the White House found that 85 percent had knowledge of the "Watergate incident" as early as mid-February.

2. Gallup Opinion Index, No. 100, October 1973, p. 11.

3. The Gallup question read, "Which of these two statements comes closer to your own view of Watergate—it's a serious matter because it reveals corruption in the Nixon administration or it's just politics, the kind of thing both parties engage in." In the Gallup survey April 6–9, 31 percent chose the first and 53 percent the second alternative. Responding to an essentially similar choice in a Harris Survey, 36 percent opted for "a serious matter" and 48 percent for "just politics."

4. Harris Survey, April 18–23, 1973.

5. Opinion Research Corporation found that 16 percent of Democrats thought Nixon was responsible compared with only 6 percent of the Republicans.

6. Gallup Survey, April 6–9, 1973. The question: "Do you think President Nixon knew about the Watergate situation in advance, or not?" The Harris question: "Do you feel that President Nixon knew about the attempt to wiretap Democratic headquarters in advance or not?"

7. Louis Harris and Associates, Inc., *The Harris Yearbook of Public Opinion; A Compendium of Current American Attitudes 1973* (New York: Author, 1976), p. 8.

8. *New York Times*, April 20, 1973.

9. *New York Times*, April 26, 1973.

10. For trends on responses to this question, see *Harris Yearbook 1973*.

11. Transcript of April 25, 1973 telephone conversation between Richard Nixon and H. R. Haldeman. *New York Times*, November 22, 1974, p. 20.

12. *New York Times*, January 31, 1973; John J. Sirica, *To Set the Record Straight* (New York: Norton, 1975), p. 71.

13. *New York Times*, February 3, 1973.

14. Josephine R. Holz, "Watergate and Mass Communication: A Case Study in Public Agenda-Setting." M. A. thesis, University of Pennsylvania, 1976.

15. Based on the Vanderbilt University Television News Archive, *Television News Index and Abstracts.* Vanderbilt University, Nashville, Tennessee.

16. Based on *Bell & Howell's Newspaper Index* for the *Chicago Tribune*, the *Los Angeles Times*, the *New Orleans Times-Picayune*, and the *Washington Post*.

17. On three previous days Ziegler was said to have dealt with over 300 reporter queries on Watergate in his regular daily briefings. Richard Nixon, *RN: The Memoirs of Richard Nixon* (New York: Grosset and Dunlap, 1978), p. 386.

18. Meg Greenfield, The Great American Flap Trap, *Washington Post*, November 25, 1981.

19. David H. Weaver, Maxwell E. McCombs, and Charles Spellman, Watergate and the Media: A Case Study of Agenda-setting," *American Politics Quarterly* (1975) 3:452–72. They explain their lack of across-the-board correlations by introducing the "need for orientation" as an intervening variable. The relatively weak effects of this variable do not preclude the simultaneous operation of the "ceiling effect" hypothesized by us.

20. Other calls for White House cooperation in clearing up the matter came from James Buckley of New York, Lowell Weicker of Connecticut, Norris Cotton of New Hampshire, and several Republican members of the House. The text of the statements quoted can be found in *The New York Times* or local newspapers.

21. Alex S. Edelstein and Diane P. Tefft, "Media Credibility and Respondent Credulity with Respect to Watergate," *Communication Research* (1976) 4:426–39.

22. A telephone poll by Harris on May 1–3 (N = 892). The agreement on "it is hard to believe . . . President Nixon did not know about the planning and the later cover-up of the affair" was 51 percent; 30 percent disagreed.

5. THE ERVIN COMMITTEE HEARINGS

1. Stanley M. Besen and Bridger M. Mitchell, *Watergate and Television.* (Santa Monica, Cal.: Rand Corporation May 1975, R-1712-MF); and, by the same authors, "Watergate and Television: An Economic Analysis," *Communication Research* (1976) 3:243–60. Also, NBC Research report.

2. CBS News, June 1, 1973.

3. David J. LeRoy, C. Edward Wotring, and Jack Lyle, "The Public Television Viewer and the Watergate Hearings," *Communication Research* (October 1974) 1:406–25.

4. *New York Times*, July 31, 1973, p. 75.

5. Sam Dash, *Chief Counsel; Inside the Ervin Committee—the Untold Story.* New York: Random House, 1976, p. 88.

6. *Newsday*, August 8, 1973. See also, P. J. McGeever, "Guilty, Yes; Impeachment, No," *Political Science Quarterly* (1974) 89:289–99.

7. Louis Harris and Associates, Inc., *The Harris Survey Yearbook of Public Opinion: A Compendium of Current American Attitudes, 1973* (New York: Author, 1976).

8. George H. Gallup, *The Gallup Poll: Public Opinion 1972–1977*. Wilmington, Del.: Scholarly Resources, Inc., 1978, vol. 1.

9. Quayle poll, reported on NBC news, August 14, 1973, and *New York Times*, August 15, 1973.

10. Harris survey, Sept. 23–25. For another replay, with similar results, see Jack McLeod, Jane D. Brown, Lee B. Becker, and Dean A. Ziemke, "Decline and Fall at the White House: A Longitudinal Study of Media Effects," *Communication Research* (1977) 4:10.

11. Timothy R. Haight and Richard A. Brody, "The Mass Media and Presidential Popularity and the News in the Nixon Administration," *Communication Research* (1977) 4:41–60; and John E. Mueller, "Presidential Popularity from Truman to Johnson," *American Political Science Review* (March 1970) 64:18–34.

12. *The Harris Yearbook*, 1973, pp. 8–9.

13. Kurt Lang and Gladys E. Lang, *Politics and Television* (Chicago: Quadrangle, 1968), pp. 137–41; also Ithiel deSola Pool, "TV: A New Dimension in Politics, in Eugene Burdick and Arthur J. Brodbeck, eds. *American Voting Behavior*, pp. 236–61 (New York: Free Press, 1969).

14. Sidney Kraus, ed. *The Great Debates* (Bloomington: Indiana University Press, 1962).

15. G. D. Wiebe, "Responses to the Televised Kefauver Hearings: Some Social Psychological Implication," *Public Opinion Quarterly* (Summer 1952) 16:179–200.

16. Eric Sevareid, *Small Sounds in the Night* (New York: Knopf, 1956), p. 217.

17. G. D. Wiebe, "The Army-McCarthy Hearings and the Public Conscience," *Public Opinion Quarterly* (Winter 1958–59) 22:490–502; G. D. Wiebe, "A New Dimension in Journalism," *Journalism Quarterly* (Fall 1954) 31:411–420.

18. Dash, *Chief Counsel*, p. 113.

19. John Dean, *Blind Ambition* (New York: Pocket Books, 1977), p. 185. See also Richard Nixon, *RN: The Memoirs of Richard Nixon* (New York: Grosset and Dunlap, 1978), p. 781.

20. Nixon, *Memoirs*, pp. 782f.

21. *New York Times*, June 5, 1973; Dash, *Chief Counsel*, pp. 140–146.

22. Dash, *Chief Counsel*, p. 125.

23. *Ibid.*, ch. 7; Sam J. Ervin Jr., *The Whole Truth* (New York: Random House, 1980), p. 115; and Fred Thompson, *At That Point in Time: The Inside Story of the Senate Watergate Committee* (New York: Quadrangle/New York Times, 1975), p. 53.

24. Nixon, *Memoirs*, p. 872.

25. Harris Survey, on Confidence in Government, September 13–22, 1973.

26. Harris Survey, release September 6, 1973.

27. *Harris Yearbook*, p. 176.

28. Gallup Survey, August 17–20.

29. Jai-Won Lee, "Mass Media's Role-Taking in Changing Societies," *Papers of the 1st International Conference on Korean Studies*, Seoul, May 15, 1980, pp. 1390–1404.

30. Dean, *Blind Ambition*, p. 288.

31. *Washington Post*, June 6, 1973. The entire column was an attack on Dean.

32. Dean, *Blind Ambition*, pp. 307f.

33. *Ibid.*, p. 329. Also Daniel Schorr, *Clearing the Air* (New York: Berkley, 1978), p. 81n.

34. Dean, *Blind Ambition*, p. 315.

35. June 28, 1973 (afternoon session).

36. One example is provided by the President's daughter Julie and her husband, David Eisenhower, who appeared on the late-night Jack Paar talk show, then on a July 10 BBC show, and gave an interview to the *Times* of London. Charles Colson was interviewed on *Face the Nation* (CBS).

37. Ervin, *The Whole Truth*, p. 209; Dash, *Chief Counsel*, pp. 174f.

38. Thompson, *At That Point in Time*, p. 84.

39. Josephine R. Holz, "Watergate and Mass Communication: A Case Study in Public Agenda-Setting." M. A. thesis, Annenberg School of Communication, University of Pennsylvania, 1976.

40. AP, Aug. 16, 1973.

41. Nixon, *Memoirs*, p. 905.

42. *New York Times*, August 19, 1973, p. 1. Regular polls by Gallup (August 17–20) and by Harris (August 18–19) show, if anything, an even more negative reaction.

43. The caption of the *New York Times* item read, "Watergate Trails Kopechne Death in National Poll" (August 4, 1973). It was based on the release of a report by Kevin Phillips, a conservative political analyst, and Albert Sindlinger, who had polled for White House assistant Charles Colson.

44. *The Harris Yearbook*, pp. 159, 169.

45. Garrett J. O'Keefe and Harold Mendelsohn, "Voter Selectivity, Partisanship and the Challenge of Watergate," *Communication Research* (October 1974) 1:345; also the review of studies in Kurt Lang and Gladys Engel Lang, "Televised Hearings: The Impact Out There," *Columbia Journalism Review*, (November–December 1973) 12:52–57.

46. LeRoy et al., "The Public Television Viewer."

47. In addition to national polls, see David H. Weaver, Maxwell E. McCombs, and Charles Spellman, "Watergate and the Media: A Case Study of Agenda-Setting," *American Politics Quarterly* (1975) 3:458–72.

48. O'Keefe and Mendelsohn, "Voter Selectivity, Partisanship, and the Challenge of Watergate," p. 356.

49. John Holm, Sidney Kraus and Arthur H. Bochner, "Communication and Opinion Formation: Issues Generated by the Watergate Hearings," *Communication Research* (October 1974) 1:368–90.

50. Michael Robinson, "Impact of the Televised Watergate Hearings," *Journal of Communication* (Spring 1974) 24(2):18.

51. Gallup press release, June 2, 1973, of the May 14–17 survey.

52. *The California Poll*, Release, September 2, 1972.

53. *Time*, August 19, 1973.

54. See chapter 9.

55. Robinson, "Impact of Watergate Hearings."

56. John P. Robinson, "Public Opinion and the Watergate Crisis," *Communication Research* (October 1974) 1:391–405.

57. The California Poll.

58. Gallup, August 3–6 (on impeachment); Harris, August 18–19 (resignation). An earlier version of the Harris question using "ordered the coverup" yielded a similar distribution.

59. May 23, 1973.

60. Dash, *Chief Counsel,* p. 43.

6. THE BATTLE OF THE POLLS

1. Congressional Quarterly, Inc., *The Presidency: 1974,* p. 2.

2. Richard M. Nixon, *RN: The Memoirs of Richard Nixon* (New York: Grosset and Dunlap, 1978), p. 972.

3. Quoted in Michael Wheeler, *Lies, Damn Lies, and Statistics* (New York: Liveright, 1962), p. 172.

4. *Ibid.,* p. xv.

5. Nixon, *Memoirs,* p. 972.

6. *Ibid.,* p. 971.

7. *Ibid.,* p. 1017.

8. Wheeler, *Lies, Damn Lies;* see also his "The Unholy Alliance," *New Times,* May 1975, pp. 39–42; Timothy Crouse, "How Many Polls Does It Take to Make a President?" *Esquire* (April, 1976), Vol. 85, pp. 16–18f.

9. Frank Mankiewicz, *U.S. v. Richard M. Nixon* (New York: Quadrangle, 1975), pp. 81–141; see also Barry Sussman, *The Great Cover-up* (New York: Thomas Y. Crowell, 1974).

10. See Samuel Dash, *Chief Counsel: Inside the Ervin Committee* (New York: Random House, 1976); also Sam J. Ervin Jr., *The Whole Truth* (New York: Random House, 1980), p. 229.

11. Nixon *Memoirs,* pp. 909–10; S. Ervin, *The Whole Truth,* p. 229.

12. See John J. Sirica, *To Set the Record Straight* (New York: Norton, 1979), ch. 8, for why he avoided the complex issues.

13. Dash, *Chief Counsel,* p. 209. The Appendix contains "A Personal Account by Senator Sam J. Ervin, Jr. of his Meeting with President Richard Nixon Regarding the Release of Transcripts of the White House Tapes," pp. 267–72; see also Ervin, *The Whole Truth,* pp. 233–41.

14. Nixon, *Memoirs,* p. 933.

15. James Doyle, *Not Above the Law* (New York: Morrow, 1977). We have also interviewed Doyle about these events and based much of our account on his excellent book. Among other main sources in putting together the pertinent facts on the Massacre have been such first-hand recollections as Richard Ben-Veniste and George Frampton Jr., *Stonewall: The Real Story of the Watergate Prosecution* (New York: Simon and Schuster, 1977); Leon Jaworski, *The Right and the Power* (New York:

Reader's Digest, 1976); and Elliot Richardson, "Saturday Night Massacre," *Atlantic,* March, 1976, pp. 40–49.

16. Marvin Barrett, ed. *Moments of Truth: The Fifth Alfred I. DuPont–Columbia University Survey of Broadcast Journalism* (New York: T. Y. Crowell, 1975), p. 29, mistakenly states that the conference was carried live on three national TV networks.

17. Doyle, *Not Above the Law*, pp. 176–78.

18. We have found versions of Cox's statement with and without the phrase "to decide." Richardson, in "The Saturday Night Massacre," ends with "to decide" and the observation that it was the American people first, and only then Congress, who decided that ours will continue a government of laws. Thus he joins the ranks of those who believe that it was public opinion that goaded Congress into action. It seems that the statement Cox dictated over the phone and disseminated by Doyle originally ended, "now it is for Congress and country." According to Mankiewicz, *U.S. v. Richard Nixon*, p. 40, it was the wire services that added the words "to decide" to draw attention to the implications. This is another instance in which a newsman's casual choice of words helped shape interpretations that affected the course of events.

19. Nixon, *Memoirs*, p. 933.

20. Doyle, *Not Above the Law*, p. 178.

21. Nixon, *Memoirs*, p. 933.

22. Sirica, *To Set the Record Straight*, p. 167.

23. Nixon *Memoirs*, p. 934.

24. NBC 90-minute Special, 11:30 P.M. EDT, October 20, 1973.

25. Doyle, *Not Above the Law*, pp. 200–1.

26. We have been unable to trace the origin of this epithet.

27. Sirica, *To Set the Record Straight*, p. 167.

28. Richardson, "Saturday Night Massacre."

29. Robert W. O'Brien and Elizabeth Jones, *The Night Nixon Spoke* (Los Alamitos, Calif.: Hwong, 1976). This estimate is based on *all* letters, postcards, and telegrams directly addressed to Nixon and Eisenhower, plus such others as found their way through local party and campaign offices to the Republican National Committee, all of which are now housed in the library of Whittier College.

30. *New York Times*, October 24, 1973, p. 31.

31. Based on the official census estimate of 141,656,000 persons 18 and older in 1974. *U.S. Statistical Abstract*.

32. *New York Times*, October 29, 1973, p. 10.

33. Nixon, *Memoirs*, p. 935.

34. Personal communication.

35. Congressional Quarterly, *Chronology of a Crisis* (Washington, D. C.: CQ, Inc., 1975), p. 355.

36. Richard Neustadt, *Presidential Power: With Reflections on Johnson and Nixon* (New York: Wiley, 1976), pp. 4–5.

37. *Congressional Quarterly*, October 27, 1973.

38. If only "normal" sampling distribution is considered, the "true" pro-impeachment sentiment after the press conference could have been as low as 23 percent or

as high as 34 percent, assuming a margin of error of ±6 percentage points. When we consider that Gallup's special telephone polls during the Watergate period had a slight bias, compared with their regular surveys, towards the "conservative" and pro-Nixon side, an estimate of 34 percent as the upper estimate is at least reasonable.

39. Louis Harris and Associates, *The Harris Yearbook of Public Opinion: A Compendium of Current American Attitudes, 1973* (New York: Author, 1976, pp. 8–9).

40. The California Poll, Field Research Corporation. Release, November 2, 1973.

41. A CBS researcher has indicated that the Opinion Research Corporation, which had polled for Nixon, was employed so as to forestall any charges of bias in the poll, whatever its results. The full report, "The President and the Media: An Evaluation of Credibility Among the Public as of November 18, 1973," was released by the Surveys and Data Services, CBS News.

42. William S. Paley, *As It Happened* (New York: Doubleday, 1979), p. 317.

43. Minnesota Poll No. 45, November 1973. From *Current Opinion* (January 1974) 2:28.

44. Nixon, *Memoirs*, p. 935.

45. Internal memo cited in Department of Communication, The American University, "Nixon's News Distortion Charge: A Coincidental Two-week Test." Unpublished report by Professor Edward Bliss, 1974, p. 11.

46. *Ibid.*

47. Bruce Herschensohn, *The Gods of Antenna* (New Rochelle, N. Y.: Arlington House, 1976), pp. 54ff.

48. Nixon, *Memoirs*, pp. 934–5.

49. Herschensohn, *The Gods of Antenna*, pp. 54ff.

50. Based on data provided by Professor Lawrence Lichty, Department of Communication Arts, University of Wisconsin, Madison.

51. Sirica, *To Set the Record Straight*, p. 182.

52. Nixon, *Memoirs*, p. 945.

53. In the ABC poll 67 percent were disbelievers. Disbelievers outnumbered believers by 57 to 23 percent in the Harris Survey fielded November 12–15.

54. Nixon, *Memoirs*, p. 946.

55. Gallup, November 30–December 3.

56. Nixon, *Memoirs*, p. 948.

57. *Ibid.*, p. 957.

58. Seven years later, the phrase was still good for a laugh on an episode of the highly popular CBS situation comedy, *House Calls*, aired March 16, 1981, when an out-patient, believing he was Richard Nixon, kept ranting "I am not a crook".

59. Harris poll, November 12–15, 1973, and January 7–10, 1974.

60. *National Observer* poll, reported in the *New York Times*, January 13, 1974, p. 13.

61. Op-Ed page, *New York Times*, May 2, 1974.

62. *New York Times*, April 30, p. 1. See also columnist James Reston, May 1, 1974, concerning the effectiveness of the speech.

63. Impeachment Inquiry, Hearings before the Judiciary Committee, House of

Representatives, 93rd Congress, Second Session, Book I (Jan. 31–May 15, 1974), pp. 403–66.

64. *The Gallup Opinion Index,* (May 1974), no. 107, pp. 2–5.

65. *Roper Reports,* (1974) no. 74–5.

66. For example, Gallup showed large pluralities in favor of releasing the tapes to properly designated persons or groups in several questions asked—August 3–6, 1973; November 2–5, 1973; and May 31–June 3, 1974.

67. Wheeler, *Lies, Damn Lies.*

68. Yankelovich, November Survey, *Time,* November 19, 1973.

69. *Roper Reports,* (1974), no. 74–4.

70. *Roper Reports,* (1973), no. 73-10.

71. William Safire, *New York Times,* November 8, 1973.

72. Nixon, *Memoirs,* p. 850.

73. *Ibid.,* p. 948.

74. *Ibid.,* p. 753.

75. *Roper Reports* (1974), no. 74–5.

76. U. S. Senate, Committee on Government Operations, *Confidence and Concern; Citizens View American Government.* December 3, 1973, part 1 (extracts).

77. Bob Woodward and Scott Armstrong, *The Brethren: Inside the Supreme Court.* (New York: Simon and Schuster, 1979).

7. TELEVISION AS AN AGENT OF LEGITIMATION

1. Monitors for the *Congressional Quarterly* put the debate time at 35 hours 46 minutes. According to Lawrence W. Lichty, University of Wisconsin, there were 43.3 hours of coverage (debate plus commentary); our own monitoring notes in Stony Brook cover 44.2 hours of broadcasting.

2. *Broadcasting,* August 4, 1974, p. 18, states that network profits were reduced by an estimated $600,000 per network per day.

3. *Ibid.*

4. E. E. Schattschneider, *The Semisovereign People: A Realist's View of Democracy* (New York: Holt, Rinehart & Winston, 1960), p. 2.

5. This approach owes much to Kenneth Burke, especially, *A Rhetoric of Motives* (New York: Prentice-Hall, 1950).

6. Interview with Francis O'Brien, HJC staff director.

7. Rodino was one of only 35 House members to have voted against Ford's confirmation as Vice President. When he justified this on the House floor as a response to the needs of his district (Ford had not approved measures designed to help urban blacks), some Republicans criticized this as a partisan act dictated only by the political insecurity of a white man representing a predominantly black district. *Congressional Quarterly,* January 26, 1974.

8. Rodino had been mentioned in taped conversations of a convicted extortionist as a source of favors for friends, but Rodino denied he ever knew the man. What mainly spawned talk of a connection with organized crime was his long friendship

with Hugh Addonizio, the former Newark Mayor, convicted and imprisoned for corruption.

9. Edward Mezvinsky, *A Term to Remember* (New York: Coward, McCann & Geoghegan, 1977), p. 90. The lawyer was Bob McCandless, Dean's former brother-in-law.

10. According to one bizarre story making the rounds, a former Congressman, serving a sentence for tax evasion, had asked Jeb Magruder, imprisoned at Allenwood, to help in "wiping out Peter Rodino" by spilling the goods on him. In return Nixon would pardon Magruder so that he could continue to practice law. Rodino was said to have learned about Magruder's proposal through the grapevine. Jimmy Breslin, *How The Good Guys Finally Won* (New York: Viking, 1975), pp. 148ff.

11. *New York Times*, July 6, 1974.

12. Interview with Francis O'Brien.

13. Books on the role of the House Judiciary Committee, especially "insider" accounts, have been fewer and less well-publicized than those emanating from the Senate Watergate Committee or the Office of the Special Prosecutor. The autobiography by Barbara Jordan and Shelby Hearon, *Barbara Jordan; a Self-Portrait* (Garden City, N.Y.: Doubleday, 1978) contains little new information. So far Mezvinsky's, *A Term To Remember*, is the one valuable account we have come across. At press time, no other member of the Committee or its staff had written a book-length version of events. Renata Adler, a writer employed by the committee, was allegedly writing a book based on her own observations, but we were able to locate only her article, "Searching for the Real Nixon Scandal: A Last Inference," *Atlantic*, December 1976, pp. 76–95.

14. Congressional Quarterly, Inc., *Watergate: Chronology of a Crisis*, (Washington, D.C., 1975), p. 503.

15. Elizabeth Drew, *Washington Journal: The Events of 1973–1974* (New York, Random House, 1975), p. 348.

16. *New York Times*, May 24, 1974.

17. *Congressional Quarterly*, January 26, 1974.

18. *New York Times*, January 15, 1974.

19. *New York Times*, January 29, 1974.

20. Adler, "Real Nixon," p. 78.

21. In March 1974, Doar and Jenner went to the U. S. Court House to pick up the secret report and briefcase of evidence left for them by the Watergate grand jury. Television coverage of their joint-trip underlined the bipartisan effort.

22. Adler, "Real Nixon," p. 79.

23. Mezvinsky, *A Term to Remember*, pp. 180f.

24. Drew, *Washington Journal*, p. 293. This account of Doar's presentation, based on what another reporter told her, has been confirmed in personal interviews with O'Brien and two members of the Committee.

25. Adler, "Real Nixon," p. 79.

26. In their syndicated column, Evans and Novak (March 4, 1974) wrote that Garrison, as part of an effort to undercut Jenner, had prepared a report presenting a narrow view of what constituted an impeachable offense which, together with a

magazine article about Jenner's lack of a "zeal to prosecute," was distributed only to Republican members of the Committee. The accuracy of the column was disputed at the time but is confirmed by Mezvinsky, *A Term to Remember*, pp. 100ff.

27. Interview with O'Brien.

28. By 1954 strong criticism of the way in which Congressmen were conducting "scientific" polls became the subject of a symposium published in the *Public Opinion Quarterly* (1954) 18:121–42.

29. Leonard A. Marascuilo and Harriett Amster, "Survey of 1961–62 Congressional Polls," *Public Opinion Quarterly* (1964) 28:497–506.

30. Report by Representative Morgan F. Murphy, of Illinois, published in the *Congressional Record*, House of Representatives, 93rd Congress, 2nd Session, June 26, 1974, p. 21300.

31. File of polls and accompanying press clippings made available by Professor Jack Orwant, Department of Communications, American University. In statistical analysis, we counted only second polls of the eight Congressmen who had polled their districts more than once during this period.

32. The timing may have been influenced by dependence on volunteer help. Many members mail out their questionnaires a month or two before the summer to coincide with the influx of summer interns, who code and tabulate the responses. There is, however, no ground for believing that Republicans were more dependent than Democrats on this kind of volunteer help.

33. Seven of the 21 Democrats (33%) and 10 of the 16 Republicans (62%) on the HJC polled their districts in the first seven months of 1974.

34. The classification into hardliners, neutrals, and zealots is from John M. Naughton, "The First Judgment," *New York Times Magazine*, April 28, 1974, pp. 27ff. Two of his "hardliners" (Hogan and Froehlich) ended up voting for the first article of impeachment.

35. The exact numbers were: 6 of 9 "hardliners" (67%); 4 of 7 Republican "neutrals" (57%); 6 of 14 Democratic "neutrals" (43%); and 1 of 7 "impeachment zealots" (14%). Harold D. Donohue, the remaining Democrat, defied categorization.

36. Office of Charles Wiggins, *Special Report* (April 1974) 8(2).

37. Saul Kohler and Miles Benson, "In the House, an Uncertain Approach to Impeachment," *Times-Picayune* National Service, no date given. Wiggins' staff included a copy of this article together with the copy of the questionnaire sent to Professor Jack Orwant. See note 31.

38. Quoted in Naughton, "The First Judgment."

39. From news clippings supplied by Representative Butler and his aides. In some cases, exact dates are not given. The quote is from an article that appeared in June.

40. Quoted in Naughton, "The Last Judgment."

41. Richard Nixon, *RN: The Memoirs of Richard Nixon* (New York, Grosset and Dunlap, p. 990). The Rangel one-liner also appeared in Naughton, "The First Judgment."

42. Mezvinsky, *A Term to Remember*, p. 189.

43. Interview with Francis O'Brien.

44. Mezvinsky, *A Term to Remember*, p. 195.

45. Drew, *Washington Journal*, p. 350.

46. Especially the NBC evening news, July 26, 1974.

47. Mezvinsky, A *Term to Remember*, p. 218.

48. The content was analyzed by Glenna Lang and Alexander von Hoffman using videotapes supplemented by audio tapes and, in the case of the complicated July 30 debate, by the printed record, *Debate on Articles of Impeachment: Hearings of the Committee on the Judiciary*, House of Representatives, 93rd Congress, Second Session. The context unit was the paragraph. If Rodino was praised as "fair" by a speaker in his opening remarks, that counted as one mention no matter how many times Rodino's name was mentioned. If that praise was repeated in summing up, however, this was counted as a second mention. Mentions of TV as "fair" or "unfair" and references to Nixon were coded in the same way.

49. Mezvinsky, A *Term to Remember*, p. 199.

50. Interview with Francis O'Brien.

51. For instance, television cameras did not focus on empty seats when members left the room. See Mezvinsky, A *Term to Remember*, p. 209. William Shawcross quotes from notes taken at a closed executive session held by Democrats on July 30 to demonstrate how cautiously members approached Article IV (*Side-Show*, New York: Pocket Books, 1977). Nothing of this could have been known by the TV viewer.

52. Mezvinsky, A *Term to Remember*, p. 223.

53. Quoted in Drew, *Washington Journal*, p. 386.

54. *Ibid.*, p. 358.

55. Robert D. Laing and Robert Stevenson, "Public Opinion Trends in the Last Days of the Nixon Administration," *Journalism Quarterly* (1976) 53.294–302.

56. *Broadcasting*, August 5, 1974, p. 7.

57. *Ibid.*, p. 18.

58. This estimate is based on our post-resignation survey on Long Island, on the Laing and Stevenson study, and on a telephone poll by *Newsday* conducted on July 30, according to which 65 percent had "watched."

59. *Newsday* poll.

60. Jack McLeod, Jane Brown, Lee B. Becker, and Dean A. Ziemke, "Decline and Fall at the White House: A Longitudinal Analysis of Media Effects," *Communication Research* (1977) 4:3–22.

61. Carl I. Hovland, F. D. Sheffield, and A. A. Lumsdaine, *Experiments in Mass Communications* (Princeton: Princeton University Press, 1949); Gladys Engel Lang and Kurt Lang, "Immediate and Delayed Responses to a Carter-Ford Debate," *Public Opinion Quarterly* (1978) 42:322–41.

62. Newspaper files, office of Representative J. Caldwell Butler.

63. *Peoria* (Ill.) *Star-Journal*, July 31, 1974.

64. *Washington Post*, September 25, 1974.

65. Interview with Representative Tom Railsback; also *Peoria Star-Journal*, July 31, 1974 and *Washington Post*, September 25, 1974.

66. Marlene Daniels, 1976, "Carbon Copy News," M. A. thesis, Department of Communication Arts, University of Wisconsin, p. 94.

67. Gallup Opinion Index, June 1974, no. 108, p. 6n.
68. *Newsday* Poll, June 24–26, 1974.
69. Laing and Stevenson, "Public Response."
70. Sam J. Ervin Jr., *The Whole Truth* (New York: Random House 1980), 282.
71. Frank Mankiewicz, *U.S. Vs. Richard Nixon: The Final Crisis.* (New York: Quadrangle/New York Times Book Co. 1975), p. 234.
72. Barry Sussman, *The Great Cover-Up* (New York: Crowell, 1974), p. 380.
73. Nixon, *Memoirs*, p. 1052.
74. *Roper Reports* (1974), no. 74–78.
75. Arthur H. Miller, Jeffrey Brudney, and Peter Joftis, "Presidential Crises and Political Support: The Impact of Watergate on Attitudes Toward Political Institutions," paper presented at the Midwest Political Science Association meetings, Chicago, 1975.

8. CEREMONIES OF TRANSITION

1. Daniel Boorstin, *The Image* (New York: Athenaeum, 1962).
2. *New York Times*, August 7, 1974.
3. Bob Woodward and Carl Bernstein, *The Final Days* (New York: Simon and Schuster, 1976, p. 418), state that the staffer writing the "confession speech" had no idea that it was to be a resignation speech.
4. *Ibid.*, for this "eyes only" memo by David Gergen.
5. See in particular Elizabeth Drew, *Washington Journal: the Events of 1973–74* (New York: Random House, 1974), p. 402; *Milwaukee Journal*, August 8, 1974, p. 4.
6. *Washington Post*, August 9, 1974. Another vivid account of the resignation watch at the White House is Edwin Diamond, "On the Last Airless Day," *Boston Phoenix*, August 20, 1974.
7. Cited by John Carmody, "Networks Held Back as Resignation Rumors Spread," *Washington Post* August 9, 1974, p. A21.
8. Based on media diaries by some of our Stony Brook students.
9. Marlene Daniels, "Carbon Copy News," M. A. thesis, Department of Communication Arts, University of Wisconsin, 1976, p. 190. The one exception was the week of October 15–19, 1973, when 84 percent of the reporters stories on ABC were about the Mideast situation.
10. Drew, *Washington Journal*, p. 409.
11. Alexander Cockburn, "End of the Mega-Story," *New Times*, September 6, 1974, p. 31.
12. Based on Nielsen ratings for the half hour before and after the speech. Nielsen reports give no national ratings for sustaining programs. *Broadcasting*, August 12, 1974, vol. 87 (6), p. 6. National news media generally estimated the audience as "up to 110,000,000."
13. The exact figures are: 74 percent watched "live," 6 percent listened "live," and 9 percent had seen or heard replays.

14. Woodward and Bernstein, *The Final Days*, p. 448.

15. Richard Nixon, *RN: The Memoirs of Richard Nixon* (New York: Grosset and Dunlap, 1978), p. 1084. Nixon described this as the briefest honeymoon of his entire political life. In what appears to be a reference to the TV-coverage that evening, he wrote that "within a few hours came the second thoughts, negative and critical."

16. *Time*, August 19, 1974, p. 74.

17. *Newsweek*, August 19, 1974, p. 77.

18. *Broadcasting*, August 19, 1973, p. 31.

19. Cockburn, "End of the Mega-Story."

20. *Nation*, August 31, 1974, p. 130.

21. *Time*, August 19, 1974.

22. *Newsweek*, August 19, 1974.

23. *Time*, August 19, 1974.

24. Larry Levine, "Content Analysis of the Network Coverage of President Nixon's Resignation," M. A. paper, Department of Communication Arts, University of Wisconsin, 1975.

25. *Broadcasting*, August 19, 1974, and *Time*, August 19, 1974.

26. Daniel Schorr, *Clearing the Air* (Boston: Houghton Mifflin, 1977), p. 114.

27. From monitoring notes.

28. Schorr, *Clearing the Air*, p. 108.

29. *Ibid.*

30. See William Barry Furlong, "Dan ('Killer') Schorr, the Great Abrasive," *New York*, June 16, 1975, pp. 41–44, and Letter by Dan Rather, *New York*, July 14, 1975, p. 59.

31. Schorr, *Clearing the Air*, p. 119.

32. Dan Rather, *The Camera Never Blinks: Adventures of a TV Journalist* (New York: Morrow, 1977).

33. David Halberstam, *The Powers That Be* (New York: Knopf, 1979), p. 704.

34. *Springfield Daily News*, August 9, 1974.

35. *New York Times*, August 10, 1974.

36. *Newsweek*, August 19, 1974, said to have been during the "days immediately following."

37. The respondent is clearly paraphrasing Nixon's explanation in his speech.

9. PUBLIC OPINION AND THE PARDON

1. Jerald ter Horst, *Gerald Ford and the Future of the Presidency* (New York: Joseph Okpaku, 1974).

2. *New York Times*, September 9, 1974, p. 26.

3. *Congressional Quarterly*, September 9, 1974.

4. *New York Times*, September 12, 1974.

5. *Roper Reports*, (1974), no. 74–8.

6. Several weeks after the pardon a poll of New Jersey residents by the Eagleton Institute showed similar distributions of opinion. (New Jersey Poll Release No. 12-11, October 7, 1974.)

7. *NBC Nightly News*, August 16, 1974.

8. *New York Times* September 10.

9. Richard Ben-Veniste and George Frampton Jr., *Stonewall: The Real Story of the Watergate Prosecution* (New York: Simon and Schuster, 1977), p. 303n.

10. Leon Jaworski, *The Right and the Power* (New York: Crowell, 1976), p. 223.

11. At a press conference on August 28, 1974 Ford had said that the Rockefeller statement coincided with his general view and that of the American public.

12. Not to be entirely ruled out is the admittedly far-out possibility that "yes" answers were erroneously coded to mean that charges should *not* be pressed and "no" answers that they should. A Gallup executive thought this unlikely but could not check it out against the processed data as these are in the sole possession of *Newsweek*, which owns them.

13. Neither of two persons on the Ford White House staff at the time, whom we interviewed and who would have paid attention to the public reaction, could remember whether this second poll had been considered.

14. 93rd Congress, *Hearings of the Senate Committee on Rules and Administration*, November 5, 1973, p. 124.

15. Press conference, August 28, 1973.

16. Cited in Ben-Veniste and Frampton, *Stonewall*, p. 238.

17. *Ibid*. p. 298f.

18. James Doyle, *Not Above the Law* (New York: Morrow, 1977), p. 360f.

19. Jaworski, *The Right and the Power*, p. 223.

20. Doyle, *Not Above the Law*, p. 368.

21. Jaworski, *The Right and the Power*, pp. 233–37.

22. Doyle, *Not Above the Law*, pp. 355, 357; Ben-Veniste and Frampton, *Stonewall*, p. 301.

23. Ben-Veniste and Frampton, *Stonewall*, p. 303.

24. ter Horst, *Gerald Ford*, p. 232.

25. Elmer E. Cornwell Jr. "The President and the Press: Phases in the Relationship." *American Academy of Political and Social Science* (1976) 427:53–64; George H. Gallup, *The Gallup Poll: Public Opinion 1935–1971* (New York: Random House, 1972).

26. *Roper Report*, (1974), no. 74–78.

27. *Roper Reports*, no. 74–8, 74-10.

28. For example, Frank Fox and Stephen Parker, "Is the Pardon Explained by the Ford-Nixon Tapes?" *New York*, October 14, 1974.

29. Ford had answered written questions submitted to him on September 17 but his answers were deemed unsatisfactory.

30. New Jersey Poll, October 7, 1974 release.

31. *Roper Report* 74-9, based on interviewing in early October.

32. Ben-Veniste and Frampton, *Stonewall*, p. 311.

33. As implied in a front-page story in the *New York Times*, September 11, 1974.

34. *New York Times*, September 12, 1974.

35. *New York Times*, August 20, 1974.

36. *Newsweek*, September 16, 1974, p. 31.

37. *New York Times*, November 3, 1974, p. 73.

38. Doyle, *Not Above the Law*, p. 392.

39. The sample consisted of students attending summer sessions at SUNY/Stony Brook, Hofstra University, C. W. Post College, Adelphi University, *and* Queens College, Queensboro Community College, and Suffolk Community College. The group is not necessarily representative of the general population or even of college students. Detailed findings are in an unpublished paper, "Crime, Guilt and Punishment."

40. Kurt Lang and Gladys Engel Lang, "Van Doren as Victim: Some Student Reactions," *Studies in Public Communication* (Summer 1961), 2:50–58. The items used in 1973 were as follows: 1. A United States Senator admitted that for several years he had received from a group of supporters a sum of money to help him meet the expenses of his office; 2. A successful candidate for the U.S. House of Representatives admitted that he had lied during the campaign about his opponent's support for and affiliation with radical causes; 3. A Federal officeholder acknowledged that public monies had been used to make capital improvements on his private residence; 4. A White House official accepted a personal gift from a firm at a time when it was bidding for a government contract; 5. A young instructor of English at a major university admitted before a Congressional Committee that he had defeated other contestants on a highly popular TV quiz show, winning $129,000, only because he had received the correct answers in advance; 6. A real estate broker reported that he had cleared a small fortune when he bought up land after being tipped off on plans for a slum clearing project on the site; 7. A college student revealed that he had copied and sold questions on an upcoming examination widely used for college admission similar to the SATs [In 1959 this had read "New York State Regents Examination"]; 8. A talented but unknown artist painted original pictures in the style of a seventeenth-century Dutch master and, after having the work certified by experts, sold them as the master's unsigned work.

41. We derived a gravity-score for each student by awarding one point for each wrongdoing judged less serious and subtracting one point for each judged more serious than Watergate, giving us a mean score of slightly over +3 within a theoretical range (based on eight comparisons) of +8 to −8. The judgments of these young people already clustered on the high side of the range a year before Nixon finally resigned, with a standard deviation of 2.66. Quite surprisingly, there was less than a one-point difference between the mean gravity scores of those favoring Nixon and those favoring McGovern.

42. *Time*, September 10, 1973, p. 19f.

43. Gerald R. Ford, *A Time to Heal*. New York: Harper & Row, 1979, p. 198f.

10. CONTINUITY AND CHANGE

1. ISR Newsletter, Summer, 1975.

2. Samuel L. Becker and Elmer Lower, "Broadcasting in Presidential Elections," in Sidney Kraus, ed. *The Great Debates*, p. 35 (Bloomington: Indiana University Press), 1962.

3. John Revett, *Advertising Age*, November 10, 1980, p. 94.

4. *Washington Post* columnist William Greider, *Newsday*, November 4, 1980, p. 52.

5. *Wall Street Journal*, November 4, 1980.

6. See especially Ronald E. Pynn, ed. *Watergate and the American Political Process* (New York: Praeger, 1974), Ralph K. Winter, *Watergate and the Law; Political Campaigns and Presidential Power* (Washington, D.C.: American Enterprise Institute, 1974); Frederic C. Mosher et al., *Watergate: Implications for Responsible Government: A Report at the Request of the Senate Select Committee on Presidential Campaign Activities* (New York: Basic Books, 1975); Philip B. Kurland, *Watergate and the Constitution* (Chicago: University of Chicago Press, 1978).

7. Jack M. McLeod, "Watergate and the 1974 Congressional Election," *Public Opinion Quarterly* (1977) 41:181–98; *Gallup Opinion Index* #116, February, 1975, p. 18.

8. *New York Times*, November 7, 1974.

9. Gerald C. Wright Jr., "Constituency Response to Congressional Behavior: the Impact of the House Judiciary Committee Impeachment Votes," *Western Political Quarterly* (1977) 30:401–10. The multiple regression equation was based on percent of two-party vote for Nixon in 1972, the voting turnout percentage in 1972, and incumbency status (a dummy variable).

10. Based on a research paper by Robert S. Resnick for a course by Professor William Adams, George Washington University.

11. The effort to involve Gerald Ford began as early as September 13, 1972, when the following exchange between Nixon and Ford was recorded. Dean: "Ford is not really taking an active interest in this matter . . . so Stans is going to see Jerry Ford and try to brief him and explain to him the problems he has." Nixon then responds: "What about Ford? . . . Ford can get the minority members. They have some weak men and women on that committee, unfortunately." Ford denied complicity while under oath during the hearings on his confirmation as Vice President.

12. Gallup Survey, September 24–27, 1974. A later survey (June 11–14, 1976) showed a 35 percent approval against 55 percent who disapproved. Among Republicans, the split was 57 to 33 percent.

13. Iowa Poll, January 12–15, 1977. *Des Moines Register*, January 23, 1977.

14. ISR Newsletter, Winter, 1972.

15. Karl Mannheim, *Man and Society in an Age of Reconstruction* (New York: Harcourt, 1940).

16. Among those who considered young people "forerunners" were Daniel Yankelovich, *The New Morality: A Profile of American Youth in the 70's* (New York: McGraw-Hill, 1974); and Ronald Inglehart, *The Silent Revolution: Changing Values and Political Styles Among Western Publics* (Princeton: Princeton University Press, 1977).

17. Arthur H. Miller, "The Institutional Focus of Political Distrust." Paper presented at the Annual Meeting of the American Political Science Association in Washington, D.C., 1979.

18. Arthur H. Miller, Jeffrey Brudney, and Peter Joftis, "Presidential Crises and Political Support: The Impact of Watergate on Attitudes Toward Political Institu-

tions." Paper presented at the Midwest Political Science Association Convention in Chicago, 1975.

19. Paul M. Sniderman, W. Russell Neuman, Jack Citrin, Herbert McCloskey, and J. Merrill Shanks, "Stability and Support for the Political System," *American Politics Quarterly* (1975) 3:437–57; Jack M. McLeod, Jane D. Brown, Lee B. Becker, and Dean A. Ziemke, "Decline and Fall at the White House: A Longitudinal Analysis of Media Effects," *Communication Research* (1977) 4:3–22.

20. Miller et al., "Presidential Crises," p. 21.

21. *Ibid.* See also McLeod et al., "Decline and Fall," who show Madison, Wisconsin voters two months after the resignation blaming Nixon and his committee for the Reelection of the President.

22. Miller et al., "Presidential Crises," p. 45.

23. The events of the 1960s have spawned a large body of literature on the subject, yet the most thorough analytic treatment is still that of Mannheim, first published in the 1920s. Karl Mannheim, *Essays on the Sociology of Knowledge* (New York: Oxford University Press, 1952), pp. 276–320. See also Herbert Hyman, *Political Socialization* (New York: Free Press, 1958), pp. 123–54, and Norman H. Ryder, "The Cohort as a Concept in the Study of Social Change," *American Sociological Review* (1965) 30:843–61.

24. Lester Milbrath, *Political Participation* (Chicago: Rand McNally, 1964), p. 18.

25. For a review of early studies of parental influence, see Hyman, *Political Socialization*, and the article by David O. Sears, "Political Socialization," in Fred Greenstein and Nelson W. Polsby, eds. *Handbook of Political Science* 2:93–144 (Reading, Mass.: Addison-Wesley, 1975).

26. Fred I. Greenstein, *Children and Politics*, rev. ed. (New Haven: Yale University Press, 1969), p. 42.

27. David Easton and Jack Dennis, *Children and the Political System: Origins of Political Legitimacy* (New York: McGraw-Hill, 1969). See also Robert D. Hess and Judith V. Torney, *The Development of Political Attitudes in Children* (Chicago: Aldine, 1967).

28. Dean Jaros, Herbert Hirsch, and Frederick Fleron Jr., "The Malevolent Leader: Political Socialization in an American Subculture," *American Political Science Review* (1968) 62:564–75.

29. Roberta Sigel, "An Exploration into Some Aspects of Political Socialization: School Children's Reactions to the Death of a President," in M. Wolfenstein and G. Kliman, eds. *Children and the Death of a President*, pp. 34–67 (Garden City, N.Y.: Doubleday, 1965).

30. Wolfenstein and Kliman, *Children and the Death of a President*.

31. F. Christopher Arterton, "The Impact of Watergate on Children's Attitudes toward Political Authority," *Political Science Quarterly* (1974) 89:269–88; F. Christoper Arterton, "Watergate and Children's Attitudes toward Political Authority Revisited," *ibid.*, (1975) 90:479–96; Kenneth D. Bailey, "Political Learning and Development: Continuity and Change in Childhood Political Orientations." Ph.D. dissertation, Department of Government and Politics, University of Maryland, 1975;

Bruce A. Campbell, "Racial Differences in the Reaction to Watergate, *Youth and Society* (1976) 7:439–60; Steven H. Chafee and Lee B. Becker, "Young Voters' Reactions to Early Watergate Issues," *American Politics Quarterly* (1975) 3:360–85; Jack Dennis and Carol Webster, "Children's Images of the President and of Government in 1962 and 1974," *American Politics Quarterly* (1975) 3:386–405; Fred I. Greenstein, "The Benevolent Leader Revisited: Children's Image of Political Leaders in Three Democracies," *American Political Science Review* (1975) 69: 1371–98; Robert P. Hawkins, Suzanne Pingree, and Donald F. Roberts, "Watergate and Political Socialization," *American Politics Quarterly* (1975) 3:406–22; Marjorie R. Hershey and David B. Hill, "Watergate and Preadults' Attitudes Toward the President," *American Journal of Political Science* (1975) 19:703–26; Michael Lupfer and Charles Kenny, "Watergate is Just a Bunch of Honky Jive," *Personality and Social Psychology Bulletin* (1974) 1:163–65; Michael B. Lupfer and Charles T. Kenny, "The Impact of Watergate on Youth's Views of the Presidency," *Public Affairs Forum* (April 1976) 5:1–8; Harrell Rodgers Jr. and Edward B. Lewis, "Student Attitudes Toward Mr. Nixon," *American Politics Quarterly*, (1975) 3:423–35; Roberta S. Sigel and Marilyn B. Hoskin, "Affect for Government and Its Relation to Policy Output among Adolescents," *American Journal of Political Science* (1977) 21:111–34.

32. Dennis and Webster, "Children's Images of the President." One discrepant piece of information is to be found in the study by Hershey and Hill of 2nd, 4th, 6th and 8th graders in Florida public schools, a state in which Nixon enjoyed greater support than in such cities as Boston, New Haven, Tacoma, etc., where other studies were conducted. On the item of "presidential responsiveness," second and fourth graders in Florida were found to be more positive in 1973–74 than the sample of Chicago second and fourth graders in 1961–62 queried by Easton and Dennis, *Children and the Political System.*

33. Arterton, "Watergate and Children's Attitudes Revisited."

34. Bailey, "Political Learning and Development."

35. Greenstein, "The Benevolent Leader Revisited." The Long Island study was conducted as part of a graduate methods course required for the M.A. in Applied Sociology taught by G. E. Lang.

36. Fernand van Langenhove, *The Growth of a Legend: A Study Based upon German Accounts of Franc-Tireurs and 'Atrocities' in Belgium* (New York: Putnam, 1916), p. 122f.

37. Louis de Jong, *The German Fifth Column: Myth or Reality?* (Amsterdam: Rijkinstituut voor Oorlogsdocumentatie, 1959).

38. Martha Wolfenstein, *Disaster: A Psychological Study* (New York: Free Press, 1957).

39. Based on a student paper by Michael Katzke for K. Lang, Fall, 1979.

40. American Political Science Association, "Watergate in Retrospect: The Forgotten Agenda," *Public Administration Review* (1976) 36:306–10.

41. Michael B. Grossmann and Francis E. Rourke, "The Media and the Presidency: an Exchange Analysis," *Political Science Quarterly* (1976) 91:455–70; see also Michael B. Grossmann and M. J. Kumar, *Portraying the President: The White House and the News Media* (Baltimore: Johns Hopkins University Press, 1981); Leon V.

Sigal, *Reporters and Officials; The Organization and Politics of Newsmaking* (Lexington, Mass.: D. C. Heath, 1973); and Colin Seymour-Ure, "Presidential Power, Press Secretaries and Communication," *Political Studies* (1980) 27:253–70.

42. CBS documentary "American Dream/American Nightmare," December 28 and 29, 1979.

43. For example, Kurland, *Watergate and the Constitution.* Chicago: University of Chicago Press, 1978, pp. 50ff.

44. Richard Ben-Veniste and George Frampton Jr., *Stonewall: The Real Story of the Watergate Prosecution.* New York: Simon and Schuster, 1977, p. 391.

45. Kurland, *Watergate and the Constitution,* p. 38; see also Sam Dash, *Chief Counsel: Inside the Ervin Committee—The Untold Story* (New York: Random House, 1976), pp. 97, 118f.

11. PUBLIC OPINION AND THE RESOLUTION OF CRISIS

1. Paul F. Lazarsfeld and Robert K. Merton, "Mass Communication, Popular Taste and Organized Social Action," in Lyman Bryson, ed. *The Communication of Ideas,* pp. 95–118. (New York: Harper, 1948).

2. Svend Ranulf, *Moral Indignation and Middle Class Psychology.* (New York: Schocken, 1964), p. 200.

3. Max Scheler, *Ressentiment* (New York: Free Press, 1961).

4. Rei Shiratori, "The Lockheed Affair: A Second Look at Democracy," *Japan Echo* (1976) 3 (2):23–30. Discussion with Professor Shiratori has helped us put the Tanaka affair into focus.

5. *New York Times,* November 26, 1974, p. 3.

6. Shiratori, "The Lockheed Affair," p. 23.

7. Jeremy Tunstall, *The Lobby Correspondents: A Sociological Study of National Political Journalism* (London: Routledge, 1970).

8. Lord Denning's Report, Cmnd. 2152.

9. Colin Seymour-Ure, *The Press, Politics and the Media.* (London: Methuen, 1968), p. 288.

10. *New York Times,* August 27, 1976.

11. *Ibid.*

12. Lyndon B. Johnson, *The Vantage Point; Perspectives of the Presidency 1963– 1969* (New York: Holt, Rinehart and Winston, 1971), pp. 427–31.

13. Herbert J. Schandler, *The Unmaking of a President: Lyndon B. Johnson and Vietnam.* (Princeton: Princeton University Press, 1977), p. 220.

14. Doris Kearns, *Lyndon Johnson and the American Dream.* New York: Harper and Row, 1976, p. 7.

15. C. Richard Hofstetter, "Watching TV-News and Support for the Military," *Armed Forces and Society* (1979) 5:261–69, addresses the question but from data collected in 1972, not 1968.

16. Peter Braestrup, *Big Story: How the American Press and Television Reported and Interpreted the Crisis of Tet in Vietnam and Washington* (Boulder, Col.: Westview Press, 1977).

17. Kearns, *Lyndon Johnson and the American Dream*, p. 336. CBS, as a corporation, did not take a stand, of course, but Walter Cronkite, in his evening news analysis February 27, 1968, said, "It seems now more certain than ever that the bloody experience in Vietnam is to end in a stalemate."

18. Gallup recorded only a minute change in pro-war sentiment between its January and February polls, Harris a striking gain of some 13 percentage points. After that, support for the Vietnam war fell and never again attained the pre-Tet levels.

19. Michael Les Benedict, *The Impeachment and Trial of Andrew Johnson*. (New York: Norton, 1973), p. 6. This account relies heavily on this book and discussion with its author.

20. *Ibid.*, p. 96.

21. Examples are from Gene Smith, *High Crimes and Misdemeanors: The Impeachment and Trial of Andrew Johnson* (New York: Morrow, 1977), ch. 13.

22. Michael Les Benedict, *A Compromise of Principle: Congressional Republicans and Reconstructions 1863–1869* (New York: Norton, 1974), p. 313. Benedict, *The Impeachment and Trial*, chapter 6.

23. Betty Schechter, *The Dreyfus Affair: A National Scandal*. (Boston: Houghton Mifflin, 1968), p. 41.

24. Nicholas Halasz, *Captain Dreyfus: The Story of Mass Hysteria* (New York: Simon and Schuster, 1955), p. 69.

25. Douglas Johnson, *Fame and the Dreyfus Affair* (London: Blandford Press, 1966), p. 113.

26. Text is as in Halasz, *Captain Dreyfus*.

27. *Ibid.*, p. 119.

28. The verdict against Zola was reversed. When a second trial ended in another conviction, Zola fled to England upon the advice of friends.

29. Halasz, *Captain Dreyfus*, p. 241.

30. Johnson, *Fame and the Dreyfus Affair*, p. 178.

31. Schechter, *The Dreyfus Affair*, p. 224.

32. David S. Lewis, *Prisoners of Honor: The Dreyfus Affair* (New York: Macmillian, 1973), p. 215.

33. Charles Peguy, *Oeuvres en Prose, 1909–1914*. Cited in Johnson, *Fame and the Dreyfus Affair*, p. 189n.

34. Halasz, *Captain Dreyfus*, p. 242.

35. Brian Inglis, *Abdication* (New York: Macmillan, 1966), p. 175.

36. Thomas Jones, *A Diary With Letters, 1931–1950* (London: Oxford University Press, 1954), p. 254 as quoted in J. Bryan III and Charles J. V. Murphy, *The Windsor Story* (New York: Morrow, 1979), p. 260.

37. Lord Beaverbrook, *The Abdication of Edward VIII* (London: Hamilton, 1966), p. 60; Bryan and Murphy, *Windsor Story*, p. 259.

38. Bryan and Murphy, *The Windsor Story*, p. 294.

39. See Inglis, *Abdication*, pp. 333–40, and Richard Hoggart, *The Uses of Literacy: Aspects of Working-Class Life with Special Reference to Publications and Entertainments* (London: Chatto and Windus, 1957), pp. 92f. on working class attitudes.

40. Edward VIII, A *King's Story: The Memoirs of the Duke of Windsor* (New York: Putnam, 1948), p. 411 for text of speech.

41. Murray Edelman, *The Symbolic Uses of Politics* (Urbana: University of Illinois Press, 1964).

42. Ranulf, *Moral Indignation.*

EPILOGUE

1. U.S. House of Representatives, House Judiciary Committee, *Report and Recommendations on Impeachment.* Report no. 93-1305, 93rd Congress, 2nd Session, 1974 contains comments on the Committee action by individual members.

INDEX